INCIDENTS OF TRAVEL
IN EGYPT, ARABIA PETRÆA,
AND THE HOLY LAND

INCIDENTS OF TRAVEL
IN EGYPT, ARABIA PETRÆA,
AND THE HOLY LAND

By John Lloyd Stephens

Edited, with an Introduction,
by Victor Wolfgang von Hagen

Chronicle Books • San Francisco

Printed in the United States of America.

ISBN 0-8118-0048-2

Library of Congress Cataloging in Publication Data

Stephens, John Lloyd, 1805-1852.
    Incidents of travel in Egypt, Arabia Petræa, and the
  Holy Land / John Lloyd Stephens ; edited, with an introduction
  by Victor Wolfgang von Hagen. – 1st pbk. ed.
        p.   cm.
    Reprint. Originally published: Norman : University of Oklahoma,
  1970.
    Includes index.
    ISBN 0-8118-0048-2
    1. Egypt–Description and travel. 2. Arabia, Roman–Description
  and travel. 3. Palestine–Description and travel. I. Von Hagen,
  Victor Wolfgang, 1908-1985. II. Title.
  [DS48.S84   1991]   91-4718
    916.204'3–dc20   CIP

Cover design: Julie Noyes Long
Cover illustration: *The Gates of the Khalif* by William Logsdail, 1887.
Reproduced by arrangement with Academy Editions London.

Distributed in Canada by Raincoast Books,
112 East Third Avenue, Vancouver, B.C. V5T 1C8

10   9   8   7   6   5   4   3   2   1

Chronicle Books
275 Fifth Street
San Francisco, CA 94103

Introduction

New York

JOHN LLOYD STEPHENS' New York in 1806[1] was only fourteen miles around, a little overgrown Dutch village of crooked and winding streets, of houses, mostly built in the high-roofed Dutch-style, with weathercocks and gables.

Yet this little old New York was cosmopolitan enough; beyond the Dutch and Americans its 60,000 population included a generous sprinkling of French, mostly emigrés from the French Revolution (of which one was Anthelme Brillat-Savarin, the author of *Physiologie du goût*) and sizable groups of Germans, Swedes, and Irish. The Battery at the tip of Manhattan was the place of promenade and elegance, while Bowling Green was the center of popular riots and popular sports, a spot which Stephens associated with his earliest recollections: "It had been my playground as a boy: hundreds of times I had climbed over the fence to get my ball. I was one of those who held it long after the city of New York invaded our rights." At that time Brooklyn was a small village, reached only by ferryboat, and Greenwich Village was a potter's field.

America still looked to Europe for its standard in manners and taste; its society was, quite naturally, a microcosm of England, and New York prided itself as being a "little London." Men dressed as they did there, albeit two seasons behind, in powdered queues, white-topped boots, silk stockings, breeches, and cocked hats. The

---

[1] Stephens was born in Shrewsbury, New Jersey, November 28, 1805, and was moved to New York at the age of thirteen months.

dress of women was "Empire," high waisted with the long, sweep skirt hiding all but the points of prunella slippers.

America was, however, no neo-Arcadia. Notwithstanding all its hustle and bustle, there were ominous rumblings over the land. New Yorkers were still nerve-strained by the aftermath of the Presidential campaign of 1804 that had sent Thomas Jefferson to the White House and Alexander Hamilton to his grave. It had been one of unbridled bitterness, reaching its climax on the heights of Weehawken; for not only had Alexander Hamilton been killed in honorable combat with Aaron Burr, but with him had died Federalism, and as a corollary in its demise the dream of Jefferson that America would continue to be a land of husbandmen "free from the corruptions of industrialism."

Pressures from abroad, the centuries-old struggle between Great Britain and France for Continental dominance, had lapped up to America's shores; impressments of sailors at sea and seizures of American vessels created hostilities that produced the Embargo Act of 1807. This act began the era of industrialization; manufacturing began to spring up almost everywhere so as to fill the void of the Continental blockade. The "corruption by industrialism" had begun.

Young John Stephens grew as America grew. He was taking his first faltering steps while the expedition of Lewis and Clark was examining the vast lands the United States had acquired with the Louisiana Purchase. He had learned to babble his first sentences when Fulton's steamboat *Clermont* anchored directly in front of his Greenwich Street home. He was a bright-eyed, mischievous boy when Pike placed his standard in the Rocky Mountains and when the Burr "Conspiracy" was at its height. As John Stephens matured, so did his country, and this left a deep impression on him. The evolving of John Lloyd Stephens in this young America gave him enthusiasm and interest and a boundless curiosity in people and places. This is discernible at an early age.

Learning in 1812 was "driven in"; young John Stephens was incessantly birched, beaten on that part which was then considered, as he remembered, "the channel of knowledge into a boy's brain."

In 1815, at the age of ten, he entered the preparatory Classical School which was the way to Columbia College. Training was classical. There were only brief excursions into analytical arithmetic, history, some mechanics and chemistry that savored of the alchemist; all the rest was the classics. "While your son remains here," the master told Benjamin Stephens, "he will be exercised in Latin and Greek composition; the higher he gets the more he will have of it." And so he did.

At the age of thirteen—there being then no intermediate school—John Stephens moved on to Columbia College. Its five faculty members arranged the admission into college by examination. "No student shall be admitted into the lowest class of Columbia College unless he be accurately acquainted with the grammar of both the Greek and Latin tongues . . . he is to be examined upon: Caesar's *Commentaries*, the *Orations* of Cicero against Catiline, the *Oration* for the Poet Archias, and the *Oration* for Marcus Marcellus; he is to know the first eight books of Virgil's *Aeneid*; the first five books of Livy; of the Gospel according to Luke and St. John and the Acts of the Apostles [for Columbia was intensely Episcopalian]; of Dalzel's *Collectanea Graeca Minora*; of the first three books of Xenophon's *Cyropaedia* and the first three books of Homer's *Iliad*. He shall also be able to translate English into grammatical Latin, and shall be versed in the first four rules of arithmetic, the rule of three direct and inverse, decimal and vulgar fractions, with Algebra as far as the end of simple equations; and with modern geography. The classical examination to be *ad aperturam libri*." Stephens was admitted to Columbia in March, 1818.

It was Charles Anthon who began Stephens' intellectualization. He was—for a full professor—relatively young, at most only eight years the senior of his students. Rich in learning, exact in his execution of it, Anthon went far beyond the bare requirements of the curriculum and introduced his students to Goethe, Schiller, Herder, and Wieland as a sort of intellectual equipoise to Shelley, Byron, Keats, and Henry Hallam. Although he was America's most famous classicist, he was also a champion of American letters and one of the earlier admirers of Edgar Allan Poe. Later, much later, when his favorite pupil John Lloyd Stephens wrote his first book and Poe was given his first New York assignment to review it, he was aided in obtaining it by Charles Anthon. Anthon was Stephens' first real influence. To his quickness of perception, Anthon must have added a dimensional depth; he gave him a sense of humanism. Under this guidance Stephens developed into a young man of intellectual curiosity with the sort of human tolerance which derives from satiated curiosity.

After four years at Columbia, Stephens was graduated. Commencement, usually held in June, had been delayed to August 14, (1822) because of an epidemic of yellow fever. It was a day over filled with orations, prayers, and music; a wearisome ordeal for the audience, who were "requested to abstain from everything which does not comport with the solemnity which ought to be observed on these occasions." In midday, as one of the "young Gentlemen of the Senior Class," John L. Stephens delivered his oration: "On the Oriental and Classical Superstitions as affecting the Imagination and Feeling."

Stephens at seventeen years of age looked now toward a profession. He elected law, and being articled out as a law clerk in the office of Mr. Daniel Lord, he began to read Blackstone. An able lawyer, this Daniel Lord ("strictly professional, no politics") had gone to Yale and then had read law at Tapping Reeve's Law School at Litchfield, Connecticut. As he believed that Stephens would make a good lawyer, he urged him to attend the school. At first Stephens did not like the idea of leaving New York with its theaters, its clubs, and its balls to go—at least for a year—into "exile" in Connecticut; but "leave" he did.

Connecticut

Litchfield, a stately, albeit isolated Connecticut town, had been in 1722 an outpost for the northwest frontier. It lay on a high plateau above the Naugatuck Valley, on the main line of post coaches, just east of the Housatonic River.

Stephens arrived in one of these great creaking red four-horse coaches which made connection with the Hudson sloops at Pough-keepsie. Careening down the main street past the dignified colonial houses framed by giant elm trees, he saw that Litchfield was cosmopolitan despite its six thousand population. Painted signs overhanging the red-brick sidewalks announced an importer, a hatter, a bookbinder; and the *Gazeteer* listed the town as having "4 forges, 1 slitting mill, one nail factory . . . 1 paper mill, comb factories, hatters and grain." It was not its modest commerciality, however, that made Litchfield cosmopolitan but the students that it drew to its schools.

Tapping Reeve's Law School by the time of Stephens' arrival had in the forty years since its founding in 1782, managed to turn out two vice-presidents of the United States, sixteen senators, fifty members of Congress, two Supreme Court justices, ten governors, five cabinet members, and countless judges, lawyers, businessmen, and even artists and writers.

The Law School was held in a small frame building adjacent to the home of Tapping Reeve. At first, in 1784, Reeve had held classes in his home; but as his fame spread and more students arrived, he built America's first law school.

The law, as taught at Litchfield, was as comprehensive as its résumé implied: ". . . every ancient and modern opinion whether over-ruled, doubted, or in any way qualified, is here systematically digested." Lectures were given in the mornings six days a week, when the students took voluminous notes. The rest of the day was spent consulting the authorities. On Saturday afternoon the students were examined on the week's lectures, and on Monday—usually in the evening—occurred the high point of the week: the students held a moot court, in which they argued hypothetical cases.

In the study of the mental growth of the man who would one day discover the Maya culture, we have a series of his letters to his father, (which somehow survived[2]) which show that his mind then was no *tabula rasa*.

[2] During my search for documentation for the writing of the only biography of Stephens (*Maya Explorer*, University of Oklahoma Press, 1947) my research carried

Every Sunday he wrote a letter to his father summarizing the week, choosing Sunday as "a principle of expediency" so as not to interfere with church attendance. He examined the law, the school, and its mentors: "One of the facts I think does me no small honour. I cannot account for my not having mentioned it before, since I can find no other reason for my omission, I must attribute it to my modesty. I called to a fact which I think I may cover without fear of contradiction; *that I am the youngest student in the class*. There are assembled here young men, from all the states of the union, between the ages of eighteen and thirty, so that my beardless face does not claim for me any very great share of *veneration* at least, from this whiskered and generally speaking gigantic race, there being among them some of the largest men I ever saw. I understand from gentlemen here, that the Law-school at Litchfield is known and its reputation well established from Main to Georgia; there are now about fifty [students] attached to it.

"Judge Gould [the other law professor at Tapping Reeve's] stands far above mediocrity, perhaps unrivalled, but it would seem from his bearing in private life, that a study so calculated to teach a man his duty to his neighbour, himself, and his country, if not to his God, and in which he so iminently excels has not taught, these fundamental principles, the want of which is unpardonable in an uneducated man, *honesty* and *honour*. Some opinion may be formed of his religious principles from a toast he gave on the 4th July 'Americans, a free people, may we know no master but the *Law*.' Judge G. is the finest looking man I ever saw. Every feature on his

---

me almost everywhere, except where I inexplicably did not look: the New York offices of the Panama Railroad Company. Why then should one find memorabilia there? Simply, that the last official position held by John Lloyd Stephens was with the Panama Railway, of which he was both founder and president. It was during the years 1847–50, when it was being built, that he contracted various infections of malaria; his liver became infected, and he died of that disease in 1852. His father, Benjamin, who survived him by thirty years, used the Panama Railroad Company as a storage place for letters, journals, and royalty payments from Harper and Brothers, Stephens' publishers. There these papers lay for almost one hundred years, until my biography somehow flushed them out. They were sold to a California bookseller, who in turn sold them to the Bancroft Library of the University of California. In 1962 the director of that library graciously turned these Stephens papers over to me.

countenance is regular and well formed, a high projecting forehead an aquiline nose, full dark eyes, which seem to read the very soul; his countenance is a faithfull index of his mind."

The law students were quartered with different families in town, at a cost of $45.00 the year (board cost $2.75 a week and fireplace wood $4.00 a cord). As for Stephens, he wrote: "I am now situated [dated August 17, 1823] in a room that I would not exchange for any in the place. The window at which I am now sitting commands a view of the larger and handsomer part of the village, while by merely turning my head, I can enjoy exclusively the beauties of the country, another window opening to one of the most picturesque landscapes in the neighbourhood. It is every way adapted to a student, not only from its beauty and situation, but from conveniences in itself, good fireplace, tight windows and walls, which will render it peculiarly comfortable; when a North Easter or a Litchfield snowstorm destroys or considerably impairs the present pleasant prospect from my windows."

Life in Litchfield was not all law and contracts. Miss Sally Pierce maintained the Female Academy, the first finishing school in America, where young ladies of good family learned drawing, music, dancing, reciting, and "other accomplishments very well adapted both to taste and delicacy of their sex." Every state of the Union and every territory of the United States was represented by the young men and women at Litchfield. The southerners were there in force, "gay blades" appearing in pink gingham frock coats and exaggerated high collars. In the winter there were sleigh rides, late suppers at the tavern, dancing to the tunes of "Black Caesar on his cracked fiddle," and occasionally dances at the big ballroom at the United States Hotel given by Miss Pierce for her pupils. And there were moments of ale-drinking at Grove Catlin's Tavern ("There was an alarm of fire last week . . . given out by old Catlin our tavern-keeper").

The young women caused Stephens less anxiety in this period than his calligraphy. "My handwriting," he wrote to his father, "being of a kind considerably different from what is ordinarily met with, I have perhaps endeavoured too much to supply in singularity what it wants in excellence." His handwriting remained throughout the year his most vexing problem. "The first observation [on this letter] will probably be the appearance of my handwriting ... which I am endeavouring to correct." Stephens then made an excursus on handwriting, which already shows a certain stylistic liveliness that would develop into that easy, laughing, prose style which gives his books their charm. "I have laboured earnestly and unweariedly; it will of course be more agreeable if I am permitted to add, successfully. A person can hardly imagine the difficulty of such an apparently trifling an operation as that of altering his writing. Every one who has the use of his fingers moves one or another when and where he chooses, and from this uncontrolled and undisputed exercise of these little members, he is apt to conclude that he can exercise as despotic a dominion over them when on paper; persons have told me as much when I have mentioned my little trouble in this matter; but I can now assure them and from actual experience that they are mistaken. A man cannot say to his fingers, on paper I mean, 'do this' and he doeth it when his fingers have been want to do otherwise, for I have said to my fingers 'make this letter so' and they make it not so and as often as I say to my fingers 'make this letter so' they make it not so. To reason correctly, on this subject as on every other we may reason from analogy, the fingers are members of the human body; and as each member being accustomed to act otherwise, the fingers after having been long exercised in some particular manner cannot well be drawn from their accustomed sphere of action. A man being accustomed from his cradle, his legs cannot well move backwards without danger to his nex, which is liable to come in contact with the ground, so to return, the fingers being used to a certain formation of letters and words and confirmed by practice in such formation are not easy to be led from their beaten track; each one seems to consider itself a Free-agent and in spite of reasoning, threats, expostulation and entreaties will have its own way.

"P.S. Please give me your opinion of my handwriting."

On September 20, 1823, Daniel Lord, the New York lawyer who

had already given Stephens a clerkship[3] made him the offer which would begin his legal career, which in turn would heighten his interest in politics and finally, as a concatenation of cause and effect, set him off on his travels. The offer was conveyed through his father, Benjamin Stephens.

"If Mr. Lord," Stephens answered, "could insure me the income he mentioned, this would be decisive of the question; but I am inclined to think he has calculated too largely. If I am not mistaken his own business after a practice of six or seven years yield him very little, if any more than the sum he named; he has been very diligent, I am very willing to allow, excels me in qualifications, and has had very active friends; friends who could interest themselves more openly for him then you could for me. Supposing you were inclining so to do, I would not have that you should run about hunting up clients for me, you might recommend a *customer* to your son, a *merchant*, but you would feel some delicacy in recommending a *client* to your son a *lawyer*; you here in a measure vouch for the capacity and qualifications of your son; in fact, you in effect say, that your son is a 'capable man' a good lawyer etc. This is perhaps carrying the point almost to an extreme, as it might imply that connections are of no use, but yet this circumstance certainly will have some operation. But to postpone this subject for the present after a few words more: when I see so many entering upon this profession which has already more than its share, so many of the finest talents unremitted application and with every incentive to exertion, and hear to many complaints of the scanty pay the law allows its followers, in a word when I see so many, and hear that there are so few clients, I am inclined to believe that he with the very teeth of prudence who rejects even a prospect of succeeding in any other business; There is no such great honour in being a lawyer

[3] In Chancery

I Daniel Lord Jr. a practising Solicitor of this Honorable Court do hereby Certify that John L. Stephens has this day commenced a Clerkship with me in my office as such Solicitor.

Dated New York November 28th A.D. 1822.   DANIEL LORD JR.

I do hereby Certify that a Certificate was this day filed in my office of which the above is a Copy—New York November 28th A.D. 1822.

ISAAC L. KIP. *Assistant Register*

that a person should sacrifice a *probability* of *doing well* at *commerce* to a *possibility* of *scraping* a *livelihood* at *law*; but on the other hand "there is a balm in Gilead; "there is comfort in the consideration of the fact, that many dull, stupid, ignoramusses etc., thrive and seem are able to live upon 'the fat of the land,' and though a mortifying idea to hope to succeed because other blockheads do, yet this very humbling reflection brightens the prospects of one who believes sincerely in the 'glorious uncertainty of the law.' "

On his eighteenth birthday, Stephens had his decision made for him. In accepting his father's decision to have him enter the office of Daniel Lord, Lawyer, he wrote:

> The Judge [Gould] laid down a principle in one of his lectures sometimes since, not indeed as matter of law, but as matter of fact, which it occured to me might be reduced to practice to very good purpose viz. that in all family concerns a Father is *Judge, Jury* and *Executioner.*
>
> I have received your last [letter], am perfectly satisfied with your decision and your reasons for it: though I cannot forbear observing that my most sanguine expectations are exceedingly limited, and even if they should be realized will fix me in quite a humble sphere; indeed there is no food for anticipation: this profession is no fairy-land in which a person can indulge to his heart; content in *building castles* in the air; facts, stubborn facts stare him too broadly in the face to suffer that he should long rove in this world of his own creation, deluding himself with hopes which can never be realized; and in the shape of hundreds of poor complaining, fortune-seeking lawyers show him the slender foundation on which his visionary fabric is erected; however as my expectations are so humble there is no danger of my suffering any pangs from disappointment; But enough of this: the Law a venerable patriarch, is now to include me in its numerous family, and now this point being fully settled I would drop it forever.
>
> P.S. I am now 2 days past eighteen: Three years yet before the law will allow me to think of living by it.
>
> Yr. affectionate son.
JOHN L. STEPHENS.

In September, 1824, John Lloyd Stephens, graduate of law and connected with one of the famous lawyers of the day, returned to New York, conveyed once again in one of those red high-wheeled coaches.

The Far West

In 1823, the Far West was still located east of the Mississippi. Although it was beginning to attract settlers, much of the Ohio, Illinois, and Indian territories were vast and vacant. One of John L. Stephens' aunts, Helena, had married a Quaker who had responded to the restlessness of the period and migrated to Illinois Territory. A pitiful letter had come to the Stephens family from their Aunt Helena Ridgway telling of the death of her child: "How shall I reveal to you my Dear sister my most unhappy moments . . . our sweet little Emma is gone, my grief is unutterable." It was generally agreed that someone of the Stephens family should visit the Ridgways, whereupon John Stephens, before he entered into his career as lawyer, elected to undertake the hazardous trip. His cousin, Charles Hendrickson also agreed; and it is he, rather than Stephens, to whom we owe the chronicles of the first adventure.

By the twenty-sixth of September the cousins were in the western reserve of Ohio. At Pittsburgh they were immediately caught up in a riot about which Charles Hendrickson wrote to his mother, who already feared the worst.

Here the plains and hills were already swarming with pioneers; Marietta, Chillicothe, and Cincinnati were rapidly emerging as cities. Conestoga wagons crawled along the dirt-bound roads, and the rivers were lined with keelboats, flatboats, and broadhorns. The human stream carried along all manner of people: farmers, trappers, traders, German professors, peddlers, and now and then an elegant French emigré. Remembering this American growth gave Stephens, when traveling in Russia, a basis for comparison; "With us a few individuals cut down the trees of the forest, or settle themselves by the banks of a stream, where they happen to find some local advantages, and build houses suited to their necessities; others come and join them, and, by degrees, the little settlement becomes a large city. But here a gigantic government, endowed almost with creative powers, says *Let there be a city!* "

By October 14, 1824, the two young men had reached Cincinnati. Charles Hendrickson had kept up a running commentary: "After starting in a keel boat [from Pittsburgh] with five passengers besides John and myself we were one week going to Wheeling [West Virginia]." Arrived in Cincinnati, they rode out to other cousins, named Lloyd ("They do not live quite as comfortable here as Folks do in Middletown [New Jersey] . . . they live in a log house"). But already Stephens was infecting his cousin with the desire for further travel down the Mississippi. This thoroughly alarmed the latter's mother: "O! my son I long to get a letter after you get to Illinois . . . . I hope you and your cousin John will have too much prudence to go to Natches for it is very Sickley there the Yellow Fevour rages."

They continued on by steamer while Charles Hendrickson tried to allay his mother's fears: "Dear Mama, I suppose you would want to know what kind of company we have fell in with we started from Cincinnati in company with Two Mr. Andersons from New York . . . one a merchant . . . the other practising law in Albany and is traveling for his health, they have been very polite to us. we also at this place fell in company with a Mr. Lewis one of our stage passengers from Wheeling to Chillicothe. . . . he introduced us to the family of Mr Martins *who are very respectable people* they are going down to Natches, to spend the winter, they gave us an invitation to wate and go down with them, we however decline[d] excepting it. . . . we intend starting tomorrow from [Louisville] . . . and take passage to Shawneetown . . . so in the course of 10 or 12 days we will be at Uncle Ridgways. . . . Traveling is very pleasant business but it takes the money out of your pocket very fast. I have no time to write more. John is dressing now and keeps all the time hurrying me to do the same."

By November 24, after "a very tegious passage," they arrived at Shawneetown and made inquiries concerning the whereabouts of Caleb Ridgway. Known as a Quaker of consequence, he had appeared in the first Illinois census in 1820, being listed as head of a family of "five white males under twenty-one and two white females over twenty-one." Mounted with a "half-breed" as a guide, the young men made their way to Carmi, which lay twenty miles from the mouth of the Little Wabash. The land was sparsely settled; they rode for hours without seeing a single house, only an occasional Indian, who silently watched them ride by.

Carmi, when they found it, was a post town with less than a square dozen of houses, although it lay, as the *Gazeteer* said, "in lands of good quality."

"It was about dusk when we arrived," Charles Hendrickson wrote to his mother, "and we decided not [to] let ourselves be known. Weed [the guide] went in and asked if we could stay there all night they informed us we could. . . . Uncle Ridgway came home . . . we talked with him some time, none of them knew us, after keeping them in suspence for about an hour we made ourselves known to the great joy of all the family. Aunt Helena said she had not spent such a pleasant Evening since she had been in Illinois, yesterday she was delivered of a fine son and I expect they will call him Benjamin. . . . I will attempt to tell you a little how they have to get along, in the first place Aunt Helena and Elizabeth have to do all the cooking and work of the house. Uncle Caleb and the boys do all the work on the farm. Uncle makes all their shoes himself, this winter he is going to keep school he has commenced and has got about Twenty scholars. You know it must be pretty hard times to drive Uncle Caleb to that. Aunt Helena has went out and worked by the days herself for the purpose of getting a little necessaries for her family which is what I never expected she would come to."

After a few days with the Ridgways they mounted again and reached St. Louis by the fourth of December ("we will take a steamboat to New Orleans") and set off down the river, a journey Stephens would recall when he floated down the Nile, though by this time the steamer had metamorphosed into a flat-bottom boat: "I remember it was the same on the Ohio and Mississippi. Several years since, when the water was low I started from Pittsburgh in a flat-bottomed boat, to float down to New-Orleans. There too we were in a habit of stopping along the banks of the river at night, or in windy and foggy weather."[4]

The Grand Tour

In 1827, Stephens journeyed to Albany, New York, where he was admitted to the bar, and at the age of twenty-one his name appeared in the New York City Directory: *John Lloyd Stephens 52 Front Street*.

New York was rapidly becoming the empire state and a financial emporium. To keep pace with its sudden growth, New York City then as now continued to change its face: "The city," wrote Philip Hone in his diary, "is now undergoing its annual metamorphosis, houses are being pulled down, others altered. Pearl Street and Broadway in particular are almost impassable by the quantities of rubbish with which they are obstructed." The "Greek Revival" relieved only somewhat the uniform solid red brick of the houses, which was the reigning style. Under the impulse of commerce, gaslight was being introduced; and bathtubs, heretofore never mentioned in polite society, were being installed within the houses, and they were common enough for the council in Philadelphia to pass an ordinance against them on sanitary grounds. New York was exhibiting a changing culture, even though scavenger pigs still ran through the streets.

In 1828, Andrew Jackson became President. A deep discontent had lain over the land, for with the rise of industrialization and the influx of immigrants slums and ghettoes had come into existence. Many voters thought there had been "a betrayal of the Jeffersonian principles of equal rights" and so elected Jackson. An economic struggle developed between Jackson and the Bank of the United States; financial panic followed. One New Yorker elbowing his way through a mob about a closed bank said, "Public opinion means something more than the drilled voices of certain political friends of General Jackson who are pledged, body and soul, to

[4] See page 98 below.

support him at all events." And this was precisely what Stephens was doing, for the law which Stephens practiced from his offices on Wall Street did not wholly hold him: "He never felt," a friend remembered, "much ardour or zeal in the practise of law. Instead his interest was directed towards politics."

This enthusiasm for politics in its curious roundabout way was to lead to great discoveries, for continued speaking engagements and "politicking" led to a throat infection, and as the *Coccaceae* in Stephens did not yield to medicine, the family doctor advised a mild trip to Europe.

An examination of Stephens' life causes one to believe in the providence of accidents. Stephens became a world traveler by accident, and he became a writer by accident. These two accidents produced the explorer, with the result that such nested accidents led to a venture of clear purpose and—no longer accidental—the discovery of the Mayan civilization. Or was it the concatenation of cause and effect of which l'abbé in *La Reine Pédauque* drolly thought was an inseparable chain of events: *Ma première pensée fut de l'embrasser; la seconde, d'admirer cet enchaînement qui m'avait conduit dans ses bras. Car enfin, monsieur, un jeune ecclésiastique, une fille de cuisine, une échelle, une botte de foin! quelle suite, quelle ordonnance! quel concours d'harmonies préétablis! quel enchaînement d'effets et de causes! quelle preuve de l'existence de Dieu!*[5]

The "mild European trip," in search of health, took Stephens to Europe, to Rome, to Naples (where he climbed Vesuvius for reasons of health), then on to Sicily (where he scaled Mount Etna for perhaps the same reason), and then to Greece in wake of the revolution against the Turks. With his head "humming with Homer and Herodotus," he went to see Mycenae, saw the mute remains of its cyclopean walls, and passed on to the Levant.

[5] "My first thought was to embrace her, the second to admire the chain of events which had led me to her arms. For, after all, monsieur, a young divine, a kitchen-maid, a ladder, a bundle of hay! What a sequence, what an ordering of things! What a meeting of pre-established harmonies, what a linking of cause and effect! What a proof of the existence of God!" Anatole France, *La Rôtisserie de la Reine Pédauque* (Paris, 1899), 158.

Smyrna

In the month of April, 1835, Stephens took ship to Smyrna, but impatient at the progress of the ship, which pushed against the desiccating winds of the sirocco, he had himself put ashore at Foggi, at the western end of the Gulf and rented a horse and took the road to Smyrna [Izmir]. "In three hours I was crossing the Caravan bridge—a bridge over the beautiful Melissus on the banks of which Homer was born—and picking my way among caravans which for ages had continued to cross this bridge laden with all the riches of the East I entered the long-looked for city of Smyrna."

On April 16, 1835, John Lloyd Stephens "the author" was born. It may have been, as Stephens said later, that it was "mere accident" that all three "letters" many pages in length written to Fenno Hoffman, editor of the *American Magazine*, had been published without his knowledge;[6] however, it seems that the "mere accident" was contrived, for in his first letter he wrote with Stephensian mockery: "But to you, my dear [Fenno] who know my *touching sensibilities* and who moreover have a tender regard for my character certainly will not publish me [?]." It must have been pre-arranged that the editor would publish anonymously; for "by an American" appears under the title of *Scenes in the Levant*.

There, under the Mussulman flag, pages of fairy scenes walked before his eyes: caravans led by turbaned Turks, camels plodding down the narrow aisles of sun-splashed streets, veiled women dressed in white, their covered faces effectively concealing every feature but bringing to "bear only the artillery of their eyes," and Tartars, Greeks, Turks, and Franks—it was like the Scheherazade. "I have just arrived at this place and I live to tell it," so he pro-

[6] "An account of my journey from Athens to Smyrna, given in a letter to friends at home, was published during my absence and without my knowledge in successive numbers of the American Monthly Magazine, and perhaps the favourable notice taken of it had some influence in inducing me to write a book."

These articles, entitled "Scenes in the Levant," appeared in the *American Monthly Magazine* as follows: Vol. I, No. 2 (October, 1835), 88–99; Vol. I, No. 3 (November, 1835), 174–83; Vol. I, No. 4 (December, 1835), 262–68; and Vol. II, No. 3 (November, 1836), 480–89.

ceeded to write in the letter that detailed his adventures from Athens to Smyrna. He wrote of Greece, Homer, and Scio, he painted verbal pictures of the land, and although at points he damned the Turks, he admitted they had "exceedingly good points: chibouks, coffee and as many wives as they please." He confessed that the ladies gave him no rest. "I never saw so much beauty . . . such eyes large dark and rolling. And they walk too, as if conscious of their high pretensions . . . under that enchanting turban charged with the whole artillery of their charms. It is a perfectly unmasked battery; nothing can stand against it. I wonder the Sultan allows it."

Stephens liked the free and easy way of the Levant, he found: "Every Stranger, upon his arrival in Smyrna, is introduced to the Casino. I went there the first time to a concert. It is a large building, erected by a club of merchants, with a suite of rooms on the lower floor, billiards, cards, reading and sitting in the ball-room, and, from what I had seen in the streets, I expected an extraordinary display of beauty; but I was much disappointed. The company consisted only of the aristocracy or higher mercantile classes. A patent of nobility in Smyrna, as in our own city, is founded upon the time since the possessor gave up selling foods, or the number of consignments he receives in the course of a year."

Stephens was also impressed with the scurrying of big business: "Society in Smyrna is purely mercantile," he wrote, "and having been so long out of the way of it, I was actually grateful once more to hear men talking with all their souls about cotton, stocks, exchanges, and other topics of interest. . . . I took up an American paper, and heard Boston, and New York, and Baltimore, and cotton, and opium, and freight, and quarter percent less bandied about, until I almost fancied myself at home." Indeed, American trading communities had been in the Levant since colonial times, as a recently published history of the area relates with pointed detail.[7]

His real interests, however, continued to lean toward the antique and history. "During one evening the young priest brought out an

---

[7] *Pioneers East: The Early American Experience in the Middle East*, by David H. Finnie (Cambridge, Harvard University Press, 1967).

edition of Homer and I surprised *him* and *myself* by being able to translate a passage in the Iliad. I translated it into French and my companion explained it in modern Greek to the young priest."

Stephens followed the Roman road to Ephesus and wandered among the ruins of one of the greatest cities of Asia. One can sense in his letter the gradual accumulative effect that the pleasure of ruins was having upon him. In a *khan*, a Turkish tavern, he set about to make himself comfortable. "And here I spent half the night musing upon the strange concatenation of circumstances which had broken up the quiet life of a practising attorney and set him a straggler from a busy money-getting land to meditate among the ruins of ancient cities, and sleep on a mud-floor with turbaned turks."

Stephens then proceeded to Constantinople "in less time," he said, "than swift-footed Achilles could have traveled it"; he went by steamboat. "Join me now in the race," he wrote in his second letter, "if your heart does not break at going by at the rate of eight to ten miles an hour, I will ship you over a piece of the most classic ground . . . in history." He sailed past the Isles of Greece, shadowed by Mount Olympus, past Sigaeum, where Homeric battles were fought, into the Hellespont—"where Leander swam for the love of Hero, and Lord Byron and Mr. Ekenhead for fun." All the while he conversed with two Americans returning from a tour of Egypt. They spoke with so much enthusiasm about the ruins that he was sorely tempted to try the Nile, but at that moment cholera was raging in Alexandria.

Constantinople was, like most of the Levantine cities, relatively new ground for an American. In 1800, Commodore William Bainbridge, bearing the annual tribute to the Dey of Algiers, had put into Constantinople, carrying for the first time the American flag into this Saracen world. Two years later a consul was appointed in the Levant, whence Turkish opium and Smyrna figs were exported to Boston. In 1831, only three years before Stephens' arrival, Commodore Porter had been raised to the rank of chargé d'affaires.

At Constantinople, Stephens had made arrangements with "an ill-smelling Tartar" to ride with him through the Balkans to France, but at the last moment there was announced the departure of a Russian government vessel, a miserable *pyroscaphe*, bound for the Black Sea and Odessa. So Stephens, following the theory of cause and effect inherent in accidents, gave up the Tartar. He went instead to Russia.

Russia and Poland

At Odessa, Stephens was immediately struck "with the military aspect of things"; in front of the examining officers the passengers paraded, one at a time—Turks, Christians, Jews, Germans, Russians, Poles, Greeks, Illyrians, Moldavians, Wallachians, Bulgarians, and one American: John Lloyd Stephens, New Yorker. They were stripped of their clothes, fumigated, and then examined by the port doctor.[8] They were also forced to pass through an involved *pratique*, including the declaration at customs of all books banned by the censors. Stephens did not declare his Byron. The author of *Childe Harold* had long been on the Russian list, for in a lyrical outburst he had lampooned "that coxcomb Tsar, that autocrat of waltzes and war." Stephens was loath to part with his Byron, for he had been, as Stephens said, "my companion in Italy, and Greece . . . so I put the book under my arm, threw my cloak over me and walked out."

Odessa, which had been a swamp until decreed a city by Empress Catherine, had been built in 1796. By 1835 it was a regal city; there was a promenade a mile in length, a palace for the governor, a casino, a theater—where Stephens witnessed a performance of the *Barber of Seville*. "I should" he confessed, "as soon thought of an opera-house at Chicago as here; but I have already found what

[8] "We were obliged to strip naked [but] the bodily examination was as delicate as the nature of the case would admit; for the doctor merely opened the door, looked in, and went out without taking his hand from the knob. It was none of my business, I know, and may be thought impertinent, but as he closed the door, I could not help calling him back to ask him whether he held the same inquisition upon the fair sex; to which he replied with a melancholy upturning of the eyes, that in the good old days of Russian barbarism this had been part of his duties, but that the march of improvements had invaded his rights and given this portion of his professional duties to a *sage femme*."

impressed itself more forcibly upon me at every step, that Russia is a country of anomalies. . . . There is no country where cities have sprung up so fast and increased so rapidly as in ours; and altogether perhaps nothing in the world can be compared with our Buffalo, Rochester, Cincinnati, etc. But Odessa has nothing of the appearance of our cities."

Stephens compared Russia with his own country: "We are both young, and both marching with gigantic strides to greatness, yet we move by different roads; and the whole face of the country, from the new city, Odessa, on the borders of the Black Sea, to the steppes of Siberia, shows a different order of government and a different constitution of Society. With us a few individuals cut down the trees of the forest, or settle themselves by the banks of a stream, where they happen to find some local advantages, and build houses suited to their necessities; others come and join them, and, by degrees, the little settlement becomes a large city. But here [in Russia] a gigantic government, endowed almost with creative powers, says *"Let there be a city!"*

A few days later Stephens moved into the Russian interior, bouncing across the steppes. He seemed to face without undue anxiety two thousand miles of travel in a springless *podorshni*. Henri, the driver, whom he had procured in Odessa, was a wild-looking Frenchman with a scar across his mouth where a saber had knocked out most of his teeth, causing him to shovel out his words from the side of his mouth. When Stephens asked him on his hire if he were French, he drew himself up with great dignity, smoothed out his coat, and replied with great hauteur, *"Monsieur, je suis Parisien."*

They bounded across Russia, dashing past miserable people who ran out at their appearance to give obeisance to what they believed must be a grand seigneur. They came into Kiev (Stephens was the first American ever to pass through it) and followed the river Dnieper on its sinuous course toward Moscow. Stephens was horrified by the abject misery of the serf. "I found in Russia [in 1835] many interesting subjects of comparison between that country and my own, but it was deep humiliation I felt that the most odious feature of the despotic government found a parallel in ours. . . . I do not hesitate to say that, abroad, slavery stands as a dark blot upon our national character . . . it will not admit of any palliation . . . I was forcibly struck with a parallel between the white serfs of Russia and the African bondsmen at home."

At this time Russia was a semi-Asiatic power; the waves of Tartar hordes had left behind a residuum of barbarism, which, despite the Westernization of Peter the Great, had diverted what should have been the normal development of the Russian people into the European concert of nations. Of Russia's fifty millions, more than one-third, in Stephens' time, were serfs bound as vassals to the aristocracy, to the church, and to the crown. Nicholas I, who succeeded Alexander, was the incarnation of the absolute: "God has placed me over Russia, and you must bow down before me, for my throne which is His altar. . . . My watchful eyes constantly detect internal evils of foreign enemies. . . . I have no need for counsel."

The entire route had neither inns, taverns, nor restaurants, and Stephens had to "trust," like Napoleon when he invaded Russia, "to make up the rest . . . of their food . . . by foraging." The only succor they received was offered by Jews who were the postmasters on the road.

Moscow in 1835 presented a magnificent vista. Six hundred churches—multiple-domed, with gilded crosses, spires, and steeples—towering above the lesser buildings gave it an extraordinary appearance. The dwellings were tastefully surrounded by gardens, a vivid contrast to the walled monasteries.

Installed in the Hotel Germania and having had a Turkish bath, Stephens toured Moscow. He was continually amazed by the paradox of Asiatic Moscow: it had an inextricable mixture of barbarism and Parisian elegance. In his hotel Stephens conversed with a French marquis, dressed in threadbare elegance, who had remained in Moscow after his capture during Napoleon's invasion. The marquis insisted, between sips of brandy, that the only difference between Russian seigneurs and serfs was that one wore his shirt inside his trousers and the other outside. "But my friend," Stephens observed, "spoke with the prejudice of twenty years of exile." The Frenchman earned his rubles by acting as a spy against foreigners. He confided to the American that he must watch not only his language but also the content of his speech. "It is almost impossible for an American to believe that even in Russia he incurs any risk in speaking what he thinks; he is apt to regard the stories of summary punishment for freedom of speech as bugbears or bygone things. In my own case, even when men looked cautiously around the room and then spoke in whispers I could not believe there was any danger. Still I had become prudent enough not to talk with any unnecessary indiscretion."

The road from Moscow to St. Petersburg—McAdam-style the whole way—was one of Europe's best; inns, regulated by tariffs, were operated by the government, and St. Petersburg, the window that Peter had built so that the Russians might look upon Europe, was splendidly conceived, with its palaces, its Hermitage, its memories of Peter and Catherine and her lover Potemkin, and its regiments of gaily uniformed soldiers. Stephens spent several days at the capital and celebrated the Fourth of July there at the American Embassy with the American minister.[9]

Leaving St. Petersburg, however, was not like entering it. On arrival, Stephens had obtained a *carte de séjour*, without which no one could remain in the capital and had submitted to routine questions of age, destination, and so on, thoroughly satisfying the authorities that he "had no intention of preaching democratic doctrines." Yet as one could not remain in St. Petersburg without permission, neither could one leave without it. He had, according to law, to advertise his intention of departing in the government gazette on three successive days. Suspicion was directed toward him because he planned to cross Poland. And for what purpose:

[9] ". . . much interesting information from home, and more than all, a budget of New-York newspapers. It was a long time since I had seen a New-York paper, and I hailed all the well-known names, informed myself of every house to let, every vessel to sail, all the cotton in market and a new kind of shaving soap for sale at Hart's Bazar; read with particular interest the sales of real estate by James Bleecker and Sons; wondered at the rapid increase of the city in creating a demand for building lots on one hundred and twenty-seventh street, and reflected that some of my old friends had probably grown so rich that they would not recognize me on my return."

Pleasure? Who, in God's name, said the exasperated police official, ever wanted to travel in Poland "for pleasure"?

Stephens left for Warsaw in company with a tall Pole, who, born in Belgium of French descent, possessed, he remembered, to a "striking degree the compound *amor patriae* incident to the relationship in which he stood to these countries." Travel was done in a *kibitka*, a round-bottomed springless box cradle on four wheels. They bounced over the same road that Napoleon had followed two decades before in his advance on Moscow. They went over the immense distances along the execrable road past the Dwina River into Minsk, and beyond it to Warsaw, which lay partially in ruins, the result of the latest revolution which had flared up over the eternal "Polish problem." On the night of November 30, 1830, the Poles had begun a badly managed revolution, led by political generals who were incompetent and irresolute. The uprising was crushed.

Stephens, too, had his problems. He had not fully recovered from the illness that had sent him to Europe for a "mild tour." In Warsaw, he was so overcome by malaise that he took to bed and from it wrote home:

> *Warsaw*, August 15, 1835:
>
> I have reached this place to be put on my back by a Polish doctor. How long he will keep me here I do not know. He promises to set me going in a week; and, as he has plenty of patients without keeping me down, I have great confidence in him. Besides having weathered a Greek, an American, and a Russian, I think I shall be too much for a Pole.

So he escaped the doctor. In time he crossed the Vistula River, and then continued to and crossed the border into Austria. Passing through Vienna, he went up the Danube into Germany, and under the cloudy November skies he took the road to Paris.[10]

Why, once in Paris, did Stephens decide to go to Egypt instead of returning to America? We do not know. It has been presumed

[10] This trip was published under the title *Incidents of Travel in Greece, Turkey, Russia, and Poland* (his second book), by Harper and Brothers in 1838, in three volumes. There was a Dublin edition (1838), British (1841), and Swedish (1841).

that it was his perusal of Léon de Laborde's book *Voyage de l'Arabie Petrée*, which had been recently published in Paris, that decided the issue; but apparently Petra was not considered until he was well up the Nile, when he raised the question of Petra while dining with some English gentlemen. "It is to them," he wrote, "that I am indebted to the first suggestion to me of the route to Petra." Where the idea of Petra came from is not even hinted at in books or letters. Whatever prompted the trip—incident or accident —it was to be one more of the concatenations of cause and effect. He would go to the Nile, to Egypt, and to Petra. This hegira was to change the course of his life. It was also to change the course of American archaeological history.

Egypt

John Lloyd Stephens was one of the six Americans to sign the consular book in Alexandria in the year 1836. Many Americans had, of course, been there long before Stephens, notably John Ledyard of Connecticut. Born in 1751, he had sailed with Captain Cook, had traveled to Russia, and then was engaged by the African Society of London "to Traverse from east to west . . . the widest part of Africa." Arriving in Cairo in 1788, he had promptly died.

Americans began to appear very early within the British business community and in Cairo and Alexandria as well at the turn of the century. By 1820 they were in sufficient number to prompt the appointment of an American consul: one such was George Gliddon, who gave much aid and direction to the travels of Stephens, for Gliddon spoke Arabic and had a knowledge of archaeology through the Society of Englishmen long since on the Nile. In later years he was to provide a source of amusement to the wits of Broadway.[11]

[11] George Gliddon (1809–1852), many years in Egypt, helped archaeological travelers. He wrote several books, among them *The American in Egypt* (1840) and *The Races of Mankind* (1851); he gathered skulls for Dr. Samuel Morton, an activity which resulted in his book *Crania Aegyptica*. He was the first person to lecture on Egyptology in America, visiting in 1837–38 and 1842–50. He gave the Lowell lectures in Boston in 1843 and created a transparent panorama of Egypt which he exhibited in the New York Chinese Museum on Broadway. He was famous, among the wits of Broadway, for the *faux pas* attending the unwrapping of an Egyptian mummy which

Stephens' Nilitic adventure was taken alone, except for the boat crew (and he remembered to keep the original contract in Arabic) and his servant Paolo (Paul). "For myself being alone and not in very good health I had some heavy moments but I have no hesitation in saying that, with a friend, a good boat well fitted out with books, guns, plenty of time and a cook like Michael, a voyage on the Nile would exceed traveling within my experience."

Stephens saw, as his "Incidents" reveal, more than the usual traveler. He had a small library containing the works of Volney, Byron, Chateaubriand, Belzoni, Herodotus, and Diodorus Siculus. He doubtlessly was intending to write a book himself, for despite his saying "that he knew nothing about archaeology," he was careful to take measurements of several of the sites.

At Dendera, which lies below Aswan and across from Qena on the Nile, Stephens came across his first Egyptian structure on the Nile, and, like everyone else, he left his graffiti on the blackened walls of the Temple. As he reveals in his *Incidents of Travel*, he next saw the Valley of Kings, marveled at the extent of the quarries of Aswan, moved on to Elephantine, and was enraptured like others before him by the ruins on the Islands of Philae, where he left his second graffiti below that of General Dessaix, conqueror of Upper Egypt, as well as that of his late friend Cornelius Bradford.

At Luxor another concatenation occurred that would eventuate in the discovery of the Mayas. He dined with "a gentleman and his lady, he an honorable and heir of an old and respectable title." They had been to Mount Sinai and the Red Sea, and they suggested Petra. "To them," he wrote *"I am indebted for the first suggestion to me of the route to Sinai and Arabia Petraea."*

It was at the Colossi of Memnon where still another incident took place. These colossi had only recently been excavated by a team of architect-archaeologists led by one Frederick Catherwood; had Stephens looked more closely at the mass of signatures that had

---

he declared to be female, but which when unwrapped proved to be a male, exhibiting in its fossil state the erected unequivocal mark of its sex. Later he was associated with E. G. Squier in the building of the Trans-Oceanic Honduras Railway, contracted malaria, and died in Panama. Squier visited his grave in 1863, which he reports in his book (*Peru*, 1877).

been cut into them, he would have seen "F. Catherwood Archt. 1832." One day, following this Liebnitzian concourse of pre-established harmonies, these two, Catherwood and Stephens, would meet, and together as author and artist would not only rediscover the Maya culture but also would later build the Panama Railway across the isthmus.

Frederick Catherwood was born in 1799, in London. After several years sketching in Italy, Sicily, and Greece, he arrived in Egypt in 1823. It was the time when Egyptianism was at its apogee because of the appearance of publications of the French savants who had accompanied Napoleon.

In the autumn of 1824, Catherwood, in company with Henry Parke and Joseph Scoles, architect-artists all, went up the Nile a thousand miles beyond the First Cataract into the Nubian country, drawing and sketching on the way. There, at considerable risk, these young architects systematically mapped the clusters of ruins on the Upper Nile. In more than one sense Catherwood's career was cast in Egypt, for later at Alexandria he met Robert Hay, a rich and titled man who had not yet made his first Nile journey. It was Catherwood's drawings that delighted him and determined his interest in Egyptology.

So Robert Hay of Linplum, heir to the marquisate of Tweeddale, with his retinue of experienced artists, architects, topographical draftsmen, and antiquarians (they were not yet archaeologists), envisioned a most ambitious archaeological program. He planned to go up the Nile and investigate each ruined site, known and unknown. He planned to have his artists draw the murals with their inscriptions at each and to have the architects make ground plans of the ruins. It was to be the greatest scientific expedition since Napoleon's. Robert Hay's expedition was composed of many men, all of whom in later years became famous for one reason or another.[12]

[12] The group included Joseph Bonomi, Francis Arundale, James Haliburton (called Burton), Charles Laver, Edward W. Lane and Sir John Gardner Wilkinson (two incipient Egyptologists), G. B. Greenough, George A. Hoskins, and, to end the impressive list, Frederick Catherwood. These young men, during the years 1824–33, were to lay down the basis of Egyptian archaeology.

Arabia Petra

On March 14, 1836, John Lloyd Stephens became "Abdel Hasis," the slave of God, and "provided myself with the unpretending and respectable costume of a Cairo merchant, a long red silk gown, with a black abbas of camels' hair over it with a green and yellow striped handkerchief rolled around it as a turban: white trousers, large red shoes, yellow slippers, blue sash, a pair of large Turkish pistols." It is precisely thus costumed that Stephens appears as an illustration in his book on Arabia Petraea in anonymity, for the illustration was titled "a Merchant of Cairo."

Stephens also had the good fortune, before he left, to meet Maurice-Adolphe Linant[13], the co-author of a celebrated book on Petra, who eleven years before had taken the route Stephens proposed to travel. His expedition in 1827 had been the second successful expedition to penetrate Petra, that intaglio city which had lain for one thousand years known only to the Bedouins. In 1806, Ulrich Seetzen, a German Orientalist traveling as an Arab, had heard a Bedouin speak of the ruins of Petra, and excited by its prospects, tried to enter it and was murdered. Johann Ludwig Burckhardt, who discovered it, spent two years in preparation, studying Arabic and learning the Koran by rote; and with Teutonic thoroughness having himself, belatedly, circumcised, for possession of foreskin was as dangerous in Arabia as possession of the Bible. Then under the pretense of being a mendicant beggar named Ibrahim Ibn Abdallah, who had vowed to slaughter a goat in honor of Aaron, he made his entrance into it in 1812.

This Petra was Stephens' goal. Cairo's seasoned travelers pointed out to him the dangers of his itinerary, for beyond the Nile, the firman of Mehemet Ali was so much paper. With an experienced camel driver and his faithful servant Paolo dressed as an Arab, Stephens mounted a vault-ribbed camel and disappeared into the desert. "I am about to cross a dreary waste of land," he wrote in his final letter home, "to pitch my tent wherever the setting sun

[13] León de Laborde and Maurice-Adolphe Linant, *Voyage de l'Arabie Petrée* (Paris, 1830; London, 1838). Stephens thought so highly of the work that he pirated all the illustrations of this book for his own.

might find me, and . . . to have for my companions the wild, rude Bedouins of the desert, to follow the wandering footsteps of children of Israel . . . to visit Mount Sinai, and then to the long-lost city of Petra, the capital of Arabia Petraea."

With his small caravan he took the Hejaz road to Mecca, passed through Suez, and followed the route along the shores of the Red Sea. The party soon lacked water, and in two days that were in utter want, "rivers were floating through my imagination when we saw a single palm-tree shading a fountain . . . and without much respect of persons, we all threw ourselves upon the fountain."

Herman Melville remembered that episode when he saw Stephens "that wonderful Arabian Traveller" in church. "For I very well remembered," Melville wrote in *Redburn*, "staring at a man myself . . . who had been in Stony Arabia and passed through strange adventures there, all of which with my own eyes I had read in the book which he wrote, an arid-looking book in a pale yellow cover.

" 'See what big eyes he has,' whispered my aunt; 'They got so big because when he was almost dead with famishing in the desert, he all at once caught sight of a date tree, with ripe fruit hanging on it.'

"Upon this I stared at him until I thought his eyes were really of an uncommon size, and stuck out from his head like lobster. I am sure my own eyes must have been magnified as I stared. When church was out, I wanted my aunt to take me along and follow the traveller home. But she said that the constables would take us up if we did; and so I never saw this wonderful Arabian traveller again. But he long haunted me; and several times I dreamt of him and thought his great eyes were grown until larger and rounder; and once I had a vision of that date tree."[14]

At Mount Sinai, Stephens' party took refuge for a few days in the ancient Monastery of St. Catherine, where Stephens scandalized the patriarch by bringing up the subject of Mohammed in the sacred precincts of Mount Sinai. Then they shaped their desert journey for Aqaba and, finally, Petra.

At the entrance to Petra was the Ain Musa, "the spring," and the

[14] Redburn: *His First Voyage* (New York, 1924), 4.

way to the city was a twisting gorge which had anciently been cut by water action. The gorge, the Wadi Musa, is narrow and vertical. It makes its sinuous way for more than two miles, then suddenly at the end of the Sîk, it opens into a wide valley. Precisely at the opening is the temple façade of El Khasna carved out of the "rosiest red of all rocks of Petra." "The first view of that superb façade," wrote Stephens, "must produce an effect which could never pass away. Even now [he was writing in 1837] that I have returned to the pursuits and thought-engrossing incidents of a life in the busiest city of the world, often in situations as widely different as light and darkness, I see before me the façade of that temple; neither the Colosseum at Rome . . . nor the ruins of the Acropolis at Athens, nor the Pyramids, nor the mighty temples of the Nile, are so often present to my memory."[15] It was here that Stephens the lawyer became Stephens the archæologist.

Within the temple a large central hall was cut into the bedrock; its undecorated walls, blackened from herdsmen's fires, were the nightstalls of nomad flocks. On the back wall Stephens discovered the names of the English travelers who had preceded him—Leigh, Bankes, Irby, and Mangles—who in 1818 had paid 1,500 piasters to gain entrance to Petra. Below these were the names of Léon, Marquis de Laborde, and Stephens' friend Maurice-Adolphe Linant. Stephens was the first American to visit Petra: "I confess that I felt what, I trust, was not an inexcusable pride, in writing upon the innermost wall of that temple, the name of an American citizen."

Petra had been built or, more accurately, carved by the Nabateans, a Semitic-speaking Arabic people. Originally a nomadic people, they turned from piracy to trade, then extended their kingdom into Jordan, parts of Syria, and down into Arabia Deserta. The first historical reference to them is on the "List of Enemies" of the Assyrians dated 647 B.C. The Romans "suggested" to Rabel II, the last of the Nabatean kings, that he have himself and Petra annexed to Rome, so in A.D. 106 the city was annexed and Hadrian renamed it "Hadriana."

[15] See page 256 below.

The relatively soft sandstone surface is harsh-colored, but once the surface is broken, the stone reveals violent colors in vivid, swirling patterns, as if modeled upon moiré silk. The Nabateans did not really build the city; they carved and hewed it out of the rock.

For once Stephens was at a loss for words. In his journal he sought for the adjectives that would describe the coloring of the rock temples. In the morning they were like great rainbows, flashing out vermillion and saffron streaked with white and crimson; at dusk, when the stone was enveloped in its last shadows, it was rose red, shot blue with porphyry.

Not all travelers were impressed, however; when Charles Doughty made his way through it in November, 1876, on his way to Arabia Deserta and literary immortality, he found it unbeautiful: "Strange and horrible as a pit in an inhuman deadness of nature, is this site of the Nabateans' metropolis; the eye recoils from the mountainous close of iron-cliffs, in which the ghastly monuments of a sumptuous barbaric art are from the first glance an eyesore."

Palestine

Stephens made his way to the Holy land over an old land route which had once been a Roman road-track. He rode through the utterly desolate Land of Edom, a formidable land passage even now. His narration, *A Journey Through Idumea*, was used by Herman Melville, who read it closely when he wrote his *Encantadas*.[16] He spoke of a desolation "which exalts them above Idumea" and again "like split Syrian gourds left withering in the sun," and finally of the desert's "emphatic uninhabitableness."

Stephens' caravan made a wide, circling movement to reach the Holy Land. He took not just another trip to the Dead Sea, since he was able to acquire a map of it, made by a Mr. Costigan ("an Irishman"), which was one of the most accurate maps since Roman

[16] *The Encantadas, or Enchanted Isles*, with an introduction, critical epilogue, and bibliographical notes by Victor Wolfgang von Hagen (San Francisco, The Grabhorn Press, 1940).

times. This map and other materials he later turned over to an official American expedition which surveyed the Jordan and the Dead Sea, and he received this acknowledgment: "To Mr. Stephens of New York, the author of one of the most interesting books of travels which our language can produce I return in this public manner my acknowledgements for a timely letter written when the equipment of the expedition was under consideration."[17]

When Stephens arrived in Jerusalem later on in 1836, he made a tour of the holy places, noted the historical facts, and yet always managed to give them a mischievous twist. (A reviewer of *Arabia Petraea* in the *Christian Examiner*, although recommending the book to his brethren, complained of the "levities with which the book is spiced and which occasionally give a queer air of irreverence . . . about sacred things." Another religious journal reviewer professed that he did not know who this "American" was, but he, too, objected to this "spice of the irreligious."

After finding the grave of his boyhood friend Cornelius Bradford, under whose graffiti he had placed his own in Egypt and at Mount Sinai,[18] he found Frederick Catherwood. He discovered him cartographically, so to speak. On this tour of Jerusalem he bought a map published by "F. Catherwood Archt., 21, Charles Square, Hoxton, London," and extolled its accuracy in the eighth edition of *Arabia Petraea*.

London

In London Stephens finally met this Mr. Catherwood in person. He was lecturing before an immense panorama called "A Description of the Ruins of Jerusalem."

In Leicester Square in the late eighteenth century a rotunda had been erected in which circular panoramic views of cities, battles, and new events of the time were exhibited—panoramas painted in continuous canvases, ofttimes two hundred feet in length and ten feet in height. The panorama had passed into the proprietorship of Robert Burford, who engaged artists to paint these panorama

[17] William F. Lynch, U.S.N., *Narrative of the United States Expedition to the River Jordan* (Washington, 1843), vi.
[18] See pages 407–409 below.

exhibits. There Stephens found the exhibition of a "Panorama of Jerusalem."

After they met, in the rare moments when Catherwood became autobiographical, Stephens learned that he had been born north of the Thames, out on Hackney Road, in the parish of Hoxton, in a house at 21 Charles Square, on February 27, 1799. He had attended some lectures at the Royal Academy, where he fell under the spell of the work of Giovanni Battista Piranesi, the Italian master of architectural invention. Later he had followed his friend Joseph Severn to Rome.

In 1823, Catherwood left for Greece, in company with other artists and architects, twenty in number, who had formed the Society of Englishmen. There Catherwood expanded his knowledge of classical architecture, but revolution was over the land; even while Catherwood was making casts of ancient sculpture, the Turks were laying siege to Athens. Dressed as a Turk, Catherwood escaped from Greece, after which he made his first tour of the Nile.

Stephens was not altogether surprised to find himself well received and known by the American consul in London. Colonel Thomas Aspinwall of Brookline, Massachusetts, was consul as well as the literary representative of Washington Irving, Fitz-Greene Halleck, and other American writers, and he had the issues of the *American Magazine* containing the "Scenes in the Levant." In Aspinwall's office Stephens met also an old friend, Rev. Dr. Francis Lister Hawks, like himself a Tapping Reeve Law School graduate. He was then laying the literary foundation for the John Jacob Astor Library of New York, and therefore believed himself possessed of a good "literary nose." When he heard Stephens speak of his adventures and later listened to a certain passage of *A Journey Through Idumea*, he remembered saying, "Stephens, you should write a book."

New York Again

The New York to which Stephens returned in 1836, to write *Arabia Petraea*, had visibly changed since he had left it in 1834 to go upon his Ulyssean wandering. Most of it was a blackened shell. The fire that had gutted it broke out on a winter's night in 1835—somewhere in the vicinity of Maiden Lane—and made an Aetna-like progress since the severe cold (the water froze in the pipes) hampered the firemen who were to stem the holocaust as it swept through Wall Street.

Yet New York, undeterred by fire or politics, was growing out of its traditional bounds; the new census placed the population at over two hundred thousand, and the city limits were stretching beyond the City Hall, once set as the optimum of expansion.

Martin Van Buren, the newly elected President, entered office with an impressive mandate from the people. He inherited Jackson's office, and promptly after taking office he also inherited the financial crash. Inflation as a concomitant of Jackson's policies had been gaining steadily since 1834; by 1837 paper money had grown far beyond the proportion of specie. There were crop failures and speculation. Credit was tightened. Gold fled the country, and America was in the grip of the worst depression it had ever known. By May, 1837, eight hundred banks had suspended payment, freezing $120,000,000 in deposits. In a single six months, one-third of the population of New York City was unemployed.

But Stephens now seemed oblivious of the financial chaos for he was writing *Arabia Petraea*. He was aware of the status of American literature. Authorship was then mostly the diversion of amateurs; moreover, it would be injurious to his law practice if it were known that he was writing a book, since writing was considered a gratification of idleness. Those who did write received little for their efforts. Emerson obtained nothing from his own publications; Nathaniel Hawthorne had published *Fanshawe* in 1828 at his own expense; Poe never did solve the problem of living by his writings; and Thoreau did not seem to need money for the type of life he lived. Prescott, who later made a sizable fortune from his "Conquests," said at the beginning of his career: "I am not obliged to write for bread and I will never write for money." Spelling books, dictionaries, notes on the Gospels, "geographies," and other such were the only types of commercial literature. It was axiomatic in publishing circles that it was deleterious to publish an American author. "But why should they anyway," questioned the English critic Sydney Smith, "why should Americans write books when a six weeks' passage brings them in their own language our sense, our science and genius in bales and hogsheads. . . . In the four quarters of the globe who reads an American book?"

Stephens, aware of all this, nonetheless in the winter of 1836 made a contract with Harper and Brothers for a publication on Egypt and Arabia Petraea in "two duodecimo volumes."[19]

The manuscript of some 180,000 words, in two volumes, with illustrations by Alexander Anderson (pirated from Léon de Laborde), was written in less than a year. It was published in the fall of 1837. Despite its light touch, the casual and droll style, *Arabia Petraea* exhibited considerable erudition, for Stephens had read widely so as to extend and enhance his own observations. Volney's *Ruins*, Keith's *Prophecies*, the "Travels of Lamartine," the researches of Pococke, and Keniker's *The Letters from Pales-*

[19] "John L. Stephens, a clever enterprising New-York lawyer, author of Travels in Russia, Greece, etc., and of Central American Antiquities, and afterwards President of Panama Railroad, made his entry into the world of literature in a rather whimsical fashion. He had been, many years ago, in Eastern Europe, upon I know not what business. After his return to New-York he happened one day to be in the publishing house of Harper Brothers, when the senior member of the firm, Mayor Harper, fell into conversation with him about literature—that is, the sort of books he sold most of, which was his special interest in the matter.

" 'Travels sell about the best of anything we get hold of,' said he. 'They don't always go with a rush, like a novel by a celebrated author, but they sell longer, and in the end, pay better. By the way you've been to Europe; why not write us a book of travels?'

" 'Never thought of such a thing,' said the lawyer. 'I travelled in out-of-the-way places and went very fast. I made no notes and should have very little to write about.'

" 'That's no matter,' said the publisher who had taken a fancy that he could get hold of something racy from the fast-talking New-Yorker; 'You went through, and saw the signs. We have got plenty of books about those countries. You just pick out as many as you want, and I will send them home for you; you can dish up something.'

"He did dish up three volumes of very amusing travels and in due time, three more, and the Harpers paid him some twenty-five thousand dollars as his portion of the enterprise—which was by no means the lion's share. Encouraged by this success, Mr. Stephens made an expedition to explore the ruins of Palenque, in Central America, taking an artist with him to do the illustrations. His work on those mysterious antiquities may be more accurate than the Oriental Travels, but it is not half so amusing, and as it was an expensive illustrated work, I doubt if it paid as well."—Thomas Low Nichols, *Forty Years of American Life, 1820–61* (New York, 1937), 211–12.

tine of Jolliffe, the *Narratives* of Legh, the published explorations of Burckhardt, Laborde, Linant, Belzoni, Bankes, and Ulrich Seetzen were read, studied, and absorbed, yet so judiciously that their presence is hardly noticeable. Stephens did not fill his travels with learned intrusions that would spoil the flow of the narrative; his humor was droll, ofttimes Boccaccian, his excursus into history masterfully done.

Arabia Petraea was widely reviewed, and without exception it was widely praised. General Lewis Cass, a former governor of Michigan and a future secretary of war, who had followed Stephens' path to Egypt in 1837, found that Stephens possessed "admirable qualities for the traveller." His review, with digressions, footnotes, paraphrases, and asides, went to seventy-five pages, of which Cass thought so highly that he published it separately. He found Stephens' style excellent ("at times rising into elevation"), and he assured the prospective purchaser of the book that he would not be bored with that "eternal affectation of *knowledge and taste.*"

But it was Edgar Allan Poe's review of *Arabia Petraea*—for he was the only critic then to have anything intelligent to say about the mechanics of writing—that helped make the book famous. In his first assignment for *The New-York Review* Poe gave the volumes a twelve-page review, a scholarly article that Poe later recalled with pride. He found the book "written with a freshness of manner evincing manliness of feeling." After twelve pages he concluded: "We take leave of Mr. Stephens with hearty respect. We hope it is not the last time we shall hear from him. He is a traveller with whom we shall like to take other journies equally free from the exaggerated sentimentality of Chateaubriand, or the sublimated, the *too* French enthusiasm of Lamartine. . . . Mr. Stephens writes like a man of good sense and sound feeling."[20]

The sales of *Arabia Petraea* reflected the reviews. The English press, including the irascible and indomitable Sydney Smith, found at last an American work it could praise. The *Athenaeum* found them "two pleasant volumes" with "not a wearisome page in the

---

[20] Poe's review of Stephens' *Arabia Petraea* was considered sufficiently important to be reprinted in his *Complete Works* (New York, 1905), 94–95, 104, 121.

whole work," echoing Poe's panegyrics on the style: "excellent, unaffected, and unpretending, with the flavor of freshness and perhaps something of the carelessness of conversation." It had both vogue and influence. The Newdigate prize poem, "Rose Red City, Half as Old as Time," written in 1845—"Match me such marvel in Eastern clime, a rose-red city, half as old as time"—was inspired by a reading of Stephens' *Arabia Petraea*. The British liked *Incidents of Travel in Arabia Petraea* so much that they were still reprinting it in 1866.

Within two years *Arabia Petraea* had sold 21,000 copies—this at a time when America's population was scarcely 20,000,000, of which only a fraction was literate so far as book reading was concerned.

An analysis of the Harper and Brothers' sales records shows that *Arabia Petraea* was in print up to 1882; forty-five years is a long life for any book. Of Stephens' four published books—the *Incidents of Travel in Egypt, Arabia Petraea, and the Holy Land*; in *Greece, Turkey, Russia, and Poland*; in *Central America, Chiapas, and Yucatán*; and in *Yucatán*—his first, *Arabia Petraea*, continued to outsell even those on the Mayas.

The Contract

The immediate result of *Arabia Petraea's* literary success (for Stephens was now better off by $25,000) was that it provided the direct means for the search for and discovery of the Maya civilization. Frederick Catherwood had arrived in New York some time in 1836 at Stephens' urging and had set about at once to become a practicing architect and at the same time to erect and operate his own Panorama. There he exhibited panoramic canvases of Thebes, Baalbek, and Jerusalem.[21]

The final Stephensian evolution from lawyer to traveler to author to archaeologist is fully chronicled by John R. Bartlett, who was widely known for his well-stocked bookstore, Bartlett and Wel-

[21] *F. Catherwood: Architect-Explorer of Two Worlds* (Barre, Mass., Barre Publishers, 1967).

ford's, in the old Astor House ("Number 7 on the ground floor").[22]

"I claim to have first suggested it [the ruins of Central America] to Mr. Stephens. No book ever awakened a deeper interest in New York than Mr. Stephens' *Incidents of Travel in Egypt, Arabia Petraea, and the Holy Land*, published in 1837. Soon after its publication I one day said to Mr. Stephens, when in my office: 'Why do you not undertake the exploration of Yucatán and Central America? There is a field that is quite unexplored where there are numerous objects of interest in ruined cities, temples and other works of art.'

"Mr. Stephens said he had never heard of these remains and would be glad to know more about them. I invited him to my house where I showed him Waldeck's work on Yucatán,[23] a beautiful work in folio, containing views of some of the ruined edifices in that country which I had imported a short time previous from Paris. Mr. Stephens called at once upon me and examined the book. At the same time, I showed him several other books on the countries in question and pointed out to him in other works references to the ancient remains in Yucatán and Central America. Mr. Stephens was greatly interested in what I showed him and took some of the books home for a more careful examination."[24]

Of a certainty Stephens talked at considerable length with Frederick Catherwood about the Central American trip, for on the seventeenth of September, 1839, Stephens drew up a contract. An absorbing document and important in the history of the Mayas, it is here reproduced for the first time:

[22] John R. Bartlett, born in Providence, R. I., in 1805 (the same month, day, and year as Stephens), came from an old Massachusetts family, who installed him after graduation from college in the banking house of Cyrus Butler. A founding member of the Providence Athenaeum, he was more interested in books than in dollars. In 1837, in conjunction with Charles Welford, he established Bartlett and Welford in the New Astor House. His literary activities embraced the universe.

His greatest contribution to bibliography was his *catalogue raisonné* of the library of John Carter Brown: *Bibliotheca Americana, in the Library of John Carter Brown* (4 vols., 1865–70). Bartlett died in 1886. His résumé of the advance of anthropology, *The Progress of Ethnology*, may still be read with profit.

[23] Jean Frédéric de Waldeck, *Voyage Pittoresque et Archéologique dans la Province d'Yucatán* (Paris, 1838).

[24] The "Journal of John R. Bartlett," deposited in the archives of the John Carter Brown Library, Providence, R.I.

Memorandum of an agreement made this day (September 9, 1839) between John L. Stephens and Frederick Catherwood.

Frederick Catherwood agrees to accompany the said Stephens on his journey to Central America, and to continue and remain with the said Stephens until the said Stephens shall finish his official duties with the government of Central America, and then to accompany the said Stephens on a tour through the provinces of Chiapas and Yucatán, and that he, the said Catherwood, will throughout the said tour exercise his skill as an artist and make drawings of the ruins of Palenque, Uxmal, Copán and such other ruined cities, places, scenes and monuments as may be considered desirable by the said Stephens, and that he will keep and preserve the said drawings to be engraved or otherwise made use of by the said Stephens for the sole use and benefit of the said Stephens, until released from his obligation by the said Stephens; and that he will not publish directly or indirectly the said drawings, nor any narration of the incidents of his journey, nor any description of places or persons, and that he will not in any way interfere with the right of the said Stephens to the absolute and exclusive use of all the information, drawings, and material collected on the said journey. And in consideration of the above, the said Stephens agrees to pay the traveling expenses of the said Catherwood from the time of his departure from New York until his return thereto and the said Stephens stipulates that the said Catherwood shall make and realize out of the materials collected on the said journey and at the disposal of the said Stephens the sum of one thousand and five hundred dollars within one year after the return of the said Stephens and Catherwood to the said city—and in case said sum shall not be so realized the said Stephens agrees to pay the same in cash—or else in lieu of the said sum of $1500 the said Stephens will deliver for Mr. Catherwood's benefit an introductive lecture or two lectures in one, two or three courses of lectures on the antiquities of Central America, and whether the said Stephens shall deliver the said lecture or lectures or not shall be agreed upon and determined by and between the said Stephens and Catherwood after their return to this city.

And the said Stephens further agrees that he will make provision for the payment of twenty-five dollars per week to Mrs. Catherwood and family during the absence of said Catherwood; it being understood that all the money which shall so be paid to Mrs. Catherwood and family shall be deducted from the above-said sum of $1500 or otherwise taken into the amount of a final settlement as so much money paid to the said Catherwood.

New York—September 1839.

Received two hundred dollars on account of the above sum of fifteen hundred. F.C.[25]

On the third of October, 1839, John Lloyd Stephens, lawyer, and Frederick Catherwood, architect, took ship on the brig *Mary Ann* at North River; its destination, Central America.

The final portion of Stephens' personal history has been thrice-told and is obtainable elsewhere.[26]

As in my edition of Stephens' *Yucatán*,[27] I have not presumed to "edit" Stephens' account, but a few mechanical alterations have been made for the convenience of the modern reader. I have corrected Egyptian and Arabic place names so that they conform to what is now standard archaeological usage. And I have allowed modern spelling for such words as "honour" and "traveller," plus some changes in punctuation for ease of reading. On request of my publisher, chapters in volume two have been renumbered to follow those of volume one and thus allow publication in a single volume. The footnotes are placed to explain without intruding on Stephens' own spirited narrative. Many of the illustrations are those of Frederick Catherwood which I found and identified in the Hays Collection, Additional Manuscripts, of the British Museum. Where there is no precise Catherwood illustration for the area, I have used engravings taken from Catherwood's originals (now lost), so that in essence we have here another of Stephens' books illustrated by his friend and collaborator Frederick Catherwood.

In the last lines of *Arabia Petraea*, John Lloyd Stephens, in the

[25] The editor extends his gratitude to the directors of the Bancroft Library, University of California, Berkeley, for their kindness in allowing him access to this and other of the J. L. Stephens Papers.

[26] *Maya Explorer: John Lloyd Stephens and the Lost Cities of Central America and Yucatán* (Norman, University of Oklahoma Press, 1947; 6th printing, 1967).

[27] *Incidents of Travel in Yucatán*, by John L. Stephens, edited by Victor Wolfgang von Hagen (2 vols., Norman, 1962).

polite form of the day, writes that he had introduced himself to his readers at Alexandria ". . . and from here, if he has not fallen from me by the way, I take my leave of him, with thanks for his courtesy"; as do I, the editor of this, to my readers.

I first met Stephens in 1932 at Chichen Itza, where the late S. G. Morley, the famed Maya scholar, gave me a copy, all foxed and battered, of *Incidents of Travel in Yucatán*. He did this then to distract me from my anguish over having lost most of my botanical collections in the río Usumacintla when my canoe overturned. His advice: "This is the man you should write about some day." In 1937, after making the first biological study of the Quetzal bird (and its capture), I wrote *Jungle in the Clouds*, in which Stephens appears briefly; in 1945, when the title was revised, the material on Stephens was extended. In 1945, at the encouragement of the late Van Wyck Brooks, in whose house I lived in Weston, Connecticut, after emerging from the army, I wrote the biography which Van Wyck remembered fifteen years later; "Victor's book on John Lloyd Stephens was largely written in my house at Weston."[28]

For thirty-five years—even while on other explorations, I have continually sought out "Stephens," keeping up a search for letters and documents, in the process trying to find the reason why one so renowned should have been buried in an unmarked grave. Even while I was off on one of my expeditions to jungle and mountains in South America, a committee that I helped arrange was giving Stephens a visible immortality. On October 9, 1947, the day Stephens' biography was published, a small group of prominent authors and archaeologists unveiled a plaque to Stephens.[29]

At the same time, from his home in Yucatán, the same place where Morley had given me that dog-eared copy of *Yucatán* fifteen years before, Morley reviewed *Maya Explorer*: "This crying bibliographic need has at last been magnificently met. . . . [The author] has done full justice to his subject." Then fifteen years after the

[28] Van Wyck Brooks, *From the Shadow of the Mountains* (New York, 1961) Chap. VIII, "At Weston," 97–99.

[29] Memorial plaque unveiled at dedication ceremonies held at New York City Marble Cemetery, October 9, 1947. Plaque executed in Monson Maine slate by John Howard Benson. The Maya glyph was taken from Frederick Catherwood.

biography further explorations in the Maya area convinced me that a new edition of *Yucatán* was needed since Stephens' books—which were once obtainable at almost all sellers of old books—had completely disappeared. In addition, we needed a new evaluation of these explorations. Accordingly it was done, and published in 1962 by the University of Oklahoma Press.[30]

One year later, the director of the Bancroft Library of the University of California called my attention to the mass of letters, statements, and memoranda of Stephens and Catherwood which had been recently purchased and housed there under the general title of "The J.L. Stephens Papers." These were the "missing papers" for which I had searched. Finally, after checking John Lloyd Stephens on the ground throughout Egypt, Sinai, Jordan, Petra, and into Palestine during my last expedition,[31] it was thought that a new edition of *Arabia Petraea* would bring Stephens into final perspective.

So now with the certainty that one more footnote has been added to the intellectual history of the early nineteenth century, I take leave of my reader with thanks for this courtesy.

John Lloyd Stephens has found his rightful place.

VICTOR WOLFGANG VON HAGEN

Begun, Dendera-on-the-Nile, February 1
Finished in Roma, December 1, 1967

[30] See note 26 above.
[31] Roman Road Expedition, partially told in *The Roads that Led to Rome* (New York, World Publishing Company, 1967).

Contents

L

Illustrations

Textual Drawings

From the original edition of Stephens' *Incidents of Travel in . . . Arabia Petraea* (1837)

Maps

Incidents of Travel
in Egypt, Arabia Petraea,
and the Holy Land

CHAPTER I

ALEXANDRIA—POMPEY'S PILLAR—THE CATACOMBS—THE WARWICK VASE
—THE PASHA'S CANAL—BOATS OF THE NILE

ON THE AFTERNOON of the —— December, 1835, after a
passage of five days from Malta, I was perched up in the
rigging of an English schooner, spyglass in hand, and earnestly
looking for the "Land of Egypt." The captain had never been there
before; but we had been running several hours along the low coast
of Barbary, and the chart and compass told us that we could not be
far from the fallen city of Alexander. Night came on, however,
without our seeing it. The ancient Pharos, the Lantern of Ptolemy,
the eighth wonder of the world, no longer throws its light far over
the bosom of the sea to guide the weary mariner. Morning came,
and we found ourselves directly opposite the city, the shipping in
the outward harbor, and the fleet of the pasha riding at anchor
under the walls of the seraglio, carrying me back in imagination to
the days of the Macedonian conqueror, of Cleopatra and the
Ptolemies. Slowly we worked our way up the difficult and dangerous
channel, unaided by a pilot, for none appeared to take us in charge.
It is a fact worthy of note, that one of the monuments of Egypt's
proudest days, the celebrated Pompey's Pillar, is even now, after a
lapse of more than two thousand years, one of the landmarks which
guide the sailor to her fallen capital. Just as we had passed the last
reef pilots came out to meet us, their swarthy faces, their turbans,
their large dresses streaming in the wind, and their little boat with
its huge latteen sail giving a strange wildness to their appearance,
the effect of which was not a little heightened by their noise and
confusion in attempting to come alongside. Failing in their first
endeavor, our captain gave them no assistance; and when they

3

came upon us again he refused to admit them on board. The last arrival at Malta had brought unfavorable accounts of the plague, and he was unwilling to run any risk until he should have an opportunity of advising with his consignee. My servant was the only person on board who could speak Arabic; and telling the wild, fly-away looking Arabs to fasten on astern, we towed our pilots in, and at about eight o'clock came to anchor in the harbor. In half an hour I was ashore, and the moment I touched it, just as I had found at Constantinople, all the illusion of the distant view was gone.

Indeed, it would be difficult for any man who lives at all among the things of this world to dream of the departed glory of Egypt when first entering the fallen city of Alexander; the present and the things of the present are uppermost; and between ambling donkeys, loaded camels, dirty, half-naked, sore-eyed Arabs, swarms of flies, yelping dogs, and apprehensions of the plague, one thinks more of his own movements than of the pyramids. I groped my way through a long range of bazars to the Frank quarter, and here, totally forgetting what I had come for, and that there were such things as obelisks, pyramids, and ruined temples, the genius of my native land broke out, and, with an eye that had had some experience in such matters at home, I contemplated the "improvements": a whole street of shops, kept by Europeans and filled with European goods, ranges of fine buildings, fine country houses, and gardens growing upon barren sands showed that strangers from a once barbarous land were repaying the debt which the world owes to the mother of arts, and raising her from the ruin into which she had been plunged by years of misrule and anarchy.

My first visit was to Mr. Gliddon, the American consul,[1] whose reception of me was such that I felt already as one not alone in a strange land. While with him an English gentleman came in—a merchant in Alexandria—who was going that night to Cairo. Mr. Gliddon introduced us; and, telling him that I too was bound for Cairo, Mr. T. immediately proposed that I should accompany him,

[1] There is a collection of spritely letters between Gliddon and Catherwood in the J. L. Stephens collections in the Bancroft Library, Berkeley, California. See also note 11 of the introduction.

4

saying he had a boat and everything ready, and that I might save myself the trouble of making any preparations, and would have nothing to do but come on board with my luggage at sundown. Though rather a short notice, I did not hesitate to accept his offer. Besides the relief from trouble in fitting out, the plague was in everyone's mouth, and I was not sorry to have so early an opportunity of escaping from a city where, above all others, "pestilence walketh in darkness, and destruction wasteth at noonday."

Having but a short time before me, I immediately mounted a donkey—an Egyptian donkey—being an animal entirely unknown to us, or even in Europe, and, accompanied by my servant, with a sore-eyed Arab boy to drive us, I started off upon a full gallop to make a hasty survey of the ruins of Alexandria. The Frank quarter is the extreme part of the city, and a very short ride brought us into another world. It was not until now, riding in the suburbs upon burning sands and under a burning sun, that I felt myself really in the land of Egypt. It was not, in fact, till standing at the base of Pompey's Pillar that I felt myself among the ruins of one of the greatest cities of the world. Reaching it through long rows of Arab huts, where poverty, and misery, and famine, and nakedness stared me in the face, one glance at its majestic height told me that this was indeed the work of other men and other times. Standing on a gentle elevation, it rises a single shaft of ninety feet, and ten feet in diameter, surmounted by a Corinthian capital ten feet high, and, independent of its own monumental beauty, it is an interesting object as marking the center of the ancient city. It stands far outside the present walls, and from its base you may look over a barren waste of sand, running from the shores of the Mediterranean to the Lake Mareotis, the boundaries of Alexandria as it was of old.

All this intermediate space of sandy hills, alternating with hollows, was once covered with houses, palaces, and perhaps with monuments, equal in beauty to that at whose base I stood. Riding over that waste, the stranger sees broken columns, crumbling walls, and fragments of granite and marble thrusting themselves above their sandy graves, as if struggling for resurrection; on one side he beholds a yawning chasm, in which forty or fifty naked Arabs are

5

toiling to disentomb a column long buried in the sand; on another an excavated house, with all its walls and apartments almost as entire as when the ancient Egyptian left it. He is riding over a mighty sepulchre, the sepulchre of a ruined city, and at every step some telltale monument is staring at him from the grave.

Riding slowly among the ruins, I passed the celebrated wells built in the time of Alexander, at the very foundation of the city, at which generation after generation have continued to slake their thirst, and ended my ride at Cleopatra's Needle,[2] a beautiful obelisk sixty feet high, full of mysterious hieroglyphics that mock the learning of the wise of our day. Time has dealt lightly with it; on one side the characters stand bold and clear as when it came from the hands of the sculptor, although, on the other, the dread sirocco, blowing upon it from the desert more than two thousand years, has effaced the sculptor's marks, and worn away the almost impenetrable granite. By its side, half-buried in the sand, lies a fallen brother, of the same size and about the same age, said to have been taken down by the English many years ago for the purpose of being carried to England; but the pasha prevented it, and since that time it has lain in fallen majesty, stretching across a deep chasm formed by excavations around it.

At six o'clock I was riding with my new friend, spurring my donkey to its utmost to get out of the city before the gate should close; and my reader will acquit me of all intention of writing a book when I tell him that, a little after dark on the same day on which I arrived at Alexandria, I was on my way to Cairo. Accident, however, very unexpectedly brought me again to Alexandria; and on my second visit, while waiting for an opportunity to return to Europe, I several times went over the same ground, more at my leisure, and visited the other objects of interest which my haste had before prevented me from seeing.

Among these were the Catacombs, situated about two miles from the city, on the edge of the Libyan Desert, and near the shore of the sea. These great repositories of the dead are so little known that we

---

[2] Cleopatra built a temple to Caesarion, her son by Julius Caesar, whom she called Ptolemy XVI, and adorned it with obelisks, called Cleopatra's needles.

had some difficulty in finding them, although we inquired of every-body whom we met. Seeing an Arab brushing some horses near an opening in the side of the rock, we went to him to inquire, and found we were at the door of the Catacombs. The real entrance is now unknown, but was probably from above. The present is a rude forced breach, and the first chamber into which we entered, a chamber built with pious regard to the repose of the dead, we found occupied as a stable for the horses of one of the pasha's regiments. My donkey-boy had taken the precaution to bring with him candles, and a line to tie at the entrance, after the manner of Fair Rosamund's clew, to save us from being lost in the labyrinth of passages; but the latter was unnecessary, as the Arabs employed about the horses had explored them so thoroughly for purposes of plunder that they were sufficiently sure guides. Taking two of them into pay, we followed with our lighted torches through two chambers, which, to me, who had then seen the tombs in Thebes, Petra, and Jerusalem, contained nothing remarkable, and came to what has been called the state chamber, a circular room about thirty feet in diameter, with three recesses, one at each side of the door and one opposite, a vaulted roof, and altogether admirably fine in its proportions. In each of the recesses were niches for the bodies of the dead, and in one of them skulls and moldering bones were still lying on the ground. Following my guides, I passed through several chambers half-filled with sand; but having by this time lost much of my ardor for wandering among tombs, and finding the pursuit unprofitable and unsatisfactory, I returned to the state chamber and left the Catacombs.

They are supposed to extend many miles under the surface, but how far will probably never be known. The excavations that have as yet been made are very trifling; and unless the enlightened pasha should need the state chamber for his horses, the sands of the desert may again creep upon them, and shut them forever from our eyes.

Near the door of the entrance, directly on the edge of the shore, are chambers cut in the rocks, which open to the sea, called by the imposing name of Cleopatra's Baths. It is rather an exposed situa-

7

tion, and, besides the view from the sea, there are several places where "peeping Tom" might have hidden himself. It is a rude place, too; and when I was there, the luxurious queen could hardly have got to her chambers without at least wetting her royal feet; in fact, not to be imposed upon by names, a lady of the present day can have a more desirable bath for a quarter of a dollar than ever the Queen of the East had in her life.

The present city of Alexandria, even after the dreadful ravages made by the plague last year, is still supposed to contain more than 50,000 inhabitants, and is decidedly growing. It stands outside the delta in the Libyan Desert, and, as Volney remarks, "It is only by the canal which conducts the waters of the Nile into the reservoirs in the time of inundation that Alexandria can be considered as connected with Egypt." Founded by the great Alexander, to secure his conquest of the East, being the only safe harbor along the coast of Syria or Africa, and possessing peculiar commercial advantages, it soon grew into a giant city. Fifteen miles in circumference, containing a population of 300,000 citizens and as many slaves, one magnificent street 2,000 feet broad ran the whole length of the city, from the Gate of the Sea to the Canopie Gate, commanding a view, at each end, of the shipping, either in the Mediterranean or in the Lake Mareotis, and another of equal length intersected it at right angles; a spacious circus without the Canopie Gate for chariot-races and on the east a splendid gymnasium, more than six hundred feet in length, with theaters, baths, and all that could make it a desirable residence for a luxurious people. When it fell into the hands of the Saracens, according to the report of the Saracen general to the Caliph Omar, "it was impossible to enumerate the variety of its riches and beauty"; and it is said to "have contained four thousand palaces, four thousand baths, four hundred theaters or public edifices, twelve thousand shops, and forty thousand tributary Jews." From that time, like everything else which falls into the hands of the Mussulman, it has been going to ruin, and the discovery of the passage to India by the Cape of Good Hope gave the death-blow to its commercial greatness. At present it stands a phenomenon in the history of a Turkish dominion. It appears once more to be raising its head from the dust. It remains to be seen whether this rise is the legitimate and permanent effect of a wise and politic government, combined with natural advantages, or whether the pasha is not forcing it to an unnatural elevation, at the expense, if not upon the ruins, of the rest of Egypt. It is almost presumptuous, on the threshold of my entrance into Egypt, to speculate upon the future condition of this interesting country; but it is clear that the pasha is determined to build up the city of Alexandria if he can: his fleet is here, his army, his arsenal, and his forts are here, and he has forced and centered here a commerce that was before divided between several places. Rosetta has lost more than two-thirds of its population, Damietta has become a mere nothing, and even Cairo the Grand has become tributary to what is called the regenerated city.[3]

Alexandria has also been the scene of interesting events in modern days. Here the long-cherished animosity of France and England sought a new battle-field, as if conscious that the soil of Europe had too often been moistened with human blood. Twice I visited the spot where the gallant Abercromby fell,[4] about two miles outside the Rosetta Gate; the country was covered with a beautiful verdure, and the Arab was turning up the ground with his plough; herds of buffalo were quietly grazing near, and a caravan of camels was slowly winding its way along the borders of a nameless lake, which empties into the Lake Mareotis. Farther on and near the sea is a large square enclosure, by some called the ruins of the palace of Cleopatra, by others the camp of Caesar. This was the French position, and around it the battle was fought. All is quiet there now, though still the curious traveler may pick up from time to time balls, fragments of shells, or other instruments of death, which tell him that war, murderous and destructive war, has been there.

My last ride was to Pompey's Pillar. Chateaubriand requested a

[3] See *Alexandria, A History and a Guide*, written originally in 1915 by E. M. Forster, "during the first world war when I was stationed in Alexandria"; see 3rd edition, Anchor Books, Doubleday & Company, 1961.

[4] Sir Ralph Abercromby (1734–1801), Scottish general. Served in the Seven Years' War and later successfully conducted the West Indian campaign in 1795 against the French. In 1801 he took over the Mediterranean command and landed at Aboukir, where he was mortally wounded.

friend to write his name upon the great pyramid, not being able to go himself, and considering this one of the duties of a pious pilgrim; but I imagine that sentimental traveler did not mean it in the sense in which "Hero" and "Beatrice," and the less romantic name of "Susannah Wilson," are printed in great black letters, six inches long, about halfway up the shaft.

There can be no doubt that immense treasures are still buried under the ruins of Alexandria; but whether they will ever be discovered will depend upon the pasha's necessities, as he may need the ruins of ancient temples for building forts or bridges. New discoveries are constantly made, and between my first and second visit a beautiful vase had been discovered, pronounced to be the original of the celebrated Warwick vase found at Hadrian's villa, near Tivoli. It was then in the hands of the French consul, who told me he would not take its weight in gold for it. I have since seen the vase at Warwick Castle; and if the one found at Alexandria is not the original, it is certainly remarkable that two sculptors, one in Egypt and the other in Italy, conceived and fashioned two separate works of art so exactly resembling each other.

But to return to the moment of my first leaving Alexandria. At dark I was on board a boat at the mouth of the Mahmudiya, the canal which connects Alexandria with the Nile; my companion had made all necessary provision for the voyage, and I had nothing to do but select a place and spread my mattress and coverlet. In a few minutes we had commenced our journey on the canal, our boat towed by our Arab boatmen, each with a rope across his breast. I have heard this canal spoken of as one of the greatest works of modern days, and I have seen it referred to as such in the books of modern travelers; and some even, as if determined to keep themselves under a delusion in regard to everything in Egypt, speak of it as they do of the pyramids, and obelisks, and mighty temples of the Upper Nile. The truth is, it is sixty miles in length, ninety feet in breadth, and eighteen in depth, through a perfectly level country, not requiring a single lock. In regard to the time in which it was made it certainly is an extraordinary work, and it could only have been done in that time, in such a country as Egypt, where the government is an absolute despotism and the will of one man is the supreme law. Every village was ordered to furnish a certain quota; 150,000 workmen were employed at once, and in a year from its commencement the whole excavation was made. As a great step in the march of public improvement, it certainly does honor to the pasha, though, in passing along its banks, our admiration of a barbarian struggling into civilization is checked by remembering his wanton disregard of human life, and the melancholy fact that it proved the grave of more than thirty thousand of his subjects.

We started in company with a Mr. Waghorn,[5] formerly in the East India Company's service, now engaged in forwarding the mails from England to India by the Red Sea. He was one of the first projectors of that route, is a man of indefatigable activity and energy, and was the first courier sent from England with despatches over land. He traveled post to Trieste, took a Spanish vessel to Alexandria, and thence by dromedary to Cairo and Suez, where, not finding the vessel which had been ordered to meet him, and having with him a compass, his constant traveling companion, he hired an open Arab boat, and, to the astonishment of his Arab crew, struck out into the middle of the Red Sea. At night they wanted, as usual, to anchor near the shore; but he sat with the helm in one hand and a cocked pistol in the other, threatening to shoot the first man that disobeyed his orders. On entering the harbor of Mocha he found an English government vessel on its way to meet him, and in the then uncommonly short time of fifty-five days, delivered his despatches in Bombay.

About eight o'clock next morning we were standing on the banks of the Nile, the eternal river, the river of Egypt, recalling the days of Pharaoh and Moses; from the earliest periods of recorded time watering and fertilizing a narrow strip of land in the middle of a sandy desert, rolling its solitary way more than a thousand miles without receiving a single tributary stream; the river which the Egyptians worshipped and the Arabs loved and which, as the

5 I find no other historical notice of Mr. Waghorn.

Mussulmans say, if Mohammed had tasted, "he would have prayed Heaven for terrestrial immortality, that he might continue to enjoy it for ever."

I cannot, however, join in the enthusiasm of the Mussulmans, for I have before me at this moment a vivid picture of myself and servant at Cairo, perched upon opposite divans covered with tawdry finery, in a huge barn of a room, with a ceiling thirty feet high, like two knights of the rueful countenance, comparing notes and bodily symptoms, and condoling with each other upon the corporeal miseries brought upon us by partaking too freely of the water of the Nile.

The appearance of the river at the mouth of the canal is worthy of its historic fame. I found it more than a mile wide, the current at that season full and strong; the banks on each side clothed with a beautiful verdure and groves of palm trees (the most striking feature in African scenery), and the village of Fouah, the stopping-place for boats coming up from Rosetta and Damietta, with its mosques, and minarets, and whitened domes, and groves of palms forming a picturesque object in the view.

Upon entering the Nile we changed our boat, the new one being one of the largest and best on the river, of the class called canjiah, about seventy feet long, with two enormous latteen sails; these are triangular in form, and attached to two very tall spars more than a hundred feet long, heavy at the end, and tapering to a point; the spars or yards rest upon two short masts, playing upon them as on pivots. The spar rests at an angle of about thirty degrees, and, carrying the sail to its tapering point, gives the boat when under way a peculiarly light and graceful appearance. In the stern a small place is housed over, which makes a very tolerable cabin, except that the ceiling is too low to admit of standing upright, being made to suit the cross-legged habits of the Eastern people. She was manned by ten Arabs, good stout fellows, and a rais or captain.

CHAPTER II

WE COMMENCED our voyage with that north wind which, books and travelers tell us, for nine months in the year continues to blow the same way, making it an easy matter to ascend from the Mediterranean to the Cataracts, even against the strong current of the river; and I soon busied myself with meditating upon this extraordinary operation of nature, thus presenting itself to my observation at the very moment of my entrance into this wonderful country. It was a beautiful ordinance of Providence in regard to the feebleness and wants of man that, while the noble river rolled on eternally in one unbroken current, another agent of Almighty power should almost as constantly fill the flowing canvas and enable navigators to stem the downward flow. I was particularly pleased with this train of reflection, inasmuch as at the moment we had the best of it. We were ascending against the current at the rate of six or seven miles an hour, with a noise and dash through the water that made it seem like nine or ten, while the descending boats, with their spars taken out and sails tied close, were crawling down almost imperceptibly, stern first, broadside first, not as the current carried them, but as the wind would let them. Our men had nothing to do; all day they lay strewed about on deck; towards evening they gathered around a large pilaf of rice, and, as the sun was setting, one after the other, turning his face towards the tomb of the Prophet, kneeled down upon the deck and prayed. And thus passed my first night upon the Nile.

In the morning I found things not quite so well ordered; the wind seemed to be giving "premonitory symptoms" of an intention to chop about, and towards noon it came in dead ahead. After my self-complacent observations of yesterday, I would hardly credit it; but when it became so strong that we were obliged to haul alongside the bank and lie to, in order to avoid being driven down the stream, I was perfectly satisfied and convinced. We saw no more of our friend Mr. Waghorn; he had a small boat rigged with oars, and while we were vainly struggling against wind and tide, he kindly left us to our fate. My companion was a sportsman, and happened to have on board a couple of guns; we went on shore with them, and the principal incident of the day that I remember is, that, instead of fowler's, I had fisherman's luck. Rambling carelessly along, we found ourselves on the bank of a stream which it was necessary to cross; on the other side we saw a strapping Arab, and called to him to come and carry us over. Like most of his tribe, he was not troubled with any superfluous clothing, and, slipping over his head the fragments of his frock, he was in a moment by our side, in all the majesty of nature. I started first, mounted upon his slippery shoulders, and went along very well until we had got more than halfway over, when I began to observe an irregular tottering movement, and heard behind me the smothered laugh of my companion. I felt my Arab slowly and deliberately lowering his head; my feet touched the water; but with one hand I held my gun above my head and with the other gripped him by the throat. I found myself going, going, deeper and deeper, let down with the most studied deliberation, till all at once he gave his neck a sudden toss, jerked his head from under me, and left me standing up to my middle in the stream. I turned round upon him, hardly knowing whether to laugh or to strike him with the butt end of my gun; but one glance at the poor fellow was enough; the sweat stood in large drops on his face and ran down his naked breast; his knees shook, and he was just ready to drop himself. He had supported me as long as he could; but, finding himself failing, and fearing we should both come down together with a splash at full length, he had lowered me as gently as possible.

The banks of the Nile from here to Cairo furnish nothing interesting. On one side is the Delta, an extensive tract of low rich land, well cultivated and watered, and on the other a narrow strip of fertile land, and then the Libyan Desert. The ruined cities which attract the traveler into Egypt, their temples and tombs, the enduring monuments of its former greatness, do not yet present themselves. The modern villages are all built of mud or of unburnt bricks, and sometimes, at a distance, being surrounded by palm-trees, make a pleasing appearance; but this vanishes the moment you approach them. The houses, or rather huts, are so low that a man can seldom stand up in them, with a hole in the front like the door of an oven, into which the miserable Arab crawls, more like a beast than a being made to walk in God's image. The same spectacle of misery and wretchedness, of poverty, famine, and nakedness, which I had seen in the suburbs of Alexandria, continued to meet me at every village on the Nile, and soon suggested the interesting consideration whether all this came from country and climate, from the character of the people, or from the government of the great reformer. At one place I saw on the banks of the river forty or fifty men, chained together with iron bands around their wrists and iron collars around their necks. Yesterday they were peaceful fellahs, cultivators of the soil, earning their scanty bread by hard and toilsome labor, but eating it at home in peace. Another day, and the stillness of their life is forever broken; chased, run down, and caught, torn from their homes, from the sacred threshold of the mosque, the sword and musket succeed the implements of their quiet profession; they are carried away to fight battles in a cause which does not concern them, and in which, if they conquer, they can never gain.

Returning to our boat on the brink of the river, a slight noise caught my ear; I turned, and saw a ragged mother kissing her naked child, while another of two years old, dirty and disgusting, was struggling to share its mother's embraces; their father I had just seen with an iron collar round his neck; and she loved these miserable children, and they loved their miserable mother, as if they were all clothed "in purple and fine raiment every day." But a few minutes after, a woman, knowing that we were "Franks," brought on board our boat a child, with a face and head so bloated

15

with disease that it was disgusting to look at. The rais took the child in his arms and brought it up to us, the whole crew following with a friendly interest. My companion gave them a bottle of brandy, with which the rais carefully bathed the face and head of the child, all the crew leaning over to help; and when they had finished to their satisfaction, these kind-hearted but clumsy nurses kissed the miserable bawling infant, and passed it, with as much care as if it had been a basket of crockery, into the hands of the grateful mother. This scene was finely contrasted with one that immediately followed. The boat was aground, and in an instant, stripping their long gowns over their heads, a dozen large swarthy figures were standing naked on the deck; in a moment more they were splashing in the river, and with their brawny shoulders under the bottom of the vessel, heaved her off the sandbank. Near this we passed a long line of excavation, where several hundred men were then digging, being part of the gigantic work of irrigating the Delta lately undertaken by the pasha.

Towards the evening of the fourth day we came in sight of the "world's great wonder," the eternal pyramids, standing at the head of a long reach in the river directly in front of us, and almost darkening the horizon; solitary, grand, and gloomy, the only objects to be seen in the great desert before us. The sun was about setting in that cloudless sky known only in Egypt; for a few moments their lofty summits were lighted by a gleam of lurid red, and, as the glorious orb settled behind the mountains of the Libyan Desert, the atmosphere became dark and more indistinct, and their clear outline continued to be seen after the whole earth was shrouded in gloom.

The next morning at seven o'clock we were alongside the Island of Roda, as the Arab boatmen called it, where the daughter of Pharaoh came down to bathe and found the little Moses. We crossed over in a small boat to Bulak, the harbor of Cairo, breakfasted with Mr. T——, the brother-in-law of my friend, an engineer in the pasha's service, whose interesting wife is the only English lady there, and mounting a donkey, in half an hour I was within the walls of Grand Cairo. The traveler who goes there with the reminiscences of Arabian tales hanging about him will nowhere see the Cairo of the caliphs; but before arriving there he will have seen a curious and striking spectacle. He will have seen, streaming from the gate among loaded camels and dromedaries, the dashing Turk with his glittering saber, the wily Greek, the grave Armenian, and the despised Jew, with their long silk robes, their turbans, their solemn beards, and various and striking costumes; he will have seen the harem of more than one rich Turk, eight or ten women on horseback, completely enveloped in large black silk wrappers, perfectly hiding face and person, and preceded by that abomination of the East, a black eunuch; the miserable santon, the Arab saint, with a few scanty rags on his breast and shoulders, the rest of his body perfectly naked; the swarthy Bedouin of the desert, the haughty janissary, with a cocked gun in his hand, dashing furiously through the crowd, and perhaps bearing some bloody mandate of his royal master; and perhaps he will have seen and blushed for his own image in the person of some beggarly Italian refugee. Entering the gate, guarded by Arab soldiers in a bastard European uniform, he will cross a large square filled with officers and soldiers, surrounded by what are called palaces, but seeing nothing that can interest him save the house in which the gallant Kléber,[1] the hero of many a bloody field, died ingloriously by the hands of an assassin. Crossing this square, he will plunge into the narrow streets of Cairo. Winding his doubtful and perilous way among tottering and ruined houses, justled by camels, dromedaries, horses, and donkeys, perhaps he will draw up against a wall, and, thinking of plague, hold his breath and screw himself into nothing, while he allows a corpse to pass, followed by a long train of howling women, dressed in black, with masks over their faces; and entering the large wooden gate which shuts in the Frank quarter for protection against any sudden burst of popular fury, and seating himself in a miserable Italian

[1] Jean Baptiste Kléber (1753–1800). Born in Strasbourg, he served first in the Austrian Army, then in the French, and he rose to brigadier general. He commanded in the Vendéan War and took Maastricht in 1794. Accompanying Napoleon to Egypt, he was wounded in Alexandria. Later as field commander he attempted a reconquest of Egypt and destroyed the Turkish Army at Heliopolis, after which he was assassinated on a terrace in Cairo, June 14, 1800.

17

locanda, he will ask himself, Where is the "Cairo of the caliphs, the superb town, the holy city, the delight of the imagination, greatest among the great, whose splendor and opulence made the Prophet smile?"

Almost immediately upon my arrival I called upon Mr. Gliddon, our vice-consul, and upon Nubar Bey, an Armenian dragoman to the pasha, to whom I had a letter from a gentleman in Alexandria. The purport of my visit to the latter was to procure a presentation to the pasha. He told me that several English officers from India had been waiting several days for that purpose; that he thought the pasha would receive them the next day, and, if so, he would ask permission to present me. Having arranged this, and not being particularly pleased with the interior, and liking exceedingly the donkeys on which it is the custom there to mount on all occasions for long and for short distances, I selected one that was particularly gay and sprightly, and followed by an Arab boy who had picked up a few Italian words, I told him to take me anywhere outside the city. He happened to take me out at the same gate by which I had entered, and I rode to Old Cairo.

Old Cairo is situated on the river, about four miles from Bulak. The road is pretty, and some of the points of view, particularly in returning, decidedly beautiful. The aqueduct which conveys water into the citadel at Cairo is a fine substantial piece of workmanship, and an item in the picture. The church and grotto in which, as tradition says, the Virgin Mary took refuge with the infant Savior when obliged to fly from the tetrarch of Judea, are among the few objects worthy of note in Old Cairo. The grotto, which is guarded with pious care by the Coptic priest, is a small excavation, the natural surface covered with smooth tiles; it is hardly large enough to allow one person to crawl in and sit upright. It is very doubtful whether this place was ever the refuge of the Virgin, but the craft or simplicity of the priests sustains the tradition; and a half-dozen Coptic women, with their faces covered and their long blue dresses, followed me down into the vault and kneeled before the door of the grotto, with a devotion which showed that they at least believed the tale.

At my locanda this morning I made acquaintance with two English parties, a gentleman, his lady, and nephew, who had been traveling in their own yacht on the Mediterranean, and the party of English officers to whom I before referred as returning from India by way of the Red Sea. They told me that they were expecting permission from the pasha to wait on him that day, and asked me to accompany them. This suited me better than to go alone, as I was not ambitious for a tête-a-tête with his highness, and merely wished to see him as one of the lions of the country. Soon after I received a note from the consul, telling me that his highness would receive me at half-past three. This, too, was the hour appointed for the reception of the others, and I saw that his highness was disposed to make a lumping business of it, and get rid of us all at once. I accordingly suggested to Mr. Gliddon that we should all go together; but this did not suit him; he was determined that I should have the benefit of a special audience. I submitted myself to his directions, and in this, as in other things while at Cairo, found the benefit of his attentions and advice.

It is the custom of the pasha upon such occasions to send horses from his own stable, and servants from his own household, to wait upon the stranger. At half-past three I left my hotel, mounted on a noble horse, finely caparisoned, with a dashing red cloth saddle, a bridle ornamented with shells, and all the decorations and equipments of a well-mounted Turkish horseman, and, preceded by the janissary and escorted by the consul, with no small degree of pomp and circumstance I arrived at the gate of the citadel. Passing through a large yard, in which are several buildings connected with the different offices of government, we stopped at the door of the palace, and, dismounting, ascended a broad flight of marble steps to a large or central hall, from which doors opened into the different apartments. There were three recesses fitted up with divans, where officers were lounging, smoking, and taking coffee. The door of the divan, or hall of audience, was open, at which a guard was stationed, and in going up to demand permission to enter, we saw the pasha at the farther end of the room, with four or five Turks standing before him.

19

Not being allowed to enter yet, we walked up and down the great hall, among lounging soldiers and officers of all ranks and grades, Turks, Arabs, and beggars, and went out upon the balcony. The view from this embraces the most interesting objects in the vicinity of Cairo, and there are few prospects in the world which include so many; the land of Goshen, the Nile, the obelisk at Heliopolis, the tombs of the caliphs, the pyramids, and the deserts of eternal sands.

While standing upon the balcony, a janissary came to tell us that the pasha would receive us, or, in other words, that we must come to the pasha. The audience-chamber was a very large room, with a high ceiling—perhaps eighty feet long and thirty high—with Arabesque paintings on the wall, and a divan all around. The pasha was sitting near one corner at the extreme end, and had a long and full view of everyone who approached him. I too had the same advantage, and in walking up I remarked him as a man about sixty-five, with a long and very white beard, strong features, of a somewhat vulgar cast, a short nose, red face, and rough skin, with an uncommonly fine dark eye, expressing a world of determination and energy. He wore a large turban and a long silk robe, and was smoking a long pipe with an amber mouthpiece. Altogether, he looked the Turk much better than his nominal master the sultan.

His dragoman, Nubar Bey, was there, and presented me. The pasha took his pipe from his mouth, motioned me to take a seat at his right hand on the divan, and with a courteous manner said I was welcome to Egypt. I told him he would soon have to welcome half the world there; he asked me why; and, without meaning to flatter the old Turk, I answered that everybody had a great curiosity to visit that interesting country; that heretofore it had been very difficult to get there, and dangerous to travel in when there; but now the facilities of access were greatly increased, and traveling in Egypt had become so safe under his government, that strangers would soon come with as much confidence as they felt while traveling in Europe; and I had no doubt there would be many Americans among them. He took his pipe from his mouth and bowed. I sipped my coffee with great complacency, perfectly satisfied with the manner in which, for the first time, I had played the courtier to royalty. Knowing his passion for new things, I went on, and told him that he ought to continue his good works, and introduce on the Nile a steamboat from Alexandria to Cairo. He took the pipe from his mouth again, and, in the tone of "Let there be light, and there was light," said he had ordered a couple. I knew he was fibbing, and I afterward heard from those through whom he transacted all his business in Europe that he had never given any such order. Considering that a steamboat was an appropriate weapon in the hands of an American, I followed up my blow by telling him that I had just seen mentioned, in a European paper, a project to run steamboats from New York to Liverpool in twelve or fourteen days. He asked me the distance; I told him, and he said nothing and smoked on. He knew America, and particularly from a circumstance which, I afterward found, had done wonders in giving her a name and character in the East, the visit of Commodore Patterson in the ship Delaware. So far I had taken decidedly the lead in the conversation; but the constant repetition of "Son Altesse" by the dragoman began to remind me that I was in the presence of royalty, and that it was my duty to speak only when I was spoken to. I waited to give him a chance, and the first question he asked was as to the rate of speed of the steamboats on our rivers. Remembering an old, crazy, five- or six-mile-an-hour boat that I had seen in Alexandria, I was afraid to tell him the whole truth, lest he should not believe me, and did not venture to go higher than fifteen miles an hour; and even then he looked as Ilderim may be supposed to have looked when the Knight of the Leopard told him of having crossed over a lake like the Dead Sea without wetting his horse's hoofs. I have no doubt, if he ever thought of me afterward, that it was as the lying American; and just at this moment, the party of English coming in, I rose and took my leave. Gibbon says, "When Persia was governed by the descendants of Sefis, a race of princes whose wanton cruelty often stained their divan, their table, and their bed with the blood of their favorites, there is a saying recorded of a young nobleman, that he never departed from the sultan's presence without satisfying him-

PALACE OF MOHAMMED ALI

self whether his head was still on his shoulders." It was in somewhat of the same spirit that, in passing, one of the Englishmen whispered to me, "Are you sure of your legs?"

During my interview with the pasha, although my conversation and attention were directed towards him, I could not help remarking particularly his dragoman, Nubar Bey. He was an Armenian, perhaps a year or two over thirty, with an olive complexion, and a countenance like marble. He stood up before us, about halfway between the pasha and me, his calm eye finely contrasted with the roving and unsettled glances of the pasha, a perfect picture of indifference, standing like a mere machine to translate words, without seeming to comprehend or take the least interest in their import; and though I had been particularly recommended to him, he did not give me a single glance to intimate that he had ever seen me before, or cared ever to see me again. He was an ambitious man, and was evidently acting, and acted well, a part suited to an Eastern court; the part necessary in his responsible and dangerous position, as the depositary of important secrets of government. He was in high favor with the pasha, and, when I left, was in a fair way of attaining any honor at which his ambitious spirit might aim. On my return to Alexandria, four months after, he was dead.

The life and character of Mohammed Ali[2] are a study and a problem. Like Bernadotte of Sweden, he has risen from the rank of a common soldier, and now sits firmly and securely on a throne of his own making. He has risen by the usual road to greatness among the Turks: war, bloodshed, and treachery. In early life his bold and daring spirit attracted the attention of beys, pashas, and the sultan himself; and having attained a prominent position in the bloody

---

[2] Mehemet Ali (1769–1849), Mohammed Ali, or Muhammad Ali. Born in Albania, he had his schooling in a Turkish regiment. In 1799 he appeared in Egypt with three hundred Albanians and first helped the French. Surviving all, he remained in Egypt and consolidated his position. He aided the Mamelukes against the Turks, then finally slaughtered them. A French consul thought he had a Machiavellian turn of mind and gave him *El Principe* to read: Of it Mehemet Ali said ". . . in the first ten pages I discovered nothing great nor new. . . . I waited. But the next ten were no better. The last ten were merely commonplace. I can learn nothing from Machiavelli." Although he was considered the founder of modern Egypt, time usurped his reason; he died insane on August 2, 1857. His son Ibrahim succeeded him.

23

wars that distracted Egypt under the Mamelukes, boldness, cruelty, intrigue, and treachery placed him on the throne of the caliphs, and neither then nor since have these usual engines of Turkish government, these usual accompaniments of Turkish greatness, for a moment deserted him.

The extermination of the Mamelukes, the former lords of Egypt as regards the number killed, is perhaps nothing in comparison with the thousands whose blood cries out from the earth against him; but the manner in which it was effected brands the pasha as the prince of traitors and murderers. Invited to the citadel on a friendly visit, while they were smoking the pipe of peace he was preparing to murder them; and no sooner had they left his presence than they were pent up, fired upon, cut down and killed, bravely but hopelessly defending themselves to the last. This cruel deed must not be likened to the slaughter of the janissaries by the sultan, to which it is often compared, for the janissaries were a powerful body, insulting and defying the throne. The sultan staked his head upon the issue, and it was not till he had been driven to the desperate expedient of unfurling the sacred standard of the Prophet, and calling upon all good Mussulmans to rally round it; in a word, it was not till the dead bodies of thirty thousand janissaries were floating down the Bosphorus, that he became master in his own dominions. Not so with the pasha; the Mamelukes were reduced to a feeble band of four or five hundred men, and could effect nothing of importance against the pasha. His cruelty and treachery can neither be forgotten nor forgiven; and when, in passing out of the citadel, the stranger is shown the place where the unhappy Mamelukes were penned up and slaughtered like beasts, one only leaping his gallant horse over the walls of the citadel, he feels that he has left the presence of a wholesale murderer.

Since that time he has had Egypt quietly to himself; has attacked and destroyed the Wahabees on the Red Sea, and subdued the countries above the Cataracts of the Nile, to Sennar and Dongola. He has been constantly aiming at introducing European improvements; has raised and disciplined an army according to European tactics; increased the revenues, particularly by introducing the culture of cotton; and has made Egypt, from the Mediterranean to the Cataracts, as safe for the traveler as the streets of New York. It remains to be seen whether, after all, he has not done more harm than good, and whether the miserable and oppressed condition of his subjects does not more than counterbalance all the good that he has done for Egypt.

One of the strongest evidences he gave of his civilizing inclinations is the tendency he once manifested to fall under petticoat government. He was passionately fond of his first wife, the sharer of his poverty and meridian greatness, and the mother of his two favorite children, Youssouff and Ibrahim Pasha;[3] and whenever a request was preferred in her name, the enamored despot would swear his favorite oath, "By my two eyes, if she wishes it, it shall be done." Fond of war, and having an eye to the islands of Crete and Cyprus, he sent a large fleet and army, commanded by his son Ibrahim Pasha, to aid the sultan in his war against Greece, and with his wild Egyptians turned the tide against that unhappy country, receiving as his reward the islands which he coveted. More recently, availing himself of a trifling dispute with the governor of Acre, he turned his arms against the sultan, invaded Syria, and, after a long siege, took and made himself master of Acre; his victorious armies under his son Ibrahim swept all Syria; Jerusalem, Damascus, and Aleppo fell into his hands; and beating the sultan's forces whenever he met them, in mid winter he led his Egyptians over Mount Taurus, defeated the grand vizier with more than 100,000 men almost under the walls of Constantinople, and would have driven the sultan from the throne of his ancestors, if the Russians, the old enemies of the Porte, had not come in to his relief. According to the policy of the Porte, that which is wrested from her and she cannot get back, she confirms in the possession of the rebel; and Palestine and Syria are now in the hands of Mohammed Ali, as the fruits of drawing his sword against his master. He still continues to pay tribute to the sultan, constrained doubtless to make the last payment by the

---

[3] Ibrahim Pasha (1789–1848), son of Mehemet Ali, governor of all Egypt south of the Delta and viceroy of Egypt, ruled all Egypt for only two months after his father became insane. See *Ibrahim of Egypt*, by Pierre Crabitès (London, 1935).

crippled state in which he was left by the terrible plague of 1834; and, without any enemy to fear, is at this moment draining the resources of his country to sustain a large army and navy. No one can fathom his intentions, and probably he does not know them himself, but will be governed, as the Turks always are, by caprice and circumstances.

On leaving the pasha, Mr. Gliddon proposed that we should call upon the governor of Cairo. We stopped at what would be called in France the "Palais de Justice," and, mounting a dozen steps, entered a large hall, at one end of which stood the governor. He was a short stout man, of about fifty-five, with a long beard, handsomely dressed, and stood gently rubbing his hands, and constantly working his jaws like an ox chewing the cud. A crowd was gathered around him, and just as we were approaching the crowd fell back, and we saw an Arab lying on his face on the floor, with two men standing over him, one on each side, with whips, like cowskins, carrying into effect the judgment of the munching governor. The blows fell thickly and heavily, the poor fellow screamed piteously, and when the full number had been given he could not move; he was picked up by his friends and carried out of doors. It was precisely such a scene as realized the reference in the Scriptures to the manners of the East in the time of our Savior, when a complaint was made to the judge, and the judge handed the offender over to justice; or the graphic accounts in the Arabian Nights, of summary justice administered by the cadi or other expounder of the law, without the intervention of lawyers or jury. The poor Arab was hardly removed before another complaint was entered; but not feeling particularly amiable towards the governor, and having seen enough of the great Turks for that day, I left the citadel and rode to my hotel.

CHAPTER III

NEARLY ALL THE TIME I was at Cairo, Paul and myself were ill, and for a few days we were in a rather pitiable condition. Fortunately, a young English army surgeon was there, on his way to India, and hearing there was a sick traveler in the house, he with great kindness called upon me and prescribed for our ailments. If this book should ever meet the eye of Dr. Forbes, he will excuse my putting his name in print, as it is the only means I have of acknowledging his kindness in saving me from what would otherwise have been a severe and most inconvenient illness. At that time there was no English physician in Cairo, and I believe none at all, except some vile, half-breed Italian or French apothecaries, who held themselves fully qualified to practice, and were certainly very successful in relieving the sick from all their sufferings. On my return I found Dr. Walne, and though for his own sake I could wish him a better lot, I hope, for the benefit of sick travelers, that he is there still.[1]

One of my first rambles in Cairo was to the slave market. It is situated nearly in the center of the city, as it appeared to me, although, after turning half a dozen corners in the narrow streets of a Turkish city, I will defy a man to tell where he is exactly. It is a large old building, enclosing a hollow square, with chambers all around, both above and below. There were probably five or six

[1] I have seen with great pleasure, in a late English paper, that Dr. Walne has been appointed English vice-consul at Cairo. In the close relation now growing up between England and Egypt by means of the Red Sea passage to India, it is a matter of no small consequence to England to have at Cairo as her representative a man of character and talents; and I am sure I but express the opinion of all who know Dr. Walne when I say that a more proper appointment could not have been made.— Stephens' note.

hundred slaves sitting on mats in groups of ten, twenty, or thirty, each belonging to a different proprietor. Most of them were entirely naked, though some, whose shivering forms evinced that even there they felt the want of their native burning sun, were covered with blankets. They were mostly from Dongola and Sennar; but some were Abyssinians, with yellow complexions, fine eyes and teeth, and decidedly handsome. The Nubians were very dark, but with oval, regularly-formed, and handsome faces, mild and amiable expressions, and no mark of the African except the color of their skin. The worst spectacle in the bazar was that of several lots of sick, who were separated from the rest and arranged on mats by themselves; their bodies thin and shrunken, their chins resting upon their knees, their long lank arms hanging helplessly by their sides, their faces haggard, their eyes fixed with a painful vacancy, and altogether presenting the image of man in his most abject condition. Meeting them on their native sands, their crouching attitudes, shrunken jaws, and rolling eyes might have led one to mistake them for those hideous animals the orangoutang and ape. Prices vary from twenty to a hundred dollars; but the sick, as carrying within them the seeds of probable death, are coolly offered for almost nothing, as so much damaged merchandise which the seller is anxious to dispose of before it becomes utterly worthless on his hands. There was one, an Abyssinian, who had mind as well as beauty in her face; she was dressed in silk, and wore ornaments of gold and shells, and called me as I passed, and peeped from behind a curtain, smiling and coquetting, and wept and pouted when I went away; and she thrust out her tongue to show me that she was not like those I had just been looking at, but that her young blood ran pure and healthy in her veins.

Cairo is surrounded by a wall; the sands of the desert approach it on every side, and every gate, except that of Bulak, opens to a sandy waste. Passing out by the Victory Gate, the contrast between light and darkness is not greater than between the crowded streets and the stillness of the desert, separated from them only by a wall. Immediately without commences the great burial-place of the city. Among thousands and tens of thousands of Mussulmans' headstones, I searched in vain for the tomb of the lamented Burck-hardt;[2] there is no mark to distinguish the grave of the enterprising traveler from that of an Arabian camel-driver. At a short distance from the gate are the tombs of the caliphs, large and beautiful buildings, monuments of the taste and skill of the Saracens.

From hence, passing around outside the walls, I entered by the Gate of the Citadel, where I saw what goes by the name of Joseph's Well, perhaps better known as the Well of Saladin. It is 45 feet wide at the mouth, and cut 270 feet deep through the solid rock to a spring of saltish water, on a level with the Nile, whence the water is raised in buckets on a wheel, turned by a buffalo.

On the 25th, with a voice that belied my feelings, I wished Paul a merry Christmas; and, after breakfast, wishing to celebrate the day, mounted a donkey and rode to the site of the ancient Helio-polis, near the village of Matariya, about four miles from Cairo, on the borders of the rich land of Goshen. The geographer Strabo[3] visited these ruins thirty years B.C., and describes them almost exactly as we see them now. A great temple of the sun once stood here. Herodotus and Plato studied philosophy in the schools of Heliopolis; "a barbarous Persian overturned her temples; a fanatic Arabian burnt her books"; and a single obelisk, sixty-seven feet high, in a field ploughed and cultivated to its very base, stands, a melancholy monument of former greatness and eternal ruin.

Passing out by another gate is another vast cemetery, ranges of tombs extending miles out into the desert. In Turkey I had admired the beauty of the graveyards, and often thought how calmly slept the dead under the thick shade of the mourning cypress. In Egypt I admired still more the solemn stillness and grandeur of a last

2 Johann Ludwig Burckhardt (1784–1817), Swiss-born, British-financed explorer of the Middle East and Africa. Sent by the African Association to explore the interior of Africa, he adopted the name of Ibrahim Ibn Abdallah and disguised as an Arab stayed at Aleppo improving his Arabic. He entered Damascus and Palmyra, but was prevented from going to the Fezzan in Libya. He traveled up the Nile to Nubia, and in 1814 made the pilgrimage to Mecca. After climbing Mount Sinai, he was preparing to join a caravan to the Fezzan in 1817 when he became sick and died in Cairo. His journals were published by the African Association.

3 Strabo (63 B.C.–A.D. 21), Greek geographer. Born at Amasya, Pontus (Turkey). His life was spent in travel in preparation for his *Geographica* (originally in forty-five volumes). He ascended the Nile in 29 B.C.

resting-place among the eternal sands of the desert. In this great city of the dead stand the tombs of the Mamelukes, originally slaves from the foot of the Caucasus, then the lords and tyrants of Egypt, and now an exterminated race; the tombs are large, handsome buildings, with domes and minarets, the interior of the domes beautifully wrought, and windows of stained glass, all going to ruins. Here, too, is the tomb of the pasha. Fallen, changed, completely revolutionized as Egypt is, even to this day peculiar regard is paid to the structure of tombs and the burial-places of the dead. The tomb of the pasha is called the greatest structure of modern Egypt. It is a large stone building, with several domes, strongly but coarsely made. The interior, still, solemn, and imposing, is divided into two chambers; in the first, in a conspicuous situation, is the body of his favorite wife, and around are those of other members of his family; in the other chamber are several tombs, covered with large and valuable cashmere shawls; several places yet unoccupied, and in one corner a large vacant place, reserved for the pasha himself. Both apartments are carpeted, and illuminated with lamps, with divans in the recesses, and little wicker chairs for the different members of the family who come to mourn and pray. Two ladies were there, sitting near one of the tombs, their faces completely covered; and, that I might not disturb their pious devotions, my guide led me in a different direction.

During the time that I had passed in lounging about Cairo, I had repeatedly been down to Bulak in search of a boat for my intended voyage up the Nile; and going one Sunday to dine on the Island of Roda with Mr. Trail, a young Englishman who had charge of the palace and garden of Ibrahim Pasha, I again rode along the bank of the river for the same purpose. In coming up from Alexandria I had found the inconveniences of a large boat, and was looking for one of the smallest dimensions that could be at all comfortable. We were crossing over one more than half-sunk in the water, which I remarked to Paul was about the right size; and while we stopped a moment, without the least idea that it could be made fit for use, an Arab came up and whispered to Paul that he could pump out the water in two hours, and had only sunk the boat to save it from the officers of the pasha, who would otherwise take it for the use of government. Upon this information I struck a bargain for the boat, eight men, a rais, and a pilot. The officers of the pasha were on the bank looking out for boats, and, notwithstanding my Arab's ingenious contrivance, just when I had closed my agreement, they came on board and claimed possession. I refused to give up my right, and sent to the agent of the consul for an American flag. He could not give me an American, but sent me an English flag, and I did not hesitate to put myself under its protection. I hoisted it with my own hands; but the rascally Turks paid no regard to its broad folds. The majesty of England did not suffer, however, in my hands, and Paul and I spent more than an hour in running from one officer to another, before we could procure the necessary order for the release of the boat. Leaving this with the rais, and the flag still flying, I went on to Roda, and spent the day there in decidedly the prettiest spot about Cairo. At the head of this island is the celebrated Nilometer, which, for no one knows how long, has marked the annual rise and fall of the Nile.

I had been ten days in Cairo without going to the pyramids. I had seen them almost every day, but my doctor,[4] who was to accompany me, had delayed my visit. He was obliged to leave Cairo, however, before I was ready to go; and as soon as he was off, like a schoolboy when the master is out of sight, I took advantage of his absence. My old friend from Alexandria had promised to go with me, and joining me at Old Cairo, we crossed over to Giza. Almost from the gates of Cairo the pyramids are constantly in sight, and, after crossing the ferry, we at first rode directly towards them; but the waters were yet so high that we were obliged to diverge from the straight road. In about an hour we separated, my guide taking one route and my friend another. With my eyes constantly fixed on the pyramids, I was not aware of our separation until I had gone too far to return, and my guide proved to be right. Standing alone on an elevated

---

[4] Stephens, while "politicking" for the election of Cornelius W. Lawrence for governor in 1835—"one of the most riotous elections ever seen in New York City"— acquired a throat infection during his speech-making. His doctor, baffled by the persistence of streptococcic throat, advised a long, mild European trip for his patient's health.

mountainous range on the edge of the desert, without any object with which to compare them, the immense size of the pyramids did not strike me with full force. Arrived at the banks of a stream, twenty Arabs, more than half-naked, and most of them blind of an eye, came running towards me, dashed through the stream, and pulling, hauling, and scuffling at each other, all laid hold of me to carry me over. All seemed bent upon having something to do with me, even if they carried me over piecemeal; but I selected two of the strongest, with little more than one eye between them, and keeping the rest off as well as I could, was borne over dryshod. Approaching, the three great pyramids and one small one are in view, towering higher and higher above the plain. I thought I was just upon them, and that I could almost touch them; yet I was more than a mile distant. The nearer I approached, the more their gigantic dimensions grew upon me, until, when I actually reached them, rode up to the first layer of stones, and saw how very small I was, and looked up their sloping sides to the lofty summits, they seemed to have grown to the size of mountains.

The base of the great pyramid is about 800 feet square, covering a surface of about eleven acres, according to the best measurement, and 461 feet high; or, to give a clearer idea, starting from a base as large as Washington Parade Ground, it rises to a tapering point nearly three times as high as Trinity Church steeple. Even as I walked around it and looked up at it from the base, I did not feel its immensity until I commenced ascending; then, having climbed some distance up, when I stopped to breathe and look down upon my friend below, who was dwindled to insect size, and up at the great distance between me and the summit, then I realized in all their force the huge dimensions of this giant work. It took me twenty minutes to mount to the summit; about the same time that it had required to mount the cones of Etna and Vesuvius. The ascent is not particularly difficult, at least with the assistance of the Arabs. There are 206 tiers of stone, from one to four feet in height, each two or three feet smaller than the one below, making what are called the steps. Very often the steps were so high that I could not reach them with my feet. Indeed, for the most part, I was obliged to climb with my knees, deriving great assistance from the step which one Arab made for me with his knee, and the helping hand of another above.

It is not what it once was to go to the pyramids. They have become regular lions for the multitudes of travelers; but still, common as the journey has become, no man can stand on the top of the great pyramid of Cheops, and look out upon the dark mountains of Moqattam bordering the Arabian desert; upon the ancient cities of the Pharaohs, its domes, its mosques and minarets, glittering in the light of a vertical sun; upon the rich valley of the Nile, and the "river of Egypt" rolling at his feet; the long range of pyramids and tombs extending along the edge of the desert to the ruined city of Memphis, and the boundless and eternal sands of Africa, without considering that moment an epoch not to be forgotten. Thousands of years roll through his mind, and thought recalls the men who built them, their mysterious uses, the poets, historians, philosophers, and warriors who have gazed upon them with wonder like his own.

For one who but yesterday was bustling in the streets of a busy city, it was a thing of strange and indescribable interest to be standing on the top of the great pyramid, surrounded by a dozen half-naked Arabs, forgetting, as completely as if they had never been, the stirring scenes of his distant home. But even here petty vexations followed me, and half the interest of the time and scene was destroyed by the clamor of my guides. The descent I found extremely easy; many persons complain of the dizziness caused by looking down from such a height, but I did not find myself so affected; and though the donkeys at the base looked like flies, I could almost have danced down the mighty sides.[5]

[5] A few years ago an unfortunate accident happened at this pyramid. An English officer, Mr. M., who had come up the Red Sea from India with his friend, had mounted to the top, and, while his friend was looking another way, Mr. M. was walking around the upper layer of stones and fell; he rolled down eight or ten steps, and caught; for a moment he turned up his face with an expression that his friend spoke of as horrible beyond all description, when his head sunk, his grasp relaxed, and he pitched headlong, rolling over and over to the bottom of the pyramid. Every bone in his body was broken; his mangled corpse was sewed up in a sack, carried to Old Cairo and buried, and his friend returned the same day to Cairo. There were at

33

The great pyramid is supposed to contain six millions of cubic feet of stone, and a hundred thousand men are said to have been employed twenty years in building it. The four angles stand exactly in the four points of the compass, inducing the belief that it was intended for other purposes than those of a sepulchre. The entrance is on the north side. The sands of the desert have encroached upon it, and, with the fallen stones and rubbish, have buried it to the sixteenth step. Climbing over this rubbish the entrance is reached, a narrow passage three and a half feet square, lined with broad blocks of polished granite, descending in the interior at an angle of 27 degrees for about 92 feet; then the passage turns to the right, and winds upward to a steep ascent of 8 or 9 feet, and then falls into the natural passage, which is 5 feet high and 100 feet long, forming a continued ascent to a sort of landing-place; in a small recess of this is the orifice or shaft called the well. Moving onward through a long passage, the explorer comes to what is called the Queen's Chambers, 17 feet long, 14 wide, and 12 high. I entered a hole opening from this crypt, and crawling on my hands and knees, came to a larger opening, not a regular chamber, and now cumbered with fallen stones. Immediately above this, ascending by an inclined plane lined with highly polished granite, and about 120 feet in length, and mounting a short space by means of holes cut in the sides, I entered the King's Chamber, about 37 feet long, 17 feet wide, and 20 feet high. The walls of the chamber are of red granite, highly polished, each stone reaching from the floor to the ceiling; and the ceiling is formed of nine large slabs of polished granite, extending from wall to wall. It is not the least interesting part of a visit to the interior of the pyramids, as you are groping your way after your Arab guide, to feel your hand running along the sides of an enormous shaft, smooth and polished as the finest marble, and to see by the light of the flaring torch chambers of red granite from the Cataracts of the Nile, the immense blocks standing around and above you, smooth and beautifully polished in places, where, if our

---

the time imputations that Mr. M. had premeditated this act, as he had left behind him his watch, money, and papers, and had been heard to say what a glorious death it would be to die by jumping from the top of a pyramid.—Stephens' note.

notions of the pyramids be true, they were intended but for few mortal eyes. At one end of the chamber stands a sarcophagus, also of red granite; its length is seven feet, six inches, depth three and a half, breadth three feet, three inches. Here is supposed to have slept one of the great rulers of the earth, the king of the then greatest kingdom of the world, the proud mortal for whom this mighty structure was raised. Where is he now? Even his dry bones are gone, torn away by rude hands and scattered by the winds of heaven.

There is something curious about this sarcophagus too. It is exactly the size of the orifice which forms the entrance of the pyramid, and could not have been conveyed to its place by any of the now known passages; consequently, it must have been deposited during the building, or before the passage was finished in its present state. The interior of the pyramid is excessively hot, particularly when surrounded by a number of Arabs and flaring torches. Leaving the King's Chamber, I descended the inclined plane, and prepared to descend the well referred to by Pliny. The shaft is small; merely large enough to permit one to descend with the legs astride, the feet resting in little niches, and hands clinging to the same. Having no janissary with me to keep them off, I was very much annoyed by the Arabs following me. I had at first selected two as my guides, and told the others to go away; but it was of no use. They had nothing else to do; a few paras would satisfy them for their day's labor; and the chance of getting these, either from charity or by importunity, made them all follow. At the mouth of the well I again selected my two guides, and again told the others not to follow; and, sending the two before me, followed down the well, being myself quickly followed by two others. I shouted to them to go back, but they paid no regard to me; so, coming out again, I could not help giving the fellow next to me a blow with a club, which sent him bounding among his companions. I then flourished my stick among them, and after a deal of expostulation and threatening gesticulation, I attempted the descent once more. A second time they followed me, and I came out perfectly furious. My friend was outside shooting, the pyramids being nothing new to him, and unfortunately I had been obliged to leave Paul at Cairo, and had no one with me but a little Nubian boy. Him I could not prevail upon to descend the well; he was frightened, and begged me not to go down; and when he saw them follow the second time, and me come out and lay about me with a club, he began to cry, and, before I could lay hold of him, ran away. I could do nothing without him, and was obliged to follow. There was no use in battling with the poor fellows, for they made no resistance; and I believe I might have brained the whole of them without one offering to strike a blow. Moreover, it was very hot and smothering; and as there was nothing particular to see, nor any discovery to make, I concluded to give it up; and calling my guides to return, in a few moments escaped from the hot and confined air of the pyramid.

At the base I found my friend sitting quietly with his gun in his hand, and brought upon him the hornet's nest which had so worried me within. The Arabs, considering their work done, gathered around me, clamorous for backsheesh, and none were more importunate than the fellows who had followed me so pertinaciously. I gave them liberally, but this only whetted their appetites. There was no getting rid of them; a sweep of my club would send them away for a moment, but instantly they would reorganize and come on again, putting the women and children in the front rank. The sheik came ostensibly to our relief; but I had doubts whether he did not rather urge them on. He, however, protected us to a certain extent, while we went into one of the many tombs to eat our luncheon. For a great distance around there are large tombs which would of themselves attract the attention of the traveler, were they not lost in the overwhelming interest of the pyramids. That in which we lunched had a deep shaft in the center, leading to the pit where the mummies had been piled one upon another. The Arabs had opened and rifled the graves, and bones and fragments were still lying scattered around. Our persecutors were sitting at the door of the tomb looking in upon us, and devouring with their eyes every morsel that we put into our mouths. We did not linger long over our meal; and, giving them the fragments, set off for a walk round the pyramid of Chephren, the second in grandeur.

This pyramid was opened at great labor and expense by the indefatigable Belzoni,[6] and a chamber discovered containing a sarcophagus, as in that of Cheops. The passage, however, has now become choked up and hardly accessible. Though not so high, it is much more difficult to mount than the other, the outside being covered with a coat of hard and polished cement, at the top almost perfectly smooth and unbroken. Two English officers had mounted it a few days before, who told me that they had found the ascent both difficult and dangerous. One of the Arabs who accompanied them, after he had reached the top, became frightened, and, not daring to descend, remained hanging on there more than an hour, till his old father climbed up and inspired him with confidence to come down.

A new attempt is now making to explore the interior of this pyramid. Colonel Vyse, an English gentleman of fortune, had devoted the last six months to this most interesting work. He has for an associate in his labors the veteran Caviglia, who returns to the pyramids rich with the experience of twenty years in exploring the temples and tombs of Upper Egypt. By a detailed report and drawing received by Mr. Gliddon (now in this country) from Caviglia himself, and by private letters of later date, it appears that they have already discovered a new passage and another chamber, containing on one of the walls a single hieroglyphic. This hieroglyphic was then under the consideration of the savans and pupils of the Champolion school in Egypt; and, whether they succeed in reading it or not, we cannot help promising ourselves the most interesting results from the enterprise and labors of Colonel Vyse and Caviglia.

The pyramids, like all the other works of the ancient Egyptians, are built with great regard to accuracy of proportion. The sepulchral chamber is not in the center, but in an irregular and out-of-

[6] Giovanni Battista Belzoni (1778–1823). Born at Padua, he went to England in 1803, where his great height of six feet, seven inches led to his being billed as "*The Patagonian Samson.*" In 1815 he went to Egypt to design hydraulic machines for Mehemet Ali. Influenced by Burckhardt, he began explorations of Egyptian antiquities. He first entered the Valley of the Kings in 1817, explored the Temple of Idfu, cleared Abu Simbel, opened the Giza pyramid, and uncovered the ruins of Berenice, a terminus of the via Hadriana nova, on the Red Sea. He died in 1823 while on the way to Timbuktu. See *The Great Belzoni* by Stanley Mayes, 1959.

the-way position in the vast pile; and some idea may be formed of the great ignorance which must exist in regard to the whole structure and its uses, from the fact that by computation, allowing an equal solid bulk for partition walls, there is sufficient space in the great pyramid for 3,700 chambers as large as that containing the sarcophagus.

Next to the pyramids, probably as old, and hardly inferior in interest, is the celebrated Sphinx. Notwithstanding the great labors of Caviglia, it is now so covered with sand that it is difficult to realize the bulk of this gigantic monument. Its head, neck, shoulders, and breast are still uncovered; its face, though worn and broken, is mild, amiable, and intelligent, seeming, among the tombs around it, like a divinity guarding the dead.

CHAPTER IV

O N THE FIRST of January I commenced my journey up the Nile. My boat was small, for greater convenience in rowing and towing. She was, however, about forty feet long, with two fine latteen sails, and manned by eight men, a rais or captain, and a governor or pilot. This was to be my home from Cairo to the Cataracts, or as long as I remained on the river. There was not a place where a traveler could sleep, and I could not expect to eat a meal or pass a night except on board; consequently, I was obliged to provide myself at Cairo with all things necessary for the whole voyage. My outfit was not very extravagant. It consisted, as near as I can recollect, of two tin cups, two pairs of knives and forks, four plates, coffee, tea, sugar, rice, macaroni, and a few dozen of claret. My bedroom-furniture consisted of a mattress and coverlet, which in the daytime were tucked up so as to make a divan. Over the head of my bed were my gun and pistols, and at the foot was a little swinging shelf, containing my Library, which consisted of the Modern Traveller on Egypt, Volney's Travels, and an Italian grammar and dictionary. My only companion was my servant; and as he is about to be somewhat intimate with me, I take the liberty of introducing him to the reader. Paolo Nuozzo, or, more familiarly, Paul, was a Maltese. I had met him at Constantinople traveling with two of my countrymen; and though they did not seem to like him much, I was very well pleased with him, and thought myself quite fortunate, on my arrival at Malta, to find him disengaged. He was a man about thirty-five years old; stout, square built, intelligent; a passionate admirer of ruins, particularly the ruins of the Nile; honest and faithful as the sun, and one of the greatest cowards that luminary ever shone upon. He called himself my dragoman, and, I remember, wrote himself such in the convent of Mount Sinai and the temple at Petra, though he promised to make himself generally useful, and was my only servant during my whole tour. He spoke French, Italian, Maltese, Greek, Turkish, and Arabic, but could not read any one of these languages. He had lived several years in Cairo, and had traveled on the Nile before, and understood all the little arrangements necessary for the voyage.

At about twelve o'clock, then, the hour when at home my friends were commencing their New Year visits, accompanied to the boat by my friend from Alexandria, my first, last, and best friend in Egypt, I embarked; and with a fair wind, and "the star-spangled banner" (made by an Arab tailor) floating above me, I commenced my journey on the Nile. It is necessary here for every stranger to place himself under the flag of his country, else his boat and men are liable to be taken at any moment by the officers of the pasha. It was the first time I had myself ever raised the banner of my country, and I felt a peculiar pride in the consciousness that it could protect me so far from home.

We started, as when I first embarked upon the Nile, with a fair wind, at sunset, and again to the gentle tap of the Arab drum we passed the great pyramids of Giza and the giant monuments of Saqqara and Dahshur. Long after sunset their dark outline was distinctly visible over the desert; I sat on the deck of my boat till their vast masses became lost in the darkness. My situation was novel and exciting, and my spirits were elate with curious expectation; but with the morrow came a very essential change. A feeling of gloom came over me when I found the wind against my progress. The current was still running obstinately the same way as before, and to be so soon deserted by the element that I needed gave rather a dreary aspect to the long journey before me. That day, however, we contrived to do something; my boat being small, my men were almost continually ashore, with ropes around their breasts, towing; and, occasionally, rowing across from side to side would give us the advantage of a bend in the river, when we would carry sail and make some progress.

The scenery of the Nile, about fifty miles from Cairo, differed somewhat from the rich valley of the Delta, the dark mountains of Moqattam in the neighborhood of Cairo bounding the valley on the Arabian side, while on the African the desert approached to the very banks of the river. Though traveling in a country in which, by poetic license, and by way of winding off a period, every foot of ground is said to possess an exciting interest, during my first day's journey on the Nile I was thrown very much upon my own resources.

My gun was the first thing that presented itself. I had bought it in Cairo, doubled-barreled and new, for fifteen dollars. I did not expect to make much use of it, and it was so very cheap that I was rather doubtful of its safety, and intended to make trial of it with a double charge and a slow match. But Paul had anticipated me; he had already put in two enormous charges, and sent one of the boatmen ashore to try it. I remonstrated with him upon the risk to which he had exposed the man; but he answered in the tone in which he (like all European servants) always spoke of the degraded inhabitants of Egypt, "Poh, he is only an Arab"; and I was soon relieved from apprehension by the Arab returning, full of praises of the gun, having killed with both shots. One thing disheartened me more than the head wind. Ever since I left home I had been in earnest search of a warm climate, and thought I had secured it in Egypt; but, wherever I went, I seemed to carry with me an influence that chilled the atmosphere. In the morning, before I rose, Paul brought in to me a piece of ice as thick as a pane of glass, made during the night; a most extraordinary, and to me unexpected circumstance. The poor Arabs, accustomed to their hot and burning sun, shrank in the cold almost to nothing, and early in the morning and in the evening were utterly unfit for labor. I suffered very much also myself. Obliged to sit with the door of my cabin closed, my coat and greatcoat on, and with a prospect of a long cold voyage, by the evening of the second day I had lost some portion of the enthusiasm

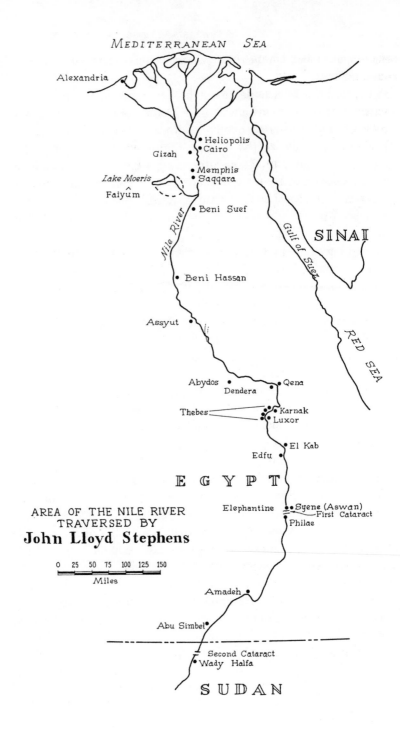

MEDITERRANEAN SEA

Alexandria

• Heliopolis
• Cairo

Gizah •

• Memphis
• Saqqara

Lake Moeris

Faiyûm

SINAI

Nile River

Gulf of Suez

• Beni Suef

• Beni Hassan

Assyut •

RED SEA

Abydos •
• Qena
Dendera

Thebes
• Karnak
• Luxor

• El Kab

Edfu •

E G Y P T

Elephantine •
• Syene (Aswan)
First Cataract

Philae

AREA OF THE NILE RIVER
TRAVERSED BY
John Lloyd Stephens

0   25   50   75   100 125 150

Miles

Amadeh •

Abu Simbel •

Second Cataract
• Wady Halfa

S U D A N

with which, under a well-filled sail, I had started the day before from Cairo.

The third day was again exceedingly cold, the wind still ahead, and stronger than yesterday. I was still in bed, looking through the many openings of my cabin, and the men were on shore towing, when I was roused by a loud voice of lamentation, in which the weeping and wailing of women predominated. I stepped out, and saw on the bank of the river the dead body of an Arab, surrounded by men, women, and children, weeping and howling over it previous to burial. The body was covered with a wrapper of coarse linen cloth, drawn tight over the head and tied under the neck, and fastened between two parallel bars, intended as a barrow to carry it to its grave. It lay a little apart before the group of mourners, who sat on the bank above, with their eyes turned towards it, weeping, and apparently talking to it. The women were the most conspicuous among the mourners. The dead man had been more happy in his connections than I imagine the Arabs generally are, if all the women sitting there were really mourning his death. Whether they were real mourners, or whether they were merely going through the formal part of an Egyptian funeral ceremony, I cannot say; but the big tears rolled down their cheeks, and their cries sounded like the overflowings of distressed hearts. A death and burial-scene is at any time solemn, and I do not know that it loses any of its solemnity even when the scene is on the banks of the Nile, and the subject a poor and oppressed Arab. Human affection probably glows as warmly here as under a gilded roof, and I am disposed to be charitable to the exhibition that I then beheld; but I could not help noticing that the cries became louder as I approached, and I had hardly seated myself at a little distance from the corpse before the women seemed to be completely carried away by their grief, and with loud cries, tearing their hair and beating their breasts, threw out their arms towards the corpse, and prayed, and wept, and then turned away with shrieks piteous enough to touch the heart of the dead.

The general territorial division of Egypt, from time immemorial, has been into upper and lower; the latter beginning at the shores of the Mediterranean, and extending very nearly to the ancient Memphis, and the former commencing at Memphis and extending to the Cataracts. Passing by, for the present, the ruins of Memphis, on the fourth day, the wind dead ahead, and the men towing at a very slow rate, I went ashore with my gun, and at about eleven o'clock in the morning walked into the town of Beni Suef. This town stands on the Libyan side of the river, on the borders of a rich valley, the Nile running close under the foot of the Arabian mountains; and contains, as its most prominent objects, a mosque and minaret, and what is here called a palace or seraglio; that is, a large coarse building covered with white cement, and having grated windows for the harem.

Here travelers sometimes leave their boats to make an excursion to Medinet el Faiyûm, the ancient Crocodilopolis, or Arsinoë, near the great Lake Moeris. This lake was in ancient days one of the wonders of Egypt. It was sixty miles long (about the size of the Lake of Geneva), and Herodotus[1] says that it was an artificial lake, and that in his time the towering summits of two pyramids were visible above its surface. The great labyrinth, too, was supposed to be somewhere near this; but no pyramids nor any ruins of the labyrinth are now to be seen. The lake is comparatively dry, and very little is left to reward the traveler.

At sundown we hauled up to the bank, alongside a boat loaded with pilgrims; and, building a fire on shore, the two crews, with their motley passengers, spent the night quietly around it. It was the first time since we had left Cairo that we had come in contact with pilgrims, although we had been seeing them from my first entering Egypt. This was the season for the pilgrimage to Mecca. The great caravan was already gathering at Cairo, while numbers, not wishing to wait, were seen on all parts of the Nile on their way to Qena, from thence to cross the desert to Quseir, and down the Red Sea to the Holy City. They were coming from all parts of the Mussulman dominions, poor and rich, old and young, women and children,

[1] Historian Herodotus (483–425 B.C.) was born in the Greek colony of Halicarnasus (Bedrum). He traveled through Asia Minor, Thrace, Persia, Tyre, and Egypt gathering materials for his *Histories*. He distinguished, as most authors did not, what he saw with "his own eyes" and what he culled from others.

almost piled upon each other, by scores, for several months exposing themselves to all manner of hardships, in obedience to one of the principal injunctions of the Koran, once in their lives to perform a pilgrimage to Mecca.

On the fifth the wind was still dead ahead; the men continued to tow, but without making much progress; and the day dragged heavily. On the sixth I saw another burial. Early in the morning Paul called me to look out. We were lying, in company with another boat, fast to a little island of sand nearly in the middle of the river. I got up exceedingly cold, and saw a dead man lying on the sand, his limbs drawn up and stiff. He was a boatman on board the other boat, and had died during the night. A group of Arabs were sitting near, making coffee, while two were preparing to wash the body previous to burial. They brought it down to the margin of the river and laid it carefully upon the sand, then washed it, pressed down the drawn-up legs, and wrapped it in fragments of tattered garments, contributed by his fellow-boatmen, who could ill spare even these scanty rags; and, laying it with great decency a little way from the river, joined the other group, and sat down with great gravity to pipes and coffee. In a few moments two of them rose, and going a little apart, with their bare hands scratched a shallow grave, and the poor Arab was left on a little sandbank in the Nile, to be covered in another season by the mighty river. He was an entire stranger, having come on board the evening before his boat set out from Cairo. In all probability, he was one of an immense mass which swarms in the crowded streets of Cairo, without friends, occupation, or settled means of living.

On the seventh the wind was still ahead and blowing strong, and the air was very cold. Having no books, no society, and no occupation except talking with Paul and my boatmen, and the stragglers on shore, I became dispirited, and sat, hour after hour, wrapped in my greatcoat, deliberating whether I should not turn back. One of the most vexatious things was the satisfaction apparently enjoyed by all around me. If we hauled up alongside another boat, we were sure to find the crew sprawling about in a most perfect state of contentment, and seemingly grateful to the adverse wind that prevented

45

their moving. My own men were very obedient, but they could not control the wind. I had a written contract with my rais, drawn up by a Copt in Cairo, in pretty Arabic characters, and signed by both of us, although neither knew a word of its contents.[2] The captain's manner of signing, I remember, was very primitive; he dipped the end of his finger in the ink, and pressed it on the paper, and in so doing seemed to consider that he had sold himself to me almost body and soul. "I know I am obliged to go if Howega says so," was his invariable answer; but, though perfectly ready to go whenever there was a chance, it was easy enough to see that they were all quite as contented when there was none. Several times I was on the point of turning back, the wind drew down the river so invitingly; but, if I returned, it was too early to go into Syria; and Thebes, "Thebes with her hundred gates," beckoned me on.

On the eighth I had not made much more than fifty miles, and the wind was still ahead, and blowing stronger than ever; indeed, it seemed as if this morning, for the first time, it had really commenced in earnest. I became desperate and went ashore, resolved to wear it out. We were lying along the bank, on the Libyan side, in company with fifteen or twenty boats wind-bound like ourselves. It was near a little mud village, of which I forget the name, and several Bedouin tents were on the bank, in one of which I was sitting smoking a pipe. The wind was blowing down with a fury I have never seen surpassed in a gale at sea, bringing with it the light sands of the desert, and at times covering the river with a thick cloud which prevented my seeing across it. A clearing up for a moment showed a boat of the largest class, heavily laden, and coming down with astonishing velocity; it was like the flight of an

[2] This contract is among the J. L. Stephens Papers, Bancroft Library. Translated, it reads: "Jacob-al-Khawaja (Mistir Astiphis) the American pays as rent 500 piasters and 100 silver paras for each complete month for the whole of it with its men, the captain, and pilot [or steersman]." The captain is obligated to listen to his [Stephens'] words wherever he may order him and whatever he may order him he is obligated to listen to and if the gentleman says whatever he says to the captain, the sailors and the pilot shall obey him on what he says. Half of the rental shall be paid on the first of the month and the second half at the end of the month. The agreement has been concluded on Ramadan 7, 1251 [December 27, 1836]. [Signed] American Mister Jacob [sic] Stephens. The Arab Captain Muhammad Musa."

enormous bird. She was under bare poles, but small portions of the sail had got loose, and the Arabs were out on the very ends of the long spars getting them in. One of the boatmen, with a rope under his arm, had plunged into the river, and with strong swimming reached the bank, where a hundred men ran to his assistance. Their united strength turned her bows around, upstream, but nothing could stop her; stern foremost, she dragged the whole posse of Arabs to the bank, and broke away from them perfectly ungovernable; whirling around, her bows pitched into our fleet with a loud crash; tore away several of the boats, and carrying one off, fast locked as in a death-grasp, she resumed her headlong course down the river. They had gone but a few rods when the stranger pitched her bows under and went down in a moment, bearing her helpless companion also to the bottom. It was the most exciting incident I had seen upon the river. The violence of the wind, the swift movement of the boat, the crash, the wild figures of the Arabs on shore and on board, one in a red dress almost on the top of the long spar, his turban loose and streaming in the wind, all formed a strange and most animating scene. I need scarcely say that no lives were lost, for an Arab on the bosom of his beloved river is as safe as in his mud cabin.

On the ninth the wind was as contrary as ever; but between rowing and towing we had managed to crawl up as far as Minia. It was the season of the Ramadan, when for thirty days, from the rising to the setting of the sun, the followers of the Prophet are forbidden to eat, drink, or even smoke, or take the bath. My first inquiry was for a bath. It would not be heated or lighted up till eight o'clock; at eight o'clock I went, and was surprised to find it so large and comfortable. I was not long surprised, however, for I found that no sooner was the sacred prohibition removed than the Turks and Arabs began to pour in in throngs; they came without any respect of persons, the haughty Turk with his pipe-bearing slave and the poor Arab boatman; in short, every one who could raise a few paras.

It was certainly not a very select company, nor over clean, and probably very few Europeans would have stood the thing as I did.

47

My boatmen were all there. They were my servants, said the rais, and were bound to follow me everywhere. As I was a Frank, and, as such, expected to pay ten times as much as anyone else, I had the best place in the bath, at the head of the great reservoir of hot water. My white skin made me a marked object among the swarthy figures lying around me; and half a dozen of the operatives, lank, bony fellows, and perfectly naked, came up and claimed me. They settled it among themselves, however, and gave the preference to a dried-up old man, more than sixty, a perfect living skeleton, who had been more than forty years a scrubber in the bath. He took me through the first process of rubbing with the glove and brush; and having thrown over me a copious ablution of warm water, left me to recover at leisure. I lay on the marble that formed the border of the reservoir, only two or three inches above the surface of the water, into which I put my hand and found it excessively hot; but the old man, satisfied with his exertion in rubbing me, sat on the edge of the reservoir, with his feet and legs hanging in the water, with every appearance of satisfaction. Presently he slid off into the water, and, sinking up to his chin, remained so a moment, drew a long breath, and seemed to look around him with a feeling of comfort.

I had hardly raised myself on my elbow to look at this phenomenon, before a fine brawny fellow, who had been lying for some time torpid by my side, rose slowly, slid off like a turtle, and continued sinking until he too had immersed himself up to his chin. I expressed to him my astonishment at his ability to endure such heat; but he told me that he was a boatman, had been ten days coming up from Cairo, and was almost frozen, and his only regret was that the water was not much hotter. He had hardly answered me before another and another followed, till all the dark naked figures around me had vanished. By the fitful glimmering of the little lamps, all that I could see was a parcel of shaved heads on the surface of the water, at rest, or turning slowly and quietly as on pivots. Most of them seemed to be enjoying it with an air of quiet, dreamy satisfaction; but the man with whom I had spoken first seemed to be carried beyond the bounds of Mussulman gravity. It operated upon him like a good dinner; it made him loquacious, and he urged me to come in, nay, he even became frolicsome; and, making a heavy surge, threw a large body of the water over the marble on which I was lying. I almost screamed, and started up as if melted lead had been poured upon me; even while standing up it seemed to blister the soles of my feet, and I was obliged to keep up a dancing movement, changing as fast as I could, to the astonishment of the dozing bathers, and the utter consternation of my would-be friend.

Roused too much to relapse into the quiet luxury of perspiration, I went into another apartment, of a cooler temperature, where, after remaining in a bath of moderately warm water, I was wrapped up in hot cloths and towels, and conducted into the great chamber. Here I selected a couch, and, throwing myself upon it, gave myself to the operators, who now took charge of me, and well did they sustain the high reputation of a Turkish bath: my arms were gently laid upon my breast, where the knee of a powerful man pressed upon them; my joints were cracked and pulled; back, arms, the palms of the hands, the soles of the feet, all visited in succession. I had been shampooed at Smyrna, Constantinople, and Cairo; but who would have thought of being carried to the seventh heaven at the little town of Minia? The men who had me in hand were perfect amateurs, enthusiasts, worthy of rubbing the hide of the sultan himself; and the pipe and coffee that followed were worthy too of that same mighty seigneur. The large room was dimly lighted, and, turn which way I would, there was a naked body, apparently without a soul, lying torpid, and tumbled at will by a couple of workmen.

I had had some fears of the plague; and Paul, though he felt his fears gradually dispelled by the soothing process which he underwent also, to the last continued to keep particularly clear of touching any of them; but I left the bath a different man; all my moral as well as physical strength was roused; I no longer drooped or looked back; and, though the wind was still blowing a hurricane in my teeth, I was bent upon Thebes and the Cataracts.

CHAPTER V

JANUARY 13. In the morning, the first thing I did was to shoot at a flock of ducks, the next to shoot at a crocodile. He was the first I had seen, and was lying on a sandbank on an island in the middle of the river. I might as well have thrown a stone at him, for he was out of range twice over, and his hard skin would have laughed at my bird-shot, even if I had hit him; but I did what every traveler on the Nile must do, I shot *at* a crocodile. I met several travelers, all abundantly provided with materials, and believe we were about equally successful. I never killed any, nor did they. During the day the wind abated considerably, and towards evening it was almost calm. My boat rowed as easily as a barge, and we were approaching Manfalut. For some time before reaching it there is a change in the appearance of the river.

The general character of the scenery of the Nile is that of a rich valley, from six to eight or ten miles wide, divided by the river and protected on either side from the Libyan and Arabian deserts by two continuous and parallel ranges of mountains. These are the strongly-marked and distinguishing features; and from Cairo to the Cataracts, almost the only variety is that occasioned by the greater or less distance of these two ranges. Before approaching Manfalut they changed their direction, and on the Arabian side the dark mountains of Moqattam advanced to the very border of the river.

Here we began to approach the eternal monuments of Egyptian industry. For a long distance the high range of rocky mountain was lined with tombs, their open doors inviting us to stop and examine

50

them; but, most provokingly, now, for the first time since the day we started, the wind was fair. It had been my peculiar bad luck to have a continuance of headwinds on a part of the river where there was nothing to see; and almost the very moment I came to an object of interest, the wind became favorable, and was sweeping us along beautifully. One of the few pieces of advice given me at Cairo, of which my own observation taught me the wisdom, was, with a fair wind never to stop going up; and though every tomb seemed to reproach me for my neglect, we went resolutely on.

In one of the tombs lives an old man, who has been there more than fifty years, and an old wife, his companion for more than half a century, is there with him. His children live in Upper Egypt, and once a year they come to visit their parents. The old man is still hale and strong; at night a light is always burning in his tomb, a basket is constantly let down to receive the offerings of the charitable, and few travelers, even among the poor Arabs, ever pass without leaving their mites for the recluse of the sepulchres.

It was dark when we arrived at Manfalut, but, being the season of the Ramadan, the Mussulman day had just begun; the bazars were open, and the cook and coffee shops thronged with Turks and Arabs, indemnifying themselves for their long abstinence. My boatmen wanted to stop for the night; but as I would not stop for my own pleasure at the tombs below, I of course would not stop here for theirs; and after an hour or two spent in lounging through the bazars and making a few necessary purchases, we were again under way.

At about eight o'clock, with a beautiful wind, I sailed into the harbor of Asyut. This is the largest town on the Nile, and the capital of Upper Egypt. Brighter prospects now opened upon me. The wind that had brought us into Asyut, and was ready to carry us on farther, was not the cold and cheerless one that for more than two weeks had blown in my teeth, but mild, balmy, and refreshing, raising the drooping head of the invalid, and making the man in health feel like walking, running, climbing, or clearing fences on horseback. Among the bourriquières who surrounded me the moment I jumped on the bank, was a beautiful bright-eyed little Arab

51

girl, about eight years old, leading a donkey, and flourishing a long stick with a grace that would have shamed the best pupil of a fashionable dancing-master. By some accident, moreover, her face and hands were clean, and she seemed to be a general favorite among her ragged companions, who fell back with a gallantry and politeness that would have done honor to the ballroom of the dancing-master aforesaid. Leaving her without a competitor, they deprived me of the pleasure of showing my preference; and, putting myself under her guidance, I followed her nimble little feet on the road to Asyut. I make special mention of this little girl, because it is a rare thing to see an Egyptian child in whom one can take any interest. It was the only time such a thing ever occurred to me; and really she exhibited so much beauty and grace, such a mild, open, and engaging expression, and such propriety of behavior as she walked by my side, urging on the donkey, and looking up in my face when I asked her a question, that I felt ashamed of myself for riding while she walked. But, tender and delicate as she looked, she would have walked by the side of her donkey and tired down the strongest man. She was, of course, the child of poor parents, of whom the donkey was the chief support. The father had been in the habit of going out with it himself, and frequently taking the little girl with him as a companion. As she grew up, she went out occasionally alone; and even among the Turks her interesting little figure made her a favorite; and when all the other donkeys were idle, hers was sure to be engaged. This and many other things I learned from her own pretty little lips on my way to Asyut.

Asyut stands about a mile and a half from the river, in one of the richest valleys of the Nile. At the season of inundation, when the river rolls down in all its majesty, the whole intermediate country is overflowed; and boats of the largest size, steering their course over the waste of waters by the projecting tops of the palm-trees, come to anchor under the walls of the city. A high causeway from the river to the city crosses the plain, a comparatively unknown and unnoticed, but stupendous work, which for more than three thousand years has resisted the headlong current of the Nile at its highest, and now stands, like the pyramids, not so striking, but an equally enduring, and perhaps more really wonderful monument of Egyptian labor. A short distance before reaching the city, on the right, are the handsome palace and garden of Ibrahim Pasha. A stream winds through the valley, crossed by a stone bridge, and over this is the entrance-gate of the city. The governor's palace, the most imposing and best structure I had seen since the citadel at Cairo, standing first within the walls, seemed like a warder at the door.

The large courtyard before the door of the palace contained a group of idlers, mostly officers of the household, all well armed, and carrying themselves with the usual air of Turkish conceit and insolence. Sitting on one side, with large turbans and long robes, unarmed, and with the large brass inkhorn by their sides, the badge of their peaceful and inferior, if not degrading profession, was a row of Copts, calling themselves, and believed to be, the descendants of the ancient Egyptians, having, as they say, preserved their blood intact during all the changes of their country. Boasting the blood of the ancient Egyptians, with the ruins of the mighty temples in which they worshipped, and the mighty tombs in which they were buried, staring them in the face, they were sitting on the bare earth at the door of a petty delegate of a foreign master, a race of degraded beggars, lifeless and soulless, content to receive, as a grace from the hands of a tyrant, the wretched privilege of living as slaves in the land where their fathers reigned as masters.

I do not believe that the contents of all the bazars in Asyut, one of the largest towns in Egypt, were worth as much as the stocks of an ordinary dealer in dry goods on Broadway. But these are not the things for which the traveler stops at Asyut. On the lofty mountains overlooking this richest valley of the Nile, and protecting it from the Libyan Desert, is a long range of tombs, the burial-place of the ancient Egyptians; and looking for a moment at the little Mohammedan burying-ground, the traveler turns with wonder from the little city he has left, and asks, Where is the great city which had its graves in the sides of yonder mountain? Where are the people who despised the earth as a burial-place, and made for themselves tombs in the eternal granite?

The mountain is about as far from the city as the river, and the

53

approach to it is by another strong causeway over the same beautiful plain. Leaving our donkeys at its foot, and following the nimble footsteps of my little Arab girl, we climbed by a steep ascent to the first range of tombs. They were the first I had seen, and are but little visited by travelers; and though I afterward saw all that were in Egypt, I still consider these well worth a visit. Of the first we entered, the entrance-chamber was perhaps forty feet square, and adjoining it on the same range were five or six others, of which the entrance-chambers had about the same dimensions. The ceilings were covered with paintings, finished with exquisite taste and delicacy, and in some places fresh as if just executed; and on the walls were hieroglyphics enough to fill volumes. Behind the principal chamber were five or six others nearly as large, with smaller ones on each side, and running back perhaps 150 feet. The back chambers were so dark, and their atmosphere was so unwholesome, that it was unpleasant, and perhaps unsafe, to explore them; if we went in far, there was always a loud rushing noise, and, as Paul suggested, their innermost recesses might now be the abode of wild beasts. Wishing to see what caused the noise, and at the same time to keep out of harm's way, we stationed ourselves near the back door of the entrance-chamber, and I fired my gun within; a stream of fire lighted up the darkness of the sepulchral chamber, and the report went grumbling and roaring into the innermost recesses, rousing their occupants to frenzy. There was a noise like the rushing of a strong wind; the light was dashed from Paul's hand; a soft skinny substance struck against my face; and thousands of bats, wild with fright, came whizzing forth from every part of the tomb to the only avenue of escape. We threw ourselves down and allowed the ugly frightened birds to pass over us, and then hurried out ourselves. For a moment I felt guilty; the beastly birds, driven to the light of day, were dazzled by the glorious sun, and, flying and whirling blindly about, were dashing themselves against the rocky side of the mountain and falling dead at its base.

Cured of all wish to explore very deeply, but at the same time relieved from all fears, we continued going from tomb to tomb, looking at the pictures on the walls, endeavoring to make out the

details, admiring the beauty and freshness of the colors, and speculating upon the mysterious hieroglyphics which mocked our feeble
knowledge. We were in one of the last when we were startled by a
noise different from any we had yet heard, and from the door leading to the dark recesses within, foaming, roaring, and gnashing his
teeth, out ran an enormous wolf: close upon his heels, in hot pursuit,
came another, and almost at the door of the tomb they grappled,
fought, growled fearfully, rolled over, and again the first broke
loose and fled; another chase along the side of the mountain, another grapple, a fierce and desperate struggle, and they rolled over
the side, and we lost sight of them. The whole affair had been so
sudden, the scene so stirring, and the interest so keen, that Paul and
I had stood like statues, our whole souls thrown into our eyes, and
following the movements of the furious beasts. Paul was the first to
recover himself; and, as soon as the wolves were fairly out of sight,
with a characteristic movement, suddenly took the gun out of my
hand, and started in pursuit. It is needless to say that he did not
go far.

But the interest of the day was not yet over. While walking along
the edge of the mountain, in spite of bats and beasts, still taking
another and another look, my ears were suddenly struck with a
loud voice of lamentation coming up from the valley below; and,
looking in the direction of the city, I saw approaching over the
elevated causeway a long funeral procession, and the voice came
from the mourners following the corpse. They were evidently coming to the Mohammedan burying-ground at the foot of the mountain, and I immediately left the tombs of the ancient Egyptians to
see the burial of one who but yesterday was a dweller in the land.

Being far beyond the regular path for descending, and wishing to
intercept the procession before its arrival at the burying-ground, I
had something like the wolfrace I had just beheld to get down in
time; unluckily, I had sent Paul back to the place where we had left
our cloaks and donkeys and the little girl with directions to ride
round the foot of the hill and meet me at the burying-ground. How
I got down I do not know; but I was quietly sitting under a large
palm-tree near the cemetery when the procession came up. It ap-

55

proached with funeral banners and devices which I could not make out, but probably containing some precept of the Koran, having reference to death, and the grave, and a paradise of houris; and the loud wailing which had reached me on the top of the mountain, here was almost deafening. First in the strange procession came the beggars, or santons, men who are supposed to lead peculiarly pure and holy lives, denying themselves all luxuries and pleasures, laboring not, and taking no heed for themselves what they shall eat or what they shall drink, and living upon the willing though necessarily stinted charity of their miserable countrymen. I could read all this at the first glance; I could see that poverty had been their portion through life; that they had drunk the bitter cup to its very dregs. Their beards were long, white, and grizzled; over their shoulders and breasts they wore a scanty covering of rags, fastened together with strings, and all with some regard to propriety. This ragged patchwork covered their breasts and shoulders only, the rest of their bodies being entirely naked, and they led the funeral procession among a throng of spectators, with heads erect and proud step, under what, anywhere else, would be called an indecent and shameless exposure of person, unbecoming their character as saints or holy beggars. Over their shoulders were slung by ropes large jars of water, which, for charity's sweet sake, and for the love of the soul of the deceased, they carried to distribute gratis at his grave. After them came a parcel of boys, then the sheiks and two officers of the town, then the corpse, tightly wrapped from head to foot in a red sash, on a bier carried by four men; then a procession of men, and more than a hundred women in long cotton dresses, covering their heads and drawn over their faces, so as to hide all except their eyes.

These were the last, but by no means the least important part of the procession, as, by general consent, the whole business of mourning devolved upon them; and the poor Arab who was then being trundled to his grave had no reason to complain of their neglect. Smiles and tears are a woman's best weapons; and she is the most to be admired, and has profited most by the advantage of education, who knows how to make the best use of them. Education and refine-

ment can no doubt do wonders; but the most skillful lady in civilized life might have taken lessons from these untutored Egyptians.
A group of them were standing near me, chattering and laughing
until the procession came up, when all at once big tears started from
their eyes, and their cries and lamentations rent the air as if their
hearts were breaking.

I was curious to see the form of a modern burial in Egypt, but I
hesitated in following. Some of the Arabs had looked rudely at me
in passing, and I did not know whether the bigoted Mussulmans
would tolerate the intrusion of a stranger and a Christian. I followed on, however, looking out for Paul, and fortunately met him
at the gate of the burying-ground. The sheik was standing outside,
ordering and arranging; and I went up to him with Paul, and asked
if there was any objection to my entering; he not only permitted it,
but, telling me to follow him, with a good deal of noise and an
unceremonious use of the scabbard of his sword, he cleared a way
through the crowd, and even roughly breaking through the ranks
of the women, so as materially to disturb their business of mourning, and putting back friends and relations, gave me a place at the
head of the tomb. It was square, with a round top, built of Nile mud,
and whitewashed; two men were engaged in opening it, which was
done simply by pulling away a few stones and scooping out the sand
with their hands. In front, but a few feet from the door, sat the old
mother, so old as to be hardly conscious of what was passing
around her, and probably long before this buried in the same grave;
near her was the widow of the deceased, dressed in silk, and sitting
on the bare earth with an air of total abandonment; her hands, her
breasts, the top of her head and her face, plastered with thick coats
of mud, and her eyes fixed upon the door of the tomb. A few stones
remained to be rolled away, and the door, or rather the hole, was
opened; the two men crawled in, remained a minute or two, came
out, and went for the corpse.

The poor widow followed them with her eyes, and when they
returned with the body, carefully and slowly dragging it within the
tomb, and the feet and the body had disappeared, and the beloved
head was about to be shut forever from her eyes, she sprang up, and

57

passionately throwing her arms towards the tomb, broke forth in a perfect frenzy of grief. "Twenty years we have lived together; we have always lived happily; you loved me, you were kind to me, you gave me bread; what shall I do now? I will never marry again. Every day I will come and weep at your tomb, my love, my life, my soul, my heart, my eyes. Remember me to my father, remember me to my brother," &c., &c. I do not remember half she said; but, as Paul translated it to me, it seemed the very soul of pathos; and all this time she was walking distractedly before the door of the tomb, wringing her hands, and again and again plastering her face and breast with mud. The mourning women occasionally joined in chorus, the santons ostentatiously crying out, "Water, for the love of God and the Prophet, and the soul of the deceased"; and a little girl about seven or eight years old was standing on top of the tomb, naked as she was born, eating a piece of sugar-cane. Paul looked rather suspiciously upon the whole affair, particularly upon that part where she avowed her determination never to marry again. "The old Beelzebub," said he; "she will marry tomorrow if anyone asks her."

Leaving the burying-ground, we returned to Asyut. On my way I made acquaintance with the governor, not only of that place, but also of all Upper Egypt, a pasha with two or three tails; a great man by virtue of his office, and much greater in his own conceit. I saw coming towards me a large, fine-looking man, splendidly dressed, mounted on a fine horse, with two runners before him, and several officers and slaves at his side. I was rather struck with his appearance, and looked at him attentively as I passed, without, however, saluting him, which I would have done had I known his rank. I thought he returned my gaze with interest; and, in passing, each continued to keep his eyes fixed upon the other to such a degree that we must either have twisted our necks off or turned our bodies. The latter was the easier for both; and we kept turning, he on horseback and I on foot, until we found ourselves directly facing each other, and then both stopped. His guards and attendants turned with him, and, silent as statues, stood looking at me. I had nothing to say, and so I stood and said nothing. His mightiness opened his lips, and his myrmidons, with their hands on their sword-hilts, looked as if they expected an order to deal with me for my unparalleled assurance. His mightiness spoke, and I have no doubt but the Turks around him thought it was with the *ne plus ultra* of dignity, and wondered that such words had not confounded me. But it was not very easy to confound me with words I could not understand, although I could perceive that there was nothing very gracious in his manner. Paul answered, and, after the governor had turned his back, told me that his first address was, "Do I owe you anything?" which he followed up by slapping his horse on the neck, and saying, in the same tone, "Is this your horse?" Paul says that he answered in a tone of equal dignity, "A cat may look at a king"; though, from his pale cheeks and quivering lips, I am inclined to doubt whether he gave so doughty a reply.

I was exceedingly amused at the particulars of the interview, and immediately resolved to cultivate the acquaintance. During the long days and nights of my voyage up the Nile, in poring over my books and maps, I had frequently found my attention fixed upon the great Oasis in the Libyan Desert. A caravan-road runs through it from Asyut, and I resolved, since I had had the pleasure of one interview with his excellency, to learn from him the particulars of time, danger, &c. I therefore hurried down to the boat for my firman, and, strong in this as if I had the pasha at my right hand, I proceeded forthwith to the palace; but my friend observed as much state in giving audience as the pasha himself. Being the season of the Ramadan, he received nobody on business until after the evening meal, and so my purpose was defeated. Several were already assembled at the gate, waiting the appointed hour; but it did not suit my humor to sit down with them and exercise my patience, and perhaps feel the littleness of Turkish tyranny in being kept to the last, so I marched back to my boat.

It was still an hour before sunset; my men had laid in their stock of bread, the wind was fair, a boat of the largest size, belonging to a Turkish officer, with a long red satin flag, was just opening her large sails to go up the river, and, bidding good-by to my little Arab girl, we cast off our fastening to the bank at Asyut. It was the first day I had spent on shore in the legitimate business of a tourist, and by far the most pleasant since I left Cairo.

CHAPTER VI

SMALL FAVORS THANKFULLY RECEIVED—SLAVERY IN EGYPT—HOW TO
CATCH A CROCODILE—AN ELABORATE JOKE—IMAGINARY PERILS—
ARABS NOT SO BAD AS THEY MIGHT BE

THE NEXT DAY, at about four o'clock, we arrived at Jidda, formerly the capital of Upper Egypt, and the largest town on the Nile. My humor for going to the Oasis had been growing upon me, and, finding that there was a track from this place also, I landed, and working my way through the streets and bazars, went to the governor's palace. As I before remarked, the palace where the governor lives is always, by extraordinary courtesy, called a palace.

The governor was not at home; he had gone to Asyut, on a visit to my handsome friend the governor there, but he had left his deputy, who gave us such an account of the journey and its perils as almost put an end to it forever, at least so far as Paul was concerned. He said that the road was dangerous, and could not be traveled except under the protection of a caravan or guard of soldiers; that the Arabs among the mountains were a fierce and desperate people, and would certainly cut the throats of any unprotected travelers. He added, however, that a caravan was about forming, which would probably be ready in four or five days, and that, perhaps, before that time the governor would return and give me a guard of soldiers. It did not suit my views to wait the uncertain movements of a caravan, nor did it suit my pocket to incur the expense of a guard. So, thanking the gentleman for his civility (he had given us pipes and coffee, as usual), I bade him good-by, and started for my boat; but I had not gone far before I found him trotting at my heels. In the palace he had sat with his legs crossed, with as much dignity as the governor himself could have displayed; but, as soon as he slid down from the divan, he seemed to have left dignity for his betters, and

61

pounced upon Paul for "backsheesh." I gave him five piasters (about equal to a quarter of a dollar), for which the deputy of the Governor of Jidda, formerly the capital of Upper Egypt, laid his hand upon his heart and invoked upon my head the blessing of Allah and the Prophet.

At Jidda, for the first time, I saw carried on one of the great branches of trade on the Nile, a trade which once stained the annals of our own country, and the fatal effects of which we still continue to experience. There were two large boat-loads—perhaps five or six hundred slaves—collected at Dongola and Sennar, probably bought from their parents for a shawl, a string of beads, or some trifling article of necessity. Born under the burning sun of the tropics, several of them had died of cold even before reaching the latitude of Lower Egypt; many were sick, and others dying. They were arranged on board the boats and on the banks in separate groups, according to their state of health. Among them was every variety of face and complexion, and it was at once startling and painful to note the gradations of man descending to the brute. I could almost see the very line of separation. Though made in God's image, there seemed no ray of the divinity within them. They did not move upon all-fours, it is true, but they sat, as I had seen them in the slave market at Cairo, perfectly naked, with their long arms wound round their legs, and their chins resting upon their knees, precisely as we see monkeys, baboons, and apes; and as, while looking at these miserable caricatures of our race, I have sometimes been almost electrified by a transient gleam of resemblance to humanity, so here I was struck with the closeness of man's approach to the inferior grade of animal existence. Nor was there much difference between the sick and well; the sick were more pitiable, for they seemed doomed to die, and death to anything that lives is terrible; but the strong and lusty, men and women, were bathing in the river; and when they came out they smeared themselves with oil, and laid their shining bodies in the sun, and slept like brutes. To such as these, slavery to the Turk is not a bitter draught; philanthropists may refine and speculate, and liberals declaim, but what is liberty to men dying for bread, and what hardship is there in being separated from the parents who have sold them, or doomed to labor where that labor is light compared with what they must endure at home?

In the East slavery exists now precisely as it did in the days of the patriarchs. The slave is received into the family of a Turk in a relation more confidential and respectable than that of an ordinary domestic; and, when liberated, which very often happens, stands upon the same footing with a free man. The curse does not rest upon him forever; he may sit at the same board, dip his hand in the same dish, and, if there are no other impediments, may marry his master's daughter.

In the evening we left Jidda, and about ten o'clock hauled up to the bank, and rested quietly till morning. Next day the wind was fair, but light, and I passed it on shore with my gun. This same gun, by-the-way, proved a better companion to me on my journey than I had expected. There were always plenty of pigeons; indeed, advancing in Upper Egypt, one of the most striking features in the villages on the Nile is the number of pigeon-cots, built of mud in the form of a sugar loaf, and whitewashed. They are much more lofty than any of the houses, and their winged tenants constitute a great portion of the wealth of the villagers. It is not, however, allowable to shoot at these, the laws regulating the right of property in animals *ferae naturae* being as well established on the banks of the Nile as at Westminster Hall; but there are hundreds of pigeons in the neighborhood of every village which no one claims. In some places, too, there is fine sport in hunting hares; and, if a man can bring himself to it, he may hunt the gazelle, and almost the whole line of the river, at least above Asyut, abounds with ducks and geese. These, however, are very wild and, moreover, very tough; and, except for the sport, are not worth shooting. No keeping and no cooking could make them tender, and good masticators were thrown away upon them.

But the standing shots on the Nile are crocodiles and pelicans. The former still abound, as in the days when the Egyptian worshipped them; and as you see one basking in the sun, on some little bank of sand, even in the act of firing at him, you cannot help going back to the time when the passing Egyptian would have bowed to him as to a god; and you may imagine the descendant of the ancient river-god, as he feels a ball rattling against his scaly side, invoking the shades of his departed worshippers, telling his little ones of the glory of his ancestors, and cursing the march of improvement, which has degraded him from the deity of a mighty people into a target for strolling tourists. I always liked to see a crocodile upon the Nile, and always took a shot at him, for the sake of the associations. In one place I counted in sight at one time twenty-one, a degree of fruitfulness in the river probably equal to that of the time when each of them would have been deemed worthy of a temple while living, and embalment and a mighty tomb when dead.

While walking by the riverside I met an Arab with a gun in his hand, who pointed to the dozing crocodiles on a bank before us, and, marking out a space on the ground, turned to the village a little back, and made me understand that he had a large crocodile there. As I was some distance in advance of my boat, I accompanied him, and found one fourteen feet long, stuffed with straw, and hanging under a palm-tree. He had been killed two days before, after a desperate resistance, having been disabled with bullets and pierced with spears in a dozen places. I looked at him with interest and compassion, reflecting on the difference between his treatment and that experienced by his ancestors, but nevertheless opened a negotiation for a purchase; and though our languages were as far apart as our countries, bargain sharpens the intellect to such a degree that the Arab and I soon came to an understanding, and I bought him as he hung, for forty piasters and a charge of gunpowder. I had conceived a joke for my own amusement. A friend had requested me to buy for him some mosaics, cameos, &c., in Italy, which circumstances had prevented me from doing, and I had written to him, regretting my inability, and telling him that I was going to Egypt, and would send him a mummy or a pyramid; and when I saw the scaly monster hanging by the tail, with his large jaws distended by a stick, it struck me that he would make a still better substitute for cameos and mosaics, and that I would box him up, and, without any advice, send him to my friend.

The reader may judge how desperately I was pushed for amusement, when I tell him that I chuckled greatly over this happy conceit; and having sent my Nubian to hail the boat as she was coming by, I followed with my little memorial. The whole village turned out to escort us, more than a hundred Arabs, men, women, and children, and we dragged him down with a pomp and circumstance worthy of his better days. Paul looked a little astonished when he saw me with a rope over my shoulder, leading the van of this ragged escort, and rather turned up his nose when I told him my joke. I had great difficulty in getting my prize on board, and, when I got him there, he deranged everything else; but the first day I was so tickled that I could have thrown all my other cargo overboard rather than him. The second day the joke was not so good, and the third I grew tired of it, and tumbled my crocodile into the river. I followed him with my eye as his body floated down the stream; it was moonlight, and the creaking of the water-wheel on the banks sounded like the moaning spirit of an ancient Egyptian, indignant at the murder and profanation of his god. It was, perhaps, hardly worth while to mention this little circumstance, but it amused me for a day or two, brought me into mental contact with my friends at home, and gave me the credit of having myself shot a crocodile, any one of which was worth all the trouble it cost me. If the reader will excuse a bad pun, in consideration of its being my first and last, it was not a *dry* joke; for, in getting the crocodile on board, I tumbled over, and, very unintentionally on my part, had a January bath in the Nile.

During nearly the whole of that day I was walking on the bank of the river; there was more tillable land than usual on the Arabian side, and I continually saw the Arabs, naked or with a wreath of grass around their loins, drawing water to irrigate the ground, in a basket fastened to a pole, like one of our old-fashioned well-poles.

On the seventeenth we approached Dendera. I usually dined at one o'clock, because it was then too hot to go on shore, and also, to tell the truth, because it served to break the very long and tedious day. I was now about four hours from Dendera by land, of which two and a half were desert, the Libyan sands here coming down to the river. It was a fine afternoon, there was no wind, and I hoped, by walking, to have a view of the great temple before night. It was warm enough then; but as it regularly became very cold towards evening, I told my Nubian to follow me with my cloak. To my surprise he objected. It was the first time he had done so! He was always glad to go ashore with me, as indeed were they all, and it was considered that I was showing partiality in always selecting him. I asked one of the others, and found that he, and, in fact, all of them, made objections, on the ground that it was a dangerous road.

This is one of the things that vex a traveler in Egypt, and in the East generally. He will often find the road which he wishes to travel a dangerous one, and, though no misadventure may have happened on it for years, he will find it impossible to get his Arabs to accompany him. My rais took the matter in hand, began kicking them ashore, and swore they should all go. This I would not allow. I knew that the whole course of the Nile was safe as the streets of London; that no accident had happened to a traveler since the pasha had been on the throne; and that women and children might travel with perfect safety from Alexandria to the Cataracts; and, vexed with their idle fears, after whipping Paul over their shoulders, who I saw was quite as much infected as any of them, I went ashore alone. Paul seemed quietly making up his mind for some desperate movement; without a word, he was arranging the things about the boat, shutting up the doors of the cabin, buttoning his coat, and with my cloak under his arm and a sword in his hand, he jumped ashore and followed me. He had not gone far, however, before his courage began to fail. The Arabs, whom we found at their daily labor drawing water, seemed particularly black, naked, and hairy. They gave dubious and suspicious answers, and when we came to the edge of the desert he began to grumble outright; he did not want to be shot down like a dog; if we were strong enough to make a stout resistance it would be another thing, &c., &c.

In truth, the scene before us was dreary enough, the desert commencing on the very margin of the river, and running back to the eternal sands of Africa. Paul's courage seemed to be going with the green soil we were leaving behind us; and as we advanced where the grass seemed struggling to resist the encroachment of the desert, he was on the point of yielding to the terror of his own imagination, until I suggested to him that we could see before us the whole extent of desert we were to cross; that there was not a shrub or bush to interrupt the view, and not a living thing moving that could do us harm. He then began to revive; it was not for himself, but for me he feared. We walked on for about an hour, when, feeling that it was safe to trust me alone, and being tired, he sat down on the bank, and I proceeded. Fear is infectious. In about half an hour more I met three men, who had to me a peculiarly cut-throat appearance; they spoke, but I, of course, could not understand them. At length, finding night approaching, I turned back to meet the boat, and saw that the three Arabs had turned too, and were again advancing to meet me, which I thought a very suspicious movement. Paul's ridiculous fears had completely infected me, and I would have dodged them if I could; but there was no bush to hide behind. I almost blushed at myself for thinking of dodging three Arabs, when I had a double-barreled gun in my hand and a pair of pistols in my sash; but I must say I was not at all sorry, before I met them again, to hear Paul shouting to me, and a moment after to see my boat coming up under full sail.

One who has never met an Arab in the desert can have no conception of his terrible appearance. The worst pictures of the Italian bandits or Greek mountain robbers I ever saw are tame in comparison. I have seen the celebrated Gasperini, who ten years ago kept in terror the whole country between Rome and Naples, and who was so strong as to negotiate and make a treaty with the pope. I saw him surrounded by nearly twenty of his comrades; and when he told me he could not remember how many murders he had committed, he looked civil and harmless compared with a Bedouin of the desert. The swarthy complexion of the latter, his long beard, his piercing coal-black eyes, half-naked figure, an enormous sword slung over his back, and a rusty matchlock in his hand, make the best figure for a painter I ever saw; but, happily, he is not so bad as he looks to be.

CHAPTER VII

SUNDAY, January 18. At eight o'clock in the morning we arrived at Qena, where, leaving my boat and crew to make a few additions to our stock, Paul and I crossed over in a sort of ferryboat to Dendera.[1]

The temple of Dendera is one of the finest specimens of the arts in Egypt, and the best preserved of any on the Nile. It stands about a mile from the river, on the edge of the desert, and, coming up, may be seen at a great distance. The temples of the Egyptians, like the chapels in Catholic countries, in many instances stand in such positions as to arrest the attention of the passer-by; and the Egyptian boatman, long before he reached it, might see the open doors of the temple of Dendera, reminding him of his duty to the gods of his country. I shall not attempt any description of this beautiful temple; its great dimensions, its magnificent propylon or gateway, portico, and columns; the sculptured figures on the walls; the spirit of the devices, and their admirable execution; the winged globe and the sacred vulture, the hawk and the ibis, Isis, Osiris, and Horus, gods, goddesses, priests, and women; harps, altars, and people clapping their hands, and the whole interior covered with hieroglyphics and paintings, in some places, after a lapse of more than two thousand years, in colors fresh as if but the work of yesterday.

It was the first temple I had seen in Egypt; and, although I

---

[1] The site of Dendera, opposite the town of Qena (which was the terminus of roads that came out of the Eastern desert), stands in magnificent solitude on the edge of the desert. It was once the capital of the sixth nome of Upper Egypt. The Temple of Dendera was begun under the Ptolemies and finished in Roman times during Nero's regime.

ought not perhaps to say so, I was disappointed. I found it beautiful, far more beautiful than I expected; but, look at it as I would, wander around it as I would, the ruins of the Acropolis at Athens rose before me; the severe and stately form of the Parthenon; the beautiful fragment of the temple of Minerva, and the rich Corinthian columns of the temple of Jupiter, came upon me with a clearness and vividness I could not have conceived. The temple is more than half-buried in the sand. For many years it has formed the nucleus of a village. The Arabs have built their huts within and around it, range upon range, until they reached and almost covered the tops of the temple. Last year, for what cause I know not, they left their huts in a body, and the village, which for many years had existed there, is now entirely deserted. The ruined huts still remain around the columns and against the broken walls. On the very top is a chamber, beautifully sculptured, and formed for other uses, now blackened with smoke, and the polished floors strewed with fragments of pottery and culinary vessels.

Nor is this the worst affliction of the traveler at Dendera. He sees there other ruins, more lamentable than the encroachments of the desert and the burial in the sand, worse than the building and ruin of successive Arab villages; he sees wanton destruction by the barbarous hand of man. The beautiful columns, upon which the skillful and industrious Egyptian artist had labored with his chisel for months, and perhaps for years, which were then looked upon with religious reverence, and ever since with admiration, have been dashed into a thousand pieces, to build bridges and forts for the great modern reformer.

It is strange how the organ of mischief develops itself when it has something to work upon. I sat down upon the sculptured fragments of a column, which perhaps at this moment forms the abutment of some bridge, and, looking at the wreck around me, even while admiring and almost reverencing the noble ruin, began breaking off the beautifully chiseled figure of a hawk, and, perhaps in ten minutes, had demolished the work of a year. I felt that I was doing wrong, but excused myself by the plea that I was destroying to preserve, and saving that precious fragment from the ruin to which it was doomed, to show at home as a specimen of the skill of the Old World. So far I did well enough; but I went farther. I was looking intently, though almost unconsciously, at a pigeon on the head of Isis, the capital of one of the front columns of the temple. It was a beautiful shot; it could not have been finer if the temple had been built expressly to shoot pigeons from. I fired: the shot went smack into the beautifully sculptured face of the goddess, and put out one of her eyes; the pigeon fell at the foot of the column, and while the goddess seemed to weep over her fallen state, and to reproach me for this renewed insult to herself and to the arts, I picked up the bird and returned to my boat.

On board I had constantly a fund of amusement in the movements of my Arab crew. During the Ramadan, a period of thirty days, no good Mussulman eats, drinks, or smokes, from the rising to the setting of the sun. My men religiously observed this severe requisition of the Koran, although sometimes they were at work at the oar under a burning sun nearly all day. They could form a pretty shrewd conjecture as to the time of the setting of the sun, but nevertheless they fell into the habit of regulating themselves by my watch, and I did not think the Prophet would be particularly hard upon them if I sometimes brought the day to a close half an hour or so before its time. Sometimes I was rather too liberal; but, out of respect for me, they considered the sun set when I told them it was; and it was interesting to see them regularly every evening, one after another, mount the upper deck, and, spreading out their cloaks, with their faces towards the tomb of the Prophet, kneel down and pray.

On the twentieth the wind was light but favorable, and part of the time the men were on shore towing with the cords. We were now approaching the most interesting spot on the Nile, perhaps in the world. Thebes, immortal Thebes was before us, and a few hours more would place us among her ruins. Towards noon the wind died away, and left us again to the slow movement of the tow-line. This was too slow for my excited humor. I could not bear that the sun should again set before I stood among the ruins of the mighty city; and, landing on the right side of the river, I set out to walk. About an hour before dark the lofty columns of the great temple at Luxor,[2] and the still greater of Karnak, were visible. The glowing descriptions of travelers had to a certain extent inflamed my imagination. Denon, in his account of the expedition to Egypt, says that when the French soldiers first came in sight of Thebes, the whole army involuntarily threw down their arms and stood in silent admiration; a sublime idea, whether true or not; but I am inclined to think that the French soldiers would have thrown down their arms, and clapped their hands with much greater satisfaction, if they had seen a living city and prospect of good quarters. For my own part, without at this moment referring to particulars, I was disappointed in the first view of the ruins of Thebes. We walked on the right side of the river, the valley, as usual, running back to the desert.

It was nearly dark when we arrived at the ruined village, which now occupies part of the site of the once magnificent city. The plough has been driven over the ruins of the temples, and grass was growing where palaces had stood. A single boat was lying along the bank; a single flag, the red cross of England, was drooping lazily against the mast; and though it be death to my reputation as a sentimental traveler, at that moment I hailed the sight of that flag with more interest than the ruined city. Since I left Cairo I had seen nothing but Arabs; for three weeks I had not opened my lips except to Paul; and, let me tell the reader, that though a man may take a certain degree of pleasure in traveling in strange and out-of-the-way places, he cannot forget the world he has left behind him. In a land of comparative savages, he hails the citizen of any civilized country as his brother; and when on the bank of the river I was accosted in my native tongue by a strapping fellow in a Turkish dress, though in the broken accents of a Sicilian servant, I thought it the purest English I had ever heard. I went on board the boat, and found two gentlemen, of whom I had heard at Cairo, who had been to Mount Sinai, from thence to Hor, by the Red Sea to Quseir, and thence

[2] Luxor, which combines the mosque Alu'l-Haggag and the Roman town, is now, as in 1836, surrounded by hotels and a bustling community. Across the Nile are the temples of Medinet Habu, Feir el Madina, The Colossi of Memnon, and the Valley of the Kings. Karnak lies three miles from Luxor; a massive complex, it has the largest assembly of temples in Egypt.

across the desert to Thebes, where they had only arrived that day. I sat with them till a late hour. I cannot flatter myself that the evening passed as agreeably to them as to me, for they had been a party of six, and I alone; but I saw them afterward, and our acquaintance ripened into intimacy; and though our lots are cast in different places, and we shall probably never meet again, if I do not deceive myself, neither will ever forget the acquaintance formed that night on the banks of the Nile.

Our conversation during the evening was desultory and various. We mounted the pyramids, sat down among the ruins of temples, groped among tombs, and, mixed up with these higher matters, touched incidentally upon rats, fleas, and all kinds of vermin. I say we touched incidentally upon these things; but, to tell the truth, we talked so much about them, that when I went to my boat I fairly crawled. I have omitted to mention that the curse provoked by Pharaoh still rests upon the land, and that rats, fleas, and all those detestable animals into which Aaron converted the sands, are still the portion of the traveler and sojourner in Egypt. I had suffered considerably during the last four days, but, not willing to lose a favorable wind, had put off resorting to the usual means of relief. Tonight, however, there was no enduring it any longer; the rats ran, shrieked, and shouted, as if celebrating a jubilee on account of some great mortality among the cats, and the lesser animals came upon me as if the rod of Aaron had been lifted for my special affliction. I got up during the night, and told Paul that we would remain here a day, and early in the morning they must sink the boat. Before I woke we were half across the river, being obliged to cross in order to find a convenient place for sinking. I was vexed at having left so abruptly my new companions; but it was too late to return. We pitched our tent on the bank, and immediately commenced unlading the boat.

On a point a little above, in front of a large house built by the French, at the south end of the temple of Luxor, and one of the most beautiful positions on the Nile, were two tents. I knew that they belonged to the companions of the two gentlemen on the opposite side, and that there was a lady with them. I rather put myself out of

72

the way for it, and the first time I met the three gentlemen on the bank, I was not particularly pleased with them. I may have deceived myself, but I thought they did not greet me as cordially as I was disposed to greet every traveler I met in that remote country. True, I was not a very inviting-looking object; but, as I said to myself, "Take the beam out of your own eye, and then—" true, too, their beards were longer, and one of them redder than mine, but I did not think that gave them any right to put on airs. In short, I left them with a sort of go-to-the-devil feeling, and did not expect to have any more to do with them. I therefore strolled away, and spent the day rambling among the ruins of the temples of Luxor and Karnak. I shall not now attempt any description of these temples, nor of the ruins of Thebes generally (no easy task), but reserve the whole until my return from the Cataracts.

At about three o'clock I returned to my tent. It was the first day of the feast of Bairam, the thirty days of fasting (Ramadan) being just ended. It was a great day at Luxor; the bazars were supplied with country products, the little cafeterias were filled with smokers, indemnifying themselves for their long abstinence, and the fellahs were coming in from the country. On my return from Karnak I for the first time saw dromedaries, richly caparisoned, mounted by well-armed Arabs, and dashing over the ground at full gallop. I had never seen dromedaries before except in caravans, accommodating themselves to the slow pace of the camel, and I did not think the clumsy, lumbering animal could carry himself so proudly and move so rapidly. Their movement, however, was very far from realizing the extravagant expression of "swift as the wind," applied to it in the East. I was somewhat fatigued on my return, and Paul met me on the bank with a smiling face, and information that the English party had sent their janissary to ask me to dine with them at six o'clock. Few things tend to give you a better opinion of a man, of his intelligence, his piety, and morals, than receiving from him an invitation to dinner. I am what is called a sure man in such cases, and the reader may suppose that I was not wanting upon this occasion.

It was an excessively hot day. You who were hovering over your coal fires, or moving about wrapped in cloaks or greatcoats, can hardly believe that on the twentieth of January the Arabs were refreshing their heated bodies by a bath in the Nile, and that I was lying under my tent actually panting for breath. I had plenty to occupy me, but the heat was too intense; the sun seemed to scorch the brain, while the sands blistered the feet. I think it was the hottest day I experienced on the Nile.

While leaning on my elbow, looking out of the door of my tent towards the temple of Luxor, I saw a large body of Arabs, on foot, on dromedaries, and on horseback, coming down towards the river. They came about halfway across the sandy plain between the temple and the river, and stopped nearly opposite to my tent, so as to give me a full view of all their movements. The slaves and pipe-bearers immediately spread mats on the sand, on which the principal persons seated themselves, and, while they were taking coffee and pipes, others were making preparations for equestrian exercises. The forms and ceremonies presented to my mind a lively picture of preparing the lists for a tournament; and the intense heat and scorching sands reminded me of the great passage of arms in Scott's Crusaders, near the Diamond of the Desert, on the shores of the Dead Sea.

The parties were on horseback, holding in their right hands long wooden spears, the lower ends resting on the sand, close together, and forming a pivot around which their movements were made. They rode round in a circle, with their spears in the sand and their eyes keenly fixed on each other, watching an opportunity to strike; chased, turned, and doubled, but never leaving the pivot; occasionally the spears were raised, crossed, and struck together, and a murmuring ran through the crowd like the cry in the fencing-scene in Hamlet, "a hit, a fair hit," and the parties separated, or again dropped their poles in the center for another round. The play for some time seemed confined to slaves and dependents, and among them, and decidedly the most skillful, was a young Nubian. His master, a Turk, who was sitting on the mat, seemed particularly pleased with his success.

The whole of this seemed merely a preliminary, designed to stir

Memorial plaque at New York Marble Cemetery, unveiled October 9, 1947, executed in Monson Maine slate by John Howard Benson. The glyph was taken from a Catherwood sketch.

Stephens' and Catherwood's signatures on the contract executed September 9, 1839.

The Giza pyramids as drawn by Catherwood about 1826.

Temple at Dendera, from Catherwood's 1833 drawing.

Catherwood's drawing of a village above Dendera, across the Nile from Qena.

The river port of Luxor as seen by Catherwood in 1833.

Luxor ruins from Theban west bank. Catherwood drawing.

Tomb interior, Valley of the Kings. Catherwood drawing.

Obelisk at Karnak. Catherwood drawing.

up the dormant spirit of the masters. For a long time they sat quietly puffing their pipes, and probably longing for the stimulus of a
battle-cry to rouse them from their torpor. At length one of them,
the master of the Nubian, slowly rose from the mat and challenged
an antagonist. Slowly he laid down his pipe, and took and raised the
pole in his hand; but still he was not more than half roused. A fresh
horse was brought him, and, without taking off his heavy cloth
mantle, he drowsily placed his left foot in the broad shovel stirrup,
his right on the rump of the horse, behind the saddle, and swung
himself into the seat. The first touch of the saddle seemed to rouse
him; he took the pole from the hand of his attendant, gave his horse
a severe check, and, driving the heavy corners of the stirrups into
his sides, dashed through the sand on a full run. At the other end
of the course he stopped, rested a moment or two, then again driving
his irons into his horse, dashed back at full speed; and when it
seemed as if his next step would carry him headlong among the
Turks on the mat, with one jerk he threw his horse back on his
haunches, and brought him up from a full run to a dead stop. This
seemed to warm him a little; his attendant came up and took off his
cloak, under which he had a red silk jacket and white trousers, and
again he dashed through the sand and back as before. This time he
brought up his horse with furious vehemence; his turban became
unrolled, he flew into a violent passion, tore it off and threw it on the
sand, and, leaving his play, fiercely struck the spear of his adversary, and the battle at once commenced. The Turk, who had seemed
too indolent to move, now showed a fire and energy, and an endurance of fatigue, that would have been terrible in battle. Both horse
and rider scorned the blazing sun and burning sands, and round and
round they ran, chasing, turning, and doubling within an incredibly
small circle, till an approving murmur was heard among the crowd.
The trial was now over, and the excited Turk again seated himself
upon the mat, and relapsed into a state of calm indifference.

The exercise finished just in time to enable me to make my toilet
for dinner. As there was a lady in the case, I had some doubt
whether I ought not to shave, not having performed that operation
since I left Cairo; but, as I had already seen the gentlemen of the

party, and had fallen, moreover, into the fashion of the country, of shaving the head and wearing the tarboosh (one of the greatest luxuries in Egypt, by-the-way), and could not in any event sit with my head uncovered, I determined to stick to the beard; and disguising myself in a clean shirt, and giving directions to my boatmen to be ready to start at ten o'clock, I walked along the bank to the tent of my new friends. I do not know whether my notion in the morning was right, or whether I had misapprehended things; but, at any rate, I had no reason to complain of my reception now; I think myself that there was a difference, which I accounted for in my own way, by ascribing to their discovery that I was an American. I have observed that English meeting abroad, though they would probably stand by each other to the death in a quarrel, are ridiculously shy of each other as acquaintances, on account of the great difference of caste at home. As regards Americans, the case is different, and to them the English display none of that feeling. After I had started on my ramble, Paul had planted my flag at the door of the tent, and, among the other advantages which that flag brought me, I included my invitation to dinner, agreeable acquaintances, and one of the most pleasant evenings I spent on the Nile. Indeed, I hope I may be pardoned a burst of national feeling, and be allowed to say, without meaning any disrespect to any other country, that I would rather travel under the name of an American than under any other known in Europe. Every American abroad meets a general prepossession in favor of his country, and it is an agreeable truth that the impression made by our countrymen abroad generally sustains the prepossession. I have met with some, however, who destroyed this good effect, and made themselves disagreeable and gave offense by a habit of intruding their country and its institutions, and of drawing invidious comparisons, with a pertinacity and self-complacency I never saw in any other people.

But to return to the dinner; a man may make a long digression before a dinner on paper, who would scorn such a thing before a dinner *de facto*. The party consisted of four, a gentleman and his lady, he an honorable and heir to an old and respectable title, a brother of the lady, an ex-captain in the guards, who changed his

name and resigned his commission on receiving a fortune from an
uncle, and another gentleman, I do not know whether of that family,
but bearing one of the proudest names in England. They were all
young, the oldest not more than thirty-five, and, not excepting the
lady, full of thirst for adventure and travel. I say not excepting the
lady; I should rather say that the lady was the life and soul of the
party. She was young and beautiful, in the most attractive style of
English beauty; she was married, and therefore dead in law; and as
we may say what we will of the dead, I venture to say that she had
shone as a beauty and a belle in the proudest circles of England, and
was now enjoying more pleasure than Almack's or drawing-rooms
could give, rambling among ruins and sleeping under a tent on the
banks of the Nile. They had traveled in Spain, had just come from
Mount Sinai and the Red Sea, and they talked of Baghdad. I had
often met on the Continent Englishmen who "were out," as they
called it, for a certain time, one year or two years, but this party had
no fixed time; they "were out" for as long as suited their humor. To
them I am indebted for the most interesting part of my journey to
the East, for they first suggested to me the route by Petra and
Arabia Petraea. We made a calculation by which we hoped, in
reference to what each had to do, to meet at Cairo and make the
attempt together. It was a great exertion of resolution that I did not
abandon my plans, and keep in company with them, but they had
too much time for me; a month or two was no object to them, but to
me a very great one.

All this and much more, including the expression of a determination, when they had finished their travels in the Old World, to visit
us in the New, took place while we were dining under the tent of the
captain and his friend. The table stood in the middle on canteens,
about eight inches from the ground, with a mattress on each side for
seats. It was rather awkward sitting, particularly for me, who was
next the lady, and in that position felt some of the trammels of conventional life; there was no room to put my legs under the table,
and, not anticipating the precise state of things, I had not arranged
straps and suspenders, and my feet seemed to be bigger than ever.
I doubled them under me; they got asleep, not the quiet and tran-

quil sleep which makes you forget existence, but the slumber of a troubled conscience, pricking and burning, till human nature could endure it no longer, and I kicked out the offending members with very little regard to elegance of attitude. The ice once broken, I felt at my ease, and the evening wore away too soon. An embargo had been laid upon my tongue so long, that my ears fairly tingled with pleasure at hearing myself talk. It was, in fact, a glorious evening; a bright spot that I love to look back upon, more than indemnifying me for weeks of loneliness. I sat with them till a late hour; and, when I parted, I did not feel as if it was the first time I had seen them, or think it would be the last, expecting to meet them a few days afterward at the Cataracts. But I never saw them again; we passed each other on the river during the night. I received several messages from them; and at Beirut, after I had finished my tour in Arabia Petraea and the Holy Land, I received a letter from them, still on the Nile. I should be extremely sorry to think that we are never to meet again, and hope that, when wearied with rambling among the ruins of the Old World, they will execute their purpose of visiting America, and that here we may talk over our meeting on the banks of the Nile. I went back to my boat to greater loneliness than before, but there was a fine wind, and in a few minutes we were again under way. I sat on deck till a late hour, smoked two or three pipes, and retired to my little cabin.

CHAPTER VIII

THE ROCK OF THE CHAIN—RAVAGES OF THE PLAGUE—DESERTED
QUARRIES—A YOUTHFUL NAVIGATOR—A RECOLLECTION OF SAM PATCH
—ANCIENT INSCRIPTIONS—A PERPLEXED MAJORDOMO—A DINNER
WITHOUT PARALLEL—AN AWKWARD DISCOVERY

THE NEXT DAY and the next still brought us favorable winds
and strong, and we were obliged to take down one of our tall
latteens, but made great progress with the other, even against the
rapid current of the river. The Nile was very wide, the water turbulent, and the waves rolling with such violence that Paul became
seasick; and, if it had not been for the distant banks, we could
hardly have believed ourselves on the bosom of a river a thousand
miles from the ocean.

In the evening we were approaching Silsila, the Rock of the
Chain, the narrowest part of the river, where the mountains of
Africa and Arabia seem marching to meet each other, and stopping
merely to leave a narrow passage for the river. Tradition says that
in ancient days an iron chain was drawn across the narrow strait,
which checked the current; and the Arab boatman believes he can
still see, in the sides of the mountains, the marks of the rings and
bolts to which the miraculous chain was fastened.

We hauled up alongside of the bank for part of the night, and the
next morning, with a strong and favorable wind, were approaching
Aswan, the last town in Egypt, standing on the borders of Ethiopia
and at the foot of the Cataracts of the Nile. For some time before
reaching Aswan the river becomes broader and the mountains again
retire, leaving space for the islands and a broad surface for the body
of the river. About three miles this side, on the Arabian bank, is the
new palace of Ibrahim, where he retired and shut himself up during
the terrible plague of last year. On the right, the top of the Libyan
mountain is crowned with the tomb of a Marabou sheik, and about

79

halfway down are the ruins of a convent, picturesque and interesting, as telling that, before the crescent came and trampled it under foot, the cross, the symbol of the Christian faith, once reared its sacred form in the interior of Africa. In front is the beautiful island of Elephantine,[1] with a green bank sloping down to the river. On the left are rugged mountains; and projecting in rude and giant masses into the river are the rocks of dark gray granite, from which came the mighty obelisks and monuments that adorned the ancient temples of Egypt. The little town of Aswan stands on the bank of the river, almost hid among palm-trees; and back at a distance on the height are the ruins of the old city.

From the deck of my boat the approach to the Cataracts presented by far the finest scene on the Nile, possessing a variety and wildness equally striking and beautiful after the monotonous scenery along the whole ascent of the river. With streamers gallantly flying I entered the little harbor, and, with a feeling of satisfaction that amply repaid me for all its vexations, I looked upon the end of my journey. I would have gone to the second cataract if time had been no object to me, or if I had had at that time any idea of writing a book, as the second cataract is the usual terminus for travelers on the Nile; and a man who returns to Cairo without having been there is not considered entitled to talk much about his voyage up the river.

I am, perhaps, publishing my own want of taste when I say that the notion of going to the great Oasis had taken such a hold of me, that it was mainly for this object that I sacrificed the voyage to the second cataract. With the feeling, therefore, that here was the end of my journey in this direction, I jumped upon the bank; and, having been pent up on board for two days, I put myself in rapid action, and, in one of the cant phrases of Continental tourists, began to "knock down the lions."

---

[1] Above Aswan (the dam, of course, not having been built in Stephens' time) were the last rocks of the cataract, and there stood Elephantine, "the town in the middle of the flood." It was ruled over by Khnum, the ram-faced god, genius of the cataract region. Elephantine controlled the eastern rock quarries; it was the gateway to Nubia, had a customs post, and was the capital of the nome. When the Persians occupied it, they allowed a Jewish colony to build a temple to Jahweh.

My first move was to the little town of Aswan; but here I found little to detain me. It was better built than most of the towns on the Nile, and has its street of bazars; the slave-bazars being by far the best supplied of any. In one of the little cafeterias opposite the slave market, a Turk, meanly dressed, though with arms, and a mouthpiece to his pipe that marked him as a man of rank, attracted my particular attention. He was almost the last of the Mamelukes, but yesterday the lords of Egypt; one of the few who escaped the general massacre of his race, and one of the very few permitted to drag out the remnant of their days in the pasha's dominions.

The ruins of the old town are in a singularly high, bold, and commanding situation, overlooking the river, the Cataracts, the island of Elephantine, and the Arabian desert. More than a thousand years ago, this city contained a large and flourishing population; and some idea may be formed of its former greatness from the fact that more than twenty thousand of its inhabitants died in one year of the plague. In consequence of the terrible ravages of this scourge, the inhabitants abandoned it; but, still clinging to their ancient homes, commenced building a new town, beginning at the northern wall of the old. The valley here is very narrow; and the desert of Arabia, with its front of dark granite mountains, advances to its bank.

The southern gate of the modern town opens to the sands of the desert, and immediately outside the walls is a large Mohammedan burying-ground, by its extent and the number of its tombstones exciting the wonder of the stranger how so small a town could pay such a tribute to the king of terrors. In many places the bodies were not more than half-buried, the loose sand which had been sprinkled over them having been blown away. Skulls, legs, and arms were scattered about in every direction; and in one place we saw a pile of skulls and bones, which seemed to have been collected by some pious hand to save them from the foot of the passing traveler. In another, the rest of the body still buried, the feet were sticking out, and the naked skull, staring at us from its sightless sockets, seemed struggling to free itself from the bondage of the grave, and claiming the promise of a resurrection from the dead.

We buried again these relics of mortality, and hoping it might not be our lot to lay our bones where the grave was so little reverenced, continued our way to the ancient granite-quarries of Syene (Aswan).

These quarries stand about half an hour's walk from the river, in the bosom of a long range of granite mountains, stretching off into the desert of Arabia. Time and exposure have not touched the freshness of the stone, and the whole of the immense quarry looks as if it was but yesterday that the Egyptians left it. You could imagine that the workman had just gone to his noonday meal; and as you look at the mighty obelisk lying rude and unfinished at your feet, you feel disposed to linger till the Egyptian shall come to resume his work, to carve his mysterious characters upon it, and make it a fit portal for some mighty temple. But the hammer and chisel will never be heard there more. The Egyptian workmen have passed away, and these immense quarries are now and forever silent and deserted.

Aside from the great interest of these ancient quarries, it is curious to notice how, long before the force of gunpowder and the art of blasting rocks were known, immense stones were separated from the sides of the mountains, and divided as the artist wished, by the slow process of boring small holes, and splitting them apart with wedges.

I returned by the old city, crossing its burying-ground, which, like that of the new town, told, in language that could not be misunderstood, that, before the city was destroyed, it too had paid a large tribute to the grave. This burying-ground has an interest not possessed by any other in Egypt, as it contains, scattered over its extended surface, many tombstones with Coptic inscriptions, the only existing remains of the language of a people who style themselves and are styled the descendants of the ancient Egyptians.

It was late in the afternoon as I stood on the height crowned by the ruins of the ancient city, with a momentary feeling of returning loneliness, and gazed upon the sun retiring with glorious splendor towards my far-distant home. I turned my eyes to my boat, and beyond it, at a distance down the river, I saw a boat coming up under full sail, bearing what my now practiced eye told me was the

English flag. I hurried down, and arrived on the bank in time to welcome to the Cataracts of the Nile the two gentlemen I had first met at Thebes.

We spent the evening together, and I abandoned my original intention of taking my own boat up the Cataracts and agreed to go up with them.

In the morning, after an early breakfast, we started for the Island of Philae, about eight miles from Aswan, and above all the Cataracts; an island singularly beautiful in situation, and containing the ruins of a magnificent temple. The road lay nearly all the way along the river, commanding a full view of the Cataracts, or rather, if a citizen of a new world may lay his innovating hand upon things consecrated by the universal consent of ages, what we who have heard the roar of Niagara would call simply the "rapids." We set off on shaggy donkeys, without saddles, bridle, or halter. A short distance from Aswan, unmarked by any monument, amid arid sands, we crossed the line which, since the days of Pharaoh, has existed as the boundary between Egypt and Ethiopia. We passed through several villages, standing alone at the foot of the granite mountains, without green or verdure around them, even to the extent of a blade of grass, and irresistibly suggesting the question, "How do the miserable inhabitants live?" It was not the first time I had had occasion to remark the effect of blood on physical character, and the strong and marked difference of races among people living under the same sun, and almost on a common soil. In the first village in Nubia, though not half an hour from Aswan, there is a difference obvious to the most superficial observer, and here, on the very confines of Egypt, it would be impossible to mistake a border Nubian for an Arab of Aswan.

Before arriving at Philae the river is filled with rocks and islands, and the view becomes singularly bold and striking. At the foot of one of the islands is a sort of ferry, with a very big boat and a very little boy to manage it; we got on board, and were astonished to see with what courage and address the little fellow conducted us among the islands washed by the Cataracts. And it was not a straight-ahead navigation either; he was obliged to take advantage of an eddy to

83

get to one point, jump ashore, tow the boat to another, again drop to another, tow her again, and so on, and all this time the little fellow was at the helm, at the oar, at the rope, leading the chorus of a Nubian song, and ordering his crew, which consisted of three boys and one little girl. In this way we worked to an island inhabited by a few miserable Nubians, and, crossing it, came to the point of the principal cataract (I continue to call it cataract by courtesy), being a fall of about two feet.

And these were the great Cataracts of the Nile, whose roar in ancient days affrighted the Egyptian boatmen, and which history and poetry have invested with extraordinary and ideal terrors! The traveler who has come from a country as far distant as mine, bringing all that freshness of feeling with which a citizen of the New World turns to the storied wonders of the Old, and has roamed over the mountains and drunk of the rivers of Greece, will have found himself so often cheated by the exaggerated accounts of the ancients, the vivid descriptions of poets, and his own imagination, that he will hardly feel disappointed when he stands by this apology for a cataract.

Here the Nubian boys had a great feat to show, viz., jump into the cataract and float down to the point of the island. The inhabitants of the countries bordering on the Nile are great swimmers, and the Nubians are perhaps the best of all; but this was no great feat. The great and ever-to-be-lamented Sam Patch would have made the Nubians stare, and shown them, in his own pithy phrase, "that some folks could do things as well as other folks"; and I question if there is a cataract on the Nile at which that daring diver would not have turned up his nose in scorn.

We returned by the same way we had come, and under the same guidance, augmented, however, by a motley collection of men and boys, who had joined us as our escort. In paying for the boat, we showed a preference for our little boy, which brought down upon him all the rest, and he had to run to us for protection. We saved him for the present, but left him exposed to one of the evils attendant upon the acquisition of money all the world over, the difficulty of keeping it, which difficulty, in his case, was so great physically, that I have no doubt he was stripped of more than half before we were out of sight.

Getting rid of them, or as many of them as we could, we again mounted our shaggy donkeys, and rode to the Island of Philae. This island makes one of the most beautiful pictures I ever saw. Perhaps the general monotony of the scenery on the Nile gives it a peculiar beauty; but I think it would be called beautiful anywhere, even among the finest scenes in Italy. It brought forcibly to my mind, but seemed to me far more lovely than, the Lake Maggiore, with the beautiful Isola Bella and Isola Madre. It is entirely unique, a beautiful *lusus naturae*, a little island about a thousand feet long and four hundred broad, rising in the center of a circular bay, which appears to be cut off from the river, and forms a lake surrounded by dark sandstone rocks; carpeted with green to the water's edge, and covered with columns, propylons, and towers, the ruins of a majestic temple. A sunken wall encircles it on all sides, on which, in a few moments, we landed.

I have avoided description of ruins when I could. The fact is, I know nothing of architecture, and never measured anything in my life; before I came to Egypt I could not tell the difference between a dromos and a propylon, and my whole knowledge of Egyptian antiquities was little more than enough to enable me to distinguish between a mummy and a pyramid. I picked up about enough on the spot to answer my purpose; but I have too much charity for my reader to impose my smattering on him. In fact, I have already forgotten more than half of the little that I then learned, and I should show but a poor return for his kindness if I were to puzzle him with the use or misuse of technical phrases. Still I must do something; the temples of Egypt must have a place here; for I might as well leave out Jerusalem in the story of a tour through the Holy Land.

The temple of Philae is a magnificent ruin,[2] 435 feet in length and 105 in width. It stands at the southwest corner of the island, close

---

[2] Philae, the ruins which caused Pierre Loti to protest the building of the canal that would submerge it, still survives its half-century immersion in the reservoir of the Aswan dam. The first temples on the island of Philae were erected by Nectanebo, one of the last kings of Egypt. The Emperor Hadrian built the last. All were dedicated to Hathor, the goddess of distant places.

85

upon the bank of the river, and the approach to it is by a grand colonnade, extending 240 feet along the edge of the river to the grand propylon. The propylon is nearly 100 feet long, and rises on each side the gateway in two lofty towers, in the form of a truncated pyramid. The front is decorated with sculpture and hieroglyphics; on each side a figure of Isis, 20 feet high, with the moon over her head, and near the front formerly stood two obelisks and two sphinxes, the pedestals and ruins of which still remain. The body of the temple contains eleven chambers, covered with sculpture and hieroglyphics, the figures tinted in the most lively colors, and the ceiling painted azure and studded with stars.

But there are other things which touch the beholder more nearly than the majestic ruins of the temple; things which carry him from the works of man to a greater and higher subject, that of man himself. On the lofty towers in front of the temple, among the mysterious and unknown writings of the Egyptians, were inscriptions in Greek and Latin, telling that they whose names were there written had come to worship the great goddess Isis; that men had lived and looked upon the sun, moon, and stars, the mountains and the rolling river, and worshipped a mute idol. And again, on the front wall was the sacred cross, the emblem of the Christian faith, and the figures of the Egyptian deities were defaced and plastered over, showing that another race had been there to worship, who scorned and trampled on the gods of the heathen. And again there was an inscription of later days, that in the ruins of the temple carried with it a wild and fearful interest; telling that the thunder of modern war had been heard above the roar of the cataract, and that the arm of the soldier, which had struck terror in the frozen regions of the north, had swept the burning sands of Africa. In the grand propylon, among the names of tourists and travelers, in a small plain hand, is written—"L'an 6 de la république, le 13 Messidor, une armée Française, commandée par Buonaparte, est descendue à Alexandrie; l'armée ayant mis, vingt jours après, les Mamelukes en fuite aux pyramides, Desaix, commandant la première division, les a poursuivi, au de-là des cataractes, où il est arrivé le 13 Ventose, de l'an 7." Near this was an inscription that to me was far more

interesting than all the rest; the name of an early friend. "C——
B——,[3] U.S. of America," written with his own hand. I did not
know that he had been here, although I knew he had been many
years from home, and I had read in a newspaper that he had died in
Palestine. A thousand recollections crowded upon me, of joys departed, never to return, and made me sad. I wrote my name under
his and left the temple.

I was glad to get back to my rascally donkey. If a man were
oppressed and borne down with mental anxiety, if he were mourning and melancholy, either from the loss of a friend or an un-
digested dinner, I would engage to cure him. I would put him on a
donkey without saddle or halter, and if he did not find himself by
degrees drawn from the sense of his misery, and worked up into a
towering passion, getting off and belaboring his brute with his stick,
and forgetting everything in this world but the obstinacy of the ass,
and his own folly in attempting to ride one, man is a more quiet
animal than I take him to be.

As I intended going the next day up the Cataracts with my companions, and expected to spend the day on board their boat, I had
asked them to dine with me in the evening. After giving the invitation, I held a council with Paul, who told me that the thing was
impossible, and, with a prudence worthy of Caleb Balderstone,
expressed his wonder that I had not worked an invitation out of
them. I told him, however, that the thing was settled, and dine with
me they must. My housekeeping had never been very extravagant,
and macaroni, rice, and fowl had been my standing dishes. Paul was
pertinacious in raising objections, but I told him peremptorily there
was no escape; that he must buy a cow or a camel, if necessary, and
left him scratching his head and pondering over the task before him.

In the hurried business of the day, I had entirely forgotten Paul
and his perplexities. Once only, I remember, with a commendable
prudence, I tried to get my companions to expend some of their
force upon dried dates and Nubian bread, which they as malicious-

---

[3] The initials of Cornelius Bradford, a New Yorker who died in Jerusalem in
August, 1830 (see p. 407 below). In 1859 a French archaeologist, incensed that Stephens should have placed his name under that of General Desaix, had the "J.L.S."
removed.

ly declined, that they might do justice to me. Returning now, at the end of nine hours' hard work, crossing rivers and rambling among ruins, the sharp exercise, and the grating of my teeth at the stubborn movements of my donkey, gave me an extraordinary voracity, and dinner, the all-important, never-to-be-forgotten business of the day, the delight alike of the ploughman and philosopher, dinner, with its uncertain goodness, began to press upon the most tender sensibilities of my nature. My companions felt the vibrations of the same chord, and, with an unnecessary degree of circumstance, talked of the effect of air and exercise in sharpening the appetite, and the glorious satisfaction, after a day's work, of sitting down to a good dinner. I had perfect confidence in Paul's zeal and ability, but I began to have some misgivings. I felt a hungry devil within me, that roared as if he would never be satisfied. I looked at my companions, and heard them talk; and, as I followed their humor with an hysteric laugh, I thought the genius of famine was at my heels in the shape of two hungry Englishmen. I trembled for Paul, but the first glimpse I caught of him reassured me. He sat on the deck of the boat, with his arms folded, coolly, though with an air of conscious importance, looking out for us. Slowly and with dignity he came to assist us from our accursed donkeys; neither a smile nor frown was on his face, but there reigned an expression that you could not mistake. Reader, you have seen the countenance of a good man lighted up with the consciousness of having done a good action; even so was Paul's. I could read in his face a consciousness of having acted well his part. One might almost have dined on it. It said, as plainly as face could speak, one, two, three, four, five courses and a dessert, or, as they say at the two-franc restaurants in Paris, Quatre plats, une demi bouteille de vin, et pain à discrétion.

In fact, the worthy butler of Ravenswood could not have stood in the hall of his master in the days of its glory, before thunder broke china and soured buttermilk, with more sober and conscious dignity than did Paul stand on the deck of my boat to receive us. A load was removed from my heart. I knew that my credit was saved, and I led the way with a proud step to my little cabin. Still I asked no questions and made no apologies. I simply told my companions we were in Paul's hands, and he would do with us as seemed to him good.

Another board had been added to my table, and my towel had been washed and dried during the day, and now lay, clean and of a rather reddish white, doing the duty of a table-cloth. I noticed, too, tumblers, knives and forks, and plates, which were strangers to me, but I said nothing; we seated ourselves and waited, nor did we wait long; soon we saw Paul coming towards us, staggering under the weight of his burden, the savory odor of which preceded him. He entered and laid before us an Irish stew. Reader, did you ever eat an Irish stew? Gracious Heaven! I shall never forget that paragon of dishes; how often in the desert, among the mountains of Sinai, in the Holy Land, rambling along the valley of Jehoshaphat, or on the shores of the Dead Sea, how often has that Irish stew risen before me to tease and tantalize me, and haunt me with the memory of departed joys! The potato is a vegetable that does not grow in Egypt. I had not tasted one for more than a month, and was almost startled out of my propriety at seeing them; but I held my peace, and was as solemn and dignified as Paul himself. Without much ceremony we threw ourselves with one accord upon the stew. I think I only do our party justice when I say that few of those famished gentlemen, from whose emerald isle it takes its name, could have shown more affection for the national dish. For my own part, as I did not know what was coming next, if anything, I felt loath to part with it. My companions were knowing ones, and seemed to be of the same way of thinking, and, without any consultation, all appeared to be approaching the same end, to wit, the end of the stew. With the empty dish before him, demonstrative to Paul that so far we were perfectly satisfied with what he had done, that worthy purveyor came forward with an increase of dignity to change our plates. I now saw that something more was coming. I had suspected from the beginning that Paul was in the mutton line, and involuntarily murmured, "this day a sheep has died"; and presently on came another cut of the murdered innocent, in cutlets, accompanied by fried potatoes. Then came boiled mutton and boiled potatoes, and then roast mutton and roast potatoes, and then came a macaroni paté. I thought this was going to damn the whole; until this I had considered the dinner as something extraordinary and recherché. But the macaroni, the thing of at least six days in the week, utterly disconcerted me. I tried to give Paul a wink to keep it back, but on he came; if he had followed with a chicken, I verily believe I should have thrown it at his head. But my friends were unflinching and uncompromising. They were determined to stand by Paul to the last, and we laid in the macaroni paté with as much vigor as if we had not already eaten a sheep. Paul wound us up and packed us down with pancakes. I never knew a man that did not like pancakes, or who could not eat them even at the end of a mighty dinner.

And now, feeling that happy sensation of fullness which puts a man above kings, princes, or pashas, we lighted our long pipes and smoked. Our stomachs were full and our hearts were open. Talk of mutual sympathy, of congenial spirits, of similarity of tastes, and all that; 'tis the dinner which unlocks the heart; you feel yourself warming towards the man that has dined with you. It was in this happy spirit that we lay like warriors, resting on our arms, and talked over the particulars of our battle.

And now, all dignity put aside and all restraint removed, and thinking my friends might have recognized acquaintances among the things at the table which were strangers to me, and thinking, too, that I stood on a pinnacle, and, come what might, I could not fall, I led the way in speculating upon the manner in which Paul had served us. The ice once broken, my friends solved many of the mysteries, by claiming this, that, and the other as part of their furniture and stores. In fact, they were going on most unscrupu- lously, making it somewhat doubtful whether I had furnished any- thing for my own dinner, and I called in Paul. But that functionary had no desire to be questioned; he hemmed, and hawed, and dodged about; but I told him to make a clean heart of it, and then it came out, but it was like drawing teeth, that he had been on a regular foraging expedition among their stores. The potatoes with which he had made such a flourish were part of a very small stock furnished them by a friend, as a luxury not to be had on the Nile; and, instead of the acknowledgments which I expected to receive on account of my dinner, my friends congratulated me rather ironically upon possessing such a treasure of a steward. We sat together till a late hour; were grave, gay, laughing, and lachrymose by turns; and when we began to doze over our pipes, betook ourselves to slumber.

CHAPTER IX

IN THE MORNING we were up betimes, expecting another stirring day in mounting the Cataracts. Carrying boats up and down the rapids is the great business of the Nubians who live on the borders of Egypt. It is a business that requires great knowledge and address; and the rais who commands the large squad of men necessary to mount a boat is an important person among them. He was already there with part of his men, the others being stationed among the islands of the Cataracts, at the places where their services would be needed. This rais was one of the most noble-looking men I ever saw. He was more than eighty, a native of Barbary, who had in early life wandered with a caravan across the Libyan Desert, and been left, he knew not why, on a little island among the Cataracts of the Nile. As the Nubian does now, firmly seated on a log and paddling with his hands, he had floated in every eddy, and marked every stone that the falling river lays bare to the eye; and now, with the experience of years, he stood among the Nubians confessedly one of their most skillful pilots through a difficult and sometimes dangerous navigation. He was tall and thin, with a beard of uncommon length and whiteness, a face dried, scarred, and wrinkled, and dark as it could be without having the blackness of a Negro. His costume was a clean white turban, red jacket, and red sash, with white trousers, red slippers, and a heavy club fastened by a string around his waist. I am particular in describing the appearance of the hardy old man, for we were exceedingly struck with it. Nothing could be finer than his look, his walk, his every movement; and the picturesque effect was admirably heightened by contrast with his swarthy assistants, most of whom were desperately ragged, and many of them as naked as they were born. The old man came on board with a dignity that savored more of a youth passed amid the polish of a European court, than on the sands of Barbary, or the rude islands of the Nile. We received him as if he had been the great pasha himself, gave him coffee and pipes, and left him to the greatest luxury of the East, perfect rest, until his services should be required.

In the meantime, with a strong and favorable wind, we started from the little harbor of Aswan, while a throng of idlers, gathered together on the beach, watched our departure with as much interest as though it were not an event of almost daily occurrence. Almost immediately above Aswan the view extends over a broad surface, and the rocks and islands begin to multiply. The strong wind enabled us to ascend some distance with the sails; but our progress gradually diminished, and at length, while our sails were yet filled almost to bursting, we came to a dead stand, struggled vainly for a while against the increasing current, and then fell astern. The old rais, who had sat quietly watching the movements of the boat, now roused himself; and, at his command, a naked Nubian, with a rope over his shoulders, plunged into the river and swam for the shore. At first he swam boldly and vigorously; but soon his strength began to fail, and the weight of the slackened rope effectually stopped his progress; when, resting for a little space, he dived like a duck, kicking his heels in the air came up clear of the rope, and soon gained the bank. A dozen Nubians now threw themselves into the water, caught the sinking rope, carried it ashore, and wound it round a rock. Again the rais spoke, and fifty swarthy bodies were splashing in the water, and in a moment more they were on the rocky bank, hauling upon the rope; others joined them, but where they came from nobody could see; and by the strength of a hundred men, all pulling and shouting together, and both sails full, we passed the first Cataract.

Above this the passage became more difficult, and the old rais seemed to rise in spirit and energy with the emergency. As we approached the second Cataract half a dozen ropes were thrown out, and the men seemed to multiply as if by magic, springing up among the rocks like a parcel of black river-gods. More than two hundred of them were hauling on the ropes at once, climbing over the rocks, descending into the river, and again mounting, with their naked bodies shining in the sun, all talking, tugging, ordering, and shouting together; and among them, high above the rest, was heard the clear voice of the rais; his noble figure, too, was seen, now scrambling along the base of a rock, now standing on its summit, his long arms thrown above his head, his white beard and ample dress streaming in the wind, until the inert mass had triumphed over the rushing river; when he again took his seat upon the deck, and in the luxury of his pipe forgot the animating scene that for a moment had cheated him back to youth.

At this season there was in no place a fall of more than two feet; though the river, breaking among the almost innumerable rocks and islands, hurried along with great violence and rapidity. In the midst of the most furious rushing of the waters, adding much to the striking wildness of the scene, were two figures, with their clothes tied above their heads, sitting upon the surface of the water apparently, and floating as if by a miracle. They were a man and his wife, crossing from one of the islands; their bark a log, with a bundle of cornstalks on each side; too frail to support their weight, yet strong enough to keep them from sinking.

And now all was over; we had passed the Cataracts, catching our dinner at intervals as we came up. We had wound round the beautiful Island of Philae, and the boat had hauled up alongside the bank to let me go ashore. The moment of parting and returning to my former loneliness had come, and I felt my courage failing. I verily believe that if my own boat had been above the Cataracts, I should have given up my own project and accompanied my English friends. Paul was even more reluctant to part than his master. He had never traveled except with a party, where the other servants and dragomen were company for him, and after these chance encounters he was for a while completely prostrated. The moment of parting came and passed; warm adieus were exchanged, and, with Paul and my own rais for company, I set out on foot for Aswan.

Directly opposite the Island of Philae is a stopping-place for boats, where dates, the great produce of Upper Egypt, are brought in large quantities, and deposited preparatory to being sent down to Cairo. All along the upper part of the Nile the palm-tree had become more plentiful, and here it was the principal and almost only product of the country. Its value is inestimable to the Nubians, as well as to the Arabs of Upper Egypt; and so well is this value known, and so general is the progress of the country in European improvements, that every tree pays an annual tax to the great reformer.

The Nubian is interesting in his appearance and character; his figure is tall, thin, sinewy, and graceful, possessing what would be called in civilized life an uncommon degree of gentility; his face is rather dark, though far removed from African blackness; his features are long and aquiline, decidedly resembling the Roman; the expression of his face mild, amiable, and approaching to melancholy. I remember to have thought, when reading Sir Walter Scott's Crusaders, that the metamorphosis of Kenneth into a Nubian was strained and improbable, as I did not then understand the shades of difference in the features and complexion of the inhabitants of Africa; but observation has shown me that it was my own ignorance that deceived me; and in this, as in other descriptions of Eastern scenes, I have been forced to admire the great and intimate knowledge of details possessed by the unequaled novelist, and his truth and liveliness of description.

The inhabitants of Nubia, like all who come under the rod of the pasha, suffer the accumulated ills of poverty. Happily, they live in a country where their wants are few; the sun warms them, and the palm-tree feeds and clothes them. The use of firearms is almost unknown, and their weapons are still the spear and shield, as in ages long past. In the upper part of Nubia the men and women go entirely naked, except a piece of leather about six inches wide, cut in strings, and tied about their loins; and even here, on the confines of Egypt, at least one-half of the Nubians appear in the same costume.

I do not know what has made me introduce these remarks upon the character and manners of the Nubians here, except it be to pave the way for the incidents of my walk down to Aswan. Wishing to get rid of my unpleasant feelings at parting with my companions, I began to bargain for one of the large heavy clubs, made of the palm-tree, which every Nubian carries, and bought what a Kentuckian would call a screamer, or an Irishman a toothpick; a large round club, about two inches in diameter, which seldom left my hand until I lost it in the Holy Land. Then seeing a Nubian riding backward and forward on a dromedary, showing his paces like a jockey at a horse-market, I began to bargain for him. I mounted him (the first time I had mounted a dromedary), and as I expected to have considerable use for him, and liked his paces, I was on the point of buying him, but was prevented by the sudden reflection that I had no means of getting him down to Cairo.

My next essay was upon more delicate ground. I began to bargain for the costume of a Nubian lady, and, to use an expressive phrase, though in this case not literally true, I bought it off her back. One of my friends in Italy had been very particular in making a collection of ladies' costumes, and, to a man curious in those things, it struck me that nothing could be more curious than this. One of the elements of beauty is said to be simplicity; and if this be not a mere poetical fiction, and beauty when unadorned is really adorned the most, then was the young Nubian girl whose dress I bought adorned in every perfection. In fact, it was impossible to be more simple, without going back to the origin of all dress, the simple fig-leaf. She was not more than sixteen, with a sweet mild face, and a figure that the finest lady might be proud to exhibit in its native beauty: every limb charmingly rounded, and every muscle finely developed. It would have been a burning shame to put such a figure into frock, petticoat, and the other et ceteras of a lady's dress. I now look back upon this, and many other scenes, as strange, of which I thought nothing at the time, when all around was in conformity. I remember, however, though I thought nothing of seeing women all but naked, that at first I did feel somewhat delicate in attempting to buy the few inches that constituted the young girl's wardrobe. Paul had no such scruples, and I found, too, that, as in the road to vice, "ce n'est que le premier pas qui coûte." In short, I bought it, and have it with me, and to the curious in such matters I have no hesitation in saying, that the costume of a Nubian lady is far more curious than anything to be found in Italy, and would make a decided sensation at a masquerade or fancy ball.

It was nearly dark, when, from the ruined height of the old city of Aswan, I saw my little boat with the flag of my country, and near it, hardly less welcome to my eyes, the red-cross banner of England. The sight of these objects, assisted by my multifarious bargainings, relieved me from the loneliness I had felt in parting from my friends; and I went on board the English boat, hoping to find a party with which I had partially arranged to set out from Cairo, and which I was every day expecting. I was disappointed, however; but found a gentleman to whom I was then a stranger, the English consul at Alexandria. He had been eighteen years in the country, closely devoted to his public and private duties, without ever having been in Upper Egypt. On the point of returning home, to enjoy in his own country and among his own people the fruits of his honorable labors, he had now for the first time ascended the Nile. He was accompanied by his daughter, who had reigned as a belle and beauty in the ancient city of Cleopatra, and her newly-married husband. Coming from home, their boat was furnished and fitted up with all kinds of luxuries. Their tea-table, in particular, made such a strong impression on me, that when I met them again at Thebes, I happened to find myself on board their boat regularly about the time for the evening meal. I was exceedingly pleased with Mr. T——; so much so, that at Thebes I gave him the strongest mark of it a man could give, I borrowed money of him; and I have reason to remember his kindness in relieving me from a situation which might have embarrassed me.

Early the next morning the sails were already loosed and the stake pulled up, when Paul, from the bank, cried out, "A sail!" and, looking down the river, I saw a boat coming up, and again the English flag. I furled my sails, fastened the stake, and waited till she came up, and found the party I had expected. I went on board and breakfasted with them. They had started from Cairo on the same day with me; but with their large boats could not keep up with me against the wind. They had heard of me along the river, and, among other things, had heard of my having shot a crocodile. Waiting to see them off for the Island of Philae, and bidding them good-by until we should meet at Thebes, I returned to my boat, and, letting fall the sails, before they were out of sight was descending the Nile.

My face was now turned towards home. Thousands of miles, it is true, were between us; but I was on the bosom of a mighty river, which was carrying me to the mightier ocean, and the waves that were rolling by my side were rapidly hurrying on, and might one day wash the shores of my native land. It was a beautiful prospect I had before me now. I could lie on the deck of my boat, and float hundreds of miles, shooting at crocodiles, or I could go ashore and ramble among modern villages, and the ruins of ancient cities, and all the time, I thought, I would be advancing on my journey. Before night, however, the wind was blowing dead ahead, and we were obliged to furl our sails and take to our oars. But it was all of no use; our boat was blown along like a feather; carried around, backward and forward, across the river, zigzag, and at last fairly driven up the stream. With great difficulty we worked down to Kom Ombo; and here, under the ruins of an ancient temple, part of which had already fallen into the river, we hauled up to the bank, and, in company with half a dozen Arab boats, lay by till morning.

Man is a gregarious animal. My boatmen always liked to stop where they saw other boats. I remember it was the same on the Ohio and Mississippi. Several years since, when the water was low, I started from Pittsburgh, in a flat-bottomed boat, to float down to New Orleans.[1] There too we were in the habit of stopping along the bank at night, or in windy or foggy weather, and the scenes and circumstances were so different that the contrast was most interesting and impressive. Here we moored under the ruins of an ancient temple, there we made fast to the wild trees of an untrodden forest; here we joined half a dozen boats with eight or ten men in each, and they all gathered round a fire, sipped coffee, smoked, and lay

[1] A reference to Stephens' and his cousin Charles Hendrickson's trip in 1824. See the section "The Far West," in the introduction. The boat, however, was a steam packet.

down quietly to sleep; there we met the dashing, roaring boys of the West, ripe for fun, frolic, or fight. The race of men "half horse, half alligator, and t'other half steamboat," had not yet passed away, and, whenever two boats met, these restless rovers must "do something"; play cards, pitch pennies, fight cocks, set fire to a house, or have a row of some description. Indeed, it always involved a long train of interesting reflections, to compare the stillness and quiet of a journey on this oldest of rivers with the moving castles and the splashing of paddle-wheels on the great rivers of the New World.

At daylight I had mounted the bank, and was groping among the ruins of the temple. The portico fronting the river is a noble ruin, nearly a hundred feet in length, with three rows of columns, five in each row, thirty feet high, and ten feet in diameter at the base. The principal figure on the walls is Osiris, with a crocodile head, and the sacred tau in his hand. The Ombites were distinguished for their worship of the crocodile, and this noble temple was dedicated to that bestial god; among the ruins are still to be seen the wall on which the sacred animal was led in religious procession, and the tank in which he was bathed.

Towards noon we were approaching Silsila, or the Rock of the Chain, the narrowest part of the river, bounded on each side by ranges of sandstone mountains. On the eastern side are ancient quarries of great extent, with the same appearance of freshness as at Aswan. Nothing is known of the history of these quarries; but they seem to have furnished material enough for all the cities on the Nile, as well as the temples and monuments that adorned them. Whole mountains have been cut away; and while the solitary traveler walks among these deserted workshops, and looks at the smooth sides of the mountains, and the fragments of unfinished work around him, he feels a respect for the people who have passed away greater than when standing among the ruins of their mighty temples; for here he has only the evidences of their gigantic industry, without being reminded of the gross and disgusting purposes to which that industry was prostituted. The roads worn in the stone by the ancient carriage-wheels are still to be seen, and somewhere among these extensive quarries travelers have found an unfinished sphinx. I remember one place where there was an irregular range of unfinished doors, which might well have been taken for the work of beginners, practicing under the eyes of their masters. Paul took a philosophic and familiar view of them, and said that it seemed as if, while the men were at work, the boys playing around had taken up the tools, and amused themselves by cutting these doors.

On the opposite side, too, are quarries, and several ranges of tombs, looking out on the river, excavated in the solid rock, with pillars in front, and images of deities in the recesses for the altars. I remember a beautiful chamber overhanging the river like a balcony. It had been part of a temple, or perhaps a tomb. We thought of stopping there to dine, but our boat had gone ahead, and our want of provisions was somewhat of an impediment.

At about four o'clock we saw at a distance the minaret of Edfu. There was no wind, the men were gently pulling at the oars, and I took one myself, much to the uneasiness of the rais, who thought I was dissatisfied. Sloth forms so prominent a feature in the composition of the Orientals, and quiet is so material an item in their ideas of enjoyment, that they cannot conceive why a man should walk when he can stand, why he should stand when he can sit, or, in short, why he should do anything when he can sit still and do nothing.

It was dark before we arrived at Edfu. I mean it was that period of time when, by Nature's laws, it should be dark; that is, the day had ended, the sun had set with that rich and burning luster which attends his departing glories nowhere but in Egypt, and the moon was shedding her pale light over the valley of the Nile. But it was a moon that lighted up all nature with a paler, purer, and more lovely light; a moon that would have told secrets; a moon—a moon—in short, a moon whose light enabled one to walk over fields without stumbling, and this was, at the moment, the principal consideration with me.

Edfu lies about a mile from the bank of the river, and, taking Paul and one of the Arabs with me, I set off to view the temple by moonlight.[2] The town, as usual, contained mud houses, many of

[2] Edfu, six miles south of Luxor, was a prosperous town in the Old Kingdom. Its

them in ruins, a mosque, a bath, bazars, the usual apology for a palace, and more than the usual quantity of ferocious dogs; and at one corner of this miserable place stands one of the magnificent temples of the Nile. The propylon, its lofty proportions enlarged by the light of the moon, was the most grand and imposing portal I saw in Egypt. From a base of nearly 100 feet in length and 30 in breadth, it rises on each side the gate, in the form of a truncated pyramid, to the height of 100 feet, gradually narrowing, till at the top it measures 75 feet in length and 18 in breadth. Judge, then, what was the temple to which this formed merely the entrance; and this was far from being one of the large temples of Egypt. It measured, however, 440 feet in length, and 220 in breadth, about equal to the whole space occupied by St. Paul's churchyard. Its dromos, pronaos, columns, and capitals all correspond, and enclosing it is a high wall, still in a state of perfect preservation. I walked round it twice, and, by means of the wall erected to exclude the unhallowed gaze of the stranger, I looked down upon the interior of the temple. Built by the Egyptians for the highest uses to which a building could be dedicated, for the worship of their gods, it is now used by the pasha as a granary and storehouse. The portico and courtyard, and probably the interior chambers, were filled with grain. A guard was stationed to secure it against the pilfering Arabs; and, to secure the fidelity of the guard himself, he was locked in at sunset, and the key left with the governor. The lofty entrance was closed by a wooden door; the vigilant guard was already asleep, and we were obliged to knock some time before we could wake him.

It was a novel and extraordinary scene, our parley with the guard at the door of the temple. We were standing under the great propylon, mere insects at the base of the lofty towers; behind us at a little distance sat a group of the miserable villagers, and leaning against a column in the porch of the temple was the indistinct figure of the guard, motionless, and answering in a low deep tone, like an

temple is well preserved and is impressive by its length and height. Ptolemy III began it in 237 B.C.; it was finished 180 years later, delayed because of revolts in the Theban region. The inscriptions that cover the wall are so many that Émile Chassinat, the French Egyptologist, has used fifteen volumes to publish them all. The temple was dedicated to the falcon-faced Horus, the sky god.

ancient priest delivering the answers of the oracles. By the mellow light of the moon everything seemed magnified; the majestic proportions of the temple appeared more majestic, and the miserable huts around it still more miserable, and the past glory and the present ruin of this once most favored land rushed upon me with a force I had not felt even at the foot of the pyramids. If the temple of that little unknown city now stood in Hyde Park or the garden of the Tuileries, France, England, all Europe would gaze upon it with wonder and admiration; and when thousands of years shall have rolled away, and they too shall have fallen, there will be no monument in those proudest of modern cities, like this in the little town of Edfu, to raise its majestic head and tell the passing traveler the story of their former greatness.

Some of the Arabs proposed to conduct me to the interior, through a passage opening from the ruined huts on the top; but, after searching a while, the miserable village could not produce a candle, torch, or taper to light the way. But I did not care much about it. I did not care to disturb the strong impressions and general effect of that moonlight scene; and though in this, as in other things, I subject myself to the imputation of having been but a superficial observer, I would not exchange the lively recollection of that night for the most accurate knowledge of every particular stone in the whole temple.

I returned to my boat, and, to the surprise of my rais, ordered him to pull up stake and drop down the river. I intended to drop down about two hours to Eileithyaspolis, or, in Arabic, El Kab. No one on board knew where it was, and, tempted by the mildness and beauty of the night, I stayed on deck till a late hour. Several times we saw fires on the banks, where Arab boatmen were passing the night, and hailed them, but no one knew the place; and though seeking and inquiring of those who had spent all their lives on the banks of the river, we passed, without knowing it, a city which once carried on an extensive commerce with the Red Sea, where the traces of a road to the emerald mines and the fallen city of Berenice are still to be seen, and the ruins of whose temples, with the beautiful paintings in its tombs, excite the admiration of every traveler.

We continued descending with the current all night, and in the morning I betook myself to my old sport of shooting at crocodiles and pelicans. At about eleven o'clock we arrived at Isna, the ancient Latopolis, so called from the worship of a fish, now containing fifteen hundred or two thousand inhabitants. Here, too, the miserable subjects of the pasha may turn from the contemplation of their degraded state to the greatness of those who have gone before them. In the center of the village, almost buried by the accumulation of sand from the desert and the ruins of Arab huts, is another magnificent temple. The street is upon a level with the roof, and a hole has been dug between two columns, so as to give entrance to the interior. The traveler has by this time lost the wonder and indignation at the barbarity of converting the wonderful remains of Egyptian skill and labor to the meanest uses; and, descending between the excavated columns, finds himself, without any feeling of surprise, in a large cleared space, filled with grain, earthen jars, and Arabs. The gigantic columns, with their lotus-leaved capitals, are familiar things; but, among the devices on the ceiling, his wandering eye is fixed by certain mysterious characters, which have been called the signs of the zodiac, and from which speculators in science have calculated that the temple was built more than six thousand years ago, before the time assigned by the Mosaic account as the beginning of the world.

But this little town contains objects of more interest than the ruin of a heathen temple; for here, among the bigoted followers of Mohammed, dwell fifty or sixty Christian families, being the last in Egypt, and standing on the very outposts of the Christian world. They exhibited, however, a melancholy picture of the religion they profess. The priest was a swarthy, scowling Arab, and, as Paul said, looked more like a robber than a pastor. He followed us for backsheesh, and, attended by a crowd of boys, we went to the house of the bishop. This bishop, as he is styled by courtesy, is a miserable-looking old man; he told us he had charge of the two churches at Isna, and of all the Christians in the world beyond it to the *south*. His flock consists of about two hundred, poor wanderers from the true principles of Christianity, and knowing it only as teaching

103

them to make the sign of the cross, and to call upon the Son, and Virgin, and a long calendar of saints. Outside the door of the church was a school; a parcel of dirty boys sitting on the ground, under the shade of some palm-trees, with a more dirty blind man for their master, who seemed to be at the work of teaching because he was not fit for anything else. I turned away with a feeling of melancholy, and almost blushed in the presence of the haughty Mussulmans, to recognize the ignorant and degraded objects around me as Christian brethren.

CHAPTER X

I T WAS NEARLY NOON, when, with a gentle breeze, we dropped
into the harbor of Thebes. The sun was beating upon it with
meridian splendor; the inhabitants were seeking shelter in their
miserable huts from its scorching rays, and when we made fast near
the remains of the ancient port, to which, more than thirty centuries
ago, the Egyptian boatman tied his boat, a small group of Arabs,
smoking under the shade of some palm-trees on a point above, and
two or three stragglers who came down to the bank to gaze at us,
were the only living beings we beheld in a city which had numbered
its millions. When Greece was just emerging from the shades of
barbarism, and before the name of Rome was known, Egypt was
far advanced in science and the arts, and Thebes the most magnificent city in the world. But the Assyrians came and overthrew forever the throne of the Pharaohs. The Persian war-cry rang through
the crowded streets of Thebes, Cambyses laid his destroying hands
upon the temples of its gods, and a greater than Babylon the Great
fell to rise no more.

The ancient city was twenty-three miles in circumference. The
valley of the Nile was not large enough to contain it, and its extremities rested upon the bases of the mountains of Arabia and
Africa. The whole of this great extent is more or less strewed with
ruins, broken columns, and avenues of sphinxes, colossal figures,
obelisks, pyramidal gateways, porticoes, blocks of polished granite,
and stones of extraordinary magnitude, while above them, "in all
the nakedness of desolation," the colossal skeletons of giant temples
are standing "in the unwatered sands, in solitude and silence. They

105

are neither gray nor blackened; there is no lichen, no moss, no rank grass or mantling ivy to robe them and conceal their deformities. Like the bones of man, they seem to whiten under the sun of the desert." The sand of Africa has been their most fearful enemy; blown upon them for more than three thousand years, it has buried the largest monuments, and, in some instances, almost entire temples.

At this day the temples of Thebes are known almost everywhere, by the glowing reports of travelers. Artists have taken drawings of all their minute details, and I shall refer to them very briefly. On the Arabian side of the Nile are the great temples of Luxor and Karnak. The temple of Luxor stands near the bank of the river, built there, as is supposed, for the convenience of the Egyptian boatmen. Before the magnificent gateway of this temple, until within a few years, stood two lofty obelisks, each a single block of red granite, more than eighty feet high, covered with sculpture and hieroglyphics fresh as if but yesterday from the hands of the sculptor. One of them has been lately taken down by the French, and at this moment rears its daring summit to the skies in the center of admiring Paris; the other is yet standing on the spot where it was first erected.

Between these and the grand propylon are two colossal statues with mitered headdresses, also single blocks of granite, buried to the chest by sand, but still rising more than twenty feet above the ground. The grand propylon is a magnificent gateway, more than two hundred feet in length at its present base, and more than sixty feet above the sand. The whole front is covered with sculpture; the battle-scenes of an Egyptian warrior, designed and executed with extraordinary force and spirit. In one compartment the hero is represented advancing at the head of his forces, and breaking through the ranks of the enemy; then standing, a colossal figure, in a car drawn by two fiery horses, with feathers waving over their heads, the reins tied round his body, his bow bent, the arrow drawn to its head, and the dead and wounded lying under the wheels of his car and the hoofs of his horses. In another place several cars are seen in full speed for the walls of a town, fugitives passing a river, horses, chariots, and men struggling to reach the opposite bank, while the hero, hurried impetuously beyond the rank of his own followers, is standing alone among the slain and wounded who have fallen under his formidable arm. At the farthest extremity he is sitting on a throne as a conqueror, with a scepter in his hand, a row of the principal captives before him, each with a rope around his neck; one with outstretched hands imploring pity, and another on his knees to receive the blow of the executioner, while above is the vanquished monarch, with his hands tied to a car, about to grace the triumph of the conqueror.

Passing this magnificent entrance, the visitor enters the dromos, or large open court, surrounded by a ruined portico formed by a double row of columns covered with sculpture and hieroglyphics; and, working his way over heaps of rubbish and Arab huts, among stately columns twelve feet in diameter, and between thirty and forty feet in height with spreading capitals resembling the budding lotus, some broken, some prostrate, some half-buried, and some lofty and towering as when they were erected, at the distance of six hundred feet reaches the sanctuary of the temple.

But great and magnificent as was the temple of Luxor, it served but as a portal to the greater Karnak. Standing nearly two miles from Luxor, the whole road to it was lined with rows of sphinxes, each of a solid block of granite. At this end they are broken, and, for the most part, buried under the sand and heaps of rubbish. But, approaching Karnak, they stand entire, still and solemn as when the ancient Egyptians passed between them to worship in the great temple of Ammon. Four grand propylons terminate this avenue of sphinxes, and, passing through the last, the scene which presents itself defies description. Belzoni remarks of the ruins of Thebes generally, that he felt as if he was in a city of giants; and no man can look upon the ruins of Karnak without feeling humbled by the greatness of a people who have passed away forever. The western entrance, facing the temple of Northern Deir on the opposite side of the river, also approached between two rows of sphinxes, is a magnificent propylon four hundred feet long and forty feet in thickness. In the language of Dr. Richardson, "looking forward from the center of this gateway, the vast scene of havoc and destruction presents itself in all the extent of this immense temple, with its columns, and walls, and immense propylons, all prostrate in one heap of ruins, looking as if the thunders of heaven had smitten it at the command of an insulted God."

The field of ruins is about a mile in diameter; the temple itself 1,200 feet long and 420 broad. It has twelve principal entrances, each of which is approached through rows of sphinxes, as across the plain from Luxor, and each is composed of propylons, gateways, and other buildings, in themselves larger than most other temples; the sides of some of them are equal to the bases of most of the pyramids, and on each side of many are colossal statues, some sitting, others erect, from 20 to 30 feet high. In front of the body of the temple is a large court, with an immense colonnade on each side, of 30 columns in length, and through the middle two rows of columns 50 feet in height; then an immense portico, the roof supported by 134 columns, from 26 to 34 feet in circumference. Next were four beautiful obelisks more than 70 feet high, three of which are still standing; and then the sanctuary, consisting of an apartment 20 feet square, the walls and ceiling of large blocks of highly-polished granite, the ceiling studded with stars on a blue ground, and the walls covered with sculpture and hieroglyphics representing offerings to Osiris, illustrating the mysterious uses of this sacred chamber, and showing the degrading character of the Egyptian worship. Beyond this is another colonnade, and again porticoes and walls to another propylon, at a distance of 2,000 feet from the western extremity of the temple.

But these are not half of the ruins of Thebes. On the western side of the river, besides others prostrate and nearly buried under the sands, but the traces of which are still visible, the temples of El Qurna, Northern Deir, Deir el Medinet, the Memnonium, and Medinet Habu, with their columns, and sculpture, and colossal figures, still raise their giant skeletons above the sands. Volumes have been written upon them, and volumes may yet be written, and he that reads all will still have but an imperfect idea of the ruins of Thebes. I will only add, that all these temples were connected by long avenues of sphinxes, statues, propylons, and colossal figures, and the reader's imagination will work out the imposing scene that was presented in the crowded streets of the now desolate city, when, with all the gorgeous ceremonies of pagan idolatry, the priests, bearing the sacred image of their god, and followed by thousands of the citizens, made their annual procession from temple to temple, and, "with harps, and cymbals, and songs of rejoicing," brought back their idol and replaced him in his shrine in the grand temple at Karnak.

The rambler among the ruins of Thebes will often ask himself, "Where are the palaces of the kings, and princes, and people who worshipped in these mighty temples?" With the devout though degraded spirit of religion that possessed the Egyptians, they seem to have paid but little regard to their earthly habitations; their temples and their tombs were the principal objects that engrossed the thoughts of this extraordinary people. It has been well said of them that they regarded the habitations of the living merely as temporary resting-places, while the tombs were regarded as permanent and eternal mansions; and while not a vestige of a habitation is to be seen, the tombs remain, monuments of splendor and magnificence, perhaps even more wonderful than the ruins of their temples. Clinging to the cherished doctrine of the metempsychosis, the immortal part, on leaving its earthly tenement, was supposed to become a wandering, migratory spirit, giving life and vitality to some bird of the air, some beast of the field, or some fish of the sea, waiting for a regeneration in the natural body. And it was of the very essence of this faith to inculcate a pious regard for the security and preservation of the dead. The whole mountainside on the western bank of the river is one vast Necropolis. The open doors of tombs are seen in long ranges, and at different elevations, and on the plain large pits have been opened, in which have been found a thousand mummies at a time. For many years, and until a late order of the pasha preventing it, the Arabs have been in the habit of rifling the tombs to sell the mummies to travelers. Thousands have been torn from the places where pious hands had laid them, and the bones meet the traveler at every step. The Arabs use the mummy-cases for firewood, the bituminous matters used in the embalment being well adapted to ignition; and the epicurean traveler may cook his breakfast with the coffin of a king. Notwithstanding the depredations that have been committed, the mummies that have been taken away and scattered all over the world, those that have been burnt, and others that now remain in fragments around the tombs, the numbers yet undisturbed are no doubt infinitely greater; for the practice of embalming is known to have existed from the earliest periods recorded in the history of Egypt; and, by a rough computation, founded upon the age, the population of the city, and the average duration of human life, it is supposed that there are from eight to ten millions of mummied bodies in the vast Necropolis of Thebes.

Leaving these resting-places of the dead, I turn for one moment to those of more than royal magnificence, called the tombs of the kings.[1] The world can show nothing like them; and he who has not seen them can hardly believe in their existence. They lie in the valley of Biban el Muluk, a dark and gloomy opening in the sandstone mountains, about three quarters of an hour from El Qurna. The road to them is over a dreary waste of sands, and their doors open from the most desolate spot that the imagination can conceive.

Diodorus Siculus[2] says that forty-seven of these tombs were entered on the sacred registers of the Egyptian priests, only seventeen of which remained at the time of his visit to Egypt, about sixty years B.C. In our own days, the industry and enterprise of a single individual, the infatigable Belzoni,[3] have brought to light one that was probably entirely unknown in the time of the Grecian traveler. The entrance is by a narrow door; a simple excavation in the side

[1] The tombs in the Valley of the Kings were first opened by Giovanni Belzoni in 1818, when he trod on mummies "as thick as leaves in Vallambrosa." Three dynasties of Sun Kings ordered their tombs hewn out of the limestone plateau. It was here that Howard Carter and Lord Carnarvon, between 1913 and 1933, found the tomb of Tutankhamen.

[2] The Greek historian of the late first century B.C. Of the forty books of his *Historical Library*, only books I–V and XI–XX are extant.

[3] Italian archaeologist Belzoni discovered the tomb of Seti I at Thebes in 1817, and moved the bust of "Young Memnon" from Thebes to Alexandria. The bust is now in the British Museum.

of the mountain, without device or ornament. The entrance hall, which is extremely beautiful, is twenty-seven feet long and twenty-five broad, having at the end a large door opening into another chamber, twenty-eight feet by twenty-five, the walls covered with figures drawn in outline, but perfect as if recently done. Descending a large staircase and passing through a beautiful corridor, Belzoni came to another staircase, at the foot of which he entered another apartment, twenty-four feet by thirteen, and so ornamented with sculpture and paintings that he called it the Hall of Beauty. The sides of all the chambers and corridors are covered with sculpture and paintings; the colors appearing fresher as the visitor advances towards the interior of the tomb; and the walls of this chamber are covered with the figures of Egyptian gods and goddesses, seeming to hover round and guard the remains of the honored dead.

Farther on is a large hall, twenty-eight feet long and twenty-seven broad, supported by two rows of square pillars, which Belzoni called the Hall of Pillars; and beyond this is the entry to a large saloon with a vaulted roof, thirty-two feet in length and twenty-seven in breadth. Opening from this were several other chambers of different dimensions, one of them unfinished, and one forty-three feet long by seventeen feet, six inches wide; in which he found the mummy of a bull; but in the center of the grand saloon was a sarcophagus of the finest oriental alabaster, only two inches thick, minutely sculptured within and without with several hundred figures, and perfectly transparent when a light was placed within it.

All over the corridors and chambers the walls are adorned with sculptures and paintings in intaglio and relief, representing gods, goddesses, and the hero of the tomb in the most prominent events of his life, priests, religious processions and sacrifices, boats and agricultural scenes, and the most familiar pictures of everyday life, in colors as fresh as if they were painted not more than a month ago; and the large saloon, lighted up with the blaze of our torches, seemed more fitting for a banqueting hall, for song and dance than a burial-place of the dead. All travelers concur in pronouncing the sudden transition from the dreary desert without to these magnificent tombs as operating like a scene of enchantment; and we may

111

imagine what must have been the sensations of Belzoni, when, wandering with the excitement of a first discoverer through these beautiful corridors and chambers, he found himself in the great saloon leaning over the alabaster sarcophagus. An old Arab who accompanied us remembered Belzoni, and pointed out a chamber where the fortunate explorer entertained a party of European travelers who happened to arrive there at that time, making the tomb of Pharaoh ring with shouts and songs of merriment.

At different times I wandered among all these tombs. All were of the same general character; all possessed the same beauty and magnificence of design and finish, and in all, at the extreme end, was a large saloon, adorned with sculpture and paintings of extraordinary beauty, and containing a single sarcophagus. "The kings of the nations did lie in glory, every one in his own house, but thou art cast out of thy grave like an abominable branch." Every sarcophagus is broken, and the bones of the kings of Egypt are scattered. In one I picked up a skull. I mused over it a moment, and handed it to Paul, who moralized at large. "That man," said he, "once talked, and laughed, and sang, and danced, and ate macaroni." Among the paintings on the walls was represented a heap of hands severed from the arms, showing that the hero of the tomb had played the tyrant in his brief hour on earth. I dashed the skull against a stone, broke it in fragments, and pocketed a piece as a memorial of a king. Paul cut off one of the ears, and we left the tomb.

Travelers and commentators concur in supposing that these magnificent excavations must have been intended for other uses than the burial, each of a single king. Perhaps, it is said, like the chambers of imagery seen by the Jewish prophet, they were the scene of idolatrous rites performed "in the dark"; and, as the Israelites are known to have been mere copyists of the Egyptians, these tombs are supposed to illustrate the words of Ezekiel: "Then said he to me, Son of man, dig now in the wall; and when I had digged in the wall, behold a door. And he said unto me, Go in, and see the abominable things that they do there. So I went in, and saw, and behold, every form of creeping thing and abominable beasts, and all the idols of the house of Israel, portrayed upon the wall round about."—Ezek. viii: 8–10.

Amid the wrecks of former greatness which tower above the plain of Thebes, the inhabitants who now hover around the site of the ancient city are perhaps the most miserable in Egypt. On one side of the river they build their mud huts around the ruins of the temples, and on the other their best habitations are in the tombs; wherever a small space has been cleared out, the inhabitants crawl in, with their dogs, goats, sheep, women, and children; and the Arab is passing rich who has for his sleeping-place the sarcophagus of an ancient Egyptian.

I have several times spoken of my intended journey to the Great Oasis. Something was yet wanting in my voyage on the Nile. It was calm, tame, and wanting in that high excitement which I had expected from traveling in a barbarous country. A woman and child might go safely from Cairo to the Cataracts; and my blood began to run sluggishly in my veins. Besides, I had a great curiosity to see an oasis; a small spot of green fertile land in the great desert, rising in solitary beauty before the eyes of the traveler, after days of journeying through arid wastes, and divided by vast sandy ramparts from the rest of the world. The very name of the Great Oasis in the Libyan Desert carried with it a wild and almost fearful interest, too powerful for me to resist. It was beyond the beaten track; and the sheik with whom I made my arrangements insisted on my taking a guard, telling me that he understood the character of his race, and an Arab in the desert could not resist the temptation to rob an unprotected traveler. For my own part, I had more fear of being followed by a party of the very unprepossessing fellows who were stealthily digging among the tombs, and all of whom knew of the preparations for our journey, than from any we might encounter in the desert. I must confess, however, that I was rather amused when I reviewed my body-guard, and, with the gravest air in the world, knocked out the primings from their guns, and primed them anew with the best of English powder. When I got through I was on the point of discharging them altogether; but it would have broken the poor fellows' hearts to disappoint them of their three piasters (about fifteen cents) per diem, dearly earned by a walk all day in the desert, and a chance of being shot at.

In the afternoon before the day fixed for my departure, I rode by the celebrated Memnons,[4] the Damy and Shamy of the Arabs. Perhaps it was because it was the last time, but I had never before looked upon them with so much interest. Among the mightier monuments of Thebes, her temples and her tombs, I had passed these ancient statues with a comparatively careless eye, scarcely bestowing a thought even upon the vocal Memnon. Now I was in a different mood, and looked upon its still towering form with a feeling of melancholy interest. I stood before it and gazed up at its worn face, its scars and bruises, and my heart warmed to it. It told of exposure, for unknown ages, to the rude assaults of the elements, and the ruder assaults of man. I climbed upon the pedestal; upon the still hardy legs of the Memnon. I pored over a thousand inscriptions in Greek and Latin. A thousand names of strangers from distant lands, who had come like me to do homage to the mighty monuments of Thebes; Greeks and Romans who had been in their graves more than two thousand years, and who had written with their own hands that they had heard the voice of the vocal Memnon. But, alas! the voice has departed from Memnon; the soul has fled, and it stands a gigantic skeleton in a grave of ruins. I returned to my boat, and, in ten minutes thereafter, if the vocal Memnon had bellowed in my ears he could not have waked me.

[4] The well-known and often illustrated Colossi of Memnon are the two seated statues of Amenhotep III. They are fifty feet in height, built of stone that was quarried in the Red Mountains. They were erected by Amenhotep, builder of the temple of Luxor. If Stephens had looked closely over the "thousand names of strangers" written on them, he would have discovered that of "F. Catherwood," who made the first accurate illustration of the monuments and who would be his collaborator in the discovery of the Maya civilization.

CHAPTER XI

THE ARABS AND THE PASHA—MARCH INTO THE DESERT—ARAB
CHRISTIANS—A COLD RECEPTION—ARAB PUNCTUALITY—A NIGHT IN
A CONVENT—AN ARAB CHRISTIAN PRIEST—SPECULATIVE THEOLOGY—
A JOURNEY ENDED BEFORE COMMENCED

EARLY IN THE MORNING I was on the bank, waiting for my caravan and guides. I had everything ready, rice, macaroni, bread, biscuit, a hare, and a few shirts. I had given instructions to my rais to take my boat down to Asyut, and wait for me there, as my intention was to go from the Great Oasis to the Oasis of Siwa, containing the ruins of the temple of Jupiter Ammon, to destroy which Cambyses had sent from this very spot an army of fifty thousand men, who, by the way, left their bones on the sands of Africa; and I need not remind the reader that Alexander the Great had visited it in person, and been acknowledged by the priests as the son of Jupiter.[1] I waited a little longer, and then, becoming impatient, mounted a donkey to ride to the sheik's. My rais and crew accompanied me a little way; they were the only persons to bid us farewell; and, as Paul remarked, if we never got back, they were the only persons to make any report of us to our friends.

The sheik's house was situated near the mountains, in the midst of the tombs forming the great Necropolis of Thebes, and we found him surrounded by fifty or sixty men, and women and children without number, all helping to fit out the expedition. There did not appear to be much choice among them; but I picked out my bodyguard, and when I looked at their swarthy visages by broad daylight, I could not help asking the sheik what security I had against them. The sheik seemed a little touched, but, pointing to the open

[1] Stephens' "Great Oasis," which lay 100 miles west of Thebes, was not the Great Oasis of Ammonium, 180 miles inland from the Mediterranean, which was visited by Alexander the Great; Ammonium Siwa lies 400 miles from Lake Moeris at Faiyûm. Stephens' "great Oasis" was Hibis (Kharga) and Dakhla, 100 miles west of Thebes.

115

doors of the tombs, and the miserable beings around us, he said he had their wives and children in his hands as pledges for my safety. Of the sheik himself I knew nothing, except that he was sheik. I knew, too, that though, by virtue of the pasha's firman, he was bound to do everything he could for me, he was no friend to the pasha or his government; for one evening, in speaking of the general poverty of the Arabs, he said that if one-fourth of them owned a musket, one charge of powder, and one ball, before morning there would not be a Turk in Egypt. However, I knew all this before.

At twelve o'clock the last sack of biscuit was packed upon the camels, and I mounted a fine dromedary, while my companions bade farewell to their wives, children, and friends; a farewell so calm and quiet, particularly for a people whose blood was warmed by the burning sun of Africa, that it seemed cold and heartless.

My caravan consisted of six camels, or rather four camels and two dromedaries, four camel-drivers armed with swords, eight men with pistols and muskets, Paul, and myself. It was the first time I had undertaken a journey in the desert. My first endeavor was to learn something of the character of my companions, and even Paul became perfectly satisfied and pleased with the journey, when, upon acquaintance, he found that their ugly outsides gave no true indication of the inward man.

Our guide, he who was to conduct us through the pathless desert, was not yet with us; he lived at a village about four miles distant, and a messenger had been sent forward to advise him of our coming. Riding for the last time among the ruined temples of Thebes, beyond the limits of the ancient city, our road lay behind the valley bordering the river, and along the edge of the desert. On one side was one of the richest and most extensive valleys of the Nile, well cultivated, and at this season of the year covered with the richest greens; on the other were barren mountains and a sandy desert.

In about four hours we saw, crossing the valley and stopping on the edge of the desert, a single Arab. It was our messenger, come to tell us that our guide would meet us at a Christian church about four hours' march in the desert. Before us, at some distance over a sandy plain, was a high range of sandstone mountains, and beyond these was the mighty waste of sand and barrenness. Towards evening we saw from afar the church at which we were to meet our guide. It was the only object that rose above the level of the sands; and as the setting sun was fast reminding us that the day was closing, it looked like a resting-place for a weary traveler.

Congratulating myself upon my unexpected good fortune in meeting with those who bore the name of Christians, I was still more happy in the prospect, for this night at least, of sleeping under a roof. As we approached we saw the figure of a man stealing along the wall, and were near enough to hear the hasty closing of the door and the heavy drawing of bolts inside. It was nine o'clock when we dismounted and knocked at the door of the convent, but received no answer; we knocked again and again without success. We then commenced a regular battery. I rattled against the door with my Nubian club in a small way, like Richard at the gate of the castle of Front de Boeuf; but my blows did not tell like the battle-axe of the Lionhearted, and the churlish inmates, secure behind their strong walls, paid no regard to us. Tired of knocking, and irritated at this inhospitable treatment from men calling themselves Christians, I walked round the building to see if by accident there was not some back door left open. The convent was enclosed by a square wall of unburnt brick, twelve or fourteen feet high, and not a door, window, or loophole was to be seen. It was built for defense against the roving Arabs, and, if we had intended to storm it, we could not have found an assailable point. I returned vexed and disappointed; and, calling away my men, and almost cursing the unchristian spirit of its inmates, I pitched my tent under its walls, and prepared to pass the night in the desert.

I had hardly stretched myself upon my mat before I heard the smart trot of a dromedary, and presently my guide, whom I had already forgotten, dismounted at the door of the tent. He was a tall, hard-faced, weather-beaten man of about fifty, the white hairs just beginning to make their appearance in his black beard. I wanted to have a good view of him, and, calling him inside, gave him a seat on the mat, a pipe, and coffee. He told me that for many years he had been in the habit of going once a year to the Oasis, on a trading voyage, and that he knew the road perfectly. Almost the first thing he said was, that he supposed I intended to remain there the next day. The Arabs, like most other Orientals, have no respect for the value of time; and among the petty vexations of traveling among them, few annoyed me more than the eternal "bokhara," "bokhara," "tomorrow," "tomorrow." When they first sent to this guide to know whether he could engage with me, he said he was ready at any moment, by which he probably meant a week's notice; and when they sent word that I had named a particular day, he probably thought that I would be along in the course of two or three thereafter, and was no doubt taken by surprise when the messenger came to tell him that I was already on the march. I, of course, had no idea of remaining there. He told me that I had better stay; that one day could not make any difference, and finally said he had no bread baked, and must have a day or two to prepare himself. I answered that he had told the sheik at Thebes that he would be ready at any moment; that it was absurd to think I would wait there in the desert; that I would not be trifled with, and, if he was not ready the next morning, I would ride over to his village and make complaint to the sheik. After a long parley, which those only can imagine who have had to deal with Arabs, he promised to be there at sunrise the next morning, and took his leave.

After supper, when, if ever, a man should feel good-natured, I began again to feel indignant at the churlish inmates of the convent, and resolved upon another effort to see what stuff these Christians were made of. I knew that the monks in these isolated places, among fanatic Mussulmans, were sometimes obliged to have recourse to carnal weapons; and telling Paul to keep a lookout, and give me notice if he saw the barrel of a musket presenting itself over the wall, I again commenced thundering at the door; almost at the first blow it was thrown wide open, with a suddenness that startled me, and a dark, surly, and half-naked Arab stood facing me in the doorway. He had been reconnoitering, and, though not sufficiently assured to come out and welcome us, he was ready to open when again summoned. With no small degree of asperity, and certainly

118

without the meekness of the character upon which I was then presuming, I asked him if that was his Christian spirit, to let a stranger and a Christian sleep outside his walls when he had a roof to shelter him; and, before he could interpose a word, I had read him a homily upon the Christian virtues that would have done credit to some pulpits. He might have retorted upon me, that with the Christian duties coming so glibly from my tongue, I was amazingly deficient in the cardinal virtue of forbearance; but I had the satisfaction of learning that I had not been excluded by the hands of Christians. The priests and monks had gone to a neighboring village, and he was left alone. I followed him through a sort of courtyard into a vestibule, where was a noble fire, with a large caldron boiling over it. He neither asked me to stay nor told me to go, and seated himself by the fire, perfectly indifferent to my movements. As soon as I had satisfied myself that he was alone, and saw that my Arabs had followed me, I thought I ran no risk in considering the building as a castle which I had stormed, and him as the captive of my bow and spear. I therefore required him to show me the interior of the convent, and he immediately took up a blazing stick from the fire, and conducted me within; and when I told him that I meant to sleep there, he said it would be for him a night "white as milk."

From the vestibule the door opened into the chapel, which consisted of a long apartment running transversely, the door in the center; the floor was covered with mats, ostrich eggs were suspended from the ceilings, and three or four recesses contained altars to favorite saints. Directly opposite the door was a larger recess, in which stood the great altar, separated by a railing, ornamented with bone and mother-of-pearl, and over the top were four pictures of St. George slaying the dragon. I walked up and down the chapel two or three times, followed in silence by my swarthy friends, not altogether with the reverential spirit of a pious Christian, but with the prudence of a man of the world, looking out for the best place to sleep, and finally deposited my mat at the foot of the great altar.

I might better have slept on the sand after all, for the walls of the church were damp, and a strong current of air from the large window above had been pouring in upon me the whole night. When

119

I first woke I felt as if pinned to the floor, and I was startled and alarmed at the recurrence of a malady, on account of which I was then an exile from home. I went outside, and found, although it was late, that the guide had not come. If he had been there I should no doubt have gone on; but, most fortunately for me, I had time to reflect. I was a changed man since the day before; my buoyancy of spirit was gone, and I was depressed and dejected. I sent a messenger, however, for the guide; and, while I was sitting under the walls, hesitating whether I should expose myself to the long and dreary journey before me, I saw four men coming across the desert towards the convent. They were the priest and three of his Christian flock; and their greeting was such as to make me reproach myself for the injustice I had done the Arab Christians, and feel that there was something in that religion, even in the corrupt state in which it existed there, that had power to open and warm the heart. The priest was a tall thin man, his dark face almost covered with a black beard and mustaches, and wore the common blue gown of the better class of Arabs, with a square black cap on his head, and his feet bare. I could not understand him, but I could read in his face that he saluted me as a brother Christian, and welcomed me to all that a brother Christian could give.

Living as we do, in a land where the only religious difference is that of sect, and all sects have the bond of a common faith, it is difficult to realize the feeling which draws together believers in the same God and the same Redeemer, in lands where power is wielded by the worshippers of a false religion. One must visit a country in which religion is the dividing line, where haughty and deluded fanatics are the masters, and hear his faith reviled, and see its professors persecuted and despised, to know and feel how strong a tie it is.

After exchanging our greetings outside, the priest led the way to the church. I do not know whether it was a customary thing, or done specially in honor of me (Paul said the latter); but, at any rate, he immediately lighted up the edifice, and, slipping over his frock a dirty white gown, with a large red cross down the back, commenced the service of the mass. His appearance and manner were extremely interesting, and very different from those of the priest I had seen at Isna. His fine head, his noble expression, his earnestness, his simplicity, his apparent piety, his long black beard and mustaches, his mean apparel and naked feet, all gave him the primitive aspect of an apostle. He was assisted by a dirty, ragged, barefooted boy, who followed him round with a censer of incense, vigorously perfuming the church from time to time, and then climbing up a stand, holding on by his naked feet, and reading a lesson from the thumbed, torn, and tattered leaves of an Arabic Bible. There were but three persons present besides myself; poor, ignorant people, far astray, no doubt, from the path of true Christianity, but worshipping in all honesty and sincerity, according to the best light they had, the God of their fathers. The priest went through many long and unmeaning forms, which I did not understand, but I had seen things quite as incomprehensible to me in the splendid cathedrals of Europe, and I joined, so far as I could, in the humble worship of these Egyptian Christians. There were no vessels of silver and gold, no imposing array of costly implements, to captivate the senses. A broken tumbler, a bottle of wine, and three small rolls of bread, formed the simple materials for the holy rite of the Lord's Supper. The three Arabs partook of it, and twice it was offered to me, but the feelings with which I had been accustomed to look upon this solemn sacrifice forbade me to partake of the consecrated elements, and never did I regret my unworthiness so bitterly as when it prevented me from joining in the holy feast with these simple-hearted Christians.

In the meantime Paul came in, and the service being ended, I fell into conversation with the priest. He was a good man, but exceedingly ignorant, weak, and of great simplicity of character. He conducted me around the little church into the several chapels, and pointed out all that he thought curious, and particularly the ornaments of bone and mother-of-pearl; and, finally, with a most imposing air, like a priest in a church in Italy, uncovering the works of the first masters, he drew the curtain from the four pieces of St. George slaying the dragon, and looked at me with an air of great satisfaction to enjoy the expression of my surprise and astonishment. I did not disappoint him, nor did I tell him that I had the night before most irreverently drawn aside the curtain, and exposed these sacred specimens of the arts to the eyes of my unbelieving Arabs; nor did I tell him that, in each of the four, St. George seemed to be making a different thrust at the dragon. There was no use in disturbing the complacency of the poor priest; he had but little of which he could be proud, and I would not deprive him of that.

Leaving him undisturbed in his exalted opinion of St. George and his dragons, I inquired of him touching the number and condition of the Christians under his charge, and their state of security under the government of the pasha; and, among other things, asked him if they increased. He told me that they remained about the same, or perhaps rather decreased. I asked him if a Mussulman ever became a Christian. He answered never, but sometimes a Christian would embrace the religion of Mohammed, and assigned a cause for this unhappy difference which I am sorry to mention, being no less than the influence of the tender passion. He told me that, in the free intercourse now existing under the government of the pasha between Christians and Mussulmans, it often happened that a Christian youth became enamored of a Moslem girl, and as they could not by any possibility marry and retain their separate religions, it was necessary that one of them should change. The Moslem dare not, for death by the hands of her own friends would be the certain consequence, while the Christian, instead of running any temporal risk, gains with his bride the protection and favor of the Mussulmans.

Paul seemed rather scandalized at this information, and began to catechise the priest on his own account. I could not understand the conversation, but could judge, from the movements, that Paul was examining him on that cardinal point, the sign of the cross. All appeared to go smoothly enough for a little while, but I soon noticed the flashing of Paul's eyes, and sundry other symptoms of indignation and contempt. I asked him several times what it was all about; but, without answering, he walked backward and forward, slapping his hands under the priest's nose, and talking louder and faster than ever, and I had to take hold of him, and ask him sharply what the plague was the matter, before I could get a word out of him. "A pretty Christian," said Paul; "fast fifty-six days for Lent, when we fast only forty-six: forty that our Savior was in the mount, and six Sundays." I told him there was not so much difference between them as I thought, as it was only ten days; he looked at me for a moment, and then, as if fearful of trusting himself, shrugged his shoulders, and marched out of the chapel. During all this time, the condition of the poor priest was pitiable and amusing; he had never been so sharply questioned before, and he listened with as much deference to Paul's questions and rebukes as if he had been listening to the pope of Rome, and, when it was over, looked perfectly crestfallen.

It was twelve o'clock when the man we had sent after the guide returned, but before this time my malady had increased to such a degree as to leave me no option; and I had resolved to abandon the Oasis, and go back to Thebes. I had great reason to congratulate myself upon my accidental detention, and still greater that the symptoms of my malady had developed themselves before I had advanced another day's journey in the desert. Still, it was with a heavy heart that I mounted my dromedary to return. I had not only the regret of being compelled abruptly to abandon a long-cherished plan, but I had great uneasiness as to what was to become of me on my arrival at Thebes. My boat was probably gone. I knew that no other could be obtained there, and, if obliged to wait for a casual opportunity, I must live in my tent on the banks of the river, or in one of the tombs. My anxieties, however, were quickly dispelled on my arrival at Thebes, where I found the English gentleman and lady whom I had met at Cairo and afterward at the Cataracts. They kindly took me on board their boat; and so ended my expedition to the Great Oasis.

CHAPTER XII

I SHALL NEVER forget the kindness of these excellent friends; and, indeed, it was a happy thing for me that my own boat had gone, and that I was thrown upon their hospitality; for, in addition to the greater comforts I found with them, I had the benefit of cheerful society under circumstances when to be alone would have been horrible. Even when we arrived at Asyut, after a voyage of seven days, they would not let me leave them, but assumed the right of physicians, and prescribed that I should be their guest until perfectly restored. I remained, accordingly, three days longer with them, my little boat following like a tender to a man-of-war, and passed my time luxuriously. I had books, conversation, and a medicine-chest. But one thing troubled me. We had a cook who looked upon his profession as a liberal and enlightened science, and had attained its very highest honors. He had served various noblemen of eminent taste, had accumulated fifty thousand dollars, and was now cooking at the rate of fifty dollars a month upon the Nile. Michel was an extraordinary man. He came from the mountains of Dalmatia, near the shores of the Adriatic; one of a small nation who had preserved the name, and form, and spirit of a republic against Italians, Hungarians, and Turks, and fell only before the irresistible arm of Napoleon. He had been a great traveler in his youth, and, besides his attainments in the culinary art, was better acquainted with history, ancient and modern, than almost any man I ever met. He had two great passions, the love of liberty and the love of the fine arts (cookery included), and it was really extraordinary to hear him, with a ladle in his hand, and tasting, from time to time, some piquant sauce, discourse of the republics of Rome and America, of the ruins of Italy, Palmyra, and Egypt. Michel's dinners, making proper allowance for the want of a daily market, would have done honor to the best lord he ever served; and I was obliged to sit down, day after day, to my tea, rice-water, biscuit, &c., and listen to the praises of his dainties while they passed untasted from me.

It was not until within two days of Cairo that we parted, with an agreement to meet at Jerusalem and travel together to Palmyra. We did meet for a few moments at Cairo, but the plague was beginning to rage, the pasha had been putting himself into quarantine, and we had barely time to renew our engagement, which a particularly unfortunate circumstance (the illness of Mrs. S.) prevented us from keeping, and we never met again. Few things connected with my compelled departure from the Holy Land gave me more regret than this; and if these pages should ever meet their eyes, they will believe me when I say that I shall remember, to the last day of my life, their kindness on the Nile.[1]

The story of my journeying on this river is almost ended. Qena was our first stopping-place on our way down; a place of considerable note, there being a route from it across the desert to El Quseir, by which many of the pilgrims, and a great portion of the trade of the Red Sea, are conveyed.[2]

At Ramaioum, not far below Asyut, we went ashore to visit a sugar-factory belonging to the pasha. This manufactory is pointed out as one of the great improvements introduced into Egypt, and, so far as it shows the capabilities of the Arabs, of which, however, no one can doubt, it may be considered useful. Formerly eighty

[1] Since this was in type, Mr. Gliddon, our consul at Cairo, has arrived in this country, and informs me that, on their way to Palmyra, Mr. S. and his whole party were robbed in the desert, and stripped of everything they had. They got back safe to Damascus, but the route to Palmyra is now entirely broken up by the atrocities of the Bedouins.—Stephens' note.

[2] From Qena (anciently Caenepolis) the Nile–Red Sea land-route moved inland across the Eastern Desert to Phoenicon. Here the road followed the Wadi Hammamat 95 miles easterly to El Quseir (Roman Leucos Linen). Along the route the rock walls are covered with pre-dynastic graffiti dating back to 2500 B.C. It is the shortest land route from the Nile to Arabia and Mecca; it has been continuously used for 4500 years (see *The Roads that Led to Rome*, by Victor W. von Hagen, New York, 1967).

Europeans were employed in the factory, but now the work is carried on entirely by Arabs. The principal was educated in France at the expense of the pasha, and is one of the few who have returned to render any service to their country and master. The enlightened pasha understands thoroughly that liberal principle of political economy which consists in encouraging domestic manufactures, no matter at what expense. The sugar costs more than that imported, and is bought by none but governors and dependents of the pasha. It is made from cane, contains a great deal of saccharine matter, and has a good taste, but a bad color. This factory, however, can hardly be considered as influential upon the general interests of the country, for its principal business is the making of rock candy for the ladies of the harem. They gave us little to taste, but would not sell any except to Mrs. S., the whole being wanted for the use of the ladies. There was also a distillery attached to the factory, under the direction of another Arab, who gave satisfactory evidence, in his own person at least, of the strength of the spirit made, being more than two-thirds drunk.

The same evening we came to at Beni Hassan,[3] and the next morning landed to visit the tombs. Like all the tombs in Egypt except those of the kings at Thebes, they are excavated in the sides of the mountain, commanding an extensive view of the valley of the Nile; but in one respect they are different from all others in Egypt. The doors have regular Doric columns, and they are the only specimens of architecture in Egypt which at all approximate to the Grecian style. This would not be at all extraordinary if they were constructed after the invasion of Alexander and the settlement of the Greeks in the country, but it is ascertained that they were built long before that time; and, indeed, it is alleged by antiquaries that these tombs and the obelisk at Heliopolis are the oldest monuments

[3] Near to Beni Hassan was the site of Antinoöpolis built by Hadrian about A.D. 135. It was erected to the memory of his friend Antinoüs who was drowned in the Nile; from that site on the Nile the *via Hadrian nova* was constructed across the desert east to the Red Sea and then south along the coast line to Berenice, which lies on the Sudan frontier. The text of the first inscription is still extant (in the Cairo Museum). It states that "Caesar Trajanus Hadrian built from Antinoöpolis to Berenice through secure and level country the New Hadrian Way . . . dated Phamenoth 1 (A.D. 138)."

in Egypt. The interiors are large and handsomely proportioned (one of them being sixty feet square and forty feet high), and adorned with paintings, representing principally scenes of domestic life. Among them Mr. S. and myself made out one, which is constantly to be seen at the present day, namely, a half-naked Egyptian, with a skin of water across his back, precisely like the modern Arab in the streets of Cairo.

We returned to our boat, and, being now within two days of Cairo, and having different places to stop at below, after dinner I said farewell to my kind friends, and returned to my own boat. My crew received me with three cheers, I was going to say, but they do not understand or practice that noisy mode of civilized welcome, and gave me the grave and quiet salutation of their country, all rising as soon as I touched the deck, and one after the other taking my hand in his, and touching it to his forehead and lips. My poor rais gave me a melancholy greeting. He had been unwell during the whole voyage, but, since we parted, had been growing worse. He told me that our stars were the same, and that misfortune had happened to us both as soon as we separated. I could but hope that our stars were not inseparably connected, for I looked upon him as a doomed man. I had saved him at Cairo from being pressed into the pasha's service; and again in descending, when he stopped at Qena, he and his whole crew had been seized in the bazars, and, in spite of their protestations that they were in the service of an American, the iron bands were put around their wrists and the iron collars round their necks. The governor afterward rode down to the river, and the American flag streaming from the masthead of my little boat procured their speedy release, and saved them from the miserable fate of Arab soldiers.

Under all the oppression of the pasha's government, there is nothing more grinding than this. The governor of a town, or the sheik of a village, is ordered to furnish so many men as soldiers. He frequently has a leaning towards his own subjects or followers, and is disposed to save them if he can; and if any unlucky stranger happens to pass before the complement is made up, he is inevitably pounced upon as one of the required number. It is useless for the poor captive to complain that he is a stranger, and that the rights of hospitality are violated; he appeals to those who are interested in tightening his bonds; and when he is transferred to the higher authorities, they neither know nor care who he is or whence he comes. He has the thews and sinews of a man, and though his heart-strings be cracking, he can bear a musket, and that is enough. For centuries Egypt has been overrun by strangers, and the foot of a tyrant has been upon the necks of her inhabitants; but I do not believe that, since the days of the Pharaohs, there has been on the throne of Egypt so thorough a despot as the present pasha.

But to return to my rais. His first request was for medicine, which, unfortunately, I could not give him. The Arabs have a perfect passion for medicine. Early in our voyage my crew had discovered that I had some on board, and one or another of them was constantly sick until they had got it all; and then they all got well except the rais; and for him I feared there was no cure.

On the eleventh, early in the morning, Paul burst into the cabin, cursing all manner of Arabs, snatched the gun from over my head, and was out again in a moment. I knew there was no danger when Paul was so valorous; and, opening my broken shutter, I saw one of my men struggling with an Arab on shore, the latter holding him by the throat with a pistol at his head. The rascal had gone on shore just at daylight to steal wood, and, while in the act of tearing down a little fence, the watchful owner had sprung upon him, and seemed on the point of correcting forever all his bad habits. His fellows ran to the rescue, with Paul at their head; and the culprit, relieved from the giant grasp of his adversary, quietly sneaked on board, and we resumed our progress.

In the course of my last day on the Nile I visited one of the greatest of its ruined cities, and, for moral effect, for powerful impression on the imagination and feelings, perhaps the most interesting of them all. So absolute, complete, and total is the ruin of this once powerful city, that antiquaries have disputed whether there is really a single monument to show where the great Memphis stood; but the weight of authority seems to be, that its stately temples and palaces, and its thousands of inhabitants, once covered the ground now occupied by the little Arab village of Metrahenny.[4] This village stands about four miles from the river; and the traveler might pass through it and around it without ever dreaming that it had once been the site of a mighty city. He might, indeed, as he wandered around the miserable village, find, half-buried in the earth, the broken fragments of a colossal statue; and, looking from the shattered relic to the half-savage Arabs around him, he might say to himself, "This is the work of other men and other times, and how comes it here?" But it would never occur to him that this was the last remaining monument of one of the greatest cities in the world. He might stop and gaze upon the huge mounds of ruins piled among the groves of palm, and ask himself, "Whence, too, came these?" But he would receive no answer that could satisfy him. In a curious and unsatisfied mood he would stroll on through the village, and from the other extremity would see, on the mountains towering before him, on the edge of the desert, a long range of pyramids and tombs, some crumbling in ruin, others upright and unbroken as when they were reared, and all stretching away for miles, one vast Necropolis; his reason and reflection would tell him that, where are the chambers of the dead, there must also have been the abodes of the living; and with wonder he would ask himself, "Where is the mighty city whose inhabitants now sleep in yonder tombs? Here are the proud graves in which they were buried; where are the palaces in which they reveled, and the temples in which they worshipped?" And he returns to the broken statue and the mounds of ruins, with the assurance that they are the sad remnants of a city once among the proudest in the world.

My movements in Egypt were too hurried, my means of observation and my stock of knowledge too limited, to enable me to speculate advisedly upon the mystery which overhangs the history of her ruined cities; but I always endeavored to come to some decision of my own, from the labors, the speculations, and the conflicting opinions of others. An expression which I had seen referred to in one of the books, as being the only one in the Bible in which Memphis was mentioned by name, was uppermost in my mind while I

[4] Helwan?

was wandering over its site. "And Memphis shall bury them." There must be, I thought, some special meaning in this expression; some allusion to the manner in which the dead were buried at Memphis, or to a cemetery or tombs different from those which existed in other cities of its day. It seems almost impossible to believe that a city, having for its burying-place the immense tombs and pyramids which even yet for many miles skirt the borders of the desert, can ever have stood upon the site of this miserable village; but the evidence is irresistible.

The plain on which this ancient city stood is one of the richest of the Nile, and herds of cattle are still seen grazing upon it, as in the days of the Pharaohs.[5] The pyramids of Saqqara stand on the edge of the desert, a little south of the site of Memphis. If it was not for their mightier neighbors, these pyramids, which are comparatively seldom honored with a visit, would alone be deemed worthy of a pilgrimage to Egypt. The first to which we came is about 350 feet high, and 700 feet square at its base. The door is on the north side, 180 feet from the base. The entrance is by a beautifully-polished shaft, 200 feet long, and inclining at an angle of about 10 degrees. We descended till we found the passage choked up with huge stones. I was very anxious to see the interior, as there is a chamber within said to resemble the tomb of Agamemnon at Mycenae; and having once made an interesting visit to that tomb of the king of kings, I wished to compare them; but it was excessively close, the sweat was pouring from us in streams, and we were suffocating with heat and dust. We came out and attempted to clamber up the side from the door to the top, but found it so difficult that we abandoned the effort, although Paul afterward mounted, with great ease, by one of the corners. While I was walking round the base I heard a loud scream from that courageous dragoman, and saw him standing about halfway up, the picture of terror, staring at a wild boar that was running away, if possible, more frightened than himself. It was

[5] Memphis, seventeen miles from Cairo, lying between the Nile and the wide plain where Upper and Lower Egypt meet, was built and named after Menes in 300 B.C. Until Alexandria was founded, Memphis was the foremost city of Egypt, an administrative capital and a site for the royal residence. The pyramid of Pepi was built at Saqqara close to Memphis.

a mystery to me what the animal could be doing there, unless he went up on purpose to frighten Paul. After he got over his fright, however, the boar was a great acquisition to him, for I always had great difficulty in getting him into any tomb or other place of the kind without a guide; and, whenever I urged him to enter a pyramid or excavation of any kind, he always threw the wild boar in my teeth, whose den, he was sure to say, was somewhere within.

There are several pyramids in this vicinity; among others, one which is called the brick pyramid, and which has crumbled so gradually and uniformly that it now appears only a huge misshapen mass of brick, somewhat resembling a beehive. Its ruins speak a moral lesson. Herodotus says that this fallen pyramid was built by King Asychis, and contained on a piece of marble the vainglorious inscription, "Do not disparage my worth by comparing me to those pyramids of stone; I am as much superior to them as Jove is to the rest of the deities."

Retracing my steps, I continued along the edge of the mountain, which everywhere showed the marks of having been once lined with pyramids and tombs. I was seeking for one of the most curious and interesting objects that exist in Egypt—not so interesting in itself, as illustrating the character of the ancient inhabitants and their superstitions—I mean the burial-place of the sacred birds. Before we reached it, my Arab guide pointed to a pyramid on our left, saying that it contained a remarkable chamber, so high that a stone hurled with a man's utmost strength could not reach the top. As this pyramid was not mentioned in my guidebook, and I had no hope, in a country so trodden as Egypt now is, to become a discoverer of new wonders, I at first paid no attention to him; but he continued urging me to visit the lofty chamber; and at last, telling him that if I did not find it as he said, I would not give him a para of backsheesh, I consented. There was no door to the pyramid; but, about a hundred feet from its base, on the north side, was a square excavation or shaft about forty feet deep, at the end of which was a little hole not more than large enough to admit a man's arm. The Arab scooped out the sand, and with his hands and feet worked his meager body through, and I followed on my back, feet foremost.

131

Though not particularly bulky, I wanted more room than the Arab, and my shoulders stuck fast. I was trying to work out again, when he grasped me by the heels, and began pulling me in with all his might; but, luckily, I had play for my legs, and, drawing them up, gave him a kick with my heavy boots that kept him from taking hold again until I had time to scramble out.

While Paul and the Arab were enlarging the hole below, the top of the pit was darkened, and, looking up, I saw two young Englishmen with whom I had dined a few days before, while coming down the river with Mr. S. and his lady. They had seen my boat, and come to join me, and I was very glad to see them; for though I had no actual apprehension of the thing, yet it occurred to me that it would be very easy for my Arab friends to roll a stone against the hole, and shut me in forever. It would have been something to be buried in a pyramid, to be sure; but even the belief that it was the tomb of a king would hardly compensate for the inconvenience of being buried alive. We left their servant, a strapping Greek, at the door, and the Arab having enlarged the hole, we went to work systematically, laid ourselves upon our backs, and, being prepared beforehand, were dragged in by the heels. The narrow part of the hole was not more than half the length of the body, and once past this, there was more room to move about than in any other of the pyramids; we could walk without stooping. Descending some hundred feet through an inclined passage excavated in the rock, with doors opening from it at regular intervals, we came to the large chamber of which the Arab had spoken. As in all the pyramids and tombs, the interior was in perfect darkness, and the feeble light of our torches gave us but an imperfect view of the apartment. The Arab immediately commenced his experiment with the stone, we could hear the whizzing as it cut through the empty space, and, after what seemed a very long time, the sound of its fall upon the rocky floor. At some distance up we could distinguish a door, and sending one of the Arabs up to it, by the flaring light of his torch, held as high as he could reach, we thought, but we were not certain, that we could make out the ceiling.

From hence it was but a short distance to the catacombs of birds;

a small opening in the side of a rock leads to an excavated chamber, in the center of which is a square pit or well. Descending the pit by bracing our arms, and putting our toes in little holes in the side, we reached the bottom, where, crawling on our hands and knees, we were among the mummies of the sacred ibis, the embalmed deities of the Egyptians. The extent of these catacombs is unknown, but they are supposed to occupy an area of many miles. The birds are preserved in stone jars, piled one upon another as closely as they can be stowed. By the light of our torches, sometimes almost flat upon our faces, we groped and crawled along the passages, lined on each side with rows of jars, until we found ourselves again and again stopped by an impenetrable phalanx of the little mummies, or rather of the jars containing them. Once we reached a small open space where we had room to turn ourselves, and knocking together two of the vessels, the offended deities within sent forth volumes of dust which almost suffocated us. The bird was still entire, in form and lineament perfect as the mummied man, and like him, too, wanting merely the breath of life. The Arabs brought out with them several jars, which we broke and examined above ground, more at our ease. With the pyramids towering around us, it was almost impossible to believe that the men who had raised such mighty structures had fallen down and worshipped the puny birds whose skeletons we were now dashing at our feet.

My last work was now done, and I had seen my last sight on the Nile. Leaving behind me for ever the pyramids of Egypt, and the mountains and sands of the Libyan Desert, I rode along the valley, among villages and groves of palm-trees, and a little before dark arrived at Giza. My boat was there; I went on board for the last time; my men took to their oars, and in half an hour we were at Bulak. It was dark when we arrived, and I had jumped on shore searching for a donkey, but none was to be had. I was almost tired out with the labors of the day, but Paul and I set off, nevertheless, on foot for Cairo. We were obliged to walk smartly, too, as the gate closed at nine o'clock; but when about halfway there we met an Arab with a donkey, cheering the stillness of the evening with a song. An extravagant price (I believe it was something like eighteen

133

and three-quarter cents) bribed him to dismount, and I galloped on to Cairo, while Paul retraced his steps to the boat. The reader may judge how completely "turned up" must have been the feelings of a quiet citizen of New York, when told that, in winding at night through the narrow streets of Grand Cairo, the citizen aforesaid felt himself quite at home; and that the greeting of Francisco, the garçon at the Locanda d'Italia, seemed the welcome of an old friend. Hoping to receive letters from home, I went immediately to the American consul, and was disappointed; there were no letters, but there was other and interesting news for me; and as an American, identified with the honor of my country, I was congratulated there, thousands of miles from home, upon the expected speedy and honorable termination of our difficulties with France. An English vessel had arrived at Alexandria, bringing a London paper containing the president's last message, a notice of the offer of mediation from the English government, its acceptance by France, and the general impression that the quarrel might be considered settled, and the money paid. A man must be long and far from home to feel how dearly he loves his country, how his eye brightens and his heart beats when he hears her praises from the lips of strangers; and when the paper was given me, with congratulations and compliments on the successful and honorable issue of the affair with France, my feelings grew prouder and prouder as I read, until, when I had finished the last line, I threw up my cap in the old city of Cairo, and shouted the old gathering-cry, "Hurrah for Jackson!"

I have heard all manners of opinion expressed in regard to a voyage on the Nile; and may be allowed, perhaps, to give my own. Mrs. S. used frequently to say that, although she had traveled in France, Switzerland, Germany, Italy, and Sicily, she had never enjoyed a journey so much before, and was always afraid that it would end too soon. Another lady's sentiments, expressed in my hearing, were just the contrary. For myself, being alone, and not in very good health, I had some heavy moments; but I have no hesitation in saying that, with a friend, a good boat well fitted up, books, guns, plenty of time, and a cook like Michel, a voyage on the Nile would exceed any traveling within my experience. The perfect freedom from all restraint, and from the conventional trammels of civilized society, form an episode in a man's life that is vastly agreeable and exciting. Think of not shaving for two months, of washing your shirts in the Nile, and wearing them without being ironed. True, these things are not absolutely necessary; but who would go to Egypt to travel as he does in Europe? "Away with all fantasies and fetters" is the motto of the tourist. We throw aside pretty much everything except our pantaloons; and a generous rivalry in long beards and soiled linen is kept up with exceeding spirit. You may go ashore whenever you like, and stroll through the little villages, and be stared at by the Arabs, or walk along the banks of the river till darkness covers the earth; shooting pigeons, and sometimes pheasants and hares, besides the odd shots from the deck of your boat at geese, crocodiles, and pelicans. And then it is so ridiculously cheap an amusement. You get your boat with ten men for thirty or forty dollars a month, fowls for three piasters (about a shilling) a pair, a sheep for half or three-quarters of a dollar and eggs almost for the asking. You sail under your own country's banner; and, when you walk along the river, if the Arabs look particularly black and truculent, you proudly feel that there is safety in its folds. From time to time you hear that a French or English flag has passed so many days before you, and you meet your fellow-voyagers with a freedom and cordiality which exist nowhere but on the Nile.

These are the little everyday items in the voyage, without referring to the great and interesting objects which are the traveler's principal inducements and rewards, the ruined cities on its banks, the mighty temples and tombs, and all the wonderful monuments of Egypt's departed greatness. Of them I will barely say, that their great antiquity, the mystery that overhangs them, and their extraordinary preservation amid the surrounding desolation, make Egypt perhaps the most interesting country in the world. In the words of an old traveler, "Time sadly overcometh all things, and is now dominant, and sitteth upon a sphinx and looketh into Memphis and old Thebes, while his sister Oblivion reclineth semisominous on a pyramid, gloriously triumphing and turning old glories into dreams. History sinketh beneath her cloud. The travel-

135

er, as he passeth amazedly through those deserts, asketh of her who builded them, and she mumbleth something, but what it is he heareth not."

It is now more than three thousand years since the curse went forth against the land of Egypt. The Assyrian, the Persian, the Greek, the Roman, the Arabian, the Georgian, the Circassian, and the Ottoman Turk have successively trodden it down and trampled upon it; for thirty centuries the foot of a stranger has been upon the necks of her inhabitants; and in bidding farewell to this once-favored land, now lying in the most abject degradation and misery, groaning under the iron rod of a tyrant and a stranger, I cannot help recurring to the inspired words, the doom of the prophecy: "It shall be the basest of the kingdoms, neither shall it exalt itself any more among the nations; and there shall be no more a prince of the land of Egypt."

CHAPTER XIII

I HAD NOW FINISHED my journey in Egypt, from the Mediterranean to the Cataracts, or, as the boundaries of this ancient
country are given in the Bible, from "Migdol to Syene, even unto
the borders of Ethiopia." For nearly two months I had been floating
on the celebrated river, with a dozen Arabs, prompt to do my slightest bidding, and, in spite of bugs and all manner of creeping things,
enjoying pleasures and comforts that are not to be found in Europe;
and it was with something more than an ordinary feeling of regret
that I parted from my worthy boatmen. I know that it is the custom
with many travelers to rail at the Arabs, and perhaps to beat them,
and have them bastinadoed; but I could not and cannot join in such
oppression of this poor and much-abused people. On the contrary,
I do not hesitate to say that I always found them kind, honest, and
faithful, thankful for the smallest favor, never surly or discontented, and always ready and anxious to serve me with a zeal
that I have not met in any other people; and when they came up in
a body to the locanda to say farewell, I felt that I was parting with
tried and trusty friends, most probably forever. That such was the
case with the rais there could be little doubt; he seemed to look upon
himself as a doomed man, and a broken cough, a sunken eye, and a
hollow cheek proclaimed him one fast hurrying to the grave.

I was now about wandering amid new and different scenes. I was
about to cross the dreary waste of sand, to exchange my quiet, easy-
going boat for a caravan of dromedaries and camels; to pitch my
tent wherever the setting sun might find me, and, instead of my
gentle Arabs of the Nile, to have for my companions the wild, rude

137

Bedouins of the desert; to follow the wandering footsteps of the children of Israel when they took up the bones of Joseph, and fled before the anger of Pharaoh, from their land of bondage; to visit the holy mountain of Sinai, where the Almighty, by the hands of his servant Moses, delivered the tables of his law to his chosen people.

But I had in view something beyond the holy mountain. My object was to go from thence to the Holy Land. If I should return to Suez, and thence cross the desert to El Arish and Gaza, I should be subjected to a quarantine of fourteen days on account of the plague in Egypt, and I thought I might avoid this by striking directly through the heart of the desert from Mount Sinai to the frontier of the Holy Land. There were difficulties and perhaps dangers on this route; but, besides the advantage of escaping the quarantine, another consideration presented itself, which, in the end, I found it impossible to resist. This route was entirely new. It lay through the land of Edom—a land that occupies a large space on the pages of the Bible; Edom denounced by God himself, once given to Esau for his inheritance, "as being of the fatness of the earth," but now a desolate monument of the Divine wrath, and a fearful witness to the truth of the words spoken by his prophets. The English friends with whom I had dined at Thebes first suggested to me this route, referring me, at the same time, to Keith on the Prophecies, in which, after showing with great clearness and force the fulfillment of prophecy after prophecy, as illustrated by the writings and reports of travelers, the learned and divine enlarges upon the prophecy of Isaiah against the land of Idumea, "None shall pass through it for ever and ever," and proves, by abundant references to the works of modern travelers, that though several have crossed its borders, none have ever passed through it. Burckhardt, he says, made the nearest approach to this achievement; but, by reference to the geographical boundaries, he maintains that Burckhardt did not pass through the land of Edom; and so strenuously does the learned divine insist upon the fulfillment of the prophecy to its utmost extent, as to contend that, if Burckhardt did pass through the land of Edom, he died in consequence of the hardships he suf-

The Colossi of Memnon, from Catherwood's 1833 *camera lucida* drawing.

Catherwood's drawing of the back of one of the Colossi. The hieroglyphs are so well executed that they can be deciphered from the drawing.

Catherwood's *camera lucida* drawing of the Temple of Horus at Edfu.

Temple of Hathor, Island of Philae, as drawn by Catherwood.

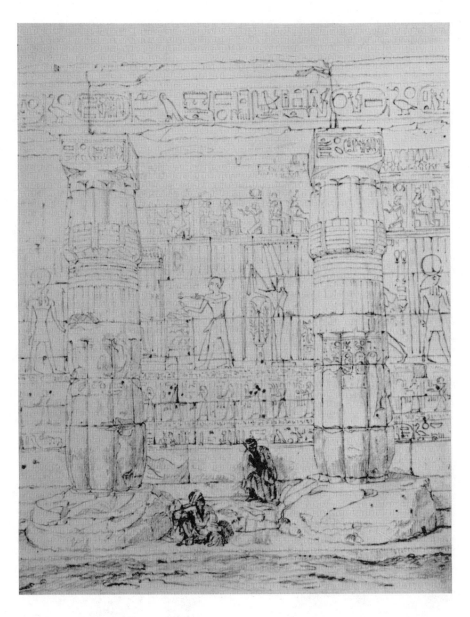

Two Arabs sitting before the lotus columns of the Temple of Isis, Philae.
Catherwood drawing.

Temple of Rameses II at Abu Simbel. Catherwood drawing.

Abu Simbel. Catherwood drawing.

View from Elephantine, just below the present Aswan dam. Catherwood drawing.

fered on that journey. I did not mean to brave the prophecy. I had already learned to regard the words of the inspired penman with an interest I never felt before; and with the evidence I had already had of the sure fulfillment of their predictions, I should have considered it daring and impious to place myself in the way of a still impending curse. But I did not go so far as the learned commentator, and to me the words of the prophet seemed sufficiently verified in the total breaking up of the route then traveled, as the great highway from Jerusalem to the Red Sea and India, and the general and probably eternal desolation that reigns in Edom.

Still, however, it added to the interest with which I looked upon this route; and, moreover, in this dreary and desolate region, far more than a thousand years buried from the eyes of mankind, its place unknown, and its very name almost forgotten, lay the long-lost city of Petra, the capital of Arabia Petraea, and the Edom of the Edomites, containing, according to the reports of the only travelers who have ever been permitted to enter it, the most curious and wonderful remains existing in the world: a city excavated from the solid rock, with long ranges of dwellings, temples, and tombs cut in the sides of the mountain, and all lying in ruins, "thorns coming up in her palaces, nettles and brambles in the fortresses thereof, a habitation of dragons, and a court for owls." Three parties had at different times visited Petra, but neither of them had passed through the land of Idumea; and, according to the reports of the few travelers who had crossed its borders, the Bedouins who roamed over the dreary sands of Idumea were the most ferocious tribe of the desert race. It will not be considered surprising, therefore, that, having once conceived the project, I was willing to fulfill it even at the cost of some personal difficulty and hazard.

I have said that this route was entirely new.[1] It was known that two Englishmen, with an Italian, long resident in Egypt, and understanding thoroughly the language and character of the Arabs, had

---

[1] Thomas Legh's *A Narrative in Egypt and the Country Beyond* was published in London in 1816. He also wrote *An Excursion from Jerusalem to Wady Musa [Petra]* (London, 1819). His name and that of Bankes, Irby, Mangles, and Stephens are found on the blackened inside chamber of El Khazneh at Petra dated "1818." Stephens placed his own name under theirs.

started from Cairo about a year before to make this journey, and, as they had been heard of afterward in Europe, it was known that they had succeeded; but no account of their journey had ever been published, and all the intelligence I could obtain of the route and its perils was doubtful and confused. The general remark was, that the undertaking was dangerous, and that I had better let it alone. Almost the only person who encouraged me was Mr. Gliddon, our vice-consul; and probably, if it had not been for him, I should have given up the idea. Besides the difficulties of the road, there were others of a more personal nature. I was alone. I could not speak the language, and I had with me a servant who, instead of leading me on and sustaining me when I faltered, was constantly torturing himself with idle fears, and was very reluctant to accompany me at all. Nor was this all; my health was far from being restored, and my friend Waghorn was telling me every day, with a warning voice, to turn my steps westward: but objections presented themselves in vain; and perhaps it was precisely because of the objections that I finally determined upon attempting the journey through the land of Idumea.

By singular good fortune the sheik of Aqaba was then at Cairo. The great yearly caravan of pilgrims for Mecca was assembling outside the walls, and he was there, on the summons of the pasha, to escort and protect them through the desert as far as Aqaba. He was the chief of a powerful tribe of Bedouins somewhat reduced by long and bloody wars with other tribes, but still maintaining, in all its vigor, the wild independence of the race, and yet strong enough to set at defiance even the powerful arm of the pasha. A system of mutual forbearance seemed to exist between them, the Bedouins knowing that, although the pasha might not subdue them, his long arm could reach and disturb them even in their sandy hills; while the pasha could not overlook the fact that the effort would cost him the lives of his best troops, and that the plunder of their miserable tents would bring him neither glory nor profit. Thus the desert was still the possession of the Bedouins; they still claimed a tribute from the stranger for permission to pass over it, and this induced the pasha annually to invite the sheik of Aqaba to Cairo, to conduct the caravan for Mecca, knowing that if not so invited, even the sacred character of the pilgrims would not protect them in passing through his country.

I found him about a mile outside the walls, near the tombs of the caliphs, on the edge of the desert, sitting on a mat under his tent, and surrounded by a dozen of his swarthy tribe, armed with long sabers, pistols, and matchlock guns. The sheik was a short stout man, of the darkest shade of bronze; his eye keen, roving, and unsettled; his teeth white; and his skin so dried up and withered that it seemed cleaving to his very bones. At the first glance I did not like his face; it wanted frankness, and even boldness; and I thought at the time, that if I had met him alone in the desert I should not have trusted him. He received me with great civility, while his companions rose, gave me their low salaam, seated me on the mat beside him, and then resumed their own cross-legged attitude, with less noise than would have attended the entrance of a gentleman into a drawing-room on a morning call. All stared at me with silent gravity; and the sheik, though desert born and bred, with an air and manner that showed him familiar with the usages of good society in Cairo, took the pipe from his mouth and handed it to me.

All being seated, the consul's janissary, who had come with me, opened the divan; but he had scarcely begun to declare my object before the whole group, sheik and all, apparently surprised out of their habitual phlegm, cried out together that they were ready to escort me, and to defend me with their lives against every danger. I said a few words, and they became clamorous in their assurances of the great friendship they had conceived for me; that life was nothing in my service; that they would sleep in my tent, guard and watch me by day and night, and, in short, that they would be my father, mother, sister, and brother, and all my relations, in the desert; and the final assurance was, that it would not be possible to travel that road except under their protection. I then began to inquire the terms, when, as before, all spoke at once, some fixed one price, some another, and for backsheesh whatever I pleased. I did not like this wild and noisy negotiation. I knew that I must make great allowance for the extravagant language of the Arabs; but there seemed to be an eagerness to get me among them which, in my eyes, was rather ominous of bad intentions. They were known to be a lawless people, and distinguished, even among their desert brethren, as a wild and savage tribe. And these were the people with whom I was negotiating to meet in the desert, at the little fortress of Aqaba, at the eastern extremity of the Red Sea; into whose hands I was to place myself, and from whom I was to expect protection against greater dangers.

My interview with them was not very satisfactory, and, wishing to talk the matter over more quietly with the sheik alone, I asked him to go with me to my hotel; whereupon the whole group started up at once, and, some on foot, and others on dromedaries or on horseback, prepared to follow. This did not suit me, and the sheik contrived to get rid of all except one, his principal and constant attendant, "his black," as he was called. He followed me on horseback, and when he came up into my room, it was, perhaps, the first time in his life that he had ever been under a roof. As an instance of his simplicity and ignorance, it may be worth mentioning here, although I did not know it until we were on the point of separating after our journey was completed, that he mistook the consul's janissary, who wore a dashing red Turkish dress, sword, &c., for an officer of the pasha's household, and, consequently, had always looked upon me as specially recommended to him by the pasha. I could not come to any definite understanding with him. The precise service that I required of him was to conduct me from Aqaba to Hebron, through the land of Edom, diverging to visit the excavated city of Petra, a journey of about ten days. I could not get him to name any sum as compensation for this service; he told me that he would conduct me for nothing, that I might give him what I pleased, &c. When I first spoke about the terms at his tent, he had said twelve dollars a camel, and, as it seemed to me, he had named this sum without the least calculation, as the first that happened to occur to him. I new referred him to this price, which he had probably forgotten, hoping to establish it as a sort of basis upon which to negotiate; but, when his attention was called to it, he insisted upon the twelve dollars, and something more for backsheesh.

A fair price for this service would have been about two dollars. I told him this did not satisfy me; that I wanted everything definitely arranged beforehand, and that I would not give the enormous price he asked, and backsheesh in proportion; but I could do nothing with him; he listened with perfect coolness; and taking his pipe from his mouth, in answer to everything I said, told me to come to him at Aqaba, come to him at his tent; he had plenty of camels, and would conduct me without any reward, or I might give him what I pleased. We parted without coming to an arrangement. He offered to send one of his men to conduct me from Mount Sinai to Aqaba; but, as something might occur to prevent my going, I would not take him. He gave me, however, his signet, which he told me every Bedouin on that route knew and would respect, and writing his name under it according to the sound, I repeated it over and over, until I could pronounce it intelligibly, and treasured it up as a password for the desert.

The next morning, under pretense that I went to see the starting of the great caravan of pilgrims for Mecca, I rode out to the sheik; and telling him that, if I came to him, I should come destitute of everything, and he must have some good tobacco for me, I slipped a couple of gold pieces into his hand, and, without further remark, left the question of my going undetermined. It was worth my ride to see the departure of the caravan. It consisted of more than thirty thousand pilgrims, who had come from the shores of the Caspian, the extremities of Persia, and the confines of Africa; and having assembled, according to usage for hundreds of years, at Cairo as a central point, the whole mass was getting in motion for a pilgrimage of fifty days, through dreary sands, to the tomb of the Prophet.

Accustomed as I was to associate the idea of order and decorum with the observance of all rites and duties of religion, I could not but feel surprised at the noise, tumult, and confusion, the strifes and battles of these pilgrim-travelers. If I had met them in the desert after their line of march was formed, it would have been an imposing spectacle, and comparatively easy to describe; but here, as far as the eye could reach, they were scattered over the sandy plain, thirty thousand people, with probably twenty thousand

143

camels and dromedaries, men, women, and children, beasts and baggage, all commingled in a confused mass that seemed hopelessly inextricable. Some had not yet struck their tents, some were making coffee, some smoking, some cooking, some eating, many shouting and cursing, others on their knees praying, and others, again, hurrying on to join the long moving stream that already extended several miles into the desert.

It is a vulgar prejudice, the belief that women are not admitted into the heaven of Mohammed. It is true that the cunning Prophet, in order not to disturb the joyful serenity with which his followers look forward to their promised heaven, has not given to women any fixed position there, and the pious Mussulman, although blessed with the lawful complement of four wives, is not bound to see among his seventy-two black-eyed houries the faces of his companions upon earth; but the women are not utterly cast out; they are deemed to have souls, and entitled to a heaven of their own; and it may be, too, that their visions of futurity are not less bright, for that there is a mystery to be unraveled beyond the grave, and they are not doomed to eternal companionship with their earthly lords. In the wildest, rudest scene where woman appears at all, there is a sweet and undefinable charm; and their appearance among the pilgrims, the care with which they shrouded themselves from every eye, their long thick veils, and their tents or four-post beds, with curtains of red silk, fastened down all around and secured on the high backs of camels, were the most striking objects in the caravan. Next to them in interest were the miserable figures of the marabous, santons, or Arab saints, having only a scanty covering of rags over their shoulders, and the rest of their bodies completely naked, yet strutting about as if clothed in purple and fine linen; and setting off utterly destitute of everything for a journey of months across the desert, safely trusting to that open-handed charity which forms so conspicuous an item in the list of Mussulman virtues. But the object of universal interest was the great box containing the presents and decorations for the tomb of the Prophet. The camel which bears this sacred burden is adorned with banners and rich housings, is watched and tended with pious care, and, when his journey is ended, no meaner load can touch his back; he has filled the measure of a camel's glory, and lives and dies respected by all good Mussulmans.

In the evening, being the last of my stay in Cairo, I heard that Mr. Linant,[2] the companion of M. Laborde[3] on his visit to Petra, had arrived at Alexandria, and, with Mr. Gliddon, went to see him. Mr. Linant is one of the many French emigrés driven from their native soil by political convulsions, and who have risen to distinction in foreign lands by military talents, and the force of that restless energy so peculiar to his countrymen. Many years before, he had thrown himself into the Arabian Desert, where he had become so much beloved by the Bedouins, that on the occasion of a dispute between two contending claimants, the customs of their tribe were waived, the pretensions of the rivals set aside, and he was elected sheik of Mount Sinai, and invested with the flattering name, which he retains to this day, of Abdel Hag, or the slave of truth. Notwithstanding his desert rank and dignity, he received me with a politeness which savored of the salons of Paris, and encouraged me in my intention of visiting Petra, assuring me that it would abundantly repay me for all the difficulties attending it; in fact, he spoke lightly of these, although I afterward found that his acquaintance with the language, his high standing among the Bedouins, and his lavish distribution of money and presents, had removed or diminished obstacles which, to a stranger without these advantages, were by no means of a trifling nature. In addition to much general advice, he counseled me particularly to wear the Turkish or Arab dress, and to get a letter from the Habeeb Effendi to the governor of the little fortress of Aqaba. Mr. Linant has been twenty years in Egypt, and is now a bey in the pasha's service; and that very afternoon, after a long interview, had received orders from the great reformer to make a survey of the pyramids, for the purpose of deciding which of those gigantic monuments, after having been respected by all

[2] Maurice-Adolphe Linant (1800–83), Arabic scholar and traveler who accompanied Léon de Laborde to Petra in 1827. He was co-author of *Voyage de l'Arabie Petrée*, published in Paris in 1830. Later he was employed by Mehemet Ali in Cairo.

[3] Léon de Laborde (1807–69), explorer, engraver, author. Artist-author of *Voyage de l'Arabie Petrée* and possibly with his brother Alexandre, co-illustrator of *Voyage Pittoresque et Historique de l'Espagne* (4 vols., elephant folio, Paris, 1806).

preceding tyrants for three thousand years, should now be demolished for the illustrious object of yielding material for a petty fortress or scarcely more useful and important bridge.[4]

Early in the morning I went into the bazars, and fitted out Paul and myself with the necessary dresses. Paul was soon equipped with the common Arab dress, the blue cotton shirt, tarboosh, and Bedouin shoes. A native of Malta, he was very probably of Arab descent in part, and his dark complexion and long black beard would enable him readily to pass for one born under the sun of Egypt. As for myself, I could not look the swarthy Arab of the desert, and the dress of the Turkish houaja or gentleman, with the necessary arms and equipments, was very expensive; so I provided myself with the unpretending and respectable costume of a Cairo merchant; a long red silk gown, with a black abbas of camel's hair over it; red tarboosh, with a green-and-yellow-striped handkerchief rolled round it as a turban; white trousers, large red shoes over yellow slippers, blue sash, sword, and a pair of large Turkish pistols.[5]

Having finished my purchases in the bazars, I returned to my hotel ready to set out, and found the dromedaries, camels, and guides, and expected to find the letter for the governor of Aqaba, which, at the suggestion of Mr. Linant, I had requested Mr. Gliddon to procure for me. I now learned, however, from that gentleman, that, to avoid delay, it would be better to go myself, first sending my caravan outside the gate, and representing to the minister that I was actually waiting for the letter, in which case he would probably give it to me immediately. I accordingly sent Paul with my little caravan to wait for me at the tombs of the caliphs, and, attended by the consul's janissary, rode up to the citadel, and stopped at the door of the governor's palace.

[4] On my return to Alexandria, I learned that Mr. Linant had reported that it would be cheaper to get stone from the quarries. After all, it is perhaps to be regretted that he had not gone on, as the mystery that overhangs the pyramids will probably never be removed until one of them is pulled down, and every stone removed, under the direction of some friend of science and the arts.—Stephens' note.

[5] Stephens had himself limned anonymously as a "Merchant of Cairo," as an illustration for *Incidents of Travel in Arabia Petraea*. As the book was published under the pseudonym of "An American," Stephens retained his anonymity in the illustration as a "Merchant of Cairo."

The reader may remember that, on my first visit to his excellency, I saw a man whipped; this time I saw one bastinadoed. I had heard much of this, a punishment existing, I believe, only in the East, but I had never seen it inflicted before, and hope I never shall see it again. As on the former occasion, I found the little governor standing at one end of the large hall of entrance, munching, and trying causes. A crowd was gathered around, and before him was a poor Arab, pleading and beseeching most piteously, while the big tears were rolling down his cheeks; near him was a man whose resolute and somewhat angry expression marked him as the accuser, seeking vengeance rather than justice. Suddenly the governor made a gentle movement with his hand; all noise ceased; all stretched their necks and turned their eager eyes towards him; the accused cut short his crying, and stood with his mouth wide open, and his eyes fixed upon the governor. The latter spoke a few words in a very low voice, to me of course unintelligible, and, indeed, scarcely audible, but they seemed to fall upon the quick ears of the culprit like bolts of thunder; the agony of suspense was over, and, without a word or look, he laid himself down on his face at the feet of the governor. A space was immediately cleared around; a man on each side took him by the hand, and, stretching out his arms, kneeled upon and held them down, while another seated himself across his neck and shoulders. Thus nailed to the ground, the poor fellow, knowing that there was no chance of escape, threw up his feet from the knee-joint, so as to present the soles in a horizontal position. Two men came forward with a pair of long stout bars of wood, attached together by a cord, between which they placed the feet, drawing them together with the cord so as to fix them in their horizontal position, and leave the whole flat surface exposed to the full force of the blow. In the meantime two strong Turks were standing ready, one at each side, armed with long whips much resembling our common cowskin, but longer and thicker, and made of the tough hide of the hippopotamus.

While the occupation of the judge was suspended by these preparations, the janissary had presented the consul's letter. My sensibilities are not particularly acute, but they yielded in this instance. I had watched all the preliminary arrangements, nerving myself

147

for what was to come; but when I heard the scourge whizzing through the air, and, when the first blow fell upon the naked feet, saw the convulsive movements of the body, and heard the first loud piercing shriek, I could stand it no longer; I broke through the crowd, forgetting the governor and everything else, except the agonizing sounds from which I was escaping; but the janissary followed close at my heels, and, laying his hand upon my arm, hauled me back to the governor. If I had consulted merely the impulse of feeling, I should have consigned him, and the governor, and the whole nation of Turks, to the lower regions; but it was all important not to offend this summary dispenser of justice, and I never made a greater sacrifice of feeling to expediency than when I re-entered his presence. The shrieks of the unhappy criminal were ringing through the chamber, but the governor received me with as calm a smile as if he had been sitting on his own divan, listening to the strains of some pleasant music, while I stood with my teeth clinched, and felt the hot breath of the victim, and heard the whizzing of the accursed whip, as it fell again and again upon his bleeding feet. I have heard men cry out in agony when the sea was raging, and the drowning man, rising for the last time upon the mountain waves, turned his imploring arms towards us, and with his dying breath called in vain for help; but I never heard such heart-rending sounds as those from the poor bastinadoed wretch before me.

I thought the governor would never make an end of reading the letter, when the scribe handed it to him for his signature, although it contained but half a dozen lines; he fumbled in his pocket for his seal, and dipped it in the ink; the impression did not suit him, and he made another; and, after a delay that seemed to me eternal, employed in folding it, handed it to me with a most gracious smile. I am sure I grinned horribly in return, and almost snatching the letter just as the last blow fell, I turned to hasten from the scene. The poor scourged wretch was silent; he had found relief in insensibility; I cast one look upon the senseless body, and saw the feet laid open in gashes, and the blood streaming down the legs. At that moment the bars were taken away, and the mangled feet fell

148

like lead upon the floor. I had to work my way through the crowd, and, before I could escape, I saw the poor fellow revive, and by the first natural impulse rise upon his feet, but fall again as if he had stepped upon red-hot irons. He crawled upon his hands and knees to the door of the hall, and here it was most grateful to see that the poor miserable, mangled, and degraded Arab yet had friends whose hearts yearned towards him; they took him in their arms and carried him away.

I was sick of Cairo, and in a right humor to bid farewell to cities, with all their artificial laws, their crimes and punishments, and all the varied shades of inhumanity from man to man, and in a few minutes I was beyond the gate, and galloping away to join my companions in the desert. At the tombs of the caliphs I found Paul with my caravan; but I had not yet escaped the stormy passions of men. With the cries of the poor Arab still ringing in my ears, I was greeted with a furious quarrel, arising from the apportionment of the money I had paid my guides. I was in no humor to interfere, and, mounting my dromedary, and leaving Paul to arrange the affair with them as he best could, I rode on alone.

It was a journey of no ordinary interest on which I was now beginning my lonely way. I had traveled in Italy, among the mountains of Greece, the plains of Turkey, the wild steppes of Russia, and the plains of Poland, but neither of these afforded half the material for curious expectation that my journey through the desert promised. After an interval of four thousand years, I was about to pursue the devious path of the children of Israel, when they took up the bones of Joseph and fled before the anger of Pharaoh, among the mountain passes of Sinai, and through that great and terrible desert which shut them from the Land of Promise. I rode on in silence and alone for nearly two hours and, just as the sun was sinking behind the dark mountains of Moqattam, halted to wait for my little caravan; and I pitched my tent for the first night in the desert, with the door opening to the distant land of Goshen.

CHAPTER XIV

THE ARRANGEMENTS for my journey as far as Mount Sinai had been made by Mr. Gliddon. It was necessary to have as my guides some of the Bedouins from around the mountains, and he had procured one known to him, a man in whom I could place the most implicit confidence; and possessing another not less powerful recommendation, in the fact that he had been with Messrs. Linant and Laborde to Petra. My caravan consisted of eight camels and dromedaries, and, as guide and camel-drivers, three young Bedouins from nineteen to twenty-two years old. My tent was the common tent of the Egyptian soldiers, bought at the government factory, easily carried, and as easily pitched; my bedding was a mattress and coverlet; and I had, moreover, a couple of boxes, about eighteen inches high, and the width of my mattress, filled with eatables, which I carried slung over the back of a camel, one upon each side, and at night, by the addition of two pieces of board, converted into a bedstead. My store of provisions consisted of bread, biscuit, rice, macaroni, tea, coffee, dried apricots, oranges, a roasted leg of mutton, and two of the largest skins containing the filtered water of the Nile.

In the evening, while we were sitting around a fire, I inquired the cause of the quarrel from which I had escaped, and this led Toualeb into an explanation of some of the customs of the Bedouins. There exists among them that community of interest and property for which radicals and visionaries contend in civilized society. The

150

property of the tribe is to a great extent common, and their earnings, or the profits of their labor, are shared among the whole. A Bedouin's wives are his own; and as the chastity of women is guarded by the most sanguinary laws, his children are generally his own; his tent, also, and one or two camels are his, and the rest belongs to his tribe. The practical operation of this law is not attended with any great difficulty; for, in general, the *rest*, or that which belongs to the tribe, is nothing; there are no hoarded treasures, no coffers of wealth, the bequest of ancestors, or the gains of enterprise and industry, to excite the cupidity of the avaricious. Poor is the Bedouin born, and poor he dies, and his condition is more than usually prosperous when his poverty does not lead him to the shedding of blood.

I did not expect to learn lessons of political economy among the Bedouin Arabs; but, in the commencement of my journey with them, I found the embarrassment and evil of trammeling individual enterprise and industry. The consul had applied to Toualeb. Toualeb was obliged to propose the thing to such of his tribe as were then in Cairo, and all had a right to participate. The consequence was, that when we were ready to move, instead of five there were a dozen camels and dromedaries, and their several owners were the men whom I had left wrangling at the tombs of the caliphs; and even when it was ascertained that only five were wanted, still three supernumeraries were sent, that all might be engaged in the work. In countries where the labor of man and beast has a per diem value, the loss of the labor of three or four men and three or four camels would be counted; but, in the East, time and labor have no value.

I do not mean to go into any dissertations on the character of the Bedouins, and shall merely refer to such traits as fell under my observation and were developed by circumstances. While I was eating my evening meal, and talking with Toualeb, the three young camel-drivers sat at the door of the tent, leaning on their hands and looking at me. I at first did not pay much attention to them, but it soon struck me as singular that they did not prepare their own meal; and, noticing them more attentively, I thought they were not looking so much at me as at the smoking pilaf before me. I asked

151

them why they did not eat their supper; and they told me that their masters had sent them away without a particle of anything to eat. I was exceedingly vexed at this, inasmuch as it showed that I had four mouths to feed more than I had prepared for; no trifling matter on a journey in the desert, and one which Paul, as my quartermaster, said it was utterly impossible to accomplish. I at first told one of them to mount my dromedary and go back to Cairo, assuring him that, if he did not return before daylight, I would follow and have both him and his master bastinadoed; but before he had mounted I changed my mind. I hated all returns and delays, and, smothering my wrath, told Paul to give them some rice and biscuit, at the risk of being obliged to come down to Arab bread myself. And so ended the first day of my journey.

Early in the morning we began our march, with our faces towards the rising sun. Before midday we were in as perfect a desert as if we were removed thousands of miles from the habitations of men; behind, before, and around us was one wide expanse of level and arid sands, although we were as yet not more than eight hours from the crowded city of Cairo; and I might already cry out, in the spirit of Neikomm's famous cavatina, "The sea, the sea, the open sea!" Indeed, in all the traveling in the East, nothing strikes one more forcibly than the quick transitions from the noise of cities to the stillness of the unpeopled waste.

It does, indeed, appear remarkable that, within so short a distance from Cairo, a city of so great antiquity and large population, and on a road which we know to have been traveled more than four thousand years, and which at this day is the principal route to the Red Sea, there is so little traveling. During the whole day we did not meet more than a dozen Arabs, with perhaps twenty or thirty camels. But a mighty change will soon be made in this particular. A railroad is about to be constructed across the desert, over the track followed by the children of Israel to the Red Sea. The pasha had already ordered iron from England for the purpose when I was in Egypt, and there is no doubt of its practicability, being only a distance of eighty miles over a dead level; but whether it will ever be finished, or whether, if finished, it will pay the expense, is much more questionable. Indeed, the better opinion is, that the pasha does it merely to bolster up his reputation in Europe as a reformer; that he has begun without calculating the costs; and that he will get tired and abandon it before it is half-completed. It may be, however, that the reader will one day be hurried by a steam-engine over the route which I was now crossing at the slow pace of a camel; and when that day comes, all the excitement and wonder of a journey in the desert will be over. There will be no more pitching of tents, or sleeping under the starry firmament, surrounded by Arabs and camels; no more carrying provisions, and no danger of dying of thirst; all will be reduced to the systematic tameness of a cotton-factory, and the wild Arab will retire farther into the heart of the desert, shunning, like our native Indians, the faces of strangers, and following forever the footsteps of his wandering ancestors. Blessed be my fortune, improvement had not yet actually begun its march.

In the course of the night I was suddenly awakened by a loud noise like the flapping of sails. A high wind had risen, and my tent not being well secured, it had turned over, so that the wind got under it and carried it away. In the civilized world, we often hear of reverses of fortune which reduce a man to such a state that he has not a roof to cover him; but few are ever deprived of the protection of their roof in so summary a way as this, and it is but fair to add that few have ever got it back so expeditiously. I opened my eyes upon the stars, and saw my house fleeing from me. Paul and I were on our feet in a moment, and gave chase, and, with the assistance of our Arabs, brought it back and planted it again; I thought of the prudent Kentuckian who tied his house to a stump to keep it from being blown away, and would have done the same thing if I could have found a stump; but tree or stump in the desert there is none.

I was not disturbed again during the night; but the wind continued to increase, and towards morning and all the next day blew with great violence. It was the dread sirocco, the wind that has forever continued to blow over the desert, carrying with it the fine particles of sand which, by the continued action of centuries, have buried the monuments, the temples, and the cities of Egypt; the

153

THE TRAVELS OF
John Lloyd Stephens
TO ARABIA PETRÆA
IN 1836

------ *route of travel*

SCALE IN MILES
0 10 20 30 40 50 60

to Beyrouth

Sour (Tyre)

Acre
Haifa (Caipha)
Mt. Carmel

Safad
Capernaum
Tiberias
Sea of Galilee
Nazareth

HOLY LAND

Jenin
Beisan

Sebastye (Samaria)
Nablus (Shechem)

Jordan River

Jaffa (Joppa)
Ramallah (Ramah)
Jericho

MEDITERRANEAN
SEA

Jerusalem
Bethlehem
Hebron

Dead Sea

Gaza

Port Said

El 'Arîsh (Rhinocolura)

DESERT

EDOM

Wadi el 'Arîsh

Petra
Jebel Harun (Mt. Hor)

from Cairo

Suez

ARABIA PETRÆA

Aqaba

Gulf of Suez

Gulf of Aqaba

Mount Sinai

Tor

Red Sea

From Victor Wolfgang von Hagen, *Maya Explorer*

sirocco always disagreeable and dangerous, and sometimes, if the reports of travelers be true, suffocating and burying whole caravans of men and camels. Fortunately for me, it was blowing upon my back; but still it was necessary to draw my Arab cloak close over my head; and even then the particles of sand found their way within, so that my eyes were soon filled with them. This was very far from being one of the worst siroccos; but the sun was obscured, the atmosphere was a perfect cloud of sand, and the tracks were so completely obliterated, that a little after midday we were obliged to stop and take shelter under the lee of a hillock of sand; occasionally we had met caravans coming upon us through the thick clouds of sand, the Arabs riding with their backs to the heads of their camels, and their faces covered, so that not a single feature could be seen.

By the third morning the wind had somewhat abated, but the sand had become so scattered that not a single track could be seen. I was forcibly reminded of a circumstance related to me by Mr. Waghorn. A short time before I met him at Cairo, in making a hurried march from Suez, with an Arab unaccustomed to the desert, he encamped about midway, and starting two hours before daylight, continued traveling, half-asleep, upon his dromedary, until it happened to strike him that the sun had risen in the wrong place, and was then shining in his face instead of warming his back; he had been more than three hours retracing his steps to Suez. If I had been alone this morning, I might very easily have fallen into the same or a worse error. The prospect before me was precisely the same, turn which way I would; and, if I had been left to myself, I might have wandered as long as the children of Israel in search of the Promised Land before I should have arrived at the gate of Suez.

We soon came in sight of the principal, perhaps the only object, which a stranger would mark in the route from Cairo to Suez. It is a large palm-tree, standing alone about halfway across, the only green and living thing on that expanse of barrenness. We saw it two or three hours; and, moving with the slow pace of our camels, it seemed as if we should never leave it behind us. A journey in the desert is so barren of incident, that wayfarers note the smallest circumstances, and our relative distance from the palm-tree, or halfway house, furnished occupation for a great part of the day.

At about twelve o'clock the next day we caught the first view of the Red Sea, rolling between the dark mountains of Egypt and Arabia, as in the days of Pharaoh and Moses. In an hour more we came in sight of Suez, a low dark spot on the shore, above the commencement of the chains of mountains on each side. About two hours before arriving, we passed, at a little distance on the left, a large khan, on the direct road to Aqaba,[1] built by the pasha as a stopping-place for the pilgrims on their way to Mecca. Three days before, more than thirty thousand pilgrims had halted in and around it, but now not a living being was to be seen. About half an hour on the hither side of Suez we came to a well, where, for the first time since we left Cairo, we watered our camels.

Even among the miserable cities of Turkey and Egypt, few present so wretched an appearance as Suez. Standing on the borders of the desert, and on the shore of the sea, with bad and unwholesome water, not a blade of grass growing around it, and dependent upon Cairo for the food that supports its inhabitants, it sustains a poor existence by the trade of the great caravan for Mecca, and the small commerce between the ports of Quseir, Jidda, and Mukha. A new project has lately been attempted here, which, it might be supposed, would have a tendency to regenerate the fallen city. The route to India by the Red Sea is in the full tide of successful experiment; the English flag is often seen waving in the harbor; and about once in two months an English steamer arrives from Bombay; but even the clatter of a steamboat is unable to infuse life into its sluggish population.

The gate was open, a single soldier was lying on a mat basking in the sun, his musket gleaming brightly by his side, and a single cannon projected over the wall, frowning with Tom Thumb greatness upon the stranger entering the city. Passing the gate, we found ourselves within a large open space crowded with pilgrims. Even the

[1] The direct route to Aqaba was laid out by the Romans in the first century A.D. The road proceeded due east from Suez to Medeia, 60 kilometers from Suez, and there the road bifurcated. The direct route to Aqaba proceeded to the Gulf.

small space enclosed by the walls was not more than one-quarter occupied by buildings, and these few were at the farthest extremity. The whole intermediate area was occupied by pilgrims, scattered about in every imaginable position and occupation, who stared at me as I passed among them in my European dress, and noticed me according to their various humors, some greeting me with a smile, some with a low and respectful salaam, and others with the black look and ferocious scowl of the bigoted and Frank-detesting Mussulmans.

We stopped in the square in front of the harbor, and inquired for an Englishman, the agent of Mr. Waghorn, to whom I had a letter, and from whom I hoped to obtain a bed; but he had arrived only two days before, and I doubt whether he had one for himself. He did all he could for me, but that was very little. I remember one thing about him, which is characteristic of a class of European residents in Egypt; he had lived fourteen years between Alexandria and Cairo, and had never been in the desert before, and talked as if he had made a voyage to Babylon or Baghdad. He had provided himself with almost everything that his English notions of comfort could suggest, and with these he talked of his three days' journey in the desert as a thing to be done but once in a man's life. I ought not to be harsh on him, however, for he was as kind as he could be to me, and in one thing I felt very sensibly the benefit of his kindness. By bad management my waterskins, instead of being old and seasoned, were entirely new; the second day out the water was injured, and the third it was not drinkable. I did not suffer so much as Paul and the Arabs did, having fallen into the habit of drinking but little, and assuaging my thirst with an orange; but I suffered from a cause much worse; my eyes were badly inflamed, and the water was so much impregnated with the noxious absorption from the leather, that it destroyed the effect of the powders which I diluted in it, and aggravated instead of relieving the inflammation. The Englishman had used kegs made for the purpose, and had more than a kegful left, which he insisted on my taking. One can hardly imagine that the giving or receiving a keg of water should be a matter of any moment; but, much as I wanted it, indeed, all-

157

important as it was to me for the rest of my journey, I hesitated to deprive him of it. Before going, however, I filled one of my skins, and counted it at the time one of the most valuable presents I had ever received. He had been in the desert, too, the same day that we suffered from the sirocco, and his eyes were in a worse condition than mine.

The first thing he did was to find me a place to pass the night in. Directly opposite the open space was a large roquel or stone building, containing a ground and upper floor, and open in the center, forming a hollow square. The whole building was divided by partitions into perhaps one hundred apartments, and every one of these and the open square outside were filled with pilgrims. The apartments consisted merely of a floor, roof, door, and walls, and sometimes one or the other of these requisites was wanting, and its deficiency supplied by the excess of another. My room was in one corner in the second story, and had a most unnecessary and uncomfortable proportion of windows; but I had no choice. I regretted that I had not pitched my tent outside the walls; but, calling to my assistance the ingenuity and contriving spirit of my country, fastened it up as a screen to keep the wind from coming upon me too severely, and walked out to see the little that was to be seen of Suez.

I had soon made a tour of the town; and, having performed this duty, I hurried where my thoughts and feelings had long been carrying me, to the shore of the sea. Half a dozen vessels of some eighty or a hundred tons, sharp built, with tall spars for latteen sails, high poops, and strangely painted, resembling the ancient ships of war, or the Turkish corsair or Arab pirate of modern days, were riding at anchor in the harbor, waiting to take on board the thousands of pilgrims who were all around me. I followed the shore till I had turned the walls, and was entirely alone. I sat down under the wall, where I had an extensive view down the sea, and saw the place where the waters divided for the passage of the Israelites. Two hours I strolled along the shore, and, when the sun was sinking behind the dark mountains of Moqattam, I was bathing my feet in the waters of the coral sea.

Early in the morning I went out on the balcony, and looking down into the open square, filled with groups of pilgrims, male and female, sleeping on the bare ground, in all manner of attitudes, I saw directly under me a dead Tartar. He had died during the night, his deathbed a single plank, and he was lying in the sheepskin dress which he wore when living. Two friends from the frozen regions of the north, companions in his long pilgrimage, were sitting on the ground preparing their morning coffee, and my Arabs were sleeping by his side, unconscious that but a few feet from them, during the stillness of the night, an immortal spirit had been called away. I gazed long and steadfastly upon the face of the dead Tartar, and moralized very solemnly—indeed, painfully—upon the imaginary incidents which my fancy summoned up in connection with his fate. Nor was the possibility of my own death, among strangers in a distant land, the least prominent or least saddening portion of my revery.

I ascribe this uncommon moping-fit to my exposing myself before breakfast. The stomach must be fortified, or force, moral and physical, is gone, and melancholy and blue devils are the inevitable consequence. After breakfast I was another creature. My acute sensibility, my tender sympathies, were gone; and, when I went out again, I looked upon the body of the dead Tartar with the utmost indifference.

The pilgrims were now nearly all stirring, and the square was all in motion. The balcony, and, indeed, every part of the old roquel, were filled with the better class of pilgrims, principally Turks, the lords of the land; and in an apartment opening on the balcony, immediately next to mine, sat a beautiful Circassian, with the regular features and brilliant complexion of her country. By her side were two lovely children, fair and beautiful as their mother. Her face was completely uncovered, for she did not know that a stranger was gazing on her, and, turning from the black visages around him to her fair and lovely face, was reveling in recollections of the beauties of his native land. And lo, the virtue of a breakfast! I, that by looking upon a dead Tartar had buried myself in the deserts of Arabia, written my epitaph, and cried over my own grave, was now ready to break a lance with a Turk to rob him of his wife.

159

THE CARAVAN FROM MECCA ENTERING THE FORTRESS OF AQABA

The balcony and staircase were thronged with pilgrims, many still asleep, so that I was obliged to step over their bodies in going down, and out of doors the case was much the same. At home I should have thought it a peculiarly interesting circumstance to join a caravan of Mussulmans on their pilgrimage to Mecca; but, long before I had seen them start from the gate of Cairo, my feelings were essentially changed. I had hired my caravan for Mount Sinai; but, feeling rather weak, and wishing to save myself six days' journey in the desert, I endeavored to hire a boat to go down the Red Sea to Tor, supposed to be the Elim, or place of palm-trees, mentioned in the Exodus of the Israelites, and only two days' journey from Mount Sinai. The boats were all taken by the pilgrims, and these holy travelers were packed together as closely as sheep on board one of our North River sloops for the New York market. They were a filthy set, many of them probably not changing their clothes from the time they left their homes until they reached the tomb of the Prophet. I would rather not have traveled with them; but, as it was my only way of going down the sea, I applied to an Arab, to hire a certain portion of space on the deck of a boat for myself and servant; but he advised me not to think of such a thing. He told me if I hired and paid for such a space, the pilgrims would certainly encroach upon me; that they would beg, and borrow, and at last rob me; and, above all, that they were bigoted fanatics, and, if a storm occurred, would very likely throw me overboard. With this character of his brethren from a true believer, I abandoned the idea of going by sea, and that the more readily, as his account was perfectly consistent with what I had before heard of the pilgrims.

The scene itself did not sustain the high and holy character of a pilgrimage. As I said before, all were abominably filthy; some were sitting around a great dish of pilaf, thrusting their hands in it up to the knuckles, squeezing the boiled rice, and throwing back their heads as they crammed the huge morsel down their throats; others packing up their merchandise, or carrying water-skins, or whetting their sabers; others wrangling for a few paras; and in one place was an Arab butcher, bare-legged and naked from the waist upward, with his hands, breast, and face smeared with blood, leaning over

161

the body of a slaughtered camel, brandishing an axe, and chopping off huge pieces of meat for the surrounding pilgrims. A little off from the shore a large party were embarking on board a small boat to go down to their vessel, which was lying at the mouth of the harbor; they were wading up to their middle, everyone with something on his shoulders or above his head. Thirty or forty had already got on board, and as many more were trying to do the same; but the boat was already full. A loud wrangling commenced, succeeded by clinching, throttling, splashing in the water, and running to the shore. I saw bright swords gleaming in the air, heard the ominous click of a pistol, and in one moment more blood would have been shed but for a Turkish aga, who had been watching the scene from the governor's balcony, and now dashing in among them with a huge silver-headed mace, and laying about him right and left, brought the turbulent pilgrims to a condition more suited to their sacred character.

At about nine o'clock I sent off my camels to go round the head of the gulf, intending to cross over in a boat and meet them. At the moment they left the roquel, two friends were holding up a quilt before the body of the dead Tartar, while a third was within, washing and preparing it for burial. At twelve o'clock I got on board my boat; she was like the others, sharp built, with a high poop and tall latteen sails, and, for the first time in all my traveling, I began to think a voyage better than a journey. In addition to the greater ease and pleasantness, there was something new and exciting in the passage of the Red Sea; and we had hardly given our large latteen sails to the wind, before I began to talk with the rais about carrying me down to Tor; but he told me the boat was too small for such a voyage, and money would not induce him to attempt it.

Late in the afternoon we landed on the opposite side, on the most sacred spot connected with the wanderings of the Israelites, where they rose from the dry bed of the sea, and, at the command of Moses, the divided waters rushed together, overwhelming Pharaoh and his chariots, and the whole host of Egypt. With the devotion of a pious pilgrim, I picked up a shell and put it in my pocket as a memorial of the place, and then Paul and I, mounting the dromedaries which my guide had brought down to the shore in readiness, rode to a grove of palm-trees, shading a fountain of bad water, called Ain Musa, or the fountain of Moses. I was riding carelessly along, looking behind me towards the sea, and had almost reached the grove of palm-trees, when a large flock of crows flew out, and my dromedary, frightened with their sudden whizzing, started back and threw me twenty feet over his head, completely clear of his long neck, and left me sprawling in the sand. It was a mercy I did not finish my wanderings where the children of Israel began theirs; but I saved my head at the expense of my hands, which sank in the loose soil up to the wrist, and bore the marks for more than two months afterward. I seated myself where I fell, and, as the sun was just dipping below the horizon, told Paul to pitch the tent, with the door towards the place of the miraculous passage. I shall never forget that sunset scene, and it is the last I shall inflict upon the reader. I was sitting on the very spot where the chosen people of God, after walking over the dry bed of the sea, stopped to behold the divided waters returning to their place and swallowing up the host of the pursuers. The mountains on the other side looked dark and portentous, as if proud and conscious witnesses of the mighty miracle, while the sun, descending slowly behind them, long after it had disappeared, left a reflected brightness, which illumined with an almost supernatural light the dark surface of the water.

But to return to the fountain of Moses. I am aware that there is some dispute as to the precise spot where Moses crossed; but, having no time for skepticism on such matters, I began by making up my mind that this was the place, and then looked around to see whether, according to the account given in the Bible, the face of the country and the natural landmarks did not sustain my opinion. I remember I looked up to the head of the gulf, where Suez or Kolsum now stands, and saw that almost to the very head of the gulf there was a high range of mountains which it would be necessary to cross, an undertaking which would have been physically impossible for six hundred thousand people, men, women, and children, to accomplish, with a hostile army pursuing them. At Suez, Moses could not have been hemmed in as he was; he could go off into the Syrian

163

Desert, or, unless the sea has greatly changed since that time, round the head of the gulf. But here, directly opposite where I sat, was an opening in the mountains, making a clear passage from the desert to the shore of the sea. It is admitted that, from the earliest history of the country, there was a caravan route from the Ramses of the Pharaohs to this spot, and it was perfectly clear to my mind that, if the account be true at all, Moses had taken that route; that it was directly opposite me, between the two mountains, where he had come down with his multitude to the shore, and that it was there he found himself hemmed in, in the manner described in the Bible, with the sea before him, and the army of Pharaoh in his rear; it was there he had stretched out his hand and divided the waters; and probably, on the very spot where I sat, the children of Israel had kneeled upon the sands to offer thanks to God for his miraculous interposition. The distance, too, was in confirmation of this opinion. It was about twenty miles across; the distance which that immense multitude, with their necessary baggage, could have passed in the space of time (a night) mentioned in the Bible. Besides my own judgment and conclusions, I had authority on the spot, in my Bedouin Toualeb, who talked of it with as much certainty as if he had seen it himself; and, by the waning light of the moon, pointed out the metes and bounds according to the tradition received from his fathers. "And even yet," said he, "on a still evening like this, or sometimes when the sea is raging, the ghosts of the departed Egyptians are seen walking upon the waters; and once, when, after a long day's journey, I lay down with my camels on this very spot, I saw the ghost of Pharaoh himself, with the crown upon his head, flying with his chariot and horses over the face of the deep; and even to this day the Arab, diving for coral, brings up fragments of swords, broken helmets, or chariot-wheels, swallowed up with the host of Egypt."

Early the next morning we resumed our journey, and traveled several hours along a sandy valley, diverging slowly from the sea and approaching the mountains on our left. The day's journey was barren of incident, though not void of interest. We met only one small caravan of Bedouins, with their empty sacks, like the children of Jacob of old, journeying from a land of famine to a land of plenty. From time to time we passed the bones of a camel bleaching on the sand, and once the body of one just dead, his eyes already picked out, and their sockets hollow to the brain. A huge vulture was standing over him, with his long talons fastened in the entrails, his beak and his whole head stained with blood. I drove the horrid bird away; but, before I had got out of sight, he had again fastened on his prey.

The third day we started at seven o'clock, and, after three hours of journeying, entered among the mountains of Sinai. The scene was now entirely changed in character; the level expanse of the sandy desert for the wild and rugged mountain pass. At eleven we came to the fountain of Marah, supposed to be that at which the Israelites rested after their three days' journey from the Red Sea. There is some uncertainty as to the particulars of this journey; the print of their footsteps did not long remain in the shifting sands; their descendants have long been strangers in the land; and tradition but imperfectly supplies the want of more accurate and enduring records. Of the general fact there is no doubt; no other road from the Red Sea to Mount Sinai has existed since the days of Moses, and there is no part of the world where the face of nature and the natural landmarks have remained so totally unchanged. Then, as now, it was a barren mountainous region, bare of verdure and destitute of streams of living water; so that the Almighty was obliged to sustain his people with manna from heaven and water from the rocks.

But travelers have questioned whether this is the fountain of Marah. The Bible account is simple and brief: "They went three days into the wilderness, and found no water; and when they came to Marah, they could not drink of the waters of Marah, for they were bitter." Burckhardt objects that the distance is too short for three days' journey, but this cavil is sufficiently answered by others; that the movements of such an immense multitude, of all ages and both sexes, with flocks and cattle, which they must have had for the sacrifice, if for no other purpose, must necessarily have been slow. Besides, supposing the habits of the people to have been the same

165

as we find them now among Orientals, the presumption is rather that they would march slowly than push on with speed, after the danger of pursuit was over. Time is thought of little consequence by the Arabs; and, as the Jews were Arabs, it is probable that the same was a feature of their character also. At all events, I was disposed to consider this the fountain, and would fain have performed the duty of a pious pilgrim by making my noonday meal at its brink; but, as in the days of Moses, we could not drink of the waters of Marah, "for they were bitter." I do not wonder that the people murmured, for even our camels would not drink of them. The ground around the fountain was white with salt. In about two hours more we came to the valley of Gherondel, a large valley with palm-trees; away at the right, in the mountains, is another spring of water, which Shaw makes the bitter fountain of Moses, the water being also undrinkable.

That night Paul was unwell; and, as it always happened with him when he had a headache, he thought he was going to die. As soon as we pitched our tent I made him lie down; and, not knowing how to deal with his real and fancied ailments, gave him some hot tea, and then piled upon him quilts, blankets, empty sacks, saddle-cloths, and every other covering I could find, until he cried for quarter. I had no difficulty in cooking my own supper, and, I remember, tried the savage taste of my Bedouins with the China weed, which they liked exceedingly when so abundantly sweetened as utterly to destroy its flavor.

CHAPTER XV

IN THE MORNING Paul was well, but I recommended a little starvation to make all sure; this, however, by no means agreed
with his opinion, or his appetite; for, as he said, a man who rode a
dromedary all day must eat or die. Late in the afternoon we passed
a hill of stones, which Burckhardt calls the tomb of a saint; but,
according to Toualeb's account, and he spoke of it as a thing within
his own knowledge, it was the tomb of a very different personage,
namely, a woman who was surprised by her kindred with a paramour, and killed and buried on the spot; on a little eminence above,
a few stones marked the place where a slave had been stationed to
give the guilty pair a timely notice of approaching danger, but had
neglected his important trust.

Our road now lay between wild and rugged mountains, and the
valley itself was stony, broken, and gullied by the washing of the
winter torrents; and a few straggling thorn-bushes were all that
grew in that region of desolation. I had remarked for some time, and
every moment impressed it more and more forcibly upon my mind,
that everything around me seemed old and in decay: the valley was
barren and devastated by torrents; the rocks were rent; the mountains cracked, broken, and crumbling into thousands of pieces; and
we encamped at night between rocks which seemed to have been
torn asunder by some violent convulsion, where the stones had
washed down into the valley, and the drifted sand almost choked
the passage. It had been excessively hot during the day, and at
night the wind was whistling around my tent as in mid-winter.

Early in the morning we were again in motion, our route lying

THE WILDERNESS OF SINAI

nearly all day in the same narrow valley, bounded by the same lofty mountains. At every step the scene became more solemn and impressive; all was still around us; and not a sound broke the universal silence, except the soft tread of our camels, and now and then the voice of one of us; but there was little encouragement to garrulity. The mountains became more and more striking, venerable, and interesting. Not a shrub or blade of grass grew on their naked sides, deformed with gaps and fissures; and they looked as if, by a slight jar or shake, they would crumble into millions of pieces. It is impossible to describe correctly the singularly interesting appearance of these mountains. Age, hoary and venerable, is the predominant character. They looked as if their great Creator had made them higher than they are, and their summits, worn and weakened by the action of the elements for thousands of years, had cracked and fallen. My days in the desert did not pass as quickly as I hurry through them here. They wore away, not slowly alone, but sometimes heavily; and, to help them in their progress, I sometimes descended to very commonplace amusements. On one occasion I remember meeting a party of friendly Bedouins, and, sitting down with them to pipes and coffee, I noticed a fine lad of nineteen or twenty, about the size of one of my party, and pitted mine against him for a wrestling match. The old Bedouins took the precaution to remove their knives and swords, and it was well they did, for the two lads throttled each other like young furies; and when mine received a pretty severe prostration on the sand, he first attempted to regain his sword, and, failing in that, sprang again upon his adversary with such ferocity that I was glad to have the young devils taken apart, and still more glad to know that they were going to travel different roads.

Several times we passed the rude burying-grounds of the Bedouins, standing alone in the waste of sand, a few stones thrown together in a heap marking the spot where an Arab's bones reposed; but the wanderer of the desert looks forward to his final rest in this wild burying-place of his tribe with the same feeling that animates the English peasant towards the churchyard of his native village, or the noble peer towards the honored tomb of his ancestors.

169

About noon we came to an irregular stone fence, running across the valley and extending up the sides nearly to the top of the adjacent mountains, built as a wall by the Bedouins of Sinai during their war with the Pasha of Egypt. Among the strong and energetic measures of his government, Mohammed Ali had endeavored to reduce these children of the desert under his iron rule; to subject them to taxes, like his subjects of the Nile, and, worse, to establish his oppressive system of military conscription. But the free spirit of the untameable could not brook this invasion of their independence. They plundered his caravans, drank his best Mocha coffee, devoured his spices from Arabia and India, and clothed themselves and their wives in the rich silks intended for the harems of the wealthy Turks. Hassan Bey was sent against them with twenty-five hundred men; four hundred Bedouins defended this pass for several days, when, craftily permitting him to force his way to the convent of Mount Sinai, the tribes gathered in force between him and the Red Sea, and held him there a prisoner until a treaty of perpetual amity had been ratified by the pasha, by which it was agreed that the pasha should not invade their territory, and that they would be his subjects, provided he would not call upon them for duties, or soldiers, or, indeed, for anything which should abridge their natural freedom; or, in other words, that he might do as he pleased with them, provided he let them have their own way. It was, in fact, the schoolboy's bargain, "Let me alone and I will let you alone," and so it has been faithfully kept by both parties, and I have no doubt will continue to be kept, until one of them shall have a strong probability of profit and success in breaking it. Upon the whole, however, the Bedouins of Mount Sinai are rather afraid of Mohammed Ali, and he has a great rod over them in his power of excluding them from Cairo, where they come to exchange their dates and apricots for grain, clothing, weapons, and ammunition. As they told me themselves, before his time they had been great robbers, and now a robbery is seldom heard of among them.

For two days we had been suffering for want of water. The skins with which I had been provided by the consul's janissary at Cairo were so new that they contaminated the water; and it had at last

170

become so bad, that, fearful of injurious effects from drinking it, and preferring the evil of thirst to that of sickness, I had poured it all out upon the sand. Toualeb had told me that some time during the day we should come to a fountain, but the evening was drawing nigh and we had not reached it. Fortunately, we had still a few oranges left, which served to moisten our parched mouths, and we were in the momentary expectation of coming to the water, when Toualeb discovered some marks, from which he told us that it was yet three hours distant. We had no apprehension of being reduced to the extremity of thirst; but, for men who had already been suffering for some time, the prolongation of such thirst was by no means pleasant. During those three hours I thought of nothing but water. Rivers were floating through my imagination, and, while moving slowly upon my dromedary, with the hot sun beating upon my head, I wiped the sweat from my face, and thought upon the frosty Caucasus; and when, after traveling an hour aside from the main track, through an opening in the mountains, we saw a single palm-tree shading a fountain, our progress was gradually accelerated, until, as we approached, we broke into a run, and dashing through the sand, and without much respect of persons, all threw ourselves upon the fountain.[1]

If any of my friends at home could have seen me then, they would have laughed to see me scrambling among a party of Arabs for a place around a fountain, all prostrate on the ground, with our heads together, for a moment raising them to look gravely at each other while we paused for breath, and then burying our noses again in the delicious water; and yet, when my thirst was satisfied, and I had time to look at it, I thought it lucky that I had not seen it before. It was not a fountain, but merely a deposit of water in a hollow sandstone rock; the surface was green, and the bottom muddy. Such as it was, however, we filled our skins and returned to the main track.

We continued about an hour in the valley, rising gently until we found ourselves on the top of a little eminence, from which we saw before us another valley, bounded also by high rocky cliffs; and directly in front, still more than a day's journey distant, standing

[1] See page xxxii of the introduction.

directly across the road, and, as has been forcibly and truly said, "looking like the end of the world," stood the towering mountains of Sinai. At the other end of the plain the mountains contracted, and on one side was an immense block of porphyry, which had fallen, probably, thousands of years ago. I could still see where it had come leaping and crashing down the mountainside, and trace its destructive course to the very spot where it now lay, itself almost a mountain, though a mere pebble when compared with the giant from which it came. I pitched my tent by its side, with the door open to the holy mountain, as many a weary pilgrim had done before me. The rock was covered with inscriptions;[2] but I could not read them. I walked round and round it with Paul at my elbow, looking eagerly for some small scrap, a single line, in a language we could read; but all were strange, and at length we gave up the search. In several places in the wilderness of Sinai the rocks are filled with inscriptions, supposed to have been made by the Jews; and finding those before me utterly beyond my comprehension, I resolved to carry them back to a respectable antiquity, and in many of the worn and faded characters to recognize the work of some wandering Israelite. I meditated, also, a desperate but noble deed. Those who had written before me were long since dead; but in this lonely desert they had left a record of themselves and of their language. I resolved to add one of my country's also. Dwelling fondly in imagination upon the absorbing interest with which some future traveler, perhaps from my own distant land, would stop to read on this lonely rock a greeting in his native tongue, I sought with great care a stone that would serve as a pencil. It made a mark which did not suit me, and I laid it down to break it into a better shape, but unluckily smashed my fingers, and in one moment all my enthusiasm of sentiment was gone; I crammed my fingers into my mouth, and danced about the rock in an agony of heroics; and so my inscription remained unwritten.

At seven o'clock of the tenth day from Cairo I was again on my

---

[2] Possibly Nabatean inscriptions similar to those found by Charles Doughty in 1875 at Madaïn Sâlih in northwestern Arabia on the Derb-el-Haj road to Mecca. (Charles Doughty, *Arabia Deserta*, I, 224–29).

dromedary, and during the whole day the lofty top of Sinai was constantly before me. We were now in a country of friendly Arabs. The Bedouins around Mount Sinai were all of the same tribe, and the escort of any child of that tribe was a sufficient protection. About nine o'clock Toualeb left me for his tent among the mountains. He was a little at a loss, having two wives living in separate tents, at some distance from each other, and he hesitated which to visit. I made it my business to pry into particulars, and found the substance of the Arab's nature not much different from other men's. Old ties and a sense of duty called him to his old wife; to her who had been his only wife when he was young and poor; but something stronger than old ties or the obligation of duty impelled him to his younger bride. Like the Prophet whom he worshipped, he honored and respected his old wife, but his heart yearned to her younger and more lovely rival.

The last was by far the most interesting day of my journey to Mount Sinai. We were moving along a broad valley, bounded by ranges of lofty and crumbling mountains, forming an immense rocky rampart on each side of us; and rocky and barren as these mountains seemed, on their tops were gardens which produced oranges, dates, and figs in great abundance. Here, on heights almost inaccessible to any but the children of the desert, the Bedouin pitches his tent, pastures his sheep and goats, and gains the slender subsistence necessary for himself and family; and often, looking up the bare side of the mountain, we could see on its summit's edge the wild figure of a half-naked Arab, with his long matchlock gun in his hand, watching the movement of our little caravan. Sometimes, too, the eye rested upon the form of a woman stealing across the valley, not a traveler or passer-by, but a dweller in the land where no smoke curled from the domestic hearth, and no sign of a habitation was perceptible. There was something very interesting to me in the greetings of my companions with the other young men of their tribe. They were just returning from a journey to Cairo, an event in the life of a young Bedouin; and they were bringing a stranger from a land that none of them had ever heard of; yet their greeting had the coldness of frosty age and the reserve of strangers;

173

twice they would gently touch the palms of each other's hands, mutter a few words, and in a moment the welcomers were again climbing to their tents. One, I remember, greeted us more warmly and stayed longer among us. He was by profession a beggar or robber, as occasion required, and wanted something from us, but it was not much; merely some bread and a charge of powder. Not far from the track we saw, hanging on a thorn-bush, the black cloth of a Bedouin's tent, with the pole, ropes, pegs, and everything necessary to convert it into a habitation for a family. It had been there six months; the owner had gone to a new pasture-ground, and there it had hung, and there it would hang, sacred and untouched, until he returned to claim it. "It belongs to one of our tribe, and cursed be the hand that touches it," is the feeling of every Bedouin. Uncounted gold might be exposed in the same way; and the poorest Bedouin, though a robber by birth and profession, would pass by and touch it not.

On the very summit of the mountain, apparently ensconced behind it as a wall, his body not more than half-visible, a Bedouin was looking down upon us; and one of my party, who had long kept his face turned that way, told me that there was the tent of his father. I talked with him about his kindred and his mountain home, not expecting, however, to discover anything of extraordinary interest or novelty. The sons of Ishmael have ever been the same, inhabitants of the desert, despising the dwellers under a roof, wanderers and wild men from their birth, with their hands against every man, and every man's hand against them. "There is blood between us," says the Bedouin when he meets in the desert one of a tribe, by some individual of which an ancestor of his own was killed, perhaps a hundred years before. And then they draw their swords, and a new account of blood is opened, to be handed down as a legacy to their children. "Thy aunt wants thy purse," says the Bedouin when he meets the stranger traveling through his wild domain. "The desert is ours, and every man who passes over it must pay us tribute."

These principal and distinguishing traits of the Bedouin character have long been known; but as I had now been with them ten days, and expected to be with them a month longer, to see them in their tents, and be thrown among different tribes, claiming friendship from those who were enemies to each other, I was curious to know something of the lighter shades, the details of their lives and habits; and I listened with exceeding interest while the young Bedouin, with his eyes constantly fixed upon it, told me that for more than four hundred years the tent of his fathers had been in that mountain. Wild and unsettled, robbers and plunderers as they are, they have laws which are as sacred as our own; and the tent, and the garden, and the little pasture-ground are transmitted from father to son for centuries. I have probably forgotten more than half of our conversation; but I remember he told me that all the sons shared equally; that the daughters took nothing; that the children lived together; that if any of the brothers got married, the property must be divided; that if any difficulty arose on the division, the man who worked the place for a share of the profits must divide it; and, lastly, that the sisters must remain with the brothers until they (the sisters) are married. I asked him, if the brothers did not choose to keep a sister with them, what became of her; but he did not understand me. I repeated the question, but still he did not comprehend it, and looked to his companions for an explanation. And when, at last, the meaning of my question became apparent to his mind, he answered, with a look of wonder, "It is impossible—she is his own blood." I pressed my question again and again in various forms, suggesting the possibility that the brother's wife might dislike the sister, and other very supposable cases; but it was so strange an idea, that to the last he did not fully comprehend it, and his answer was still the same—"It is impossible—she is his own blood." Paul was in ecstasies at the noble answers of the young savage, and declared him the finest fellow he had ever met since he left Cairo. This was not very high praise, to be sure; but Paul intended it as a compliment, and the young Bedouin was willing to believe him, though he could not exactly comprehend how Paul had found it out.

I asked him who governed them; he stretched himself up and answered in one word, "God." I asked him if they paid tribute to the pasha; and his answer was, "No, we take tribute from him." I asked him how. "We plunder his caravans." Desirous to understand my exact position with the sheik of Aqaba, under his promise of protection, I asked him if they were governed by their sheik; to which he answered, "No, we govern him." The sheik was their representative, their mouthpiece with the pasha and with other tribes, and had a personal influence, but not more than any other member of the tribe. I asked him, if the sheik had promised a stranger to conduct him through his territory, whether the tribe would not consider themselves bound by his promise. He said no; they would take the sheik apart, ask him what he was going to do with the stranger; how much he was going to get; and, if they were satisfied, would let him pass; otherwise they would send him back; but they would respect the promise of the sheik so far as not to do him any personal injury. In case of any quarrel or difference between members of a tribe, they had no law or tribunal to adjust it; but if one of them was wounded—and he spoke as if this was the regular consequence of a quarrel—upon his recovery he made out his account, charging a per diem price for the loss of his services, and the other must pay it. But what if he will not? "He *must*," was the reply, given in the same tone with which he had before pronounced it "impossible" for the brother to withhold protection and shelter from his sister. If he does not he will be visited with the contempt of his tribe, and very soon he or one of his near relations will be killed. They have a law which is as powerful in its operations as any that we have, and it is a strange and not uninteresting feature in their social compact, that what we call public opinion should be as powerful among them as among civilized people, and that even the wild and lawless Bedouin, a man who may fight, rob, and kill with impunity, cannot live under the contempt of his tribe.

In regard to their yet more domestic habits, he told me that though the law of Mohammed allowed four wives, the Bedouin seldom took more than one, unless that one was barren or could not make good bread, or unless he fell in love with another girl, or could afford to keep more than one; with these and some few other exceptions, the Bedouin married but one wife; and the chastity of women was protected by sanguinary laws, the guilty woman having her head cut off by her own relations, while her paramour, unless caught in the act, is allowed to escape; the Arabs proceeding on the ground that the chastity of the woman is a pearl above all price; that it is in her own keeping; and that it is but part of the infirmity of man's nature to seek to rob her of it.

The whole day we were moving between parallel ranges of mountains, receding in some places, and then again contracting, and at about midday entered a narrow and rugged defile, bounded on each side with precipitous granite rocks more than a thousand feet high. We entered at the very bottom of this defile, moving for a time along the dry bed of a torrent, now obstructed with sand and stones, the rocks on every side shivered and torn, and the whole scene wild to sublimity. Our camels stumbled among the rocky fragments to such a degree that we dismounted, and passed through the wild defile on foot. At the other end we came suddenly upon a plain table of ground, and before us towered in awful grandeur, so huge and dark that it seemed close to us and barring all farther progress, the end of my pilgrimage, the holy mountain of Sinai. On our left was a large insulated stone, rudely resembling a chair, called the chair of Moses, on which tradition says that Moses rested himself when he came up with the people of his charge; farther on, upon a little eminence, are some rude stones which are pointed out as the ruins of the house of Aaron, where the great high-priest discoursed to the wandering Israelites. On the right is a stone, alleged to be the petrified golden calf. But it was not necessary to draw upon false and frivolous legends to give interest to this scene; the majesty of nature was enough. I felt that I was on holy ground; and, dismounting from my dromedary, loitered for more than an hour in the valley. It was cold, and I sent my shivering Bedouins forward, supposing myself to be at the foot of the mountain, and lingered there until after the sun had set. It was after dark as alone, and on foot, I entered the last defile leading to the holy mountain. The moon had risen, but her light could not penetrate the deep defile through which I was toiling slowly on to the foot of Sinai. From about halfway up it shone with a pale and solemn lustre, while below

177

all was in the deepest shade, and a dark spot on the side of the mountain, seeming perfectly black in contrast with the light above it, marked the situation of the convent. I passed a Bedouin tent, under which a group of Arabs were sleeping around a large fire, and in a few moments stood at the foot of the convent wall. My camels were lying down eating their evening meal, and my Bedouins were asleep on the ground close under the walls.

Knowing that they would not be admitted themselves, they had not demanded entrance; and as I had not told them to do so, they had not given notice of my coming. The convent was a very large building, and the high stone walls surrounding it, with turrets at the corners, gave it the appearance of a fortress. Exposed as they are to occasional attacks by the Bedouins, the holy fathers are sometimes obliged to have recourse to carnal weapons. The walls are accordingly mounted with cannon, and there is no entrance except by a subterraneous passage under the garden, or by a small door in one of the walls, about thirty feet from the ground. My Bedouins had stopped under this door, and here we commenced shouting for admission, first singly, and then all together, in French, English, and Arabic; but no one came to admit us. I was strongly reminded of the scene under the walls of the little convent in the desert, on my attempted expedition to the Great Oasis. Then, as now, it was a moonlight night, and the scene was a convent, a lonely habitation of Christians, with its door closed against a fellow-*Christian*. I remember that then I had to force my way in and make my own welcome, and I resolved that no trifle should keep me from an entrance here. The convent belonged to the Greek church. I did not know how many monks were in it, or what was the sanctity of their lives, but I wished that some of them had slept with more troubled consciences, for we made almost noise enough to wake the dead; and it was not until we had discharged two volleys of firearms that we succeeded in rousing any of the slumbering inmates. On one side were two or three little slits or portholes, and a monk, with a long white beard and a lighted taper in his hand, cautiously thrust out his head at one of them, and demanded our business. This was soon told; we were strangers and Christians, and wanted admission; and

178

had a letter from the Greek patriarch at Cairo. The head disappeared from the loophole, and soon after I saw its owner slowly open the little door, and let down a rope for the patriarch's letter. He read it by the feeble glimmer of his lamp, and then again appeared at the window, and bade us welcome. The rope was again let down; I tied it around my arms; and after dangling in the air for a brief space, swinging to and fro against the walls, found myself clasped in the arms of a burly, long-bearded monk, who hauled me in, kissed me on both cheeks, our long beards rubbing together in friendly union, and, untwisting the rope, set me upon my feet, and passed me over to his associates.

By this time nearly all the monks had assembled, and all pressed forward to welcome me. They shook my hand, took me in their arms, kissed my face; and if I had been their dearest friend just escaped from the jaws of death, they could not have received me with a more cordial greeting. Glad as I was, after a ten days' journey, to be received with such warmth by these recluses of the mountains, I could have spared the kissing. The custom is one of the detestable things of the East. It would not be so bad if it were universal, and the traveler might sometimes receive his welcome from rosy lips; but, unhappily, the women hide their faces and run away from a stranger, while the men rub him with their bristly beards. At first I went at it with a stout heart, flattering myself that I could give as well as take; but I soon flinched and gave up. Their beards were the growth of years, while mine had only a few months to boast of, and its downward aspirations must continue many a long day before it would attain the respectable longitude of theirs.

During the kissing scene, a Bedouin servant came from the other end of the terrace with an armful of burning brush, and threw it in a blaze upon the stony floor. The monks were gathered around, talking to me and uttering assurances of welcome, as I knew them to be, although I could not understand them; and, confused and almost stunned with their clamorous greeting, I threw myself on the floor, thrust my feet in the fire, and called out for *Paul*. Twice the rope descended and brought up my tent, baggage, &c.; and the third time it brought up Paul, hung round with guns, pistols, and swords,

179

like a traveling battery. The rope was wound up by a windlass, half a dozen monks, in long black frocks with white stripes, turning it with all their might. In the general eagerness to help, they kept on turning until they had carried Paul above the window, and brought his neck up short under the beam, his feet struggling to hold on to the sill of the door. He roared out lustily in Greek and Arabic; and while they were helping to disencumber him of his multifarious armor, he was cursing and berating them for a set of blundering workmen, who had almost broken the neck of as good a Christian as any among them. Probably, since the last incursion of the Bedouins, the peaceful walls of the convent had not been disturbed by such an infernal clatter.

The monks had been roused from sleep, and some of them were hardly yet awake; the superior was the last who came, and his presence quickly restored order. He was a remarkably noble-looking old man, of more than sixty. He asked me my country, and called me his child, and told me that God would reward me for coming from so distant a land to do homage on the holy mountain; and I did not deny the character he ascribed to me, or correct his mistake in supposing that the motive of my journey was purely religious; and, looking upon me as a devout pilgrim, he led me through a long range of winding passages, which seemed like the streets of a city, into a small room spread with mats, having a pile of coverlets in one corner, and wearing an appearance of comfort that could be fully appreciated by one who had then spent ten nights in the desert. I threw myself on the mats with a feeling of gratitude, while the superior renewed his welcome, telling me that the convent was the pilgrim's home, and that everything it contained was mine for a week, a month, or the rest of my days. Nor did he neglect my immediate wants, but, with all the warmth and earnestness of a man who could feel for others' woes in so important a matter as eating, expressed his regret that meat was always a forbidden thing within the walls of the convent, and that now, during their forty days of fasting even fish and eggs were proscribed. I told him that I was an invalid, and wanted only the plainest and simplest viands, but insinuated that speed was of more importance than richness of fare, having eaten only a biscuit and an orange since morning. The cook of the convent, however, a lay brother in his novitiate, was not used to do things in a hurry, and before he was ready I felt myself goaded by the fiend of famine; and when he came with a platter of beans and a smoking pilaf of rice, I made such an attack upon them as made the good superior stare with wonder and admiration; and I have no doubt that, before I had done, he must have thought a few more such invalids would bring him and the whole brotherhood to actual starvation.

The superior was a Greek by birth, and though it was forty years since he had first come to the convent at Sinai, and twenty years since he entered it for the last time, he was still a Greek in heart. His relations with his native land were kept up by the occasional visits of pilgrims. He had heard of their bloody struggle for liberty, and of what America had done for her in her hour of need,[3] and he told me that, next to his own country, he loved mine; and by his kindness to me as an individual, he sought to repay, in part, his country's debt of gratitude. In my wanderings in Greece, I had invariably found the warmest feeling towards my country. I had found it in the offices of government, in my boatmen, my muleteer, and I remember a ploughman on immortal Marathon sang in my greedy ears the praises of America. I had seen the tear stream down the manly cheeks of a mustached Greek when he talked of America. I had seen those who had received directly from the hands of my countrymen the bounty that came from home. One, I remember, pointed me to a family of sons and daughters who, he told me, were saved from absolute starvation by our timely help; and so dearly was our country loved there, that I verily believe the mountain robber would have spared the unprotected American.

I knew that this feeling existed in Greece, but I did not expect to find it thus glowing in the wilderness of Sinai. For myself, different

[3] The Greeks rose in 1821 against the Turks, their masters. This war, without rules, went on for eight years and attracted widespread sympathy. Under the name of "Philhellenes" volunteers flocked to Greece—Napoleonic veterans, students, Russian mystics, Englishmen, and a scattering of Americans. No struggle, save its own, had so aroused America. Huge sums of money were raised in the United States for Greek independence.

in this respect from most other travelers, I liked the Greeks. Travelers and strangers condemn the whole people as dishonest, because they are cheated by their boatmen or muleteers, without ever thinking of their four centuries of bitter servitude; but when I remembered their long oppression and galling chains, instead of wondering that they were so bad, I wondered that they were not worse. I like the Greeks; and when I talked of Greece and what I had seen there, of the Bavarians lording it over the descendants of Cimon and Miltiades, the face of the superior flushed and his eyes flashed fire; and when I spoke of the deep interest their sufferings and their glorious struggle had created in America, the old man wept. Oh, who can measure the feeling that binds a man to his native land! Though forty years an exile, buried in the wilderness, and neither expecting nor wishing to revisit the world, he loved his country as if his foot now pressed her soil, and under his monkish robe there glowed a heart as patriotic as ever beat beneath a soldier's corslet. The reader will excuse an unusual touch of sensibility in me when he reflects upon my singular position, sitting at the base of Mount Sinai, and hearing from the lips of a white-bearded Greek the praises of my beloved country. He sat with me till the ringing of the midnight bell for prayers, when I threw myself upon the mat, and, before the hollow sounds had died away in the cloisters, I was fast asleep.

CHAPTER XVI

T HE NEXT DAY was one of the most interesting of my life. At eight o'clock I was breakfasting; the superior was again at my side; again offering me all the convent could give, and urging me to stay a month, a fortnight, a week, at least spend that day with him, and repose myself after the fatigues of my journey; but from the door of the little room in which I sat I saw the holy mountain, and I longed to stand on its lofty summit. Though feeble and far from well, I felt the blood of health again coursing in my veins, and congratulated myself that I was not so hackneyed in feeling as I had once supposed. I found, and I was happy to find, for the prospective enjoyment of my farther journey, that the first tangible monument in the history of the Bible, the first spot that could be called holy ground, raised in me feelings that had not been awakened by the most classic ground of Italy and Greece, or the proudest monuments of the arts in Egypt.

Immediately after breakfast I rose to ascend the mountain. The superior conducted me through the convent, which, even more than at night, seemed like a small city, through long galleries built of stone, with iron doors, and finally through a long subterraneous passage to the other garden, a beautiful spot in the midst of the surrounding barrenness, now blooming with almonds and oranges, lemons, dates, and apricots, and shaded by arbors of grape-vines to the extreme end of the walls. At this moment I gave but a passing glance at the garden; and hurrying on to the walls, where a trusty Arab was sitting as sentinel, I descended by a rope, the superior, or papa, as he is called, bidding me farewell, and telling me not to

183

fatigue myself or be long away. At the foot of the wall I found
Toualeb waiting orders for my final departure. He said that he must
consult with his tribe before he could make any bargain; and I told
him to come to the convent in two days, prepared to start upon
the third.

Immediately behind the wall of the convent we began to ascend.
A Bedouin dwarf, the first specimen of deformity I had seen among
the Arabs, led the way, with a leather bag of refreshments on his
back. An old monk followed, with long white hair and beard, supporting himself by a staff; after him came a young novice from
Corfu, who spoke Italian, and then Paul and myself. For some time
the ascent was easy. Ever since the establishment of the convent, it
had been the business of the monks to improve the path to the top
of the mountain; and for about twenty minutes we continued
ascending by regular steps. In half an hour we came to a beautiful
fountain under an overhanging rock. Besides the hallowed localities
in and around the mountain, consecrated by scenes of Bible history,
almost every spot has some monkish legend, of which that connected with the fountain is a specimen. Taking a long draught from
its stony bed, our younger companion began the story somewhat in
the usual Eastern form. "Once there was a poor shoemaker" who,
in making his pilgrimage to the holy mountain, on a hot day, sat
down under the shade of the impending rock. He was an industrious
man, and, while resting himself, took out his cobbling materials,
and began to cobble; he was a good man, and while he sat there at
his work, he thought of the wickedness of the world and its temptations, and how the devil was always roaming about after poor cob-
blers, and resolved to leave the world forever, and live under that
rock. There was no water near it then; but, as soon as he had made
this resolution, the water gushed forth, and a living fountain has
remained there ever since. The same year there was a dispute between the Greek and Armenian patriarchs at Cairo, and the pasha
gave notice that he would decide in favor of him who should perform
a miracle. This was more than either had power to do; but the Greek
dreamed one night of the poor cobbler, and the next morning des-
patched a messenger to the mountain with a dromedary, and a

request that the holy man should come and perform a miracle. The cobbler was a modest man, and said he would be glad to make a pair of shoes for the patriarch, but could not perform a miracle. The messenger, however, insisted upon taking him to Cairo, where, roused into a belief of his own powers, he ordered a mountain to approach the city. The obedient mountain marched till it was told to stop, and there it stands to the present day.

In half an hour more we came to a little chapel dedicated to the Virgin, to which, some two or three hundred years ago, certain holy men, who wished to separate themselves more completely from the world, had withdrawn from the convent, and here lived and died upon the mountain. The chapel had been fitted up several times, but the Bedouins had always entered and destroyed everything it contained. The situation was well suited for retirement; quiet and isolated, but not dreary, and fitted for a calm and contemplative spirit. Paul was particularly struck with it; and, in a moment of enthusiasm, said he would like to end his days there; and, with his characteristic prudence, asked if he could get his meals from the convent. The monk did not approve his enthusiasm, and told him that his inspiration was of the devil and not of God, but suddenly said that there were no hermits now; that all men thought too much of eating and drinking, and indulging in luxuries; sighed, kissed the cross, asked Paul for a cigar, and then walked on again. Passing through a defile of precipitous rocks, we soon reached a gate about three feet wide, where formerly, when pilgrimages to this place were more frequent, a guard was stationed, to whom it was necessary to show a permission from the superior of the convent. A little beyond this was another narrow passage secured by a door, where it was formerly necessary to show a pass from the keeper of the gate, and where a dozen men could make a good defense against a thousand. Soon after we entered a large open space, forming a valley surrounded on all sides by mountains; and on the left, high above the others, rose the lofty peak of Sinai. It is this part of the mountain which bears the sacred name of Horeb. In the center, enclosed by a stone fence, is a tall cypress, the only tree on the mountain, planted by the monks more than a hundred

185

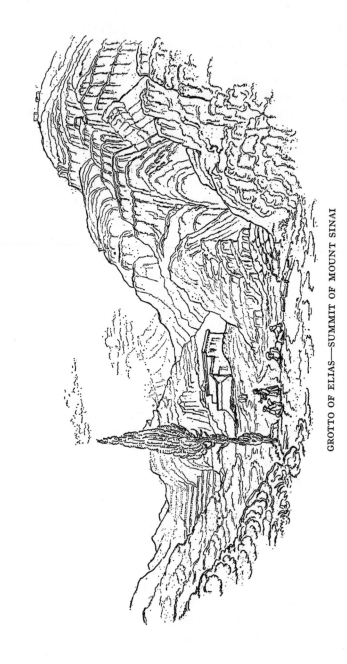

GROTTO OF ELIAS—SUMMIT OF MOUNT SINAI

years ago. Near it is a fountain, called the fountain of Elias, which the prophet dug with his own hands when he lived in the mountain, before he was ordered by the Lord to Jerusalem. According to the monks, the prophet is still living somewhere in the world, wandering about with Enoch, and preparing for the great final battle with Antichrist. A little above is an old church, with strong walls and iron doors, now falling and dilapidated, and containing a grotto, called the grotto of Elias, which, according to the legend, formed the prophet's sleeping chamber. I crawled into the rocky cell, and, thanks to my traveling experience, which had taught me not to be fastidious in such matters, found the bedroom of the prophet by no means an uncomfortable place; often in the desert I would have been thankful for such a shelter.

Here our dwarf left us, and continuing our ascent, the old monk still leading the way, in about a quarter of an hour came to a table of rock standing boldly out, and running down almost perpendicularly an immense distance to the valley. I was expecting another monkish legend, and my very heart thrilled when the monk told me that this was the top of the hill on which Moses had sat during the battle of the Israelites and the Amalekites, while Aaron and Hur supported his uplifted hands, until the sun went down upon the victorious arms of his people. From the height I could see, clearly and distinctly, every part of the battle-ground, and the whole vale of Rephidim and the mountains beyond; and Moses, while on this spot, must have been visible to the contending armies from every part of the field on which they were engaged.

Some distance farther on the old monk stopped, and, prostrating himself before a stone, kissed it devoutly, and then told me its history. He said that the last time the monks in the convent were beset by the Arabs, when their communication with Cairo was cut off, and death by the sword or famine staring them in the face, the superior proposed that they should put on their holiest vestments, and, under the sacred banner of the cross, ascend in a body, and for the last time sing their Te Deum on the top of the mountain. On their return, at this stone they met a woman with a child, who told them that all their danger was over; and, in accordance with her words, when they returned to the convent they found the Arabs gone, and forty camels from Cairo laden with provisions standing under the walls. Since that time they had never been molested by the Arabs, "and there is no doubt," continued the old monk, "that the woman was the mother of God, and the child the Saviour of the world."

But away with monkish superstition. I stand upon the very peak of Sinai, where Moses stood when he talked with the Almighty. Can it be, or is it a mere dream? Can this naked rock have been the witness of that great interview between man and his Maker? where, amid thunder and lightning, and a fearful quaking of the mountains, the Almighty gave to his chosen people the precious tables of his law, those rules of infinite wisdom and goodness, which, to this day, best teach man his duty towards his God, his neighbor, and himself?

The scenes of many of the incidents recorded in the Bible are extremely uncertain. Historians and geographers place the garden of Eden, the paradise of our first parents, in different parts of Asia; and they do not agree upon the site of the tower of Babel, the mountain of Ararat, and many of the most interesting places in the Holy Land; but of Sinai there is no doubt. This is the holy mountain; and, among all the stupendous works of Nature, not a place can be selected more fitted for the exhibition of Almighty power. I have stood upon the summit of the giant Etna, and looked over the clouds floating beneath it, upon the bold scenery of Sicily, and the distant mountains of Calabria; upon the top of Vesuvius, and looked down upon the waves of lava, and the ruined and half-recovered cities at its foot; but they are nothing compared with the terrific solitudes and bleak majesty of Sinai. An observing traveler has well called it "a perfect sea of desolation." Not a tree, or shrub, or blade of grass is to be seen upon the bare and rugged sides of innumerable mountains, heaving their naked summits to the skies, while the crumbling masses of granite around, and the distant view of the Syrian desert, with its boundless waste of sands, form the wildest and most dreary, the most terrific and desolate picture that imagination can conceive.

The level surface of the very top, or pinnacle, is about sixty feet square. At one end is a single rock about twenty feet high, on which, as said the monk, the spirit of God descended, while in the crevice beneath his favored servant received the tables of the law. There, on the same spot where they were given, I opened the sacred book in which those laws are recorded, and read them with a deeper feeling of devotion, as if I were standing nearer and receiving them more directly from the Deity himself.

The ruins of a church and convent are still to be seen upon the mountain, to which, before the convent below was built, monks and hermits used to retire, and, secluded from the world, sing the praises of God upon his chosen hill. Near this, also in ruins, stands a Mohammedan mosque; for on this sacred spot the followers of Christ and Mohammed have united in worshipping the true and living God. Under the chapel is a hermit's cell, where, in the iron age of fanaticism, the anchorite lingered out his days in fasting, meditation, and prayer.

In the East, the fruitful parent of superstition, occurred the first instances of monastic life. A single enthusiast withdrew himself from the society of his fellow-men, and wandered for years among the rocks and sands of the desert, devoting himself to the service of his Maker by the mistaken homage of bodily mortification. The deep humility of the wanderer, his purity and sincerity, and the lashes and stripes he inflicted upon his worn and haggard body excited the warm imaginations of the Christians of the East. Others, tortured by the same overpowering consciousness of sin, followed his example, emulating each other in self-punishment; and he was accounted the most holy, and the most worthy to be received at the right hand of God, who showed himself most dead to all the natural feeling of humanity. The deserts of the Thebaid were soon covered with hermits; and more than seventy thousand anchorites were wasting their lives in the gloomy wilds of Sinai, startling the solitude with the cries of their self-inflicted torture. The ruins of their convents are still to be seen upon the rudest mountain-side, in the most savage chasm, or upon the craggiest top; and, strange as the feeling may seem, my very soul cleaved to the scene around me. I too felt myself lifted above the world, and its petty cares and troubles, and almost hurried into the wild enthusiasm which had sent the tenants of these ruined convents to live and die among the mountains.

Blame me not, reader, nor think me impious, that, on the top of the holy mountain of Sinai, half-unconscious what I did, I fired at a partridge. The sound of my gun, ringing in frequent echoes from the broken and hollow rocks, startled and aroused me; and, chasing the bird down the mountain-side, I again reached "the place in Horeb," and threw myself on the ground under the palm-tree, near the fountain of Elias.

I always endeavored to make my noonday meal near some rock or ruin, some tree or fountain; and I could not pass by the fountain of the prophet. My Arab dwarf had anticipated my wants; and now prepared some of the genuine Mocha, which every Arabian (and an Arabian only) knows how to prepare, exhaling an aroma that refreshes and invigorates the wearied frame; and, in the desert, a cordial more precious than the finest wines of France or Madeira. Seated under the palm-tree, monks, Bedouins, Paul, and myself, all together, eating our frugal meal of bread and fruit, accompanied with long draughts from the fountain of Elias, I talked with the Bedouins about the mountain, consecrated in the eyes of all true Mussulmans by the legend of Mohammed and his camel.

In one respect I was very unlucky in this journey. I had no guide-books. Having formed no definite plan in my wanderings, I never knew with what books to provide myself, and therefore carried none, trusting to chance for finding what I wanted. As might be supposed, when I needed them most it was utterly impossible to obtain any; and from the borders of Egypt to the confines of the Holy Land I was in some measure groping in the dark; the Bible was my only guide; and though the best a man could have in his pilgrimage through life, and far better than any other in this particular journey, yet others would have been exceedingly valuable, as illustrating obscure passages in the sacred book; and particularly as referring, besides, to circumstances and traditions other than scriptural, connected with the holy mountain.

In the book of one of the modern travelers, I believe of the lamented Burckhardt, I remembered to have seen a reference to a tradition among the Mussulmans, that Mohammed had ascended the mountain on the back of his camel, and from its lofty summit had taken his departure to the seventh heaven, and that the prints of the beast's footsteps were still to be seen on the surface of the rock. I questioned the Arab about this story. In the more engrossing interest of the scene, I had forgotten to look for the prints of the camel's feet, and told him, with great truth, that I had examined everything carefully, but had not seen them. The old monk, who had sat quietly munching his bread and figs, scandalized at my inquiring into such a profane story, and considering the holy mountain in a manner his property, broke out unceremoniously, and denounced it as a wicked invention of the Arabs, averring that everybody knew that, before Mohammed got halfway up, the camel stumbled, fell, and broke the neck of the Prophet. This was equally new and monstrous to the Arab, who swore that the legend was true, for it was written in the Koran, and that he himself had often seen the print of the foot; and he accounted for my not seeing it by the very sensible and satisfactory explanation that it was visible only to the eyes of true believers. The good father was completely roused by this obstinate resistance in the scandal; and a reckless Bedouin and an old Bulgarian monk, sitting by a fountain among the deserts of Sinai, were soon disputing with as much clamor and bitterness as if they had been brought up in the midst of civilization, to harangue from opposing pulpits, the preachers of the promises and the denouncers of the curses of rival churches. One thing the pious father especially insisted on; the strong point in his argument, and particularly ludicrous, as coming from such an old bundle of superstitions, was the impossibility of a camel's foot making an impression on stone; and, judging from this alone, one might have suspected him of having had in his youth some feeble glimmerings of common sense; but a few minutes after he told me the legend of Mount St. Catherine.

Mount St. Catherine is the great rival of Sinai in the range of mountains in the Arabian peninsula. They rise like giant twin brothers, towering above every other; and the only thing which detracts in the slightest degree from the awful supremacy of Sinai, is the fact that Mount St. Catherine is somewhat the highest. The legend is, that in the early days of the Christian church, the daughter of a king of Alexandria became converted. While her father remained a pagan, she tried to convert him; but, indignant at the attempt, he cast her in prison, where she was visited by the Savior, who entered through the keyhole, and married her with a ring which is now in the hands of the Empress of Russia. Her father cut her head off, and angels carried her body to the top of the mountain and laid it on the rock. For centuries no one knew where it was deposited, the Christians believing that it had been carried up into heaven, until about two centuries ago, when a monk at the convent dreamed where it had been laid. The next morning he took his staff and climbed to the top of the mountain; and there, on the naked rock, fresh and blooming as in youthful beauty, after a death of more than a thousand years, he found the body of the saint. The monks then went up in solemn procession, and, taking up the body, bore it in pious triumph to the convent below, where it now lies in a coffin with a silver lid, near the great altar in the chapel, and receives the homage of all pious pilgrims.

It was nearly dark when I returned to the convent; and, in no small degree fatigued with the labors of the day, I again threw myself on the mat and welcomed rest. In the evening the superior came to my room, and again we mingled the names of Greece and America. I was weary, and talked with the old man when I would rather have been asleep; but with his own hands he drew mats and cushions around me, and made me so comfortable, that I could not refuse to indulge him with the rare luxury of conversation on the subject of his native land, and of the world from which he was shut out forever. He was single-hearted and simple, or, perhaps I should rather say, simple and ignorant; I remember, for instance, when we had been embarrassed for a time by the absence of the younger monk who served as our interpreter, the old man told me very gravely, and as a new thing, which I could not be expected to know, but which he did not think the less of me for not knowing, that formerly, in the time of Adam, all mankind spoke but one tongue;

and that men became wicked, and built a tower to reach heaven (he had forgotten its name), and that God had destroyed it and confounded the impious builders with a variety of tongues. I expressed my astonishment, as in duty bound, and denounced, in good set terms, the wickedness of our fathers, which now prevented us from enjoying at our ease the sweets of friendly converse.

Before breakfast the next morning he was with me again; with a striped abbas over his black gown, and a staff in his hand, prepared to accompany me outside the walls. I was surprised. He had told me that he had not left the convent for more than three years, when he had accompanied a great apostolic vicar, holding a distinguished situation in the church of France; and this was the last and only time he had ever bestowed such attention on a stranger. The kind-hearted old man intended it as an act of extraordinary kindness; I received it as such; and, as such, he told me I could mention it to my friends in America. Humble and unimportant as was that old monk in the drama of life, I felt proud of his kindness—prouder than I should have been of a reception at a European court, or a greeting from royal lips—and my pride was the greater that I did not ascribe it to any merits of my own. My only claim was that possessed by all my countrymen—I was an American; my country had heard the cry of his in her distress, and from her seat across the broad Atlantic had answered that cry.

We passed, as before, through the subterraneous passages into the garden. The miserable Bedouins who were gathered around outside, waiting for the bread which they received daily from the convent, surprised at the unexpected but welcome appearance of the superior, gathered around him and kissed his hands and the hem of his garment. He had provided himself with an extra sack of bread, which he distributed among them, and which they seemed to receive with peculiar pleasure from his hands. The monks of Mount Sinai are now no longer obliged to have recourse to carnal weapons for protection; peace reigns between them and the Bedouins; and part of the price of peace is the distribution of twenty-five hundred rolls of bread among the poor around the mountain. I did not think so much of this price when I saw the

193

bread, hard, black, and mouldy, and such as the meanest beggar in our country would not accept from the hand of charity. But the Bedouins took it, and thanked God and the monks for it.

Hurrying away from these grateful pensioners, we descended by the defile through which we had entered; and again passing the ruins of the house of Aaron, and the spot from which he preached to the assembled people, we came to a long flat stone, with a few holes indented in its surface, which the superior pointed out as that on which Moses threw down and broke the tablets of the law when he descended from the mountain and found the Israelites worshipping the golden calf. About half an hour farther on was another stone much holier than this; at first I understood from the interpreter that it was the petrifaction of the golden calf; but gathered, with some difficulty, from the superior, that it was the mold in which the head of the golden calf was run. He pointed out to me the prints of the head, ears, and horns, clear even to the eyes of a man of sixty; and told me the story of the golden calf somewhat differently from the Bible account. He said that the people, wanting another god, came up with one accord and threw their golden ornaments upon that stone, and agreed by acclamation that when it was melted they would worship whatever should come out; three times it came out the head of a calf; and then they fell down and worshipped it.

Some distance farther on we passed on our right a Hebrew burying-ground; "The burial-place," said the superior, "of the Israelites who died in their forty years wandering among the mountains of Sinai." The old man had heard these things so long, and had told them so often, and believed them so firmly, that it would have broken his heart—besides shaking his confidence in my Christian principle—if I had intimated the slightest doubt. I asked whether the Jews ever came in pilgrimage to the mountain of their fathers; and he told me that, four years ago, two Asiatic Jews had come disguised as Europeans, and attempted to pass themselves as Christians; "but," said the priest, with a vindictive spirit lighting his usually mild eye, "I detected them under their sheep's clothing, and they did not stay long in the convent." Yet I remember seeing

194

on the wall of the convent, and with no small degree of interest, the name of an American Jew.

Farther on, turning into a valley which opened between the mountains on the left, we came to a garden belonging to the convent, which presented a strange appearance in the midst of the surrounding desolation, producing all kinds of fruits; where one might almost wonder to see a blade of grass put forth, the orange, the date, the fig, and the vine are growing in rich luxuriance. The soil is formed from the debris of rocks washed from the mountains; and, though too light for strong products, for fruit it is better than the rich valley of the Nile. Sitting under the shade of the fig-tree, the superior pointed out to me a rent in the mountain opposite, which, he said, was caused by an earthquake, that had swallowed up two friends and servants of Moses of whom I had never heard before, and who were so swallowed up for disobeying the orders of their earthly master.

The superior, unused to such a task as he had imposed upon himself, here completely gave out, and I left him panting under the shade of his fig-tree, while I went on to the valley of Rephidim; and, passing another garden, came to the rock of Horeb, the stone which Moses struck with his rod, and caused the waters to gush out. The stone is about twelve feet high, and on one side are eight or ten deep gashes from one to three feet long, and from one to two inches wide, some of which were trickling with water. These gashes are singular in their appearance, though probably showing only the natural effect of time and exposure. They look something like the gashes in the bark of a growing tree, except that, instead of the lips of the gash swelling and growing over, they are worn and reduced to a polished smoothness. They are, no doubt, the work of men's hands, a clumsy artifice of the early monks to touch the hearts of pious pilgrims; but the monks of the convent, and the Greek pilgrims who go there now, believe in it with as much honesty and sincerity as in the crucifixion.

Will the reader forgive me if I say that this rock had in my eyes an interest scarcely less than that which the rod of Moses gave it? Three names were written on it: one of a German, the second of an

Englishman, and the third of my early friend [Cornelius Bradford], the same which I had seen above the Cataracts of the Nile. When, a few years since, he bade me farewell in my native city, little did I think that I afterward should trace him beyond the borders of Egypt, and through the wilderness of Sinai, to his grave in Jerusalem.

Again I wrote my name under his,[1] and, returning by the way I came, found the superior still sitting under the fig-tree, and, moving on, we soon reached the convent. He hurried away to his official duties, and I retired to my room. I stayed there three or four hours, poring over the scriptural account of the scenes that hallowed the wilderness of Sinai with an attention that no sound disturbed. Indeed, the stillness of the convent was at all times most extraordinary; day or night not a sound was to be heard but the tolling of the bell for prayers, or occasionally the soft step of a monk stealing through the cloisters.

In the afternoon I lounged around the interior of the convent. The walls form an irregular quadrangle, of about 130 paces on each side, and, as I before remarked, it has the appearance of a small city. The building was erected by the Empress Helena, the mother of the first Christian emperor, and I might almost call her the mother of the Holy Land. Her pious heart sent her, with the same spirit which afterward animated the crusaders, to search out the holy places referred to in the Bible; and when she found one, she erected a monument to mark it for the guidance of future Christians; and the pilgrim may see the fruits of her pious labors from the mountain where God spake in thunder down to the place where the cock crew when Peter denied his master. The convent is capable of containing several hundred people. It was originally built as a place of defense; but the necessity of keeping it fortified has passed away; a parcel of rusty guns are lying in a sort of armory, and a few small cannon are frowning from the walls. The cells of the monks, compared with anything else I had seen in the East, are exceedingly comfortable; on one side, raised about a foot from the

---

[1] Stephens' name has been all but buried under other names and dates on the stone, the last part only being still visible.

floor, is a stone platform, on which the monk spreads his mat and coverlet, and the furniture includes a table, chairs, sometimes two or three books, and the fragment of a looking-glass. There are twenty-four chapels erected to different saints, in which prayers are said regularly in rotation. I went through them, but saw nothing to interest me until I came to the church of the convent. Here I was surprised to find the handsomest Greek church I had seen, except in Russia; the floor and steps were of marble; and distributed around in various places were pillars and columns, the works of ancient artists, plundered from heathen temples, and sent to this lonely spot in the desert by the active piety of the early Christian emperors.

The convent was raised in honor of the transfiguration, and the dome of the altar contains a coarse but antique painting of the holy scene. In front, near the great altar, in a coffin covered with rich palls and a silver lid, are the bones of St. Catharine, the patroness of the convent. Among the chapels, one, I remember, is dedicated to Constantine and Helena, and another to Justinian and his wife; but the great object of interest is the holy of holies, the spot where God appeared to Moses in the burning bush. A chapel is now erected over it, and the pilgrim, on entering, hears at this day almost the same words which God addressed to Moses, "Put thy shoes from thy feet, for the ground whereon thou treadest is holy ground." I pulled off my shoes and followed my conductor. The place is now bedizened with Grecian ornaments; the rude simplicity of nature which beheld the interview between God and his servant is utterly gone, and the burning bush is the last thing one would think of on the spot where it grew.

There are but few objects of interest besides. In one of the chapels are a copy of the Evangelists, written in letters of gold by the Emperor Theodosius, and portraits of the four evangelists and the twelve apostles, and all the psalms of David, written in an inconceivably small space by a young virgin who came out and died in the desert.

The condition and character of the monks formed a subject of no little interest for my speculating observation, and I investigated their habits and dispositions as closely as bienséance and my inability for conversing with them, except through an interpreter, would permit. So far as I could judge, they seemed perfectly contented; but they were, for the most part, mere drones and sluggards, doing little good for themselves or others, and living idly upon the misapplied bounty of Christian pilgrims. I do not mean to say that they were bad men. Most of them were too simple to be bad; and, if there was evil in their nature, they had no temptation to do evil; and, after all, the mere negative goodness which does no harm is not to be lightly spoken of, in a world so full of restlessness and mischief as this of ours. Many of them had been a long time in the convent, some as much as twenty or thirty years, and one, who was now 105 years old, had been seventy-five years worshipping the Lord, after his fashion, at the foot of Sinai. Among them were a baker, shoemaker, and tailor; they baked, cooked, made and mended for themselves, and had but one other duty to perform, and that was four times daily to kneel down and pray. Nothing could be more dull and monotonous than their lives, and none but the most sluggish or the most philosophic spirit could endure it. They were philosophers without knowing it, and dozed away their existence in one unvarying round of prayer, and meals, and sleep.

Their discipline was not rigid, save in one particular, and that a matter in regard to which there has been much discussion with us; they never ate meat; no animal food of any kind is permitted to enter the walls of the convent. During all the various periods of their abode in the convent, some thirty, some forty, and one more than seventy-five years, not one of them had eaten a particle of animal food; and yet I never saw more healthy-looking men. Hardier men I have seen, for they are indolent in their habits, take but little exercise, and in most cases show a strong disposition to corpulency; but I had some little opportunity of testing their ability to endure fatigue; and, though the superior soon walked himself out of breath, the monk who guided us up the mountain, and who was more than sixty years old, when he descended, after a hard day's labor, seemed less tired than either Paul or myself. I am aware that climate may make a difference; but, from my own observation and experience, I am perfectly satisfied that, even in our climate, invalids and persons of sedentary habits, and, indeed, all except laboring men, would be much benefited by a total abstinence from animal food. I have traveled for a week at a time, night and day, not under the mild sky of the East, but in the rough climate of Russia, and found myself perfectly able to endure the fatigue upon bread and milk diet; and I have been told that the Tartars who ride post from Constantinople to Baghdad in an incredibly short time, never sleeping, except on horseback, during the whole of their immense journey rigidly abstain from anything more solid and nutritious than eggs.

The night of my return from the top of Sinai, I was awake when the bell tolled for midnight prayers; and, wrapping myself in my Arab cloak, took a small lamp in my hand, and, groping my way along the passage, descended to the chapel, where the monks were all assembled. I leaned behind a protecting pillar and watched their proceedings; and it was an event of no common interest, thus, at the dead hour of night, to be an unobserved witness of their sincerity, and earnest though erroneous devotion. There was not one among them who did not believe he was doing God good service, and that his works would find acceptance at the throne of Grace, and obtain for him that blessed immortality which we are all seeking.

CHAPTER XVII

T HE NEXT DAY was Sunday, and early in the morning the superior sent for me to come down and take my meal with the holy brotherhood. The monks were all at the table, and it was the first time I had had so good an opportunity of seeing them together. They were about thirty in number, mostly old men with long white beards, all Greeks, and some with faces as noble as Grecian chisel ever traced. There was not a beard at table less than eight inches long; and my own, though it would have been rather distingué at home, blushed more than its natural red at its comparative insignificance. The table was a long naked board; the vessels were all of metal, and before each man were a wooden spoon, and a drinking-cup in the form of a porringer. It was Lent, the season of forty or fifty days' fasting, during which even fish, eggs, and oil are prohibited. A large basin of boiled beans was set before each of the monks; and, besides this, there were black olives, beans in water, salad, vinegar, salt, dates, and bread. My companions had never been pampered with luxuries, and ate their bread and beans with as keen a relish as if they were feasting on turtle and venison, and drank their water as freely as though it was Tokay or Burgundy. The meal was eaten in silence, all appearing of opinion that they came simply to eat; and the only unusual circumstance I remarked was the civility of my immediate neighbors in pushing the tempting viands before me. It was curious to see how they found the way to their mouths through such a wilderness of beard, and the spoon disappearing in a huge red opening, leaving the handle projecting from a bush of hair. The room in which we ate was perhaps sixty feet long, having at one end a chapel and altar, and a reading-desk close by, in which, during the whole of the meal, a monk was reading aloud from the lives of the saints.

After dinner the monks all rose, and, wiping their mouths, walked in a body to the foot of the altar, and two of them commenced burning incense. One of my neighbors took me by the hand, and led me up with them. There they kneeled, prayed, and chanted, and went through a long routine of ceremonies, in which, so far as it was practicable, they carried me with them. They could not get me up and down as fast as they moved themselves, but they flung the incense at me as hard as at the worthiest of them all. I supposed this to be a sort of grace after meat, and that there it would end; but, to my surprise and great regret, I found that this was merely preparatory to the administration of the sacrament. It was the second time I had been placed in the same situation; and a second time, and even more earnestly than before, I wished for that state of heart which, according to the notions of its solemnity in which I had been brought up, would have permitted me to join in the sacred rite. I refused the consecrated bread, and the monk, after pausing some moments, apparently in astonishment, passed on to the next. After he had completed the circle, the superior crossed and brought him back again to me; I could not wound the feelings of the good old man, and ate the consecrated bread and drank the wine. May God forgive me if I did wrong; but, though rigid censors may condemn, I cannot believe that I incurred the sin of "the unworthy partaker" by yielding to the benevolent importunity of the kind old priest. After this we walked out on the terrace, under the shade of some venerable grape-vines, and, sitting down along the wall, took coffee. The reading-desk was brought out, and the same monk continued reading for more than two hours.

I had noticed that monk before; for he was the same who had conducted me through the church, had visited me in my room, and I had seen him in his cell. He was not more than thirty-five, and his face was as perfect as art could make it; and the sunbeams occasionally glancing through the thick foliage of the vines, and lighting up his pale and chiseled features and long black beard, made him one of those perfect figures for a sketch which I had often dreamed of, but had never seen. His face was thin, pale, and emaciated; the excitement of reading gave it a hectic flush, and he looked like a man who, almost before the springtime of life was over, had drained the cup of bitterness to its dregs. If I am not deceived, he had not always led so peaceful and innocent a life, and could unfold a tale of stirring incident, of wild and high excitement, and perhaps of crime. He was from the Island of Tinos, but spoke Italian, and I had talked with him of the islands of Greece, and the ports in the Mediterranean and the Black Sea, with many of which he seemed familiar; and then he spoke of the snares and temptations of the world, and his freedom from them in the convent, and, above all, of the perils to which men are exposed by the wiles and witcheries of the sex; and I could not but imagine that some beautiful Grecian girl, not less false than fair, had driven him to the wilderness. One of the other monks told me that it was about the time when the last of the pirates were swept from the Mediterranean that the young islander had buried himself in the walls of the convent. They told me, too, that he was rich, and would give all he had to the fraternity. Poor fellow! they will soon come into possession.

In the garden of the convent is the cemetery of the monks. Though not of a particularly melancholy humor, I am in a small way given to meditation among the tombs; and, in many of the countries I have visited, the burial-places of the dead have been the most interesting objects of examination. The superior had promised to show me his graves; and something in the look of the reader reminding me of death and burial, I now told the old man of his promise, and he hobbled off to get the key; for it appeared that the cemetery was not to be visited without his special permission. At the end of a long arbor of grape-vines, a narrow staircase cut in the rock, which I had not seen before, led down to an excavated square of about twenty feet; on the left of which was a small door opening into a vault, where formerly the bodies of the dead monks were laid on an iron bedstead, and there suffered to remain until all the corruptible part was gone, and only the dry bones remained. Now they are buried for about three years, or as long as may be necessary to

INTERIOR OF THE CONVENT

ARABS OF THE DESERT

effect the same object; and, when the flesh and muscles have disappeared, the bones are deposited in the great cemetery, the door of which is directly opposite. Within the door is a small antechamber, containing a divan and a portrait of some saint who wandered eighteen years in the desert without meat or drink. From this the door opens into the cemetery, which was so different from any I had ever seen, that I started back on the threshold with surprise. Along the wall was an excavation about thirty feet in length, but of what depth I could not tell. It was enclosed by a fence, which was three or four feet above the ground, and filled with human skulls; and in front, extending along the whole width of the chamber, was a pile of bones about twenty feet high, and running back I could not tell how far. They were very regularly disposed in layers, the feet and shoulders being placed outward alternately, and by the side of the last skeleton was a vacant place for the next that should be ready.

I had seen thousands of Egyptian mummies, and the catacombs of Kiev, the holy city of Russia, where the bodies of the saints are laid in rows, in open coffins, clothed in their best apparel, and adorned with gold and jewels; and in that extraordinary burial-place I had seen, too, a range of small glasses in a dead stone wall, where wild and desperate fanatics had made their own tombs, with their own hands building themselves in an upright position against the walls, leaving a small hole open in front by which to receive their bread and water; and when they died, the small opening was closed with a piece of glass, and the body of the saint was left thus buried. I had seen the catacombs of the Capuchin convent at Syracuse, where the bodies of the monks are dried and laid in open coffins, or fixed in niches in the walls, with their names labeled on their breasts; and in the vault of the convent at Palermo I had seen the bodies of nobles and ladies, the men arranged upright along the walls, dressed as in life, with canes in their hands and swords by their sides; and the noble ladies of Palermo lying in state, their withered bodies clothed in silks and satins, and adorned with gold and jewels; and I remember one among them, who, if then living, would have been but twenty, who two years before had shone in the bright constellation of Sicilian beauty, and, lovely as a light from heaven, had led the dance in the royal palace; I saw her in the same white dress which she had worn at the ball, complete even to the white slippers, the belt around her waist, and the jeweled mockery of a watch hanging at her side, as if she had not done with time forever; her face was bare, the skin dry, black, and shriveled, like burnt paper; the cheeks sunken; the rosy lips a piece of discolored parchment; the teeth horribly projecting; the nose gone; a wreath of roses around her head; and a long tress of hair curling in each hollow eye.

I had seen these things, and even these did not strike me so powerfully as the charnel-house at the convent of Mount Sinai. There was something peculiarly and terribly revolting in this promiscuous heaping together of mortal relics; bones upon bones; the old and young; wise men and fools; good men and bad; martyrs and murderers; masters and servants; bold, daring, and ambitious men—men who would have plucked bright honor from the moon, lying pell-mell with cowards and knaves. The superior told me that there were more than thirty thousand skeletons in the cemetery— literally an army of dead men's bones. Besides the pile of skulls and bones, in a chamber adjoining were the bones of the archbishops, in open boxes, with their names and ages labeled on them, and those of two sons of a king of Persia, who came hither on pilgrimage and died in the convent; their iron shirts, the only dress they wore on their long journey from their father's court, are in the same box. Other skeletons were lying about, some in baskets, and some arranged on shelves, and others tied together and hanging from the roof. In one corner were the bones of St. Stephen—not the martyr who was stoned to death at Jerusalem, but some pious anchorite of later and less authentic canonization.

As to the effect upon the mind of such burial-places as this, or the catacombs to which I have referred, I can say from my own experience that they destroy altogether the feeling of solemnity with which we look upon the grave. I remember once, in walking through long rows of dead, arranged like statues in niches of the wall, I remarked to the friar who accompanied me that he promenaded every day among his old acquaintances; and he stopped and opened a box, and took out piecemeal the bones of one who, he said, had been his closest friend, and laughed as he pulled them about, and told me of the fun and jokes they two had together.

Returning to the convent, and passing through the great chapel on the way to my room, I met one who, in the natural course of things, must soon be borne to the charnel-house I had just left. It was the aged monk of whom I have before spoken; he whose years exceeded by thirty-five the seventy allotted to man. I had desired an opportunity of speaking with him, and was curious to know the workings of his mind. The superior had told me that he had out-lived every feeling and affection; that he spent all his time in prayer, and had happily arrived at a new and perfect state of inno-cence; and I remember, that after comparing him to the lamb, and every other emblem of purity, the good superior ended, with a sim-plicity that showed his own wonderful ignorance of human nature, by declaring that the old monk was as innocent as a young girl. It occurred to me that this might be a dubious comparison; but as I knew that the monastic life of the old eulogist, and his long seclusion from the world, had prevented him from acquiring any very accu-rate knowledge of young girls, I understood him to mean the per-fection of innocence.

I looked upon the old monk with exceeding interest, as a vener-able relic of the past. For more than seventy-five years he had wandered around the holy mountain, prostrating himself daily at the foot of the altar, and, with three generations of men, had sung the praises of God under the hallowed peak of Sinai. I approached him, and told him my pleasure in knowing so old and holy a man, and the wonder with which his story would be heard in my own far-distant country. But the old man listened with impatience. The other monks were rather pleased when I stopped to talk with them, but he seemed anxious to get away, and stood, as I supposed, with his hand on his heart, as if pleading some religious duty as an excuse for his haste; but it turned out that he was merely complaining of the emptiness of his stomach, and was hungering for his evening meal. I was sorry to have the interesting picture I had conceived of this monkish Methuselah marred and effaced by so matter-of-fact an incident; but I describe him as I found him, not as I would have wished him to be.

Ever since I had left Cairo I had been troubled with misgivings touching my ability to undertake the journey by Petra. I had hoped to recruit during my few days' residence at the convent, but I was obliged to acknowledge to myself that I was, to say the least, no better. The route through Idumea was difficult and dangerous, requiring all the energy of mind and body that perfect health could give; and a wrong movement from the point where I now was might place me in a position in which the loudest cry of distress could never be heard. It is not necessary to inflict upon the reader all my hesitations; it is enough to say, that with one of the strongest efforts of resolution I was ever called upon to make, I abandoned my cherished project of visiting Petra and the land of Idumea; and, with a heavy heart, wrote to Mr. Gliddon that I was a broken reed, and was bound on the safe and direct road to Gaza. My kind friend the superior would not hear of my leaving the convent; but I resisted his importunities, and laughingly told him I did not like that unchristian way of burial, cutting up and piling away a man's bones like sticks of firewood to dry. Finding me resolved, he took me to his room, and gave me from his little store of treasures some shells and petrifications (which I threw away when out of sight), engravings of Mount Sinai, and incidents of which it has been the scene, the rudest and most uncouth conceptions that ever were imagined, and a small box of manna, the same, as he religiously believed, which fed the Israelites during their sojourn in the wilderness. He gave me, too, a long letter, written in modern Greek, and directed to the governor of Gaza, certifying that I was a pilgrim from America; that I had performed all the duties of the pilgrim age, and was now traveling to the holy city of Jerusalem. The letter contained, also, a warm and earnest recommendation to all the Greek convents in the Holy Land to receive and comfort, feed and clothe, and help and succor me in case of need. Last of all, he put on my finger a ring of the simplest form and substance, and worthy to accompany the palmer's staff of an older age. Every pilgrim to Mount Sinai receives one of these rings; and, like the green turban of the Mussul-

207

man, which distinguishes the devout hadji who has been to Mecca, among the Christians of the East it is the honored token of a complete and perfect pilgrimage.

At eight o'clock in the morning the whole convent was in commotion, preparing for my departure. My old Bedouin guide had been out among his tribe, and arrived the night before with three times as many men and camels as I wanted, ready to conduct me to Aqaba or Gaza. I took my leave of the holy brotherhood, who now sped me on my way as kindly and warmly as they had welcomed me on my arrival; and, after a long and most affectionate parting with the good old superior,[1] who told me that in all probability he should never see me again, but should always remember me, and begged me not to forget him—assuring me that there in the desert I always had a home, and telling me that if, when I returned to my own country, misfortune should press upon me, and I should find my kindred gone and friends standing aloof, I must shake the dust from off my feet, and come back and live with him in the wilderness—I fastened the rope around me, and was let down for the last time to the foot of the convent-wall. A group of Bedouins, beggars, and dependents upon the charity of the convent gathered around, and invoked blessings upon me as I started. Twice since my arrival

---

[1] In 1839, Stephens sent the "President Neofite," Prior of the Holy Brotherhood of the Fathers at the Convent of Mount Sinai, copies of *Arabia Petraea* and other gifts. His acknowledgment, preserved in the J. L. Stephens Papers of the Bancroft Library, reads as follows in translation:

To the most honored etc. etc. John Stephens, in the American City of New York.

With the greatest pleasure and satisfaction we have received your most honored letter, sent us through our good friend Mr. Geo. K. Gliddon, the American consul, together with two books, a spyglass, all sent by you. These were received by us with the greatest pleasure, while we thank you exceedingly for the gift, as well as for your recollection of us—particularly for the friendly eulogiums you make to us, and to the Convent of St. Catharine. We do not merit these praises, never having done anything for your worship, in comparison with the merits of your person; and this proceeds therefore from your goodness, and we return you our thanks for your kind memory. We cannot reciprocate any of the kind expressions or honors you make to us, beyond praying to God and to St. Catharine to give you a long life, and every blessing, which could be desired, as well to yourself, as to your family. With every respect we salute you.

From Mount Sinai, March 22, 1839 (old style)

The President Neofite and the Holy Brotherhood of the Fathers at the Convent of Mount Sinai.

there had been rain. In that dry and thirsty desert, every drop of water falls upon the earth like precious ointment, and "welcome," says the Arab, "is the stranger who brings us rain."

I turned my back upon the rising sun, and felt by comparison on my homeward way; but a long journey was still before me; I had still to cross "the great and terrible desert" of the Bible, which spread before the wandering Israelites its dreary and eternal sands, from the base of Sinai to the Promised Land.

CHAPTER XVIII

MY CARAVAN consisted of five camels, four Arabs, Paul, and myself.[1] We moved silently down the valley, and I tried hard to fasten my thoughts upon Gaza, the strong city of the Philistines, the city of Delilah and Samson, and to amuse my discontented spirit with imagining the gates which he carried away, and the temple which he pulled down; but it would not do; Petra, the rock of Edom, the excavated city, was uppermost in my mind. We had been marching in perfect silence about four hours, and I was sitting carelessly on my dromedary, thinking of everything but what I saw, when Toualeb pointed to a narrow opening in the mountain as the road to Aqaba. I raised my head unconsciously, and it struck me, all of a sudden, that I was perfectly recovered, and fit for any journey. It was a day such as can only be seen in the mountainous desert of Arabia, presenting a clearness and purity in the atmosphere, and a gentle freshness in the air, which might almost bring to life a dying man. I stretched myself and brandished my Nubian club; my arm seemed nerved with uncommon vigor; I rose in my saddle strong as the slayer of the Philistines, and, turning the head of my dromedary towards the opening in the mountains, called out briefly and decidedly, to "Aqaba and Petra."

Paul was astonished; he took the pipe from his mouth, and for a moment paused; then knocking out the ashes, he slipped from his dromedary and ran up to the side of mine, looking up in my face with an expression of countenance that seemed to intimate strong suspicions of my sanity. After gazing at me as steadfastly as he

[1] This chapter is chapter I of volume II in the original two-volume set.

210

could without being impertinent, he went away, still apparently in doubt, and I soon saw him following with Toualeb, in earnest conversation. Toualeb was even more astonished than Paul. The Arabs are not used to any of these mercurial changes of humor; and, according to their notion, if a man sets out for Gaza he must go to Gaza; they cannot conceive how one in his right reason can change his mind; and Toualeb would have been very easily persuaded that an evil spirit was hurrying me on, particularly as, like Paul, from the beginning he had opposed my going by Petra and Idumea. Finding me resolute, however, he soon began to run, and brought back the camels, which were some distance in advance, and for several hours we moved on in perfect silence through the wild and rugged defile.

The mountains on each side were high, broken, and rugged, and ever presenting the same appearance of extreme old age. The road, if road it might be called, was rougher than any I had yet traveled; it was the only opening among the mountains by which we could pass at all, made by the hand of Nature, and so encumbered with fallen rocks that it was exceedingly difficult for our camels to advance. I did not intend to push far that day; and a little before dark I proposed to encamp in a narrow pass between the mountains, where there was barely room to pitch our tents; but appearances threatened rain, and Toualeb, pointing to the accumulation of stones and rocks which had fallen from the mountain and been washed through the pass, told me it would be a dangerous place to spend the night in. There was no earth to drink the falling rain, and, pouring down the hard and naked mountain sides, it formed a torrent in the pass, which hurried and dashed along, gathering force at every moment, and carrying with it bodies of sand and stones that would have crushed to atoms any obstruction they might meet in their resistless progress. I felt at once the force of the suggestion; and as I had no idea of being disturbed in the night by such a knock at the door of my tent as one of these gigantic missiles would have made, we kept on our difficult way.

At dark we were still in the ravine. Toualeb was right in his apprehensions; for some time before we reached the end of the pass the rain was falling in torrents, the rocks and stones were washing under our feet, and we heard the loud roar of thunder, and saw the forked lightning play among the mountain-tops. It was two hours after dark before we reached a place where it was prudent to encamp. We pitched our tent in the open valley; the thunder was rumbling, and ever and anon bursting with a terrific crash among the riven mountains, and the red lightning was flashing around the hoary head of Sinai. It was a scene for a poet or painter; but, under the circumstances, I would have given all its sublimity for a pair of dry pantaloons. Thunder and lightning among mountains are exceedingly sublime, and excellent things to talk about in a ballroom or by the fireside; but, my word for it, a man traveling in the desert has other things to think of. Everything is wet and sloppy; the wind catches under his tent before he can get it pinned down; and when it is fastened, and he finds his tight canvas turning the water like a cemented roof, and begins to rub his hands and feel himself comfortable, he finds but the beginning of trouble in a wet mat and coverlet.

I was but poorly prepared for a change like this, for I had been so long used to a clear, unclouded sky, that I almost considered myself beyond the reach of the changing elements. It was the beauty of the weather more than anything else that had tempted me to turn off from the road to Gaza; and, hardly equal to this change of scene, my heart almost sank within me. I reproached myself as if for a willful and unjustifiable disregard of prudence, and no writer on moral duties could have written a better lecture than I inflicted upon myself that evening. In wet clothes I was literally sitting on the stool of repentance. Drooping and disheartened, I told Paul that I was already punished for my temerity, and the next morning I would go back and resume the road to Gaza. For the night, however, there was but one thing to be done, and that was to sleep if I could, and sleep I did. A man who rides all day upon a dromedary must sleep, come what may, and even thunder among the mountains of Sinai cannot wake him. Daylight brought back my courage; the storm was over; the sun was shining brightly as I ever saw it even in the East; and again there was the same clear and refreshing atmosphere that had beguiled me from my prudent resolution. I too was changed again; and, in answer to the suggestion of Paul, that we should retrace our steps, I pointed towards Aqaba, and gave the brief and emphatic order, "Forward!"

We continued for several hours along the valley, which was closely bounded on either side by mountains, not high, but bare, cracked, and crumbling into fragments. The tops had apparently once been lofty and pointed, but time, and the action of the elements, had changed their character. The summits had crumbled and fallen, so as to expose on every side a rounded surface, and the idea constantly present to my mind was, that the whole range had been shaken by an Almighty hand; shaken so as to break the rugged surface of the mountains, but not with sufficient force to dash them into pieces; I could not help thinking that, with another shock, the whole mass would fall in ruins. I had often remarked the silence and stillness of the desert; but never had I been so forcibly impressed with this peculiarity as since I left the convent. The idea was constantly present to my mind, "How still, how almost fearfully still!" The mountains were bare of verdure; there were no shrubs or bushes, and no rustling of the wind, and the quiet was like that of the ocean in a perfect calm, when there is not a breath of air to curl a wave, or shake the smallest fold in the lazy sail that hangs useless from the yard. Occasionally we disturbed a hare or a partridge, but we had not met a human being since we left the convent. Once we saw the track of a solitary dromedary, the prints of his feet deeply bedded in the sand, as if urged by one hurrying with hot haste; perhaps some Bedouin robber flying to his tent among the mountains with the plunder of some desert victim; we followed it for more than an hour, and when we lost sight of it on the rocky road, I felt as if we were more lonely than before.

I was thinking what an incident it would be in the life of one used to the hurrying bustle of steamboats and railroads, to travel for days through this oldest of countries without meeting a living being; and, as far as I could understand, it might well be so; there was no trade even for small caravans, and years passed by without any person, even an Arab, traveling this road. Toualeb had been over it

213

INCIDENTS OF TRAVEL

but once, and that was ten years before, when he accompanied M. Laborde on his way to Petra. I knew that there were Bedouin tents among the mountains, but, unless by accident, we might pass through without seeing any of them; and I was speculating on the chances of our not meeting a single creature, when Paul cried out that he saw a woman; and, soon after repeating the exclamation, dismounted and gave chase. Toualeb ran after him, and in another moment or two I caught a glimpse and followed.

I have before mentioned that, among these barren and desolate mountains, there was frequently a small space of ground, near some fountain or deposit of water, known only to the Arabs, capable of producing a scanty crop of grass to pasture a few camels and a small flock of sheep or goats. There the Bedouin pitches his tent, and remains till the scanty product is consumed; and then packs up his household goods, and seeks another pasture-ground. The Bedouins are essentially a pastoral people; their only riches are their flocks and herds, their home is in the wide desert, and they have no local attachments; today they pitch their tent among the mountains, tomorrow in the plain; and wherever they plant themselves for the time, all that they have on earth, wife, children, and friends, are immediately around them. In fact, the life of the Bedouin, his appearance and habits, are precisely the same as those of the patriarchs of old. Abraham himself, the first of the patriarchs, was a Bedouin, and four thousand years have not made the slightest alteration in the character and habits of this extraordinary people. Read of the patriarchs in the Bible, and it is the best description you can have of pastoral life in the East at the present day.

The woman whom we had pursued belonged to the tent of a Bedouin not far from our road, but completely hidden from our view; and, when overtaken by Toualeb, she recognized in him a friend of her tribe, and in the same spirit, and almost in the same words which would have been used by her ancestors four thousand years ago, she asked us to her tent, and promised us a lamb or a kid for supper. Her husband was stretched on the ground in front of his tent, and welcomed us with an air and manner that belonged to the desert, but which a king on his throne could not have ex-

214

celled. He was the embodied personification of all my conceptions of a patriarch. A large loose frock, a striped handkerchief on his head, bare legs, sandals on his feet, and a long white beard formed the outward man. Almost immediately after we were seated he took his shepherd's crook, and, assisted by his son, selected a lamb from the flock for the evening meal; and now I would fain prolong the illusion of this pastoral scene. To stop at the door of an Arab's tent, and partake with him of a lamb or kid prepared by his hospitable hands, all sitting together on the ground, and provided with no other implements than those which Nature gave us, is a picture of primitive and captivating simplicity; but the details were such as to destroy forever all its poetry, and take away all relish for patriarchal feasts. While we were taking coffee the lamb lay bleating in our ears, as if conscious of its coming fate. The coffee drunk and the pipe smoked, our host arose and laid his hand upon the victim; the long sword which he wore over his shoulder was quickly drawn; one man held the head and another the hind legs; and, with a rapidity almost inconceivable, it was killed and dressed, and its smoking entrails, yet curling with life, were broiling on the fire.

I was the guest of the evening, and had no reason to complain of the civility of my entertainer; for, with the air of a well-bred host, and an epicure to boot, he drew from the burning coals one of the daintiest pieces, about a yard and a half in length, and rolling one end between the palms of his hands to a tapering point, broke off about a foot and handed it to me. Now I was by no means dainty. I could live upon the coarsest fare, and all the little luxuries of tables, knives, and forks were of very little moment in my estimation. I was prepared to go full length in this patriarchal feast. But my indifference was not proof against the convivial elegances of my Bedouin companions; and as I saw yard after yard disappear, like long strings of macaroni, down their capacious throats, I was cured of all poetical associations and my appetite together.

In the tent of the Arabian patriarch, woman, the pride, the ornament, and the charm of domestic life, is the mere household drudge. In vain may one listen for her light footstep, or look to find her by the side of her natural lord, giving a richer charm to the hospitality he is extending to a stranger. It would repay one for much of the toil and monotony of a journey in the desert, if, when by chance he found himself at a Bedouin tent, he could be greeted by her sunny smile. Dark and swarthy as she is, and poor and ignorant, it would pay the traveler for many a weary hour to receive his welcome from the lips of an Arabian girl. But this the customs of the tribes forbid. When the stranger approaches the woman retires; and so completely is she accustomed to this seclusion, that, however closely he may watch, he can never catch her even peeping at him from behind a screen or partition of the tent; curiosity, which in civilized life is so universally imputed to the daughters of Eve, seems entirely unknown to the sex in this wild region. Nor is this the worst of her lot. Even when alone the wife of the Bedouin is not regarded as his equal; the holy companionship of wedded life has between them no existence. Even when no guest is present, she never eats with him. I have seen the father and sons sit down together, and when they had withdrawn from the tent, the mother and daughters came in to what was left.

Away, then, with all dreams of superior happiness in this more primitive condition of society. Captivating as is the wild idea of roving abroad at will, unfettered by the restraints of law or of conventional observances, the meanest tenant of a log hut in our western prairies has sources of happiness which the wandering Arab can never know. A spirit of perfect weariness and dissatisfaction with the world might drive a man to the desert, and, after having fallen into the indolent and mere animal habits of savage life, he might find it difficult to return to the wholesome restraints and duties of society; but I am satisfied that it is sheer affectation or ignorance, in which a member of the civilized family sighs, or pretends to sigh, for the imagined delights of an untried freedom. For my own part, I had long been satisfied of this truth, and did not need the cumulative evidence of my visit to the Bedouin's tent. He would have had me sleep under its shelter; but I knew that in all the Bedouin tents there were multitudes of enemies to rest; creatures that murder sleep; and I preferred the solitude of my own.

One word as to the hospitality of the Arabs. I had read beautiful descriptions of its manifestation, and in some way or other had gathered up the notion that the Bedouin would be offended by an offer to reward his hospitality with a price; but, feeling naturally anxious not to make a blunder on either side of a question so delicate, I applied to my guide Toualeb for information on the subject. His answer was brief and explicit. He said there was no obligation to give or pay, it being the custom of the Bedouins (among friendly tribes) to ask the wayfaring man into his tent, give him food and shelter, and send him on his way in the morning; that I could give or not, as I pleased; but that, if I did not, the hospitable host would wish his lamb alive again; and from the exceeding satisfaction with which that estimable person received my parting gift, I am very sure that in this instance, at least, I did better in taking Toualeb's knowledge of his people for my guide than I should have done by acting upon what I had read in books. It may be that, if I had gone among them poor and friendless, I should have been received in the same manner, and nothing would have been expected or received from me; but I am inclined to think, from what I saw afterward, that in such case the lamb would have been spared for a longer term of existence, and the hospitality confined to a dip into the dish and a mat at the door of the tent.

Early in the morning we left the tent of our Bedouin landlord. We were still among mountains; at every moment a new view presented itself, wild, fanciful, and picturesque; and in the distance was still visible the long range of dark mountains bordering the Red Sea. Our course was now directly for this sea, but the mountain range appeared so contiguous and unbroken that there seemed no way of getting to it but by crossing their rugged summits. There was a way, however; an opening which we could not distinguish at so great a distance, and for some time Toualeb was at a loss. He was so purblind that he could scarcely distinguish me from one of his dark companions, yet he could read the firmament like a book, and mark the proportion of the almost shapeless mountains; but he was uncertain how to hit precisely the opening by which we must pass through. There was no danger of our losing ourselves, and the only hazard was that of wasting a day in the search; but, fortunately, at the commencement of our perplexity, we came upon a Bedouin whose tent was at the foot of the mountain; and, under his instructions, we pushed on with confidence and ultimate success.

CHAPTER XIX

I T WAS LATE in the afternoon when our little caravan entered the narrow opening, presenting itself like a natural door between precipitous rocks several hundred feet in height. Passing this, and continuing onward to a vast amphitheater, or hollow square of lofty rocks, through a larger opening on our left, we again saw the dark waters of the Red Sea. About midway across I dismounted from my dromedary to survey the scene around me; and, among the many of high interest presented to the traveler in the wilderness of Sinai, I remember none more striking and impressive. It was neither so dreary and desolate, nor so wild and terrible as others I had seen, but different from all. The door by which we entered was undistinguishable, the rocks in the background completely closing it to the sight; on all sides except towards the sea, and forming almost a perfect square, were the naked faces of the rock, lofty, smooth, and regular, like the excavated sides of an ancient quarry, and quiet to that extraordinary and indescribable degree of which I have already spoken. Descending towards the opening that led to the sea, directly under us was an extensive and sandy plain, reaching to its very margin; and nearly opposite, rising abruptly from the clear waters, a long unbroken range of stern and rugged mountains, their dark irregular outline finely contrasted with the level surface at their feet, while the sea itself extended on the right and left as far as the eye could reach in that clear atmosphere; but the first stage of my journey, the head of the gulf, and the little fortress of Aqaba, were still invisible.

We rode about an hour along the shore, passing at a distance the tents of some Bedouins; and, about an hour before dark, encamped in a grove of wild palm-trees, so near the sea that the waves almost reached the door of my tent. When the moon rose I walked for an hour along the shore, and, musing upon the new scenes which every day was presenting me, picked up some shells and bits of coral as memorials of the place. I am no star-gazer, but I had learned to look up at the stars; and though I knew most of them merely by sight, I felt an attraction towards them as faces I had seen at home; while the Great Bear with his pointers, and the North Star, seemed my particular friends.

Returning to my tent, I found my Bedouins, with some strangers from the tents which we had passed, sitting round a fire of the branches of palm-trees, smoking, and telling stories as extravagant as any in the Arabian Nights' Entertainments. I sat down with them for a few moments, then entered my tent and lay down on my mat on the very shore of the sea, and was lulled to sleep by the gentle murmur of its waters.

In the morning Paul told me that there was a strange Arab outside, who wanted to see me. When we first came down from the mountain on the preceding day, a Bedouin had come out and requested me to turn aside and visit a sick man in his tent. In their perfect ignorance of the healing art, the Arabs believe every stranger to be a hakim; and so great is their confidence in the virtue of medicine, and so great their indifference to the hands from which they receive it, that the path of the traveler is constantly beset with applications from the sick or their friends. I had been so often besought and entreated to cure blindness, deafness, and other maladies beyond even the reach of medical skill, that now I paid little attention to such applications; and when this last request was made, after inquiring into the symptoms of the case, I told the messenger that I could do the sick man no good, and passed on. This morning Paul told me that the patient himself had come over during the night, and was then at the door, begging me to cure him. Paul had told him of my utter inability, but he would not be satisfied; and when I went out of my tent he was sitting directly before the door, a thin, ghastly figure; and opening his mouth and attempting an inarticulate jabber, there fell out a tongue so festered to the very throat, that the sight of it made me sick. I told him that it was utterly out of my power to help him; that I knew no more of the healing art than he did himself; and that the only advice I could give him was to endeavor to get to Cairo and put himself under the hands of a physician. I shall never forget the poor fellow's look, and almost blamed myself for not giving him some simple preparation, which might have cheated him, at least for a few days, with the hope that he might escape the tomb to which he was hurrying. His hands fell lifeless by his side, as if he had heard a sentence of death; he gave me a look which seemed to say that it was all my fault, and fell senseless on the ground. His two companions lifted him up; his faithful dromedary kneeled to receive him; and, as he turned away, he cast a reproachful glance towards me, which made me almost imagine myself guilty of his death. I have no doubt that, long before this, the poor Arab is dead, and that in his dying moments, when struggling with the king of terrors, he has seen, in his distracted visions, the figure of the hard-hearted stranger, who, as he thought, might have saved him, but would not.

Anxious to escape an object so painful to my feelings, I walked on and was soon busily engaged in picking up shells and coral; of the former I never saw so many as at this place. Some were particularly beautiful, but exceedingly delicate, and difficult to be carried. The first day I could have loaded a camel with them. The coral, too, such as it was, lay scattered about in lavish profusion. I remember, the first piece Paul found, he rubbed his hands like the toiling and untiring alchemist, when he thinks he has discovered the philosopher's stone; but when he came to a second he threw away the first, in the same spirit in which the Irishman, on his arrival in our country, the El Dorado of his dreams, threw down a sixpence which he had picked up in the street, assuring himself that there was more where that came from. Some of this coral was exceedingly beautiful; we did not know its value, but I did not think very highly of it, merely from the circumstance of its lying there in such abundance. It was not the rock or branch coral, but a light porous substance, resembling very much the honeycomb. Paul

221

gathered a large quantity of it, and contrived to carry it to Jerusalem, though it got very much broken on the way. He had the satisfaction of knowing, however, that he had not sustained any great loss; for, on our first visit to the Church of the Holy Sepulchre, we found in the porch a green-turbaned Mussulman, who, returning from his pilgrimage to Mecca, had thought to indemnify himself for the expense and fatigue of his long and dreary journey with this treasure of the sea. Paul took up a large piece and asked him the price, when the Mussulman, with an air as dejected in telling as was that of Paul in hearing it, told him two paras, a para being about one-eighth of a cent; and the next day I saw before the door of the convent at which we were staying a large heap of the coral which Paul had been so careful in carrying; and after that he talked only of his shells, the value of which was not yet ascertained.

At about twelve o'clock, close by the shore, we came to a stunted wild palm-tree, with a small stone fence around it; and, looking down from my dromedary, I saw extended on the ground the figure of an Arab. I at first thought he was dead; but, at the noise of our approach, he raised his head from a stone which served him as a pillow, and the first greeting he gave us was to ask for bread. Among all the habitations of hermits I had yet seen, in caves, among rocks or mountains, there was none which could be compared with this by the shore of the sea; a small fence, but little higher than his recumbent body, protected him from the wind; the withered branches of the palm-tree were his only covering; his pillow a stone, and the bare earth his bed; and when he crawled out and stood before us, erect as age and infirmity would allow, I thought I had never seen such a miserable figure. I could not have believed, without seeing it, that anything so wretched, made in God's image, existed on the earth.

He was more than sixty; his face was dried, and seamed with the deep wrinkles of age and exposure; his beard long and white; and his body thin to emaciation. Over his shoulders and breast was a miserable covering of rags, but the rest of his body was perfectly naked; his skin was dry, horny, and covered with blotches resembling large scales, which, on his legs, and particularly over his knees, stood out like the greaves of an ancient coat of mail; and he looked like one who literally crawled on his belly and licked the dust of the earth. He reminded me of the wild hermit of Engaddi, who came out upon the Saracen emir when he journeyed with the Knight of the Leopard on the shore of the Dead Sea. And this man was a saint, and my Arabs looked on him with respect and reverence; and when he died a public tomb would be erected over him, and they upon whose charity he now lived would resort to it as a shrine of prayer. We gave him some bread, and left him in his solitary den; and, before we had got out of sight, he had crawled back under his palm-leaves, and was again resting upon his pillow of stone. In our busy and stirring world, we cannot imagine the possibility of existing in such a dronish state; but, in all probability, that man would lie there till the bread we gave him was exhausted, and, when he had taken his last morsel, again lie down in hope that more would come.

About an hour afterward we came upon a fisherman stealing along the shore with his net in his hand, looking into the sea, and ready to throw it when he saw any fish. The process, like everything else that one sees here, is perfectly primitive, and carries the beholder back to the early days of this ancient country. Carrying the net on his left arm crooked, cleared and prepared for a throw, with the one end in his right hand, and taking advantage of ripples made by the wind, and the sun throwing his shadow behind him, he runs along the shore until he sees a school of fish, when, with a gentle jerk, and without any noise, he throws his net, which opens and spreads as it falls, so that a little thing, which could be put easily into a hat, expands sufficiently to cover a surface of twenty or thirty feet. While running along with us he threw several times; and, as he managed his craft with skill, never throwing until he saw something, he was always successful. I could not make anything out of the Arabic name of the fish; but I have the flavor of them still on my tongue; a flavor at the moment finer than that of the sole or turbot of Paris, or the trout of Long Island.

In the afternoon the weather changed. Since we first struck the sea, our road along its shore had been one of uncommon beauty, and my time passed very pleasantly, sometimes allowing my dromedary to cool his feet in the clear water, sometimes dismounting to pick up a shell, and all the time having a warm sun and a refreshing breeze; but it was my fortune to see this ancient country under every hue of the changing elements. The sun was now obscured; a strong wind came down the sea directly in our teeth; the head of the gulf was cut off from our view; the sea was troubled, and the white caps were dancing on its surface; the dark mountains looked darker and more lonely; while before us a rainbow was forming over the point of Aqaba, which threw itself across the gulf to the east, marking in the firmament, with its rich and varied colors, the figure of the crescent. Soon after we were in the midst of a perfect hurricane. Several times during the day I had wished to float upon the bosom of the tranquil sea, and had looked in vain for some boat or fisherman's skiff to carry me up the gulf; but I now shrank from the angry face of the deep, and, under the shelter of an impending rock, listened to the fierce whistling of the wind and the crashing of the thunder among the mountains.

In the morning the storm was over, and the atmosphere pure, clear, and refreshing as before; but, as a set-off to the pleasure of returning sunshine, Toualeb told me that we had passed the boundaries of the friendly tribes, and that we must look to our weapons, for we were now among strangers, and perhaps enemies. Here, too, for the first time, I put on my Turkish dress, being that of a merchant of Cairo, with the addition of pistols and sabre; but, fearful of taking cold, I cut down an old coat and tied up a pair of pantaloons, so as to have a complete suit under the large white trousers and red silk gown which formed the principal items of my dress. The red tarboosh I had worn ever since I had been in Egypt; but I now rolled round it a green and yellow striped handkerchief, to which Toualeb gave the proper twist; and, with my yellow slippers and red shoes over them, sash, pistols, sword, and a long beard, I received the congratulations and compliments of my friends upon my improved appearance.

Indeed, I played the Turk well. Different from my notions of the appearance of the Turk, they have generally light and florid complexions; and, if I could have talked their language, dressed as a

Turk, they could not have judged from my appearance that I had ever been outside the walls of old Istanbul. There is no exaggeration in the unanimous reports of travelers of the effect which the costumes of the East give to personal appearance; and, having seen and known it even in my own person, I am inclined to believe that there is fallacy in the equally prevalent opinion of the personal beauty of the Turks. Their dress completely hides all deformity of person, and the variety of colors, the arms and the long beard, divert the attention of the observer from a close examination of features. The striking effect of costume is strongly perceptible in the soldiers of the sultan, and the mongrel, half-European uniform in which he has put them, and in which they are not by any means an uncommonly fine-looking set of men. These soldiers are taken wherever they are caught, and, consequently, are a fair specimen of the Turkish race; and any English regiment will turn out finer men than the best in the sultan's army. Following my example, Paul also slipped into his Bedouin shirt, and could hardly be distinguished from the best Arab of them all.

MERCHANT OF CAIRO WITH PISTOLS & SABRE
This is Stephens dressed in the manner he describes in his text.

225

Again our road lay along the shore, so near that sometimes we had to dismount and pick our way over the rocks, and at others our dromedaries bathed their feet in the water. In one place the side of the mountain rose so directly and abruptly from the water's edge that we had to turn aside and pass around it, coming again to the shore after about an hour's ride. Here we saw the gulf narrowing towards its extremity; and on the opposite side a cluster of palm-trees, within which, and completely hidden from our view, was the end of our first stage, the fortress of Aqaba. Never was the sight of one of the dearest objects on earth, home to the wanderer, land to the sailor, or a mistress to the lover, more welcome than the sight of those palm-trees to me. The malady under which I had been laboring had grown upon me every day; and, in spite of all that was rich and interesting, time after time I had regretted my rashness in throwing myself so far into the desert. The repose, therefore, which awaited me at Aqaba, seemed the most precious thing on earth.

Towards evening we could see Aqaba more distinctly, though still on the opposite side of the gulf, and still at a formidable distance to me. A brisk trot would have carried me there in an hour; but this was more than I could bear, supported as I was by a mattress on each side of me, and barely able to sustain the slow and measured movement of a walk. Night was again coming on, and heavy clouds were gathering in the east. I was extremely anxious to sleep within the fortress that night; and, fearful that a stranger would not be admitted after dark, I sent Paul on ahead with my compliments to the governor, and the modest request that he would keep the gates open till I came.

A governor is a governor all the world over. Honor and respect attend him wherever he may be; whether the almost regal governor-general of India, the untitled chief magistrate of our own democratic state, or the governor of a little fortress on the shores of the Red Sea. But there are some governors one may take a liberty with, and others not; and of the former class was my friend of Aqaba. His name was Suliman, his title aga, and therefore he was called Suliman Aga. He had his appointment by favor of the pasha, and permission to retain it by favor of the Bedouins around; he had under him nominally a garrison of Mogrebbin soldiers, but they were as restive as some of our own unbroken militia; and, like many a worthy disciplinarian among us, he could do just as he pleased with them if he only let them have their own way. He was, in short, an excellent governor, and I gave him two dollars and a recommendation at parting.

But I am going too fast. I arrived before dark, and in such a state that I almost fell from my dromedary in dismounting at the gate of the fortress. The first glance told me that this was not the place of rest I had promised myself. Half a dozen Mogrebbins from the shores of Morocco, the most tried and faithful of the hired troops of the pasha, were sitting on a mat within the gate, smoking their long pipes, with their long guns, swords, and pistols hanging above their heads. They rose and gave me a seat beside them, and the whole of the little population of the fortress, and the Bedouins living under the palm-trees outside, gathered around to gaze at the stranger. The great caravan of pilgrims for Mecca had left them only three days before; and, except upon the passing and return of the caravan, years pass by without a stranger ever appearing at the fortress. They had heard of my coming, for the sheik had waited two days after the departure of the caravan, and had only gone that morning, leaving directions with the governor to send for him as soon as I arrived. I was somewhat surprised at his confidence in my coming, for, when I saw him, I was very far from being decided; but in the miserable condition in which I found myself, I hailed it as a favorable omen. The governor soon came, and was profuse in his offers of service, beginning, of course, with coffee and a pipe, which I was forced to decline, apologizing on the ground of my extreme indisposition, and begged to be conducted to a room by myself. The governor rose and conducted me, and every Bedouin present followed after; and when I came to the room by *myself*, I had at least forty of them around me. Once Paul prevailed on some of them to go out; but they soon came back again, and I was too ill to urge the matter.

The very aspect of the room into which I was shown prostrated the last remains of my physical strength. It was eighty or a hundred feet long, forty feet wide, and about as many high, having on one side a dead wall, being that of the fortress, and on the other two large windows without shutters and the door; the naked floor was of mud, and so were the walls and ceiling. I looked for one spot less cheerless than the rest; and finding at the upper end a place where the floor was elevated about a foot, with a feeling of despondency I have seldom known, I stretched my mattress in the extreme corner, and, too far gone to have any regard to the presence of the governor or his Arab soldiers, threw myself at full length upon it. I was sick in body and soul; for, besides the actual and prostrating debility under which I was laboring, I had before me the horrible certainty that I was completely cut off from all medical aid, and from all the comforts which a sick man wants. I was ten days from Cairo; to go there in person was impossible; and, if I should send, I could not obtain the aid of a physician in less than twenty-five or thirty days, if at all; and before that I might be past his help.

When I left Cairo Dr. Walne had set me up, so that I held out tolerably well until I reached Mount Sinai; and, moreover, had given me sundry medicines, with directions for their use under particular circumstances; but my symptoms had so completely changed, that the directions, if not the medicines themselves, were entirely useless. In a spirit of desperation, however, I took them out; and, not knowing where to begin, resolved to go through the whole catalogue in such order as chance might direct. I began with a double dose of cathartic powders; and, while lying on my mat, I was diverted from the misery of my own gloomy reflections by the pious conversation of the Mussulman governor. If God willed, he said, I would soon get well; himself and his wife had been ill three months, and had no physician, but God willed that they should recover, and they did; and as I looked in his believing face and those of the Bedouins, I found myself gradually falling into the fatalism of their creed. I shall never forget the manner in which I passed that night, and the somber fancies that chased each other through my brain. A single lamp threw a dim and feeble light through the large apartment, scarcely revealing the dusky forms of the sleeping Bedouins, with their weapons by their sides, and I was the only one awake. Busy memory called up all the considerations that ought to have prevented my taking such a journey, and the warning voice of my friend at Cairo, "turn your steps westward," again rang in my ears. I saw the figure of the dead Tartar at Suez, like me, a wanderer from home, and buried by strangers in the sandy desert; and so nervous and desponding had I become, that the words of the prophet in regard to the land of Idumea, "none shall pass through it for ever and ever," struck upon my heart like a funeral knell. I was now upon the borders of Edom; and, in the despondency of sickness, I looked upon myself as rash and impious in undertaking what might be considered a defiance of the prophetic denunciations inspired by God himself.

In the morning I was worse; and, following up my almost desperate plan of treatment, commenced the day with a double emetic. The governor came in; and though I tried to keep the door shut, another and another followed, till my room was as public as any part of the fortress. Indeed, it was by far the most public, for all the rest was stripped of its bronzed figures to ornament my room. Annoyed to death by seeing twenty or thirty pairs of fiery black eyes constantly fixed upon me, I remembered, with feelings of envy, my tent in the desert. There I could at least be alone, and I resolved, at all hazards, not to pass another night in the fortress.

In the midst of my exceeding perplexities, the sheik of Aqaba, my friend of Cairo, made his appearance. I was in a pitiable condition when he entered, under the immediate operation of my emetic, with the whole of the Mogrebbin guard and every beggarly Bedouin about the fortress staring at me. He looked surprised and startled when he saw me; but, with a glimmering of good sense, though, as I thought, with unnecessary harshness, told me that I would die if I stayed there, and that he was ready to set out with me at a moment's notice. By the advice of Mr. Gliddon, my plan had been to make this my place of negotiation and arrangement, and not to proceed farther without having all things definitely explained and settled. But I was in no condition to negotiate, and was ready to do anything to get away from the fortress. He was exceedingly anxious to start immediately, and gave me a piece of information that almost lifted me from the ground; namely, that he could provide me with a horse of the best blood of Arabia for the whole of the journey. He could not have given me more grateful intelligence, for the bare idea of again mounting my dromedary deprived me of all energy and strength. I had endeavored to procure a sort of palanquin, to be swung between two camels; but so destitute was the fortress of all kinds of material, that it was impossible to make it. When he spoke to me, then, of a horse, it made me a new man; and, without a moment's hesitation, I told him that if he would give me till five o'clock in the afternoon, I would be ready to set out with him. One thing I did not like. I wished and designed to take with me my faithful Toualeb; but he had told me that he did not believe that the El Alouins would allow it; and, when he spoke to the sheik, the latter had positively refused, pretending that all was arranged between us at Cairo. I was fain, therefore, to abandon the idea, not having energy to insist upon anything that was disputed, and to trust everything to fortune and the sheik. I told Paul to do all that was necessary; and, begging to be left alone for a few hours, I laid myself down upon my mat, and, worn out with the watching of the last night, and the excitement of thinking and deciding on my future movements, quickly fell asleep.

At five o'clock the sheik returned, punctual to his appointment; I had slept soundly, and awoke somewhat refreshed. The room was again filled with the Bedouins, and I was as ready to go as he was to take me. He had ordered what was necessary upon the journey for man and beast, and provisions for six camels and ten men for ten days. I gave Paul my purse, and told him to pay, and, walking to the gate of the fortress, a dozen Arabs helped me to my saddle; they would have taken me up in their arms and carried me, and, when I had mounted, they would have taken up the horse and carried him too, so great a friendship had they already conceived for me. But the friendship was not for what I was, but for what I had. They had welcomed me as they would have welcomed a bag of gold; and I had scarcely mounted before they all, governor, Mogrebbin soldiers, and Bedouins, began to clamor for backsheesh. Ten years before, M. Laborde had passed along this route, and stopped at the fortress

230

while waiting for the sheik who was to guide and protect him to Petra; and having in view the purpose of preparing the great work which has since given him such merited reputation, he had scattered money and presents with a most liberal hand. M. Laborde himself was not personally known to any of those now at the fortress; but his companion, Mr. Linant, of whom I have before spoken, was known to them all; and they all had heard of the gold shower in which M. Laborde appeared among them. They therefore expected the same from me; and, when Paul had got through his distribution, I was startled at perceiving the dissatisfied air with which they received a backsheesh that would have overwhelmed any other Arabs with joy and gratitude.

But I must not hurry the reader from Aqaba with the same eagerness which I displayed in leaving it. This little fortress is seldom visited by travelers, and it is worth a brief description.[1] It stands at the extremity of the eastern or Elanitic branch of the Red Sea, at the foot of the sandstone mountains, near the shore, and almost buried in a grove of palm-trees, the only living things in that region of barren sands. It is the last stopping-place of the caravan of pilgrims on its way to Mecca, being yet thirty days' journey from the tomb of the Prophet, and, of course, the first at which they touch on their return. Except at the time of these two visits, the place is desolate from the beginning of the year to its close; the arrival of a traveler is of exceedingly rare occurrence, and seldom does even the wandering Bedouin stop within its walls; no ship rides in its harbor, and not even a solitary fishing-boat breaks the stillness of the water at its feet. But it was not always so desolate, for this was the Ezion-geber of the Bible, where, three thousand years ago, King Solomon made a navy of ships, which brought from Ophir gold and precious stones for the great temple at Jerusalem; and again, at a later day, a great city existed here, through which, at this distant point in the wilderness, the wealth of India was conveyed to imperial Rome.[2] But all these are gone, and there are no

[1] The fortress, built in the fourteenth century, has the arms of the Hashemite family (and tribal head) carved above the main door. Only the central gateway still stands. It is described by T. E. Lawrence in *Seven Pillars of Wisdom*.

[2] Aqaba is listed as "Addianam" in the Peutinger Tablum, a fourth-century Roman

relics or monuments to tell of former greatness; like the ships which once floated in the harbor, all have passed away. Still, ruined and desolate as it is, to the eye of feeling the little fortress is not without its interest; for, as the governor told me, it was built by the heroic Saladin.

I had taken leave of my trusty Toualeb, and was again in the hands of strangers; and I do not deceive myself when I say, that on the very borders of Edom I noticed a change for the worse in the appearance of the Bedouins. According to the reports of travelers and writers, those with whom I now set out from Aqaba belonged to one of the most lawless tribes of a lawless race; and they were by far the wildest and fiercest-looking of all I had yet seen; with complexions bronzed and burnt to blackness; dark eyes, glowing with a fire approaching to ferocity; figures thin and shrunken, though sinewy; chests standing out, and ribs projecting from the skin, like those of a skeleton.

The sheik, like myself, was on horseback, dressed in a red silk gown like my own, and over it a large cloak of scarlet cloth, both the gifts of Messieurs Linant and Laborde; a red tarboosh with a shawl rolled round it, long red boots, and a sash; and carried pistols, a sword, and a spear about twelve feet long, pointed with steel at both ends; his brother, too, wore a silk gown, and carried pistols and sword, and the rest were armed with swords and matchlock guns and wore the common Bedouin dress; some of them almost no dress at all.

We had moved some distance from the fortress without a word being uttered, for they neither spoke to me nor with each other. I was in no humor for talking myself, but it was unpleasant to have more than a dozen men around, all bending their keen eyes upon me, and not one of them uttering a word. With a view to making

---

itinerary. It is also known under the Nabatean name of "Alia." It was the entrepôt for trade ships carrying produce, cloves, nutmeg, ginger root, pepper, "a Roman passion," pearls from India, diamonds, slaves, and ivory. There are, however, no ruins of Roman buildings. No inscriptions have been found, nor sunken docks or warehouses. It was also the terminus of Trajan's road that went from Aqaba to Petra and beyond to Gerash and Damascus. (See Victor W. von Hagen, *The Roads That Led to Rome* [New York, 1967].)

some approach to acquaintance, and removing their jealousy of me as a stranger, I asked some casual question about the road; but I might better have held my peace, for it seemed that I could not well have hit upon a subject more displeasing. My amiable companions looked as black as midnight, and one of them, a particularly swarthy and truculent-looking fellow, turned short around, and told me that I had too much curiosity, and that he did not understand what right a Christian had to come there and hunt up their villages, take down their names, &c. But the sheik came in as mediator, and told them that I was a good man; that he had been to my house in Cairo, and that I was no spy; and so this cloud passed off.

I did not mean to go far that afternoon, for I had left the fortress merely to get rid of the crowd, and return to fresh air and quiet; and in less than an hour I again pitched my tent in the desert. Finding plenty of brush, we kindled a large fire, and all sat down around it. It was a great object with me to establish myself on a good footing with my companions at the outset; and, more fortunate on my second attempt, before one round of coffee and pipes was over, the sheik turned to me, and, with all the extravagance of Eastern hyperbole, said he thanked God for having permitted us again to see each other's face, and that I had been recovering since I saw his face; and, turning his eyes to heaven, with an expression of deep and confiding piety, he added, "God grant that you may soon become a strong man"; and then the others all took their pipes from their mouths, and, turning up their eyes to heaven, the whole band of breechless desperadoes added, "Wallah-Wallah," "God grant it."

CHAPTER XX

PROPHECY AND FULFILLMENT—UNPLEASANT SUGGESTIONS—THE
DENOUNCED LAND—MANAGEMENT—A RENCOUNTER—AN ARAB'S
CUNNING—THE CAMEL'S HUMP—ADVENTURE WITH A LAMB—
MOUNT HOR—DELICATE NEGOTIATIONS—APPROACH TO PETRA

I HAD NOW CROSSED the borders of Edom. Standing near the shore of the Elanitic branch of the Red Sea, the doomed and accursed land lay stretched out before me, the theatre of awful visitations and their more awful fulfillment; given to Esau as being the fatness of the earth, but now a barren waste, a picture of death, an eternal monument of the wrath of an offended God, and a fearful witness to the truth of the words spoken by his prophets. "For my sword shall be bathed in heaven: behold, it shall come down upon Idumea, and upon the people of my curse, to judgment." "From generation to generation it shall lie waste; none shall pass through it for ever and ever. But the cormorant and the bittern shall possess it; the owl also and the raven shall dwell in it; and he shall stretch out upon it the line of confusion and the stones of emptiness. They shall call the nobles thereof to the kingdom, but none shall be there, and all her princes shall be nothing. And thorns shall come up in her palaces, nettles and brambles in the fortresses thereof; and it shall be a habitation of dragons, and a court for owls. The wild beasts of the desert shall also meet with the wild beasts of the island, and the satyr shall cry to his fellow: the screech-owl also shall rest there, and find for herself a place of rest. There shall the great owl make her nest, and lay, and hatch, and gather under her shadow: there shall the vultures also be gathered, every one with her mate. Seek ye out the book of the Lord, and read: no one of these shall fail, none shall want her mate: for my mouth it hath commanded, and his spirit it hath gathered them. And he hath cast the lot for them, and his hand hath divided it unto them by line: they shall possess it for ever; from generation to generation shall they dwell therein."—Isaiah xxxiv.

I read in the sacred book prophecy upon prophecy and curse upon curse against the very land on which I stood. I was about to journey through this land, and to see with my own eyes whether the Almighty had stayed his uplifted arm, or whether his sword had indeed come down "upon Idumea, and the people of his curse, to judgment." I have before referred to Keith on the Prophecies, where, in illustrating the fulfillment of the prophecies against Idumea, "none shall pass through it for ever and ever," after referring to the singular fact that the great caravan routes existing in the days of David and Solomon, and under the Roman empire, are now completely broken up, and that the great hadji routes to Mecca from Damascus and Cairo lie along the borders of Idumea, barely touching and not passing through it, he proves by abundant references that to this day no traveler has ever passed through the land.

The Bedouins who roam over the land of Idumea have been described by travelers as the worst of their race. "The Arabs about Aqaba," says Pococke, "are a very bad people and notorious robbers, and are at war with all others." Mr. Joliffe alludes to it as one of the wildest and most dangerous divisions of Arabia; and Burckhardt says, "that for the first time he had ever felt fear during his travels in the desert, and his route was the most dangerous he had ever traveled," that he had "nothing with him that could attract the notice or excite the cupidity of the Bedouins," and was "even stripped of some rags that covered his wounded ankles." Messrs. Legh and Banks, and Captains Irby and Mangles, were told that the Arabs of Wadi Musa, the tribe that formed my escort, "were a most savage and treacherous race, and that they would use their Frank's blood for a medicine"; and they learned on the spot that "upward of thirty pilgrims from Barbary had been murdered at Petra the preceding year by the men of Wadi Musa; "and they speak of the opposition and obstruction from the Bedouins as resembling the case of the Israelites under Moses, when Edom refused to give them passage through his country. None of these had passed through it, and unless the two Englishmen and Italian before referred to succeeded in their attempt, when I pitched my tent on the borders of Edom no traveler had ever done so.

The ignorance and mystery that hung over it added to the interest with which I looked to the land of barrenness and desolation stretched out before me; and I would have regarded all the difficulties and dangers of the road merely as materials for a not unpleasant excitement, if I had only felt a confidence in my physical strength to carry me through. But some idea may be formed of my unhappy condition from the circumstance that, in the evening, my servant, an honest and faithful fellow, who, I believe, was sincerely attached to me, while I was lying on my mat, with many apologies, and hoping I would not think hard of him, and praying that no accident might happen to me, told me that he was a poor man, and it would be very hard for him to lose his earnings, and that an English traveler had died in Syria the year before, and his consul had taken possession of his effects, and to this day his poor servant had never received his wages. I at first thought it unkind of him to come upon me at that moment with such a suggestion; but I soon changed my mind. I had not paid him a cent since he had been with me, and his earnings were no trifle to him; and, after all, what was I to him except a debtor? In any event I should leave him in a few months, and, in all probability, should never see him again. I told him that he knew the circumstances under which we had left Cairo; that I had brought with me barely enough to pay my expenses on the road; nor could I give him what he wanted, an order upon my consul at Beirut; but, after he had gone out, with somewhat the same feelings that may be supposed to possess a man in extremis writing his own will, I wrote an order, including a gratuity which he richly deserved, upon a merchant in Beirut, upon whom I had a letter of credit; but the cheerlessness and helplessness of my situation never struck me so forcibly as when I reflected that, in the uncertain position in which I was placed, it was not prudent to give it into his hands. At that moment I mistrusted everybody; and, though I had not then, nor at any subsequent time, the slightest reason to doubt his faith, I did not dare to let him know that he could in any event be a gainer by my death. I considered it necessary to make him suppose that his interest was identified with my safety, and therefore folded up the paper, enclosed it in the letter of credit directed to the merchant, and put it back in my trunk; and I need not say that it was a great satisfaction to me that the validity of the draught was never tested.

When I awoke in the morning, the first thing I thought of was my horse. It almost made me well to think of him, and it was not long before I was on his back.

Standing near the shore of this northern extremity of the Red Sea, I saw before me an immense sandy valley, which, without the aid of geological science, to the eye of common observation and reason, had once been the bottom of a sea or the bed of a river. This dreary valley, extending far beyond the reach of the eye, had been partly explored by Burckhardt; sufficiently to ascertain and mention it in the latest geography of the country, as the great valley of El Ghor, extending from the shores of the Elanitic gulf to the southern extremity of the Lake Asphaltites or the Dead Sea; and it was manifest, by landmarks of Nature's own providing, that over that sandy plain those seas had once mingled their waters, or, perhaps more probably, that before the cities of the plain had been consumed by brimstone and fire, and Sodom and Gomorrah covered by a pestilential lake, the Jordan had here rolled its waters. The valley varied from four to eight miles in breadth, and on each side were high, dark, and barren mountains, bounding it like a wall. On the left were the mountains of Judea, and on the right those of Seir, the portion given to Esau as an inheritance; and among them, buried from the eyes of strangers, the approach to it known only to the wandering Bedouins, was the ancient capital of his kingdom, the excavated city of Petra, the cursed and blighted Edom of the Edomites. The land of Idumea lay before me, in barrenness and desolation; no trees grew in the valley, and no verdure on the mountain-tops. All was bare, dreary, and desolate.

But the beauty of the weather atoned for this barrenness of scene; and mounted on the back of my Arabian, I felt a lightness of frame and an elasticity of spirit that I could not have believed possible in my actual state of health. Patting the neck of the noble

237

animal, I talked with the sheik about his horse; and, by warm and honest praises, was rapidly gaining upon the affectations of my wild companions. The sheik told me that the race of these horses had been in his family more than four hundred years, though I am inclined to think, from his not being able to tell his own age, that he did not precisely know the pedigree of his beasts. If anything connected with my journey in the East could throw me into ecstasies, it would be the recollection of that horse. I felt lifted up when on his back, and snuffed the pure air of the desert with a zest not unworthy of a Bedouin. Like all the Arabian horses, he was broken only to the walk and gallop, the unnatural and ungraceful movement of a trot being deemed unworthy the free limbs of an Arab courser.

The sheik today was more communicative. Indeed, he became very fond of talking; suspicious as I was, and on the watch for anything that might rouse my apprehensions, I observed that he regularly settled down upon the same topics, namely, the dangers of the road, the bad character of the Arabs, his great friendship for me the first moment he saw me, and his determination to protect me with his life against all dangers. This was well enough for once or twice, but he repeated it too often, and overshot the mark, as I did when I first began to recommend myself to them. I suspected him of exaggerating the dangers of the road to enhance the value of his services; and, lest I should entertain any doubt upon the subject, he betrayed himself by always winding up with a reference to the generosity of Monsieur Linant. The consequence was, that, instead of inspiring me with fear, he gave me confidence; and, by the end of my first day's journey, I had lost nearly all apprehensions of the dangers of the road, and acquired some distrust and contempt for my protector. We were all getting along very well, however. Paul had been playing a great game among the men, and, by his superior knowledge of mankind, easily circumvented these ignorant Bedouins; and his Arabic name of "Osman" was constantly in someone's mouth. I forgot to mention that, very early in my journey in the desert, my companions, unable to twist my name to suit their Arabic intonations, had called me Abdel Hasis (literally, the slave of the good God),[1] and Paul, Osman.

In the evening, while making a note in a little memorandum-book, and on the point of lying down to sleep, I heard a deep guttural voice at some distance outside, and approaching nearer, till the harsh sounds grated as if spoken in my very ears. My Bedouins were sitting around a large fire at the door of the tent, and through the flames I saw coming up two wild and ferocious-looking Arabs, their dark visages reddened by the blaze, and their keen eyes flashing; and hardly had they reached my men, before all drew their swords, and began cutting away at each other with all their might. I did not feel much apprehension, and could not but admire the boldness of the fellows, two men walking up deliberately and drawing upon ten. One of the first charges Toualeb gave me on my entrance into the desert was, if the Arabs composing my escort got into any quarrel, to keep out of the way and let them fight it out by themselves; and, in pursuance of this advice, without making any attempt to interfere, I stood in the door watching the progress of the fray.

The larger of the two was engaged with the sheik's brother, and their swords were clashing in a way that would soon have put an end to one of them, when the sheik, who had been absent at the moment, sprang in among them, and knocking up their swords with his long spear, while his scarlet cloak fell from his shoulders, his dark face reddened, and his black eyes glowed in the firelight, with a voice that drowned the clatter of the weapons, roared out a volley of Arabic gutturals which made them drop their points, and apparently silenced them with shame. What he said we did not know; but the result was a general cessation of hostilities. The sheik's brother had received a cut in the arm, and his adversary helped to bind up the wound, and they all sat down together round the fire to pipes and coffee, as good friends as a party of Irishmen with their heads broken after a Donnybrook fairing. I had noticed, in this flurry, the exceeding awkwardness with which they used their swords, by their overhand blows constantly laying themselves open,

---

[1] Abdel Hasis or Hazis is a well-known name throughout the Arab world. Emirs and sheiks bore it. Charles Doughty wrote it as Abh-el-Aziz (many streets are named such). It is more accurately translated "beloved slave."

so that any little Frenchman with his toothpick of a rapier would have run them through before they could have cried quarter. After the thing was all over, Paul went out and asked the cause; but the sheik told him that it was an affair of their own, and with this satisfactory answer we were obliged to rest content.

Though all was now quiet, the elements of discord were still existing. The newcomer was a ferocious fellow; his voice was constantly heard, like the hoarse croaking of some bird of evil omen, and sometimes it was raised to the pitch of high and deadly passion. Paul heard him ask if I was a European, to which the sheik answered no; I was a Turk. He then got upon the railroad to Suez, and the poor benighted Bedouin, completely behind the age in the march of improvement, having never read Say's Political Economy or Smith's Wealth of Nations, denounced it as an invasion of the natural rights of the people, and a wicked breaking up of the business of the camel-drivers. He cursed every European that ever set foot in their country; and, speaking of Mr. Galloway, the engineer of the proposed railroad, hoped that he might some day meet him, and swore he would strangle him with his own hands.

In the morning we were again under way. Our quarrelsome friend of the night before was by our side, perched on the bare back of a dromedary, and, if possible, looking more grim and savage by daylight. His companion was mounted behind him, and he kept near the sheik, occasionally crossing my path, looking back at me, and croaking in the sheik's ear as he had done the night before. Two or three times he crossed my path, as if with the intention of going into the mountains; and then, as if he found it impossible to tear himself away, returned to the sheik. At length he did go, and with the most discontented and disconsolate air, and after he had gone, the sheik told us that, when they came up to the fire, they demanded tribute or backsheesh from the stranger passing over the Bedouins' highway; that his brother had refused to pay it, which had been the cause of the quarrel; and that, when he himself came up, he had told the demanders of tribute that he had undertaken to protect me from injury through the desert; that he had given his head to Mohammed Ali for my safety, and would defend me with his life against every danger; but that, finally, he had pacified them by giving them a couple of dollars apiece. I did not believe this. They looked too disconsolate when they went away, for the four dollars would have made the hearts of two beggarly Bedouins leap for joy; and I could not help asking him if we were obliged to buy our peace when only two came upon us, what we should do when a hundred should come; to which he answered that they must all be paid, and that it was impossible to pass through the desert without it.

We got through the day remarkably well, the scene being always precisely the same; before us, the long, desolate, sandy valley, and on each side the still more desolate and dreary mountains. Towards evening we encamped; and, after sitting some time around a fire with my companions, I entered my tent. Soon after, the sheik, in pursuance of his pitiful plan of exciting my fears and raising his own value, sent in for my gun and pistols, telling me that there were Arabs near; that he heard the barking of a dog, and intended to keep watch all night. I had already seen so much of him, that I knew this was a mere piece of braggadocio; and I met it with another, by telling him that no man could use my pistols better than myself, and that all he had to do was, upon the first alarm, to give me notice, and I would be among them. About an hour afterward I went out and found them all asleep; and I could not help making Paul rouse the sheik, and ask him if he did not want the pistols for his vigilant watch.

In the morning we started at half-past six. The day was again beautiful and inspiriting; my horse and myself had become the best friends in the world; and, though I was disgusted with the sheik's general conduct, I moved quietly along the valley, conversing with him or Paul, or with any of the men, about anything that happened to suggest itself. I remember I had a long discourse about the difference between the camel and the dromedary. Buffon gives the camel two humps, and the dromedary one; and this, I believe, is the received opinion, as it had always been mine; but, since I had been in the East, I had remarked that it was exceedingly rare to meet a camel with two humps. I had seen together at one time, on the starting of the caravan of pilgrims to Mecca, perhaps twenty

241

thousand camels and dromedaries, and had not seen among them more than half a dozen with two humps. Not satisfied with any explanation from European residents or travelers, I had inquired among the Bedouins; and Toualeb, my old guide, brought up among camels, had given such a strange account that I never paid any regard to it. Now, however, the sheik told me the same thing, namely, that they were of different races, the dromedary being to the camel as the blood-horse is to the cart-horse; and that the two humps were peculiar neither to the dromedary nor the camel, or natural to either; but that both are always born with only one hump, which, being a mere mass of flesh, and very tender, almost as soon as the young camel is born a piece is sometimes cut out of the middle for the convenience of better arranging the saddle; and, being cut out of the center, a hump is left on either side of the cavity; and this, according to the account given by Toualeb, is the only way in which two humps ever appear on the back of a camel or dromedary. I should not mention this story if I had heard it only once; but, precisely as I had it from Toualeb, it was confirmed with a great deal of circumstantial detail by another Bedouin, who, like himself, had lived among camels and dromedaries all his life; and his statement was assented to by all his companions. I do not give this out as a discovery made at this late day in regard to an animal so well known as the camel; indeed, I am told that the Arabs are not ignorant of that elegance of civilized life called "quizzing." I give it merely to show how I whiled away my time in the desert, and for what it is worth.[2]

Towards midday the sheik dashed across the plain, with his long lance poised in his hand, and his scarlet dress streaming in the wind; and about an hour afterward we came to his spear stuck in the sand, and a little Bedouin boy sitting by it to invite us to his father's tent. We turned aside, and, coming to the tent, found the sheik sitting on the ground refreshing himself with long draughts of goat's milk. He passed the skin to us; but, as master of the ceremonies, he declined the regular Arab invitation to stay and eat a lamb. He could not,

[2] In spite of Stephens' information, zoologists still classify camels as Dromedary (one hump) and Bactrian (two humps).

however, neglect the goods the gods provided, and told our host that we would take a lamb with us for our evening meal. The lamb was caught, and, with his legs tied, was thrown into a sack, where he made music for us the rest of the day. To the Bedouin, next to the pleasure of eating a lamb is that of knowing he has one to eat; and so the bleating of the doomed innocent was merely a whetter of appetite. After we had gone some distance from the tent, we set down the lamb on the ground, and I never saw a creature so perfectly the emblem of helplessness. At first he ran back a little way from us; then stopped; and apparently feeling the loneliness of his condition, returned and followed us, and in a few moments was under the feet of the camels, a part of our caravan unwittingly moving to the slaughter. The tent was hardly pitched before he lay bleeding on the ground; and the fire was no sooner kindled than his entrails, liver, &c., were in the burning brush; and in a few moments the Arabs were greedily devouring the meal into which he had been so speedily converted. The whole scene which I have before described was repeated; and, as before, in the morning the skin was the only part of the lamb to be seen.

One thing in the sheik was particularly disagreeable. He was constantly talking with Paul about the sacrifice he made in accompanying me; his confident expectation that I would pay him well for it; and the generosity of Mr. Linant; always winding up with asking what backsheesh I intended to give him. Paul told me all that passed, and it was evident that the sheik and his men were making extravagant calculations. I had estimated with Mr. Gliddon the probable expenses to Jerusalem, founded on the rate of hire for camels which the sheik had named at Cairo; and as it was not beyond the range of possibilities that I should be stripped on the way, I had brought with me barely enough to cover my probable expenses; and, consequently, I saw that my means were very likely to fall short of the sheik's expectations. I did not want any disappointment at the last, and that night I called him to my tent, resolved upon coming to an understanding. I told him that, knowing it was a dangerous road, and that I was subject to the risk of being robbed, I had brought with me a specific sum of money, all of which I intended for him, and that all he scattered along the road would be so much taken from his own pocket in the end. He was evidently startled, and expressed his surprise that a howaga, or gentleman, should have any bottom to his pocket, but promised to economize in future.

The next day the general features of the scene were the same, eternal barrenness and desolation; and, moving to the right, at one o'clock we were at the foot of the mountains of Seir; and towering above all the rest, surmounted by a circular dome, like the tombs of the sheiks in Egypt, was the bare and rugged summit of Mount Hor, the burial-place of Aaron, visible in every direction at a great distance from below, and on both sides the great range of mountains, and forming one of the marks by which the Bedouin regulates his wanderings in the desert. Soon after we turned in among the mountains, occasionally passing small spots of verdure, strangely contrasting with the surrounding and general desolation. Towards evening, in a small mountain on our left, we saw an excavation in the rock, which the sheik said had been a fortress; and, as of every other work of which the history is unknown, its construction was ascribed to the early Christians. It was a beautiful afternoon; gazelles were playing in the valleys, and partridges running wild up the sides of the mountains, and we pitched our tent partly over a carpet of grass, with the door open to the lofty tomb of the great high-priest of Israel.

In the evening the sheik came to my tent for money, having been very pertinacious on that tender subject all day with Paul, asking him how much he thought I had with me, and how much I intended to give him. He began by asking me for pay for the camels, at the price agreed upon in Cairo. If he had asked me before starting from Aqaba, I should probably have paid him; but, after what I had seen, and what had passed between him and Paul, I did not like his asking for it now. He told me, too, that we were now at the door of Petra, and that it would be necessary to pay a backsheesh or tribute on entering, but he could not tell how much would be required, as that would depend altogether on circumstances. There was always a guard stationed at the entrance of the defile leading to Petra, and the amount to be paid would depend upon the number we might happen to find when we entered. These were never less than thirty or forty; and if there should not be more, the tribute exacted would not be more than thirty or forty dollars, but there might be two or three hundred; and, at all events, I had better give him my purse, and he would return me what was left.

I suspected that, as he could not find out from Paul either how much I had with me or what I intended to give him, this story of the tribute was merely a pretext to levy an immediate contribution. The precise danger I had to fear was, that he would get my money from me piecemeal, and, when we came among Bedouins where it would be necessary to buy my peace, go off and leave me to their mercy. I did not want to have any rupture with him, particularly at the moment when I was at the very door of Petra, and might lose all that I had been endeavoring with so much personal difficulty to accomplish; and therefore told him, as to the backsheesh for entering Petra, that I expected; and, when we should arrive there and learn how much it was, would be ready to pay it; but, in the meantime, for any little casual expense that might be incurred, I would give him a purse of five hundred piasters, or twenty-five dollars. Touching the hire of camels, I said that I did not expect to pay it until we should arrive at Hebron; and, hurling back upon him one of his own flourishes, told him that it was distrusting my honor to ask it now. I reminded him of our conversation at Cairo, remarking that I had come into the desert upon the faith of his promise; and he replied very impertinently, if not menacingly, that one word here was worth a hundred at Cairo. I was somewhat roused at this, and, determined not to be dragooned into compliance, forgot for a moment my prudential plan, and told him that I would not be driven into that or anything else; and that, sooner than submit to his demand, I would turn back here, at the very door of Petra, and return to Cairo. This had its effect, for he was no more disposed to proceed to extremities than myself; and when I found him giving way a little, I threw in a powerful argument, which I had several times before hinted at, namely, that there were two parties on the Nile who were exceedingly anxious to make the same journey, and

245

who would be governed altogether by the report I should make. I saw that his avarice and hope of future gain were rapidly getting the better of his eagerness to touch his money before it was earned; and, without inflicting upon the reader a full account of our long negotiation, made up principally of blustering and exaggeration, with some diplomatic concessions on both sides, it is enough to say that at last, to my great relief, he withdrew his demand and took what I offered.

Before daybreak the next morning we had struck our tent, and sending it and the other baggage by another route, the sheik being afraid to take with us anything that might tempt the Bedouins, and leaving behind us several of our men, the sheik, his brother, three Arabs, Paul, and myself, with nothing but what we had on, and provisions for one day, started for Wadi Musa and the city of Petra. Our course was a continued ascent. I have found it through-out difficult to give any description which can impart to the reader a distinct idea of the wild and desolate scenes presented among these mountainous deserts.[3] I have been, too, in so many of the same general nature, that particular ones do not present themselves to my mind now with the force and distinctness of perfect recollection; and, in the few rough and hurried notes which I made on the spot, I marked rather the effect than the causes which produced it. I re-member, however, that the mountains were barren, solitary, and desolate, and that, as we ascended, their aspect became more and more wild and rugged, and rose to grandeur and sublimity. I re-member, too, that among these arid wastes of crumbling rock there were beautiful streams gushing out from the sides of the mountains; and sometimes small valleys, where the green grass, and shrubs, and bushes were putting forth in early spring; and that, altogether, I saw among the stony mountains of Arabia Petraea more verdure

[3] There were, anciently, two north roads toward Petra. The Nabatean way followed the desert west to Wadi Musa, and caravans entered it from the western end of the rock-cliff city. Trajan, however, laid his road along the Wadi-el-Butm; the soldiers of Legio IX Hispaña built the road to bypass Petra on the east side, thus rendering use-less the strategically placed Nabatean-controlled spice route through the heart of Petra (see maps by Laborde and Harding). Stephens entered by way of the Roman road into the ruins of Petra.

than I had observed since I left the banks of the Nile. I remember, moreover, that the ascent was difficult; that our camels toiled laboriously; and that even our sure-footed Arabian horses often slipped upon the steep and rugged path. Once the sheik and myself, being in advance of the rest, sat down upon an eminence which overlooked, on one side, a range of wild and barren mountains, and, on the other, the dreary valley of El Ghor; above us was the venerable summit of Mount Hor; and near us a stone blackened with smoke, and surrounded by fragments of bones, showing the place where the Arabs had sacrificed sheep to the Prophet Aaron. From this point we wound along the base of Mount Hor, which, from this great height, seemed just beginning to rise into a mountain; and I remember, that, in winding slowly along its base, as our companions had objected to our mounting to the tomb of Aaron, Paul and I were narrowly examining its sides for a path, and making arrangements to slip out as soon as they should all be asleep, and ascend by moonlight. Not far from the base of Mount Hor we came to some tombs cut in the sides of the rocks, and standing at the threshold of the entrance to the excavated city. Before entering this extraordinary place, it would not be amiss, in few words, to give its history.

CHAPTER XXI

PETRA, the excavated city, the long-lost capital of Edom, in the Scriptures and profane writings, in every language in which its name occurs, signifies a rock; and, through the shadows of its early history, we learn that its inhabitants lived in natural clefts or excavations made in the solid rock. Desolate as it now is, we have reason to believe that it goes back to the time of Esau, "the father of Edom"; that princes and dukes, eight successive kings, and again a long line of dukes, dwelt there before any king "reigned over Israel"; and we recognize it from the earliest ages as the central point to which came the caravans from the interior of Arabia, Persia, and India, laden with all the precious commodities of the East, and from which these commodities were distributed through Egypt, Palestine, and Syria, and all the countries bordering on the Mediterranean, even Tyre and Sidon deriving their purple and dies from Petra. Eight hundred years before Christ, Amaziah, the king of Judea, "slew of Edom in the Valley of Salt ten thousand, and took Selah [the Hebrew name of Petra] by war." Three hundred years after the last of the prophets and nearly a century before the Christian era, the "King of Arabia" issued from his palace at Petra, at the head of fifty thousand men, horse and foot, entered Jerusalem, and, uniting with the Jews, pressed the siege of the temple, which was only raised by the advance of the Romans; and in the beginning of the second century, though its independence was lost, Petra was still the capital of a Roman province. After that time it rapidly declined; its history became more and more obscure; for more than a thousand years it was completely lost to the civilized world; and, until its discovery by Burckhardt in 1812, except to the wandering Bedouins its very site was unknown.[1]

And this was the city at whose door I now stood. In a few words, this ancient and extraordinary city is situated within a natural amphitheatre of two or three miles in circumference, encompassed on all sides by rugged mountains five or six hundred feet in height. The whole of this area is now a waste of ruins, dwelling-houses, palaces, temples, and triumphal arches, all prostrate together in undistinguishable confusion. The sides of the mountains are cut smooth, in a perpendicular direction, and filled with long and continued ranges of dwelling-houses, temples, and tombs, excavated with vast labor out of the solid rock; and while their summits present Nature in her wildest and most savage form, their bases are adorned with all the beauty of architecture and art, with columns, and porticoes, and pediments, and ranges of corridors, enduring as the mountains out of which they are hewn, and fresh as if the work of a generation scarcely yet gone by.

Nothing can be finer than the immense rocky rampart which encloses the city. Strong, firm, and immovable as Nature itself, it seems to deride the walls of cities and the puny fortifications of skillful engineers. The only access is by clambering over this wall of stone, practicable only in one place, or by an entrance the most extraordinary that Nature, in her wildest freaks, has ever framed. The loftiest portals ever raised by the hands of man, the proudest monuments of architectural skill and daring, sink into insignificance by the comparison. It is, perhaps, the most wonderful object in the world, except the ruins of the city to which it forms the entrance.

[1] Petra was built by the Nabateans, speaking a language close to Semitic. The first historical reference to them is on the "List of Enemies" compiled by the Assyrians in 647 B.C. In time, the territory of the Nabateans spread from Damascus to the Red Sea; they seized and fortified the mountain fastness of Petra some time in the second century B.C. Strabo, the Greek historian, wrote about Petra from information gathered from Ahendorous, who was born in Petra and was a friend of Augustus. Pliny wrote of it, accurately mentioning the stream of water drawn from the Ain Musa "running through it." It was conquered by Trajan in A.D. 106. It was Romanized by Hadrian, who paved the El Sîk with a stone-laid road. He called it Hadriana. After the Arab conquest in the seventh century it was lost to human memory until Burckhardt entered it. (See A. V. Domaszewski, *Die Provinicia Arabia* [2 vols., Strasbourg, 1904].)

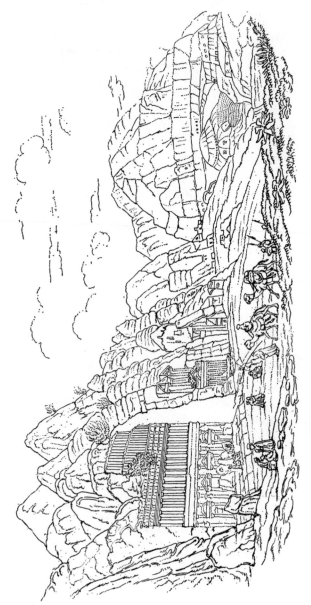

GENERAL VIEW OF PETRA FROM THE NORTHEAST

Unfortunately, I did not enter by this door, but by clambering over the mountains at the other end; and when I stood upon the summit of the mountain, though I looked down upon the vast area filled with ruined buildings and heaps of rubbish, and saw the mountainsides cut away so as to form a level surface, and presenting long ranges of doors in successive tiers or stories, the dwelling and burial places of a people long since passed away; and though immediately before me was the excavated front of a large and beautiful temple, I was disappointed. I had read the unpublished description of Captains Irby and Mangles. Several times the sheik had told me, in the most positive manner, that there was no other entrance; and I was moved to indignation at the marvellous and exaggerated, not to say false representations, as I thought, of the only persons who had given any account of this wonderful entrance.

I was disappointed, too, in another matter. Burckhardt had been accosted, immediately upon his entry, by a large party of Bedouins, and been suffered to remain but a very short time. Messrs. Legh, Banks, Irby, and Mangles had been opposed by hundreds of Bedouins, who swore "that they should never enter their territory nor drink of their waters," and "that they would shoot them like dogs if they attempted it." And I expected some immediate opposition from at least the thirty or forty, fewer than whom, the sheik had told me, were never to be found in Wadi Musa. I expected a scene of some kind; but at the entrance of the city there was not a creature to dispute our passage; its portals were wide open, and we passed along the stream down into the area, and still no man came to oppose us. We moved to the extreme end of the area; and, when in the act of dismounting at the foot of the rock on which stood the temple that had constantly faced us, we saw one solitary Arab, straggling along without any apparent object, a mere wanderer among the ruins; and it is a not uninteresting fact, that this poor Bedouin was the only living being we saw in the desolate city of Petra. After gazing at us for a few moments from a distance, he came towards us, and in a few moments was sitting down to pipes and coffee with my companions. I again asked the sheik for the other entrance, and he again told me there was none; but I could not believe him, and set out to look for it myself; and although in my search I had already seen enough abundantly to repay me for all my difficulties in getting there, I could not be content without finding this desired avenue.

In front of the great temple, the pride and beauty of Petra,[2] of which more hereafter, I saw a narrow opening in the rocks, exactly corresponding with my conception of the object for which I was seeking. A full stream of water was gushing through it, and filling up the whole mouth of the passage. Mounted on the shoulders of one of my Bedouins, I got him to carry me through the swollen stream at the mouth of the opening, and set me down on a dry place a little above, whence I began to pick my way, occasionally taking to the shoulders of my follower, and continued to advance more than a mile. I was beyond all peradventure in the great entrance I was seeking. There could not be two such, and I should have gone on to the extreme end of the ravine, but my Bedouin suddenly refused me the further use of his shoulders. He had been some time objecting and begging me to return, and now positively refused to go any farther; and, in fact, turned about himself. I was anxious to proceed, but I did not like wading up to my knees in the water, nor did I feel very resolute to go where I might expose myself to danger, as he seemed to intimate. While I was hesitating, another of my men came running up the ravine, and shortly after him Paul and the sheik, breathless with haste, and crying in low gutturals, "El Arab! el Arab!"—"The Arabs! the Arabs!" This was enough for me. I had heard so much of El Arab that I had become nervous. It was like the cry of Delilah in the ears of sleeping Samson, "The Philistines be upon thee." At the other end of the ravine was an encampment of the El Alouins; and the sheik, having due regard to my communication about money matters, had shunned this entrance to avoid bringing upon me this horde of tribute-gatherers for a participation in the spoils. Without any disposition to explore farther, I turned towards the city; and it was now that I began to feel the powerful and indelible impression that must be produced on entering, through this mountainous passage, the excavated city of Petra.

[2] See page 34 of the introduction for Charles Doughty's different impression.

RAVINE LEADING TO PETRA AND TOMB WITH GREEK INSCRIPTION

For about two miles it lies between high and precipitous ranges of rocks, from five hundred to a thousand feet in height, standing as if torn asunder by some great convulsion, and barely wide enough for two horsemen to pass abreast. A swelling stream rushes between them; the summits are wild and broken; in some places overhanging the opposite sides, casting the darkness of night upon the narrow defile; then receding and forming an opening above, through which a strong ray of light is thrown down, and illuminates with the blaze of day the frightful chasm below. Wild fig-trees, oleanders, and ivy were growing out of the rocky sides of the cliffs hundreds of feet above our heads; the eagle was screaming above us; all along were the open doors of tombs, forming the great Necropolis of the city; and at the extreme end was a large open space, with a powerful body of light thrown down upon it, and exhibiting in one full view the façade of a beautiful temple, hewn out of the rock, with rows of Corinthian columns and ornaments, standing out fresh and clear as if but yesterday from the hands of the sculptor.[3] Though coming directly from the banks of the Nile, where the preservation of the temples excites the admiration and astonishment of every traveler, we were roused and excited by the extraordinary beauty and excellent condition of the great temple at Petra. Even in coming upon it, as we did, at disadvantage, I remember that Paul, who was a passionate admirer of the arts, when he first obtained a glimpse of it, involuntarily cried out, and moving on to the front with a vivacity I never saw him exhibit before or afterward, clapped his hands, and shouted in ecstasy. To the last day of our being together he was in the habit of referring to his extraordinary fit of enthusiasm when he first came upon that temple; and I can well imagine that, entering by this narrow defile, with the feelings roused by its extraordinary and romantic wildness and beauty, the first view of that superb façade must produce an effect which could never pass away. Even now, that I have returned to the pursuits and thought-engrossing incidents of a life in the busiest city in the world, often in situations

[3] El Khasna is sculptured out of the rosiest red of all the base-rock of Petra. The style of the architecture is Greek, the period first century. It is not built but sculptured out of the sandstone like a miniature tholos.

INTERIOR VIEW OF THE KHASNA

as widely different as light from darkness, I see before me the façade of that temple; neither to Colosseum at Rome, grand and interesting as it is, nor the ruins of the Acropolis at Athens, nor the Pyramids, nor the mighty temples of the Nile, are so often present to my memory.

The whole temple, its columns, ornaments, porticoes, and porches, are cut out from and form part of the solid rock; and this rock, at the foot of which the temple stands like a mere print, towers several hundred feet above, its face cut smooth to the very summit, and the top remaining wild and misshapen as Nature made it. The whole area before the temple is perhaps an acre in extent, enclosed on all sides except at the narrow entrance, and an opening to the left of the temple, which leads into the area of the city by a pass through perpendicular rocks five or six hundred feet in height.

It is not my design to enter into the details of the many monuments in this extraordinary city; but, to give a general idea of the character of all the excavations, I cannot do better than go within the temple. Ascending several broad steps, we entered under a colonnade of four Corinthian columns, about thirty-five feet high, into a large chamber of some fifty feet square and twenty-five feet high. The outside of the temple is richly ornamented, but the interior is perfectly plain, there being no ornament of any kind upon the walls or ceiling; on each of the three sides is a small chamber for the reception of the dead; and on the back wall of the innermost chamber I saw the names of Messrs. Legh, Banks, Irby, and Mangles, the four English travelers who with so much difficulty had effected their entrance to the city; of Messieurs Laborde and Linant, and the two Englishmen and Italian of whom I have before spoken; and two or three others, which, from the character of the writing, I supposed to be the names of attendants upon some of these gentlemen. These were the only names recorded in the temple; and, besides Burckhardt, no other traveler had ever reached it. I was the first American who had ever been there. Many of my countrymen, probably, as was the case with me, have never known the existence of such a city; and, independently of all personal considerations, I confess that I felt what, I trust, was not an inexcusable pride, in writing upon the innermost wall of that temple the name of an American citizen; and under it, and flourishing on its own account in temples, and tombs, and all the most conspicuous places in Petra, is the illustrious name of Paolo Nuozzo, dragoman.[4]

Leaving the temple and the open area on which it fronts, and following the stream, we entered another defile much broader than the first, on each side of which were ranges of tombs, with sculptured doors and columns; and on the left, in the bosom of the mountain, hewn out of the solid rock, is a large theater, circular in form, the pillars in front fallen, and containing thirty-three rows of seats, capable of containing more than three thousand persons. Above the corridor was a range of doors opening to chambers in the rocks, the seats of the princes and wealthiest inhabitants of Petra, and not unlike a row of private boxes in a modern theatre.

The whole theatre is at this day in such a state of preservation, that if the tenants of the tombs around could once more rise into life, they might take their old places on its seats, and listen to the declamation of their favorite player. To me the stillness of a ruined city is nowhere so impressive as when sitting on the steps of its theatre; once thronged with the gay and pleasure-seeking, but now given up to solitude and desolation. Day after day these seats had been filled, and the now silent rocks had echoed to the applauding shout of thousands; and little could an ancient Edomite imagine that a solitary stranger, from a then unknown world, would one day be wandering among the ruins of his proud and wonderful city, meditating upon the fate of a race that has for ages passed away. Where are ye, inhabitants of this desolate city? ye who once sat on the seats of this theatre, the young, the high-born, the beautiful, and brave; who once rejoiced in your riches and power, and lived as if there was no grave? Where are ye now? Even the very tombs, whose open doors are stretching away in long ranges before the eyes of the wondering traveler, cannot reveal the mystery of your doom:

---

[4] All of these names are faintly visible on the right-hand wall of El Khasna directly within the darkened portals, but they are all but obscured by countless later names.

VIEW OF PETRA FROM THE TOP OF THE THEATRE

your dry bones are gone; the robber has invaded your graves, and your very ashes have been swept away to make room for the wandering Arab of the desert.

But we need not stop at the days when a gay population were crowding to this theatre. In the earliest periods of recorded time, long before this theatre was built, and long before the tragic muse was known, a great city stood here. When Esau, having sold his birthright for a mess of pottage, came to his portion among the mountains of Seir; and Edom, growing in power and strength, became presumptuous and haughty, until, in her pride, when Israel prayed a passage through her country, Edom said unto Israel, "Thou shalt not pass by me, lest I come out against thee with the sword."

Amid all the terrible denunciations against the land of Idumea, "her cities and the inhabitants thereof," this proud city among the rocks, doubtless for its extraordinary sins, was always marked as a subject of extraordinary vengeance. "I have sworn by myself, saith the Lord, that Bozrah (the strong or fortified city) shall become a desolation, a reproach, and a waste, and a curse, and all the cities thereof shall be perpetual waste. Lo, I will make thee small among the heathen, and despised among men. Thy terribleness hath deceived thee, and the pride of thy heart, oh thou that dwellest in the clefts of the rocks, that holdest the height of the hill; though thou shouldest make thy nest as high as the eagle, I will bring thee down from thence, saith the Lord."[5] "Thy shall call the nobles thereof to the kingdom, but none shall be there, and all her princes shall be nothing; and thorns shall come up in her palaces, nettles and brambles in the fortresses thereof, and it shall be a habitation for dragons, and a court for owls."[6]

I would that the skeptic could stand as I did among the ruins of this city among the rocks, and there open the sacred book and read the words of the inspired penman, written when this desolate place was one of the greatest cities in the world. I see the scoff arrested, his cheek pale, his lip quivering, and his heart quaking with fear, as

[5] Jeremiah xlix., 13, 16.—Stephens' note.
[6] Isaiah xxxiv., 14, 15.—Stephens' note.

CORINTHIAN TOMB, PETRA

the ruined city cries out to him in a voice loud and powerful as that of one risen from the dead; though he would not believe Moses and the prophets, he believes the handwriting of God himself in the desolation and eternal ruin around him. We sat on the steps of the theatre, and made our noonday meal; our drink was from the pure stream that rolled down at our feet. Paul and myself were alone. We scared the partridge before us as we ascended, and I broke for a moment the stillness of the desolate city by the report of my gun.

All around the theatre, in the sides of the mountains, were ranges of tombs; and directly opposite they rose in long tiers one above another. Having looked into those around the theatre, I crossed to those opposite; and, carefully as the brief time I had would allow, examined the whole range. Though I had no small experience in exploring catacombs and tombs, these were so different from any I had seen that I found it difficult to distinguish the habitations of the living from the chambers of the dead. The façades or architectural decorations of the front were everywhere handsome; and in this they differed materially from the tombs in Egypt; in the latter the doors were simply an opening in the rock, and all the grandeur and beauty of the work within; while here the door was always imposing in its appearance, and the interior was generally a simple chamber, unpainted and unsculptured.

I say that I could not distinguish the dwellings from the tombs; but this was not invariably the case; some were clearly tombs, for there were pits in which the dead had been laid, and others were as clearly dwellings, being without a place for the deposit of the dead. One of these last particularly attracted my attention. It consisted of one large chamber, having on one side, at the foot of the wall, a stone bench about a foot high, and two or three broad, in form like the divans in the East at the present day; at the other end were several small apartments, hewn out of the rock, with partition walls left between them, like stalls in a stable, and these had probably been the sleeping apartments of the different members of the family, the mysteries of bars and bolts, of folding doors and third stories, being unknown in the days of the ancient Edomites. There were no paintings or decorations of any kind within the chamber; but the rock out of which it was hewn, like the whole stony rampart that encircled the city, was of a peculiarity and beauty that I never saw elsewhere, being a dark ground, with veins of white, blue, red, purple, and sometimes scarlet and light orange, running through it in rainbow streaks; and within the chambers, where there had been no exposure to the action of the elements, the freshness and beauty of the colors in which these waving lines were drawn gave an effect hardly inferior to that of the paintings in the tombs of the kings at Thebes. From its high and commanding position, and the unusual finish of the work, this house, if so it may be called, had no doubt been the residence of one who had strutted his hour of brief existence among the wealthy citizens of Petra. In front was a large table of rock, forming a sort of court for the excavated dwelling, where probably, year after year, in this beautiful climate, the Edomite of old sat under the gathering shades of evening, sometimes looking down upon the congregated thousands and the stirring scenes in the theatre beneath, or beyond upon the palaces and dwellings in the area of the then populous city.

Farther on in the same range, though, in consequence of the steps of the streets being broken, we were obliged to go down and ascend again before we could reach it, was another temple, like the first, cut out of the solid rock, and, like the first too, having for its principal ornament a large urn, shattered and bruised by musket balls; for the ignorant Arab, believing that gold is concealed in it, day after day, as he passes, levels at it his murderous gun, in the vain hope to break the vessel and scatter a golden shower on the ground.

But it would be unprofitable to dwell upon details. In the exceeding interest of the scene around me, I hurried from place to place, utterly insensible to physical fatigue; and being entirely alone, and having a full and undisturbed range of the ruins, I clambered up broken staircases and among the ruins of streets; and, looking into one excavation, passed on to another and another, and made the whole circuit of the desolate city. There, on the spot, everything had an interest which I cannot give in description; and if the reader has followed me so far, I have too much regard for him to drag him about after me as I did Paul. I am warned of the consequences by what occurred with that excellent and patient follower; for, before the day was over, he was completely worn out with fatigue.

The shades of evening were gathering around us as we stood for the last time on the steps of the theatre. Perfect as has been the fulfillment of the prophecy in regard to this desolate city, in no one particular has its truth been more awfully verified than in the complete destruction of its inhabitants; in the extermination of the race of the Edomites. In the same day, and by the voice of the same prophets, came the separate denunciations against the descendants of Israel and Edom, declaring against both a complete change of their temporal condition; and while the Jews have been dispersed in every country under heaven, and are still, in every land, a separate and unmixed people, "the Edomites have been cut off forever, and there is not any remaining of the house of Esau."

"Wisdom has departed from Teman, and understanding out of the mount of Esau"; and the miserable Arab who now roams over the land cannot appreciate or understand the works of its ancient inhabitants. In the summer he cultivates the few valleys in which seed will grow, and in the winter makes his habitation in the tombs; and, stimulated by vague and exaggerated traditionary notions of the greatness and wealth of the people who have gone before him, his barbarous hand is raised against the remaining monuments of their arts; and, as he breaks to atoms the sculptured stone, he expects to gather up their long-hidden treasures. I could have lingered for days on the steps of that theatre, for I never was at a place where such a crowd of associations pressed upon my mind. But the sheik was hurrying me away. From the first he had told me that I must not pass a night within the city; and begging me not to tempt my fortune too rashly, he was perpetually urging me to make my retreat while there was yet time. He said that, if the Arabs at the other end of the great entrance heard of a stranger being there, they would be down upon me to a man, and, not content with extorting money, would certainly prevent my visiting the tomb of Aaron. He had touched the right chord; and considering that weeks or months could not impress the scene more strongly on my mind, and that I was no artist, and could not carry away on paper the plans and

263

models of ancient art, I mounted my horse from the very steps of the theatre, and followed the sheik in his progress up the valley. Turning back from the theatre, the whole area of the city burst upon the sight at once, filled with crumbling masses of rock and stone, the ruined habitations of a people long since perished from the face of the earth, and encompassed on every side by high ranges of mountains; and the sides of these were cut smooth, even to the summit, hundreds of feet above my head as I rode past, and filled with long-continued ranges of open doors, the entrances to dwellings and tombs, of which the small connecting staircases were not visible at a distance, and many of the tenements seemed utterly inaccessible.

Every moment the sheik was becoming more and more impatient; and, spurring my horse, I followed him on a gallop among the ruins. We ascended the valley, and rising to the summit of the rocky rampart, it was almost dark when we found ourselves opposite a range of tombs in the suburbs of the city. Here we dismounted; and selecting from among them one which, from its finish and dimensions, must have been the last abode of some wealthy Edomite, we prepared to pass the night within its walls. I was completely worn out when I threw myself on the rocky floor of the tomb. I had just completed one of the most interesting days in my life; for the singular character of the city, and the uncommon beauty of its ruins, its great antiquity, the prophetic denunciations of whose truth it was the witness, its loss for more than a thousand years to the civilized world, its very existence being known only to the wandering Arab, the difficulty of reaching it, and the hurried and dangerous manner in which I had reached it, gave a thrilling and almost fearful interest to the time and place, of which I feel it utterly impossible to convey any idea.

In the morning Paul and I had determined, when our companions should be asleep, to ascend Mount Hor by moonlight; but now we thought only of rest; and seldom has the pampered tenant of a palace laid down with greater satisfaction upon his canopied bed than I did upon the stony floor of this tomb in Petra. In the front part of it was a large chamber, about twenty-five feet square and ten feet high; and behind this was another of smaller dimensions, furnished with receptacles for the dead, not arranged after the manner of shelves extending along the wall, as in the catacombs I had seen in Italy and Egypt, but cut lengthwise in the rock, like ovens, so as to admit the insertion of the body with the feet foremost.

We built a fire in the outer chamber, thus lighting up the innermost recesses of the tombs; and, after our evening meal, while sipping coffee and smoking pipes, the sheik congratulated me upon my extreme good fortune in having seen Petra without any annoyance from the Bedouins; adding, as usual, that it was a happy day for me when I saw his face at Cairo. He told me that he had never been to Wadi Musa without seeing at least thirty or forty Arabs, and sometimes three or four hundred; that when Abdel Hag (Mr. Linant) and Mr. Laborde visited Petra the first time, they were driven out by the Bedouins after remaining only five hours, and were chased down into the valley, Mr. Linant changing his dromedary every three hours on the way back to Aqaba; that there he remained, pretending to be sick, for twenty-four days, every day feasting half the tribe; and during that time sending to Cairo for money, dresses, swords, guns, pistols, ammunition, &c., which he distributed among them so lavishly that the whole tribe escorted him in triumph to Petra. This is so different from Mr. Laborde's account of his visit, that it cannot be true. I asked him about the visit of Messrs. Legh and Banks, and Captains Irby and Mangles; and drawing close to me, so as not to be overheard by the rest, he told me that he remembered their visit well; that they came from Karak with three sheiks and three or four hundred men, and that the Bedouins of Wadi Musa turned out against them more than two thousand strong. His uncle was then the sheik, and he himself a young man; and, if his account is true, which cannot, however, be, as it is entirely different from theirs, he began the life of a knave so young, that, though he had no great field for exercise, he ought then to have been something of a proficient; he said, that while they were negotiating and parleying, one of the strange Arabs slipped into his hands a purse with a hundred pieces of gold, which he showed to his uncle, and proposed to him that they should use their

265

influence to procure the admission of the strangers, and divide the money between them; and so wrought upon the old man that he procured their entrance, telling the tribe that one of the strangers was sick, and, if they did not admit them into Wadi Musa, he would take them to his tent; and, added the sheik, his eyes sparkling with low cunning, my uncle and I ate the whole of that gold without any one of the tribe ever knowing anything about it.

One piece of information he gave me, which I thought very likely to be true; that the road to Petra, and thence through Idumea in any direction, never could be pursued with assurance of safety, or become a frequented route, because the Bedouins would always be lying in wait for travelers, to exact tribute or presents; and although a little might sometimes content them, at others their demands would be exorbitant, and quarrels and bad consequences to the traveler would be almost sure to follow; and he added, in reference to our visit, that, as soon as the Arabs should hear of a stranger having been at Petra, they would be down in swarms; and perhaps even now would follow us into the valley. I was satisfied that I had made a fortunate escape, not, perhaps, from personal danger, but from grinding exactions, if not from robbery; and, congratulating myself upon my good fortune so far, I began to feel my way for what I now regarded as important as before I had thought the journey to Petra, namely, a visit to the tomb of Aaron.

My companions opposed my going to it, saying that no Christian had ever done so; and that none but Mussulmans went there, and they only to sacrifice a sheep upon the tomb. I told them that I also designed to sacrifice; and that, like them, we regarded Aaron as a prophet; that my visit to Petra was nothing unless I made the sacrifice; and that my conscience would not be at ease unless I performed it according to my vow. This notice of my pious purpose smoothed some of the difficulties, as the Arabs knew that after the sacrifice the sheep must be eaten. The sheik was much more liberal or more indifferent than the rest, and my desire was finally assented to; although, in winding up a long discussion about the pedigree of Aaron, one of them held out to the last that Aaron was a Mussulman, and would not believe that he lived before Mohammed. He had an indefinite idea that Mohammed was the greatest man that ever lived, and in his mind this was not consistent with the idea of anyone having lived before him.

My plans for the morrow being all arranged, the Bedouins stretched themselves out in the outer chamber, while I went within; and seeking out a tomb as far back as I could find, I crawled in feet first, and found myself very much in the condition of a man buried alive. But never did a man go to his tomb with so much satisfaction as I felt. I was very tired; the night was cold, and here I was completely sheltered. I had just room enough to turn round; and the worthy old Edomite for whom the tomb was made never slept in it more quietly than I did. Little did he imagine that his bones would one day be scattered to the winds, and a straggling American and a horde of Bedouins, born and living thousands of miles from each other, would be sleeping quietly in his tomb, alike ignorant and careless of him for whom it was built.

CHAPTER XXII

A MAN RISING from a tomb with all his clothes on does not require much time for the arrangement of his toilet. In less than half an hour we had breakfasted, and were again on our way. Forgetting all that had engrossed my thoughts and feeling the day before, I now fixed my eyes upon the tomb of Aaron, on the summit of Mount Hor. The mountain was high, towering above the rest, bare and rugged to its very summit, without a tree or even a bush growing on its sterile sides; and our road lay directly along its base. The Bedouins again began to show an unwillingness to allow my visit to the tomb; and the sheik himself told me that it would take half the day, and perhaps be the means of bringing upon me some of the horde I had escaped. I saw that they were disposed to prevent me from accomplishing my object; and I felt sure that, if we met any strange Arabs, my purpose would certainly be defeated. I suspected them of stratagem, and began to think of resorting to stratagem for myself. They remembered the sheep, however, and told me that the sacrifice could as well be performed at the base as on the summit of the mountain; but this, of course, would not satisfy my conscience.

With my eyes constantly fixed on the top of the mountain, I had thought for some time that it would not be impracticable to ascend from the side on which I was. Paul and I examined the localities as carefully as a couple of engineers seeking an assailable place to scale the wall of a fortified city; and afraid to wait till they had matured some plan of opposing me, I determined to take them by surprise; and throwing myself from my horse, and telling Paul to

268

say that we would climb the mountain here and meet them on the other side, I was almost out of hearing before they had recovered from their astonishment. Paul followed me, and the sheik and his men stood for some time without moving, irresolute what to do; and it was not until we had advanced considerably on the mountain that we saw the caravan again slowly moving along its base. None of them offered to accompany us, though we should have been glad to have one or two with us on our expedition.

For some distance we found the ascent sufficiently smooth and easy—much more so than that of Mount Sinai—and, so far as we could see before us, it was likely to continue the same all the way up. We were railing at the sheik for wanting to carry us around to the other side, and congratulating ourselves upon having attempted it here, when we came to a yawning and precipitous chasm, opening its horrid jaws almost from the very base of the mountain. From the distance at which we had marked out our route, the inequalities of surface could not be distinguished, but here it was quite another thing. We stood on the brink of the chasm, and looked at each other in blank amazement; and at a long distance, as they wound along the base of the mountain, I thought I could see a quiet smile of derision lighting up the grim visages of my Bedouin companions. We stood upon the edge of the chasm, looking down into its deep abyss, like the spirits of the departed lingering on the shores of the Styx, vainly wishing for a ferryman to carry us over, and our case seemed perfectly hopeless without some such aid. But the days when genii and spirits lent their kind assistance to the sons of men are gone; if a man finds himself in a ditch, he must get out of it as well as he can, and so it was with us on the brink of this chasm. Bad, however, as was our prospect in looking forward, we had not yet begun to look back; and as soon as we saw that there was no possibility of getting over it, we began to descend; and groping, sliding, jumping, and holding on with hands and feet, we reached the bottom of the gully; and, after another hard half hour's toil, were resting our wearied limbs upon the opposite brink, at about the same elevation as that of the place from which we had started.

This success encouraged us; and, without caring or thinking how

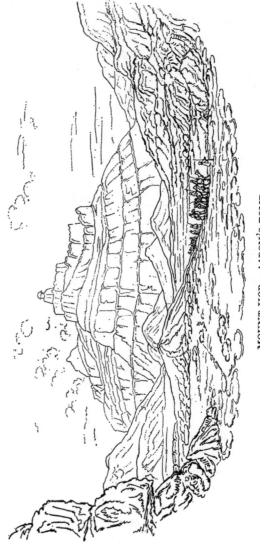

MOUNT HOR—AARON'S TOMB

we should come down again, we felt only the spirit of the seaman's cry to the trembling sailor boy, "Look aloft, you lubber"; and looking aloft, we saw through a small opening before us, though still at a great distance, the white dome that covered the tomb of the first high-priest of Israel. Again with stout hearts we resumed our ascent; but, as we might reasonably have supposed, that which we had passed was not the only chasm in the mountains. What had appeared to us slight inequalities of surface we found great fissures and openings, presenting themselves before us in quick succession; not, indeed, as absolute and insurmountable barriers to farther progress, but affording us only the encouragement of a bare possibility of crossing them. The whole mountain, from its base to its summit, was rocky and naked, affording not a tree or bush to assist us; and all that we had to hold on by were the rough and broken corners of the porous sandstone rocks, which crumbled in our hands and under our feet, and more than once put us in danger of our lives.

Several times, after desperate exertion, we sat down perfectly discouraged at seeing another and another chasm before us, and more than once we were on the point of giving up the attempt, thinking it impossible to advance any farther; but we had come so far, and taken so little notice of our road, that it was almost as impossible to return; and a distant and accidental glimpse of the whitened dome would revive our courage, and stimulate us to another effort. Several times I mounted on Paul's shoulders, and with his helping reached the top of a precipitous or overhanging rock, where, lying down with my face over the brink, I took up the pistols, swords, &c., and then helped him up in turn; sometimes, again, he was the climber, and my shoulders were the stepping-stone; and, in the rough grasps that we gave each other, neither thought of the relation of master and servant. On the sides of that rugged mountain, so desolate, so completely removed from the world, whose difficult ascent had been attempted by few human footsteps since the days when "Moses and Aaron went up in sight of all the congregation," the master and the man lay on the same rock, encountering the same fatigues and dangers, and inspired by the same hopes and fears. My dress was particularly bad for the occasion; for, besides the en-

271

cumbrance of pistols and a sword, my long silk gown and large sleeves were a great annoyance, as I wanted every moment a long reach of the arm and full play of the legs; even our light Turkish slippers were impediments in our desperate scramble, and we were obliged to pull them off, for the better hold that could be taken with the naked feet.

It will be remembered that we were ascending on the eastern side of the mountain; and in one of our pauses to breathe, when about halfway up, we looked back upon the high rampart of rocks that enclosed the city of Petra; and on the outside of the rock we saw the façade of a beautiful temple, resembling in its prominent features, but seeming larger and more beautiful than, the Khasne of Pharaoh opposite the principal entrance of the city. I have no doubt that a visit to that temple would have abundantly repaid me for the day I should have lost; for, besides its architectural beauty, it would have been curious to examine, and, if possible, discover why it was constructed, standing alone outside of the city, and, as it appeared, apart from everything connected with the habitations of the Edomites. But as yet we had work enough before us. Disencumbering ourselves of all our useless trappings, shoes, pistols, swords, tobacco-pouch, and water-sack, which we tied together in a sash and the roll of a turban, by dint of climbing, pushing, and lifting each other, after the most arduous upward scramble I ever accomplished, we attained the bald and hoary summit of the mountain; and, before we had time to look around, at the extreme end of the desolate valley of El Ghor, our attention was instantly attracted and engrossed by one of the most interesting objects in the world, and Paul and I exclaimed at the same moment, "The Dead Sea!" Lying between the barren mountains of Arabia and Judea, presenting to us from that height no more than a small, calm, and silvery surface, was that mysterious sea which rolled its dark waters over the guilty cities of Sodom and Gomorrah; over whose surface, according to the superstition of the Arabs, no bird can fly, and in whose waters no fish can swim; constantly receiving in its greedy bosom the whole body of the Jordan, but, unlike all other waters, sending forth no tribute to the ocean. A new idea entered my mind.

I would follow the desert valley of El Ghor to the shores of the Dead Sea, along whose savage borders I would coast to the ruined Jericho and the hallowed Jordan, and search in its deadly waters for the ruins of the doomed and blasted cities.

If I had never stood on the top of Mount Sinai, I should say that nothing could exceed the desolation of the view from the summit of Mount Hor, its most striking objects being the dreary and rugged mountains of Seir, bare and naked of trees and verdure, and heaving their lofty summits to the skies, as if in a vain and fruitless effort to excel the mighty pile, on the top of which the high priest of Israel was buried. Before me was a land of barrenness and ruin; a land accursed by God, and against which the prophets had set their faces; the land of which it is thus written in the Book of Life: "Moreover, the word of the Lord came unto me, saying, Son of man, set thy face against Mount Seir, and prophesy against it, and say unto it, Thus saith the Lord God, Behold, oh Mount Seir, I am against thee, and I will stretch out mine hand against thee, and I will make thee most desolate. I will lay thy cities waste, and thou shalt be desolate; and thou shalt know that I am the Lord. Because thou hast had a perpetual hatred, and hast shed the blood of children of Israel by the force of the sword in the time of their calamity, in the time that their iniquity had an end: therefore, as I live, saith the Lord God, I will prepare thee unto blood, and blood shall pursue thee: sith thou hast not hated blood, even blood shall pursue thee. Thus will I make Mount Seir most desolate, and cut off from it him that passeth out and him that returneth. And I will fill his mountains with his slain men: in thy hills, and in thy valleys, and in all thy rivers shall they fall that are slain with the sword. I will make thee perpetual desolations, and thy cities shall not return: and ye shall know that I am the Lord."[1]

The Bible account of the death of Aaron is—"And the children of Israel, even the whole congregation, journeyed from Kadesh, and came unto Mount Hor. And the Lord spake unto Moses and Aaron in Mount Hor, by the coast of the land of Edom, saying, Aaron shall be gathered unto his people: for he shall not enter into the land

---

[1] Ezekiel xxxv.—Stephens' note.

which I have given unto the children of Israel, because ye rebelled against my word at the water of Meribah. Take Aaron and Eleazer his son, and bring them up unto Mount Hor; and strip Aaron of his garments, and put them upon Eleazer his son: and Aaron shall be gathered unto his people, and shall die there. And Moses did as the Lord commanded: and they went up into Mount Hor, in the sight of all the congregation. And Moses stripped Aaron of his garments, and put them upon Eleazer his son; and Aaron died there in the top of the mount: and Moses and Eleazer came down from the mount. And when all the congregation saw that Aaron was dead, they mourned for Aaron thirty days, even all the house of Israel."[2]

On the very "top of the mount," reverenced alike by Mussulmans and Christians, is the tomb of Aaron. The building is about thirty feet square, containing a single chamber; in front of the door is a tombstone, in form like the oblong slabs in our churchyards, but larger and higher; the top rather larger than the bottom, and covered with a ragged pall of faded red cotton in shreds and patches. At its head stood a high round stone, on which the Mussulman offers his sacrifices. The stone was blackened with smoke; stains of blood and fragments of burnt brush were still about it; all was ready but the victim; and when I saw the reality of the preparations, I was very well satisfied to have avoided the necessity of conforming to the Mussulman custom. A few ostrich eggs, the usual ornaments of a mosque, were suspended from the ceiling, and the rest of the chamber was perfectly bare.

After going out, and from the very top of the tomb surveying again and again the desolate and dreary scene that presented itself on every side, always terminating with the distant view of the Dead Sea, I returned within; and examining once more the tomb and the altar, walked carefully around the chamber. There was no light except what came from the door; and, in groping in the extreme corner on one side, my foot descended into an aperture in the floor. I put it down carefully, and found a step, then another, and another, evidently a staircase leading to a chamber below. I went down till my head was on the level of the floor, but could see nothing; all was

[2] Numbers xx.—Stephens' note.

dark, and I called to Paul to strike a light. Most provokingly, he had no materials with him. He generally carried a flint and steel for lighting his pipe with; but now, when I most wanted it, he had none. I went back to the staircase, and, descending to the bottom of the steps, attempted to make out what the place might be; but it was utterly impossible. I could not see even the steps on which I stood. I again came out, and made Paul search in all his pockets for the steel and flint. My curiosity increased with the difficulty of gratifying it; and in a little while, when the thing seemed to be utterly impossible, with this hole unexplored, Petra, Mount Hor, and the Dead Sea appeared to lose half their interest. I ran up and down the steps, inside and out, abused Paul, and struck stones together in the hope of eliciting a spark; but all to no purpose. I was in an agony of despair, when I found myself grasping convulsively the handle of my pistol. A light broke suddenly upon me. A pile of dry brush and cotton rags lay at the foot of the sacrificial altar; I fired my pistol into it, gave one puff, and the whole mass was in a blaze. Each seized a burning brand, and we descended. At the foot of the steps was a narrow chamber, at the other end an iron grating, opening in the middle, and behind the grating a tomb cut in the naked rock, guarded and reverenced as the tomb of Aaron. I tore aside the rusty grating, and thrusting in my arm up to the shoulders, touched the hallowed spot. The rocks and mountains were echoing the discharge of my pistol, like peals of crashing thunder; and while, with the burning brand in one hand, I was thrusting the other through the grating, the deafening reverberations seemed to rebuke me for an act of sacrilege, and I rushed up the steps like a guilty and fear-struck criminal.

Suddenly I heard from the foot of the mountain a quick and irregular discharge of firearms, which again resounded in loud echoes through the mountains. It was far from my desire that the bigoted Mussulmans should come upon me, and find me with my pistol still smoking in my hand, and the brush still burning in the tomb of the prophet; and, tearing off a piece of the ragged pall, we hurried from the place and dashed down the mountain on the opposite side with a speed and recklessness that only fear could give. If there was room for question between a scramble or a jump, we gave the jump; and, when we could not jump, our shoes were off in a moment, one leaned over the brow of the precipice, and gave the other his hand, and down we went, allowing nothing to stop us. Once for a moment we were at a loss; but Paul, who, in the excitement of one successful leap after another, had become amazingly confident, saw a stream of water, and made for it with the glorious boast that where water descended we could; and the suggestion proved correct, although the water found much less difficulty in getting down than we did. In short, after an ascent the most toilsome, and a descent the most hairbrained and perilous it was ever my fortune to accomplish, in about half an hour we were at the base of the mountain, but still hurrying on to join our escort.

We had only to cross a little valley to reach the regular camel-track, when we saw from behind a slightly elevated range of rocks the head and long neck of a dromedary; a Bedouin was on his back, but, riding sidewise, did not see us. Another came, and another, and another; then two or three, and finally, half a dozen at a time, the blackest, grimmest, and ugliest vagabonds I had ever yet seen. A moment before, Paul and I had both complained of fatigue, but it is astonishing how the sight of these honest men revived us; anyone seeing the manner in which we scoured along the side of the mountain would have thought that all our consciousness was in our legs. The course we were pursuing when we first saw them would have brought us on the regular camel-track a little in advance of them, but now our feet seemed to cling to the sides of the mountain. We were in a humor for almost calling on the rocks to fall upon us and cover us; and, if there had been a good dodging-place, I am afraid I should here have to say that we had taken advantage of it until the very unwelcome caravan passed by; but the whole surface of the country, whether on mountainside or in valley's depth, was bare and naked as a floor; there was not a bush to obstruct the view; and soon we stood revealed to these unpleasant witnesses of our agility. They all shouted to us at once; and we returned the salute, looking at them over our shoulders, but pushing on as fast as we could walk. In civilized society, our course of proceeding would have been considered a decided cut; but the unmannerly savages did not know when they received a civil cut, and were bent on cultivating our acquaintance. With a loud shout, slipping off their camels and whipping up their dromedaries, they left the track, and dashed across the valley to intercept us. I told Paul that it was all over, and now we must brazen it out; and we had just time to turn around and reconnoiter for a moment, before we were almost trodden under foot by their dromedaries.

With the accounts that we had read and heard of these Bedouins, it was not a pleasant thing to fall into their hands alone; and, without the protection of the sheik, we had reason to apprehend bad treatment. We were on a rising ground; and, as they came bounding towards us, I had time to remark that there was not a gun or pistol among them; but every one, old and young, big and little, carried an enormous sword slung over his back, the hilt coming up towards the left shoulder, and in his hand a large club, with a knot at the end as large as a doubled fist. Though I had no idea of making any resistance, it was a satisfaction to feel that they might have some respect for our firearms; as even a Bedouin's logic can teach him, that though a gun or pistol can kill but one, no man in a crowd can tell but that he may be that one. Our armory, however, was not in the best condition for immediate use. I had fired one of my pistols in the tomb of Aaron and lost the flint of the other; and Paul had burst the priming cap on one of his barrels, and the other was charged with bird-shot.

It seemed that there was nothing hostile in their intentions; for though they came upon us with a wild and clamorous shout, their dark eyes appeared to sparkle with delight as they shook us by the hand, and their tumultuous greeting, to compare small things with great, reminded me of the wild welcome which the Arabs of Saladin gave to the litter of the Queen of England, when approaching the Diamond of the Desert on the shores of the Dead Sea. Nevertheless, I looked suspiciously upon all their demonstrations of good-will; and, though I returned all their greetings, even to the kiss on their black faces, I would rather have been looking at them through the bars of an iron grating. But Paul behaved like a hero, although he was a supreme coward, and admitted it himself.[3] I knew that everything depended upon him; but they had come upon us in such a hurry, and so few words had passed between us, that I had no idea how he stood affected. His first words reassured me; and really, if he had passed all his life in taming Bedouins, he could not have conducted himself more gallantly or sensibly. He shook hands with one, took a pipe from the mouth of another, kicked the dromedary of a third, and patted his owner on the back, smoking, laughing, and talking all the time, ringing the changes upon the Sheik El Alouin, Habib Effendi, and Abdel Hasis. I knew that he was lying from his remarkable amplitude of words, and from his constantly mixing up Abdel Hasis (myself) with the Habib Effendi, the prime minister of the pasha; but he was going on so smoothly that I had not the heart to stop him; and besides, I thought he was playing for himself as well as for me, and I had no right to put him in danger by interfering. At length, all talking together, and Paul's voice rising above the rest, in force as well as frequency, we returned to the track, and proceeded forward in a body to find the sheik.

Not to be too heavy on Paul for the little wanderings of his tongue, I will barely mention such as he remembered himself. Beginning with a solemn assurance that we had not been in Wadi Musa or Petra (for this was his cardinal point), he affirmed that I was a Turk making a pilgrimage to the tomb of Aaron under a vow; and that, when Sheik El Alouin was at Cairo, the Habib Effendi had taken me to the sheik's tent, and had told him to conduct me to Djebel Haroun, or Mount Hor, and from thence to Hebron (Khalil), and that, if I arrived in safety, he, the Habib Effendi, would pay him well for it. We went on very well for a little while; but by-and-by the Bedouins began talking earnestly among themselves, and a fine, wicked-looking boy, leaning down from the hump of his barebacked dromedary, with sparkling eyes thrust out his

[3] Paul's explanation of his cowardice was somewhat remarkable, and perhaps veracious. He said that he was by nature brave enough, but that, when traveling in Syria, about three years before, with Mr. Wellesley—a natural son of the Duke of Wellington—their party was stopped by Arabs, and their two kervashes, without any parley, raised their muskets and shot two of the poor savages dead before his face; which had such an effect upon his nerves as to give him a horror of lead and cold steel ever since.—Stephens' note.

hand and whispered backsheesh; an old dried-up man echoed it in a hoarse voice directly in my ears; and one after another joined in, till the whole party, with their deep-toned gutturals, were croaking the odious and ominous demand that grated harshly on my nerves. Their black eyes were turned upon me with a keen and eager brightness; the harsh cry was growing louder every moment; and I had already congratulated myself upon having very little about my person, and Paul was looking over his shoulders, and flourishing the Habib Effendi and the Sheik El Alouin with as loud a voice as ever, but evidently with a fainting heart; backsheesh, backsheesh, backsheesh was drowning every other noise, when a sudden turn in the road brought us upon the sheik and his attendants. The whole party were in confusion; some were descending the bare sides of the mountains, others were coming down with their dromedaries upon a full run; the sheik's brother, on my horse, was galloping along the base; and the sheik himself, with his long red dress streaming in the wind, and his spear poised in the air, was dashing full speed across the plain. All seemed to catch a glimpse of us at the same moment, and at the same moment all stopped. The sheik stood for a little space, as if astonished and confounded at seeing us attended by such an escort; and then spurring again his fiery horse, moved a few paces towards us, and dismounting, struck his spear in the sand, and waited to receive us. The men came in from all quarters; and, almost at the same moment, all had gathered around the spear. The sheik seemed more alarmed than any of us, and Paul said he turned perfectly green. He had heard the report of the pistol, which had given him much uneasiness; the men had answered, and scattered themselves abroad in search of us; and now seeing us come up in the midst of such a horde of Bedouins, he supposed that we had opened an account which could only be settled with blood.

The spirit of lying seemed to have taken possession of us. Thinking it would not be particularly acceptable to my pious friends to hear that I had been shooting in the tomb of Aaron, I told Paul to say that we had shot at a partridge. Even before saluting the strangers, with a hurried voice and quivering lip, the sheik asked the cause of our firing; and when Paul told him, according to my

279

instructions, that the cause was merely a simple bird, he was evidently relieved, although, unable to master his emotion, he muttered, "Cursed be the partridge, and cursed the gun, and cursed the hand that fired it." He then saluted our new companions, and all sat down around his long spear to smoke and drink coffee. I withdrew a little apart from them, and threw myself on the ground, and then began to suffer severely from a pain which, in my constant excitement since the cause of it occured, I had not felt. The pistol which I fired in the tomb had been charged by Paul with two balls, and powder enough for a musket; and in the firing it recoiled with such force as to lay open the back of my hand to the bone. While I was binding it up as well as I could, the sheik was taking care that I should not suffer from my withdrawal.

I have mentioned Paul's lying humor, and my own tendency that way; but the sheik cast all our doings in the shade; and particularly, as if it had been concerted beforehand, he averred most solemnly, and with the most determined look of truth imaginable, that we had not been in Wadi Musa; that I was a Turk on a pilgrimage to Mount Hor; that when he was in Cairo waiting for the caravan of pilgrims, the pasha sent the Habib Effendi to conduct him to the citadel, whither he went, and found me sitting on the divan by the side of the pasha; that the pasha took me by the hand, told him that I was his (the pasha's) particular friend, and that he, Sheik El Alouin, must conduct me first to Mount Hor, and then to Khalil or Hebron, and that he had given his head to Mohammed Ali for my safety. Paul was constantly moving between me and the group around the spear, and advising me of the progress of affairs; and when I heard who I was, and of my intimacy with the pasha, thinking that it was not exactly the thing for the particular friend of the Viceroy of Egypt to be sprawling on the sand, I got up, and, for the credit of my friend, put myself rather more upon my dignity. We remained there half an hour, when, seeing that matters became no worse, I took it for granted that they were better; and, after moving about a little, I began to arrange the saddle of my horse; and, by-and-by, as a sort of declaration of independence, I told them that I would ride on slowly, and they could follow at their convenience.

The sheik remained to settle with my new friends. They were a caravan belonging to the El Alouin tribe, from the tents at the mouth of the entrance to Petra, now on their way to Gaza; and the sheik got rid of them by paying them something, and assuring them that we had not been in Petra.

Early in the afternoon a favorite camel was taken sick, stumbled, and fell; and we turned aside among the mountains, where we were completely hidden from the view of any passing Bedouins. The camel belonged to a former female slave of the sheik, whom he had manumitted and married to "his black," and to whom he had given a tent and this camel as a dowry. He had been very anxious to get away as far as possible from Wadi Musa that night; but, as soon as the accident happened, with the expression always uppermost in the mouth of the followers of the Prophet, "God wills it," he began to doctor the animal. It was strange to be brought into such immediate contact with the disciples of fatalism. If we did not reach the point we were aiming at, God willed it; if it rained, God willed it; and I suppose that, if they had happened to lay their black hands upon my throat, and stripped me of everything I possessed, they would have piously raised their eyes to heaven, and cried, "God willed it." I remember Mr. Wolff,[4] the converted Jew missionary, told me an anecdote illustrating most strikingly the operation of this fatalist creed. He was in Aleppo during an earthquake, and saw two Turks smoking their pipes at the base of a house then tottering and ready to fall. He cried out to them and warned them of their peril; but they turned their eyes to the impending danger, and crying, "Allah el Allah," "God is merciful," were buried under the ruins.

[4] The Rev. Joseph Wolff is now in this country, and has taken orders in the Episcopal Church here. When I left Egypt he had set out on his long-projected journey to Timbuctu. He was taken sick in Abyssinia, and, unable to continue his progress, under great personal hardship and suffering, crossed the desert to the Red Sea, and went down to Bombay. It is greatly to be regretted that Mr. Wolff's health failed him. From his extensive travels in Asia and Africa, and his intimate knowledge of the languages and customs of the wild tribes that roam over their deserts, he was probably better qualified, and had a better chance of reaching that city, than any other man now living. It will probably be long before the attempt is made by another. Mr. Wolff has not, however, abandoned his purpose. As soon as his health will permit he intends to resume his journey, and, if the difficulties and dangers are not greater than man can overcome, we may yet hear from him in the heart of Africa.—Stephens' note.

It was not more than four o'clock when we pitched our tent. The Arabs all came under the shade to talk more at ease about our ascent of Mount Hor, and our adventure with the Bedouins of Wadi Musa; and wishing to show them that we Christians conceived ourselves to have some rights and interests in Aaron, I read to them, and Paul explained, the verses in the Bible recording his death and burial on the mountain. They were astonished and confounded at finding anything about him in a book, records of travel being entirely unknown to them, and books, therefore, regarded as of unquestionable veracity. The unbeliever of the previous night, however, was now as obstinate as if he had come from the banks of the Zuyder Zee. He still contended that the great high-priest of the Jews was a true follower of the Prophet; and I at last accommodated the matter by allowing that he was not a Christian.

That evening Paul and the sheik had a long and curious conversation. After supper, and over their pipes and coffee, the sheik asked him, as a brother, why we had come to that old city, Wadi Musa, so long a journey through the desert, spending so much money; and when Paul told him it was to see the ruins, he took the pipe from his mouth, and said, "That will do very well before the world; but, between ourselves, there is something else"; and when Paul persisted in it, the sheik said to him, "Swear by your God that you do not come here to search for treasure"; and when Paul had sworn by his God, the sheik rose, and, pointing to his brother as the very acme of honesty and truth, said, after a moment's hesitation, "Osman, I would not believe it if that brother had sworn it. No," he continued, "the Europeans are too cunning to spend their money in looking at old stones. I know there is treasure in Wadi Musa; I have dug for it, and I mean to dig for it again"; and then again he asked Paul whether he had discovered any, and where, telling him that he would aid in removing it, without letting any of the rest of the tribe know anything of the matter.

CHAPTER XXIII

E ARLY in the morning we continued our descent down the mountain. Every turn was presenting us with a new view of wild, barren, and desolate scenery; and yet frequently, in little spots watered by the mountain streams, we saw shrubs, and patches of green grass, and odoriferous bushes. At about nine o'clock we were again at the foot of the mountains of Seir, again moving along the great desert valley of El Ghor; and again I saw, in imagination, at the extreme end of the valley, that mysterious sea which I had first looked upon from the summit of Mount Hor. I had spoken to the sheik before, and again I tried to prevail upon him to follow the valley directly to its shores; but he told me, as before, that he had never traveled that road, and the Bedouins (whom he had last night declared to be total strangers) were deadly enemies of his tribe; in short, it was impossible to prevail upon him; and, as I found afterward, it would have been physically impossible to proceed along the mountainous borders of the sea.

We pursued the route which I had originally contemplated, through the land of Idumea. In regard to this part of my journey I wish to be particularly understood. Three different parties, at different times and under different circumstances, after an interval of twenty years from its discovery by Burckhardt, had entered the city of Petra, but not one of them had passed through the land of Idumea. The route of the two Englishmen and Italian before referred to was not precisely known; and, with the exception of these three, I was the first traveler who had ever attempted to pass through the doomed and blighted Edom.[1] In very truth, the prophecy of Isaiah, "None shall pass through it for ever and ever," seemed in a state of literal fulfillment. And now, without considering that I was perhaps braving the malediction of Heaven, but stimulated by the interest of associations connected with the denounced region, and the excitement of traveling over a new and unbeaten track, I was again moving along the desert valley of El Ghor.

In the present state of the world, it is an unusual thing to travel a road over which hundreds have not passed before. Europe, Asia, and even the sands of Africa, have been overrun and trodden down by the feet of travelers; but in the land of Idumea, the oldest country in the world, the aspect of everything is new and strange, and the very sands you tread on have never been trodden by the feet of civilized human beings. The Bedouin roams over them like the Indian on our native prairies. The road along which the stranger journeys was far better known in the days of David and Solomon than it is now; and when he tires with the contemplation of barrenness and ruin, he may take the Bible in his hand, and read what Edom was, and how God, by the mouth of his prophets, cursed it; and see with his own eyes whether God's words be true. "Also Edom shall be a desolation; every one that goeth by it shall be astonished, and shall hiss at all the plagues thereof. As in the overthrow of Sodom and Gomorrah, and the neighboring cities thereof, saith the Lord, no man shall abide there, neither shall a son of man dwell in it. Therefore, hear the counsel of the Lord that he hath taken against Edom; and his purposes that he hath purposed against the inhabitants of Teman; surely the least of the flock shall draw them out; surely he shall make their habitations desolate with them. The earth is moved at the noise of their fall, at the cry, the noise thereof was heard in the Red Sea."[2] And again. "Thus saith the

---

[1] It is fully possible that Stephens' claim that his was the first party within historical memory to ride through the Idumea (Edom) is true. There was an ancient Nabatean track that began at Aqaba moving westward of the Wadi Musa. Some of the way-stops were preserved when the Romans included this desert track in their road system; three are known—Ad Dianam, Tartare, and Mampis—on the road that reached Hebron. There is also a lateral from the via Trajana, which courses through Jordan and which begins at El Rabba.

[2] Jeremiah xlix.—Stephens' note.

Lord God: Because that Edom hath dealt against the house of
Judah by taking vengeance, and hath greatly offended, and re-
venged himself upon them; therefore, thus saith the Lord God, I
will also stretch out mine hand upon Edom, and will cut off man
and beast from it; and I will make it desolate from Teman."[3]
"Edom shall be a desolate wilderness."[4] "For three transgressions
of Edom, and for four, I will not turn away the punishment thereof."[5] "Thus saith the Lord God concerning Edom: Behold, I have
made thee small among the heathen: thou art greatly despised. The
pride of thine heart hath deceived thee, thou that dwellest in the
clefts of the rock, whose habitation is high; that saith in his heart,
Who shall bring me down to the ground? Though thou exalt thyself
as the eagle, and though thou set thy nest among the stars, thence
will I bring thee down, saith the Lord. Shall I not in that day, saith
the Lord, even destroy the wise men out of Edom, and understanding out of the mount of Esau? And they mighty men, oh Teman,
shall be dismayed, to the end that every one of the mount of Esau
may be cut off by slaughter."[6]

All that day the sheik was particularly disagreeable. He was
constantly talking of the favorable circumstances under which I
had seen Petra, the bad character of the Bedouins, his devotion to
me, and the generosity of Mr. Laborde and Abdel Hag. Ever since
we started, one of his standing subjects of conversation with Paul
had been what he expected from me; and today he pressed him
particularly, to learn how much money I had brought with me. In
the evening he came to my tent. He was in the habit of coming in
every evening; and, though I did not like him, I was in the habit
of talking with him; and, according to the Arab custom, I always
asked him to take a share of my meal. In general, appease the
stomach, and you gain the heart of the Arab; but the viscera of my
sheik were of impenetrable toughness. They produced none of that
delicious repose, that "peace on earth, and good-will towards all
men" spirit, which comes over an honest man after dinner. "A child

[3] Ezekiel xxv.—Stephens' note.
[4] Joel iii., 19.—Stephens' note.
[5] Amos i., 11.—Stephens' note.
[6] Obadiah i.—Stephens' note.

might play with me," said the good-hearted son of Erin, as he threw himself back in his chair after dinner; but it was not so with my sheik. While he was eating my bread, he was plotting against me. I had smoked my pipe, and was lying on my mat reading, while a long conversation was going on between him and Paul, and my suspicions were aroused; for, on the part of the sheik, it was carried on in a low whisper. Though he knew I could not understand a word, he had the indefinite fear that indicates a guilty intention; and, as I looked up occasionally from my book, I saw his keen and cunning eyes turned towards me, and withdrawn as soon as they met mine. He remained there more than an hour, conversing in the same low whisper; I, meanwhile, watching his looks from time to time; and when he had gone I asked what it all meant.

At first Paul hesitated, but finally said that it was the old story about Abdel Hag's generosity, and what he expected from me; for himself, the sheik expected at least $250; his brother would not expect so much; but that he was on an entirely different footing from the men; and he had concluded, by attempting to bribe Paul, to find out how much money I had with me, and how much I intended to give him; and, in going out, had slipped a couple of pieces into Paul's hand as an earnest. I have not troubled the reader with the many petty difficulties I had with the sheik, nor the many little circumstances that were constantly occurring to irritate me against him. I had been several times worked up to such a pitch that it was difficult to keep within the bounds of prudence; and I now broke through all restraints. From the beginning he had been exaggerating the danger of the road, and making a parade of devotion of the value of his services; and only the last night I had been driven out of my tent by four enormous fires which he had built at the four corners, as he said, for the men to sleep by and keep guard. I could hardly restrain myself then; but merely telling him that I would rather be robbed than roasted, I reserved myself for a better moment. The fact is, from the beginning I had been completely mistaken in my opinion touching the character of the chief of a powerful tribe of Bedouins. I had imagined him like the chief of a tribe of our own Indians, wild, savage, and lawless, but generous and true when he had once offered his protection; one who might rob or even murder, but who would never descend to the meanness of trickery and falsehood.

I had been smothering my feelings of contempt through the whole journey; but now I had seen Petra and Mount Hor, and it was a relief to have something to justify me in my own eyes in breaking through all restraint. I had caught him in the very act of baseness and villany, corrupting the faith of my servant; bribing under my own eyes, and while eating my bread, the only man on whom I could rely at all; and the proof of his treason, the accursed gold, was before me. With a loud voice I called him back to the tent, and charged him with his baseness, reproaching him that I had come into the desert upon the faith of his promises, and he had endeavored to corrupt my servant before my eyes; I told him that he was false and faithless; that I had before distrusted him, but that I now despised him, and would not give him a para till we got to Hebron, nor would I tell him how much I would give him then; but that, if he would take himself off and leave me alone in the desert, I would pay him the price of his camels; I assured him that, bad as he represented them, I did not believe there was a worse Arab in all his tribe than himself; and finally, throwing open my trunk, I told him that I did not fear him or all his tribe; that I had there a certain sum of money, which should belong to the man who should conduct me to Hebron, whoever he might be, and clothes which would not suit an Arab's back; that I knew I was in his power; but that, if they killed me, they could not get more than they could without it; and added, turning my pistols in my belt, that they should not get it while I could defend it.

All this, passing through an interpreter, had given me time to cool; and, before coming to my grand climax, though still highly indignant, I was able to observe the effect of my words. At the first glance I saw that I had the vantage ground, and that the consciousness of being detected in his baseness sealed his lips. I am inclined to think that he would have been disgraced in the eyes of his tribe if they had been acquainted with the circumstances; for, instead of resenting my passionate language, he earnestly begged me to lower

287

my voice, and frequently looked out of the tent to see if any of his companions were near. Keep cool is a good maxim, generally, in a man's walk through life, and it is particularly useful with the Bedouins in the desert; but there are times when it is good to be in a passion, and this was one of them. Without attempting to resent what I said, even by word or look, he came up to me, kissed my hand, and swore that he would never mention the subject of backsheesh again until we got to Hebron, and he did not. I retained my command over him through the whole journey, while he was constantly at my side, taking my horse, holding my stirrup, and in every way trying to make himself useful. I am not sure, however, but that, in his new character of a sycophant, he was worse than before. A sycophant in civilized life, where the usages of society admit, and perhaps demand, a certain degree of unmeant civility, is the most contemptible thing that crawls; but in a wild Arab it was intolerable. I really despised him, and made no secret of it; and sometimes, rash and imprudent as was the bare thought, it was with the greatest difficulty that I could keep from giving him my foot. After he had gone out that night, Paul sewed twenty gold pieces in the collar of my jacket, and I left the rest of my money open in my trunk.

I have frequently been astonished at the entire absence of apprehension which accompanied me during the whole of this journey. I fortunately observed, at the very first, an intention of exaggerating its danger; and this and other litle things carried me into the other extreme to such a degree, that perhaps my eyes were closed against the real dangers. Among all the pictures and descriptions of robbers and bandits that I have seen, I have never met with anything so unprepossessing as a party of desert Arabs coming down upon the traveler on their dromedaries; but one soon gets over the effect of their dark and scowling visages; and, after becoming acquainted with their weapons and bodily strength, a man of ordinary vigor, well armed, feels no little confidence in himself among them. They are small in stature, under our middle size, and thin almost to emaciation. Indeed, the same degree of spareness in Europeans would be deemed the effect of illness or starvation; but with them it seems to be a mere drying up of the fluids, or, as it were, an attraction between skin and bone, which prevents flesh from insinuating itself between. Their breast-bones stand out very prominently; their ribs are as distinctly perceptible as the bars of a gridiron, and their empty stomachs seem drawn up till they touch the back-bone; and their weapons, though ugly enough, are far from being formidable. The sheik was the only one of our party who carried pistols, and I do not believe they could have been discharged without picking the flints once or twice; the rest had swords and matchlock guns; the latter, of course, not to be fired without first striking a light, which is not the work of a moment; and although these inconvenient implements do well enough for contests with their brother Bedouins, the odds are very much against them when they have to do with a well-armed Frank; two pairs of good pistols and a double-barreled gun would have been a match for all our matchlock muskets.

Besides all this, one naturally feels a confidence in himself after being some time left to his own resources; a development of capacities and energies which he is entirely unconscious of possessing, until he is placed in a situation to call them out. A man must have been in the desert alone, and beyond the reach of help, where his voice can never reach the ears of his distant friends, with a strong and overwhelming sense that everything depends upon himself, his own coolness and discretion; and such is the elasticity of the human character, that his spirit, instead of sinking and quailing as it would once have done under difficulties and dangers incomparably less, rises with the occasion; and as he draws his sash or tightens his sword belt, he stretches himself to his full length, and is prepared and ready for any emergency that may befall him. Indeed, now that I have returned to the peaceful occupation of civilized life, I often look back with a species of mirthful feeling upon my journey in the desert as a strange and amusing episode in my life; and, when laying my head on my quiet pillow, I can hardly believe that, but a few months ago, I never slept without first placing my pistols carefully by my side, and never woke without putting forth my hand to ascertain that they were near and ready for instant use.

I had scarcely mounted the next morning before one of the men came up to me, and, telling me that he intended to return home, asked for his backsheesh. I looked at the sheik, who was still sitting on the ground, enjoying a last sip of coffee, and apparently taking no notice of us, and it immediately occurred to me that this was another scheme of his to find out how much I intended to give. The idea had no sooner occurred to me than I determined to sustain the tone I had assumed the night before; and I therefore told the fellow that I should not pay any one a piaster until I arrived at Hebron. This occasioned a great clamor; the sheik still remained silent, but all the others took up the matter, and I do not know how far it would have gone if I had persisted. I was the only one mounted; and, having given my answer, I turned my horse's head, and moved on a few paces, looking over my shoulder, however, to watch the effect; and when I saw them still standing, as if spellbound, in the unfinished act, one of mounting a dromedary, another of arranging the baggage, and all apparently undecided what to do, I reflected that no good could come from the deliberations of such men, and began to repent somewhat of the high tone I had assumed. I only wanted a good excuse to retrace my steps; and, after a moment's reflection, I laid hold of something plausible enough for immediate use. The man who wanted to return was rather a favorite with me—the same who had carried me on his shoulders up the stream in the entrance of Petra—and, returning suddenly, as if the thing had just occurred to me, I called him to me, and told him that, although I would not pay him for accompanying me on my journey, as it was not yet ended, still, for his extra services in Petra, I would not let him go home destitute; that I loved him—by which I meant that I liked him, an expression that would have been entirely too cold for "the land of the East and the clime of the sun," or, as I should rather say, for the extravagant and inflated style of the Arabs—that if the same thing had happened with any of the others, I would not have given him a para; and now he must understand that I only paid him for his services in Petra.

This seemed natural enough to the other Bedouins, for they all knew that this man and I had returned from the defile the best friends in the world, calling each other brother, &c.; and, in the end, the whole affair turned out rather fortunately; for, under-standing me literally that I paid only for the day in Petra, although not understanding the rule of three as established in the books of arithmetic, they worked out the problem after their own fashion, "If one day gives so much, what will so many days give?" and were exceedingly satisfied with the result. Indeed, I believe I might at any time have stopped their mouths, and relieved myself from much annoyance, by promising them an extravagant sum on my arrival at Hebron; but this I would not do. I had not, from the first, held out to them any extravagant expectations, nor would I do so then; perhaps, after all, not so much from a stern sense of principle, as from having conceived a feeling of strong though smothered in-dignation and contempt for the sheik. Indeed, I should not have considered it safe to tell him what I intended to give him, for I soon saw that the amount estimated by Mr. Gliddon and myself was very far from being sufficient to satisfy his own and his men's extrava-gant expectations. My apparent indifference perplexed the sheik, and he was sorely confounded by my valiant declaration, "There is my trunk; all that is in it is yours when we arrive at Hebron; rob me or kill me, and you get no more"; and, though he could not con-ceal his eagerness and rapacity, he felt himself trammeled; and my plan was to prolong his indecision, and postpone our denouement until our arrival at Hebron. Still, it was very unpleasant to be travel-ing upon these terms with my protectors, and I was exceedingly glad when the journey was over.

We were again journeying along the valley in an oblique direc-tion. In the afternoon we fell in with a caravan for Gaza. It may be that I wronged the sheik; but I had the idea that, whenever we saw strangers, his deep and hurried manner of pronouncing El Arab, his fixing himself in his saddle, poising his spear, and getting the cara-van in order, frequently accompanying these movements with the cautioning words not to be afraid, that he would fight for me till death, were intended altogether for effect upon me. Whether he had any influence or not with the caravan for Gaza, I cannot say; but I know that I would have been glad to leave the wandering tribes of the land of Idumea, and go with my new companions to the ancient city of the Philistines. While we moved along together, Paul and myself got upon excellent terms with them, and consulted them to take us under their escort. I have no doubt they would have done it willingly, for they were a fine, manly set of fellows; but we were deterred by the fear of involving them in a quarrel, if not a fight, with our own men.

The valley continued the same as before, presenting sandy hillocks, thorn-bushes, gullies, the dry beds of streams, and furnishing all the way incontestible evidence that it had once been covered with the waters of a river. To one traveling along that dreary road as a geologist, every step opens a new page in the great book of Nature; carrying him back to the time when all was chaos, and darkness covered the face of the earth; the impressions it conveys are of a confused mass of matter settling into "form and substance," the earth covered with a mightly deluge, the waters retiring, and leaving bare the mountains above him, and a rolling river at his feet; and, by the regular operation of natural causes, the river contracting and disappearing, and for thousands of years leaving its channel-bed dry. And again, he who, in the wonders around him, seeks the evidences of events recorded in the sacred volume, here finds them in the abundant tokens that the shower of fire and brimstone which descended upon the guilty cities of Sodom and Gomorrah stopped the course of the Jordan, and formed it into a pestilential lake, and left the dry bed of a river in the desolate valley in which he is journeying. This valley is part of the once populous land of Idumea; in the days of Solomon, the great traveled highway by which he received the gold of Ophir for the temple; and by which, in the days of imperial Rome, the wealth of India was brought to her doors.

About the middle of the day, as usual, the sheik rode ahead, and, striking his spear in the sand, he had coffee prepared before we came up. While we were sitting around the spear, two of our camels so far forgot the calm dignity of their nature, and their staid, quiet habits, as to get into a fight; and one of them, finding himself likely to come off second best, took to his heels, and the other after him; they were baggage camels, one being charged with my boxes of provisions and housekeeping apparatus, and his movements indicated death to crockery. I will not go into particulars, for eggs, rice, macaroni, and lamp-oil make a bad mixture; and though the race and fight between the loaded camels were rather ludicrous, the consequence was by no means a pleasant thing in the desert.

The next morning we had another camel scene; for one of the combatants was stretched upon the sand, his bed of death. The Bedouins had examined him, and, satisfied that the hand of death was upon him, they left him to breathe his last alone. The camel is to the Arab a treasure above all price. He is the only animal by nature and constitution framed for the desert, for he alone can travel several days without eating or drinking. Every part of him is useful; his milk is their drink, his flesh their food, and his hair supplies material for their rude garments and tents. Besides this, the creature is domesticated with the Bedouins; grows up in his tent, feeds from his hand, kneels down to receive his burden, and rises as if glad to carry his master, and, in short, is so much a part of a Bedouin's family, that often, in speaking of himself, the Bedouin will say that he has so many wives, so many children, and so many camels. All these things considered, when this morning they knew that the camel must die, I expected, in a rough way, something like Sterne's picture of the old man and his ass. But I saw nothing of the kind; they left him in the last stages of his struggle with the great enemy with as much indifference, I was going to say, as if he had been a brute; and he was a brute; but it was almost worth a passing tear to leave even a brute to die alone in the desert; one that we knew, that had traveled with us, and formed part of our little world; but the only lament the sheik made was, that they had lost twenty dollars, and we left him to die in the sand. I could almost have remained myself to close his eyes. The vultures were already hovering over him, and once I went back and drove them away; but I have no doubt that, before the poor beast was dead, the horrid birds had picked out his eyes, and thrust their murderous beaks into his brain.

It was, as usual, a fine day. Since we left Aqaba we had a continued succession of the most delightful weather I had ever experienced. I was, no doubt, peculiarly susceptible to the influence of weather. With a malady constantly hanging about me, if I drooped, a bright sun and an unclouded sky could at any time revive me; and more than once, when I have risen flushed and feverish, and but little refreshed with sleep, the clear, pure air of the morning has given me a new life. From dragging one leg slowly after the other, I have fairly jumped into the saddle, and my noble Arabian, in such cases, always completed what the fresh air of the morning had begun. Indeed, I felt then that I could not be too thankful for those two things, uncommonly fine weather and an uncommonly fine horse; and I considered that it was almost solely those two that sustained me on that journey. It is part of the historical account of the Bedouins' horses that the mares are never sold. My sheik would have sold his soul for a price; and, as soon as he saw that I was pleased with my mare, he wanted to sell her to me; and it was singular and amusing, in chaffering for this animal, to mark how one of the habits of bargain-making, peculiar to the horse-jockey with us, existed in full force among the Arabs; he said that he did not want to sell her; that at Cairo he had been offered $250, a new dress, and arms complete, and he would not sell her; but if *I* wanted her, there being nothing he would not do for me, &c., I might have her.

The sheik's was an extraordinary animal. The saddle had not been off her back for thirty days; and the sheik, himself a most restless creature, would dash off suddenly a dozen times a day, on a full run across the valley, up the sides of a mountain, round and round our caravan, with his long spear poised in the air, and his dress streaming in the wind; and when he returned and brought her to a walk at my side, the beautiful animal would snort and paw the ground as if proud of what she had done, and anxious for another course. I could almost imagine I saw the ancient warhorse of Idumea, so finely described by Job—"His neck clothed with thunder. Canst thou make him afraid as a grasshopper? the glory of his nostrils is terrible. He paweth in the valley, and rejoiceth in his strength; he goeth on to meet the armed men. He mocketh at fear, and is not affrighted; neither turneth he back from the sword.

The quiver rattleth against him, the glittering spear and the shield. He swalloweth the ground with fierceness and rage; neither believeth he that it is the sound of the trumpet. He saith among the trumpets, ha, ha; and he smelleth the battle afar off, the thunder of the captains, and the shouting."

Nothing showed the hardiness of these horses more than their drinking. Several times we came to deposits of rainwater left in the hollow of a rock, so foul and dirty that I would not have given it to a dog; and while their sides were white with foam, the sheik would take the bits out of their mouths, and sit down with the bridle in his hands, and let them drink their fill; and I could not help thinking that a regular-bred English groom, accustomed to insinuate a wet sponge in the mouth of a heated horse, would have been amazed and horrified at such a barbarian usage. These two horses were twelve and twenty years old respectively; and the former was more like a colt in playfulness and spirit, and the other like a horse of ten with us; and the sheik told me that he could count upon the services of both until they were thirty-five. Among all the recommendations of the Arabian horse, I know none greater than this; I have known a man, from long habit, conceive a liking for a vicious jade that no one else would mount; and one can imagine how warm must be the feeling, when, year after year, the best of his race is the companion of the wandering Arab, and the same animal may bear him from the time when he can first poise a spear until his aged frame can scarcely sustain itself in the saddle.

Before leaving the valley, we found in one of the gullies a large stone veined in that peculiar manner which I had noticed at Petra; it had been washed down from the mountains of Wadi Musa and the Arab told me that stone of the same kind was found nowhere else. Towards evening we had crossed the valley, and were at the foot of the mountains of Judea, in the direction of the southern extremity of the Dead Sea. That evening, I remember, I noticed a circumstance which called to my mind the wonderful accounts handed down to us by Strabo and other ancient historians, of large cities built of salt having stood at the southern extremity of the Dead Sea and the valley beyond. In the escapade of our runaway camels, bringing about the catastrophe which one of them had since expiated with his life, they had mingled together in horrible confusion, contrary to all the rules of art, so many discordant ingredients, that a great portion of my larder was spoiled; and, among other things, salt, almost as necessary to man as bread, had completely lost its savor. But the Bedouins, habituated to wanting almost everything, knew where to find all that their barren country could give; and one of them leaving the tents for a few moments, returned with a small quantity that he had picked up for immediate use, being a cake or incrustation about as large as the head of a barrel; and I afterward saw regular strata of it, and in large quantities, in the sides of the mountains.

CHAPTER XXIV

WE STARTED at six o'clock the next day, the morning rather cool, though clear and bracing; we were again among the mountains, and at about eleven a track scarcely distinguishable to my eye turned off to Gaza.[1] To a traveler from such a country as ours, few of the little every-day wonders he is constantly noticing strike him more forcibly than the character of the great public roads in the East. He makes allowance for the natural wildness of the country, the impossibility of using wheel-carriages on the mountains, or horses in the desert as beasts of burden, but still he is surprised and disappointed. Here, for instance, was a road leading to the ancient city of Gaza, a regular caravan route for four thousand years, and yet so perfect in the wildness of nature, so undistinguishable in its appearance from other portions of the wilderness around, that a stranger would have passed the little opening in the rocks probably without noticing it, and certainly without imagining that the wild track, of which it formed the entrance, would conduct him to the birthplace and ancient capital of David, and the holy city of Jerusalem. The solitary trail of the Indian over our prairies and forests is more perfectly marked as a road than either of the great routes to Gaza or Jerusalem, and yet, near the spot where these two roads diverge, are the ruins of an ancient city.

Little, if anything, has been known in modern days concerning the existence and distinguishing features of this road; and it is

---

[1] The track is known. Stephens would have left at Oleatha and turned northwest to enter a larger site called Birosaba (Bershabee). The road was serviced with wells way-stops on the way to Gaza.

completely a terra incognita to modern travelers. All the knowledge
possessed of it is that derived from the records of ancient history;
and from these we learn that in the time of David and Solomon, and
the later days of the Roman empire, a great public road existed
from Jerusalem to Aqaba, the ancient Eloth or Ezion-geber; that
several cities existed upon it between these terminating points, and
that their ruins should still be visible. Believing that I am the first
traveler who has ever seen those ruins, none can regret more than
myself my inability to add to the scanty stock of knowledge already
in possession of geographers. If my health had permitted, I might
have investigated and explored, noted observations, and treasured
up facts and circumstances, to place them in the hands of wiser
men for their conclusions; but I was not equal to the task. The
ruins which I saw were a confused and shapeless mass, and I rode
among them without dismounting; there were no columns, no blocks
of marble, or large stones which indicated any architectural greatness, and the appearance of the ruins would answer the historical
description of a third- or fourth-rate city.

About three hours farther on, and half a mile from our path, on
the right, was a quadrangular arch with a dome; and near it was a
low stone building, also arched, which might have been a small
temple. The Bedouins, as usual, referred it to the times of the
Christians. For about a mile, in different places on each side of us,
were mounds of crumbling ruins; and directly on the caravan-track
we came to a little elevation, where were two remarkable wells, of
the very best Roman workmanship, about fifty feet deep, lined with
large hard stones, as firm and perfect as on the day in which they
were laid. The uppermost layer, round the top of the well, which
was on a level with the pavement, was of marble, and had many
grooves cut in it, apparently worn by the long-continued use of
ropes in drawing water. Around each of the wells were circular
ranges of columns, which, when the city existed, and the inhabitants
came there to drink, might and probably did support a roof similar
to those now seen over the fountains in Constantinople. No remains
of such roof, however, are existing; and the columns are broken,
several of them standing not more than three or four feet high, and

the tops scooped out to serve as troughs for thirsty camels. On the other side, a little in the rear of the wells, is a hill overlooking the scattered ruins below, which may, some hundred years ago, have been the Acropolis of the city. A strong wall seems to have extended around the whole summit level of the hill. I remember that I rode up to the summit, winding around the hill, and leaped my horse over the broken wall; but there was nothing to reward me for the exertion of the undertaking. The enclosure formed by the wall was filled with ruins, but I could give form or feature to none of them; here, too, I rode among them without dismounting; and from here I could see the whole extent of the ruins below. As in the ruined city I had just passed, there was not a solitary inhabitant, and not a living being was to be seen but my companions watering their camels at the ancient wells. This, no doubt, was another of the Roman cities;[2] and although it was probably never celebrated for architectural or monumental beauty, it must have contained a large population.

We were now coming into another country, and leaving the desert behind us; a scanty verdure was beginning to cover the mountains; but the smiling prospect before me was for a moment overclouded by an unfortunate accident. Paul had lent his dromedary to one of the men; and riding carelessly on a baggage-camel, in ascending a rough hill the girths of the saddle gave way, and Paul, boxes, and baggage, all came down together, the unlucky dragoman completely buried under the burden. I was the first at his side; and when I raised him up he was senseless. I untied his sash and tore open his clothes. The Bedouins gathered around, all talking together, pulling, and hauling, and one of them drew his sword, and was bending over my prostrate interpreter, with its point but a few inches from his throat. Poor Paul! with his mortal antipathy to cold steel, if he could have opened his eyes at that moment, and seen the fiery orbs of the Bedouins, and the point of a sharp sword apparently just ready to be plunged into his body, he would have uttered one groan and given up the ghost. It was a startling movement to me; and for

[2] This could have been the ruins of Asoa (kh el-meshash) five kilometers west on this road after Oleatha (see *Cairo Carte Internationale del' Empire Roman ay L: I000000* Pub. Survey of Egypt, Gaza, July 1934).

a moment I thought they were going to employ in his behalf that mercy which is sometimes shown to a dying brute, that of killing him to put him out of misery. I pressed forward to shield him with my own body; and in the confusion of the moment, and my inability to understand what they meant, the selfish feeling came over me of the entire and absolute helplessness of my own condition if Paul should die. But Paul was too good a Catholic to die out of the pale of the church; he could never have rested quietly in his grave, unless he had been laid there amid the wafting of incense and the chanting of priests. "The safety of the patient often consists in the quarrels of the physicians," says Sancho Panza, or some other equally great authority, and perhaps this saved Paul; the Arabs wanted to cut open his clothes and bleed him; but I, not liking the looks of their lancets, would not suffer it; and, between us both, Paul was let alone and came to himself. But it was a trying moment, while I was kneeling on the sand supporting his senseless head upon my knee. No parent could have waited with more anxiety the return to life of an only child, or lover watched the beautiful face of his adored and swooning mistress wtih more earnestness than I did the ghastly and grizzled face of my faithful follower; and when he first opened his eyes, and stared wildly at me, the brightest emanations from the face of beauty could not at that moment have kindled warmer emotions in my heart. I never thought I should look on his ugly face with so much pleasure. I put him on my horse, and took his dromedary; and in half an hour we came to a Bedouin encampment in one of the most singular and interesting spots I ever saw.

We should have gone on two hours longer, but Paul's accident made it necessary to stop as soon as we found a proper place; and I should have regretted exceedingly to pass by this without a halt. There was something interesting even in our manner of approaching it. We were climbing up the side of a mountain, and saw on a little point on the very summit the figure of an Arab, with his face towards the tomb of the prophet, kneeling and prostrating himself in evening prayer. He had finished his devotions, and was sitting upon the rock when we approached, and found that he had literally been praying on his house-top, for his habitation was in the rock beneath. Like almost every old man one meets in the East, he looked exactly the patriarch of the imagination, and precisely as we would paint Abraham, Isaac, or Jacob. He rose as we approached, and gave us the usual Bedouin invitation to stop and pass the night with him; and, leading us a few paces to the brink of the mountain, he showed us in the valley below the village of his tribe.

The valley began at the foot of the elevation on which we stood, and lay between ranges of broken and overhanging rocks, a smooth and beautiful table of green, for perhaps a quarter of a mile, and beyond that distance broke off and expanded into an extensive meadow. The whole of this valley, down to the meadow, was filled with flocks of sheep and goats; and, for the first time since I left the banks of the Nile, I saw a herd of cows. I did not think I should ever be guilty of a sentiment at beholding a cow, but so it was; after my long journey in the desert, my feelings were actually excited to tenderness by the sight of these old acquaintances.

But where were the dwellings of the pastors, the tents in which dwelt the shepherds of these flocks and herds? In Egypt I had seen the Arabs living in tombs, and among the ruins of temples; in the desert I had seen them dwelling in tents; but I had never yet seen them making their habitations in the rude crevices of the rocks. Such, however, were their habitations here. The rocks in many places were overhanging; in others there were chasms or fissures; and wherever there was anything that could afford a partial protection from the weather on one side, a low, rough, circular wall of stone was built in front of it, and formed the abode of a large family. Within the small enclosure in front, the women were sitting winnowing or grinding grain, or rather pounding and rubbing it between two stones, in the same primitive manner practiced of old, in the days of the patriarchs. We descended and pitched our tents in the middle of the valley; and my first business was to make some hot tea for Paul, roll him up in blankets and coverlets, and thus repeat the sweating operation that had done him so much good before. He was badly hurt, and very much frightened. The boxes had fallen upon him, and the butt of a heavy gun, which he held in his left hand, had struck with all the momentum of its fall against his breast.

301

He thought his ribs were all broken; and when I persuaded him that they were as good as ever, he was sure there was some inward bruise, that would be followed by mortification; and, until we separated, especially when we had any hard work before us, he continued to complain of his hurts by this unlucky misadventure.

Having disposed of Paul, I strode out to examine more particularly the strange and interesting scene in the midst of which we were. The habitations in the crevices of the rocks, bad as they would be considered anywhere else, I found much more comfortable than most of the huts of the Egyptians on the banks of the Nile or the rude tents of the Bedouins. It was not sheer poverty that drove these shepherds to take shelter in the rocks, for they were a tribe more than three hundred strong, and had flocks and herds such as are seldom seen among the Bedouins; and they were far better clad, and had the appearance of being better fed than my worthy companions. Indeed, they were a different race from mine; and here, on the borders of the desert, I was again struck with what had so forcibly impressed me in crossing the borders of Ethiopia, the strong and marked difference of races in the East. The Bedouins among whom we were encamped were taller, stouter, and had longer faces than the El Alouins; and sometimes I thought I saw in them strong marks of the Jewish physiognomy. Above all, they were whiter; and this, with the circumstances of the women being less particular in keeping their faces covered, enabled me to pass an hour before dark with much satisfaction.

The change from the swarthy and bearded visages of my traveling companions to the comparatively fair and feminine countenances of these pastoral women was striking and agreeable, and they looked more like home than anything I had seen for a long time, except the cows. I cannot help thinking what a delight it would have been to meet, in that distant land, one of those beautiful fairies, lovely in all the bewitching attractions of frocks, shoes, stockings, clean faces, &c., of whom I now meet dozens every day, with the calm indifference of a stoic, since, even in spite of bare feet and dirty faces, my heart warmed towards the women of the desert. I could have taken them all to my arms; but there was one among them who might be accounted beautiful even among the beautiful women of my own distant home. She was tall, and fairer than the most of her tribe; and, with the shepherd's crook in her hand, she was driving her flock of goats up the valley to the little enclosure before the door of her rocky dwelling. There was no color in her cheek, but there was gentleness in her eye and delicacy in every feature; and, moving among us, she would be cherished and cared for as a tender plant, and served with all respect and love; but here she was a servant; her days were spent in guarding her flock, and at night her tender limbs were stretched upon the rude floor of her rocky dwelling. I thought of her much, and she made a deep impression upon me; but I was prevented from attempting to excite a correspondent feeling in her gentle bosom by the crushed state of Paul's ribs and my own inability to speak her language.

In the evening the men and women, or, to speak more pastorally, the shepherds and shepherdesses, came up one after another, with their crooks in their hands and their well-trained dogs, driving before them their several flocks. Some entered the little enclosures before their rude habitations; but many, destitute even of this miserable shelter, slept outside in the open valley, with their flocks around them, and their dogs by their side, presenting the same pastoral scenes which I had so often looked upon among the mountains of Greece; but unhappily, here, as there, the shepherds and shepherdesses do not in the least resemble the Chloes and Phyllises of poetic dreams. In the evening we seated ourselves round a large bowl of cracked corn and milk, so thick as to be taken with the hands, unaided by a spoon or ladle, followed by a smoking marmite of stewed kid; and, after this exercise of hospitality to the strangers, some withdrew to their rocky dwellings, others laid themselves down around the fire, and I retired to my tent. All night I heard from every part of the valley the lowing of cattle, the bleating of lambs and goats, and the loud barking of the watch-dogs.

Early in the morning, while the stars were yet in the sky, I was up and out of my tent. The flocks were still quiet, and the shepherds and shepherdesses were still sleeping with the bare earth for their bed and the canopy of heaven their only covering. One after the

303

other they awoke; and, as the day was breaking, they were milking the cows and goats, and at broad daylight they were again moving, with their crooks and dogs, to the pasture-ground at the foot of the valley.

We set off at an early hour, Paul again on my horse and I on his dromedary; the patriarchal figure who had welcomed being the last to speed me on my way. At every step we were now putting the desert behind us, and advancing into a better country. We had spent our last night in the wilderness; and were now approaching the Holy Land; and no pilgrim ever approached its borders with a more joyous and thankful heart than mine.

At nine o'clock we came to another field of ruins, where the relics of an Arab village were mingled with those of a Roman city.[3] The hands of the different builders and residents were visible among them; two square buildings of large Roman stone were still standing like towers, while all the rest had fallen to pieces, and the stones which once formed the foundations of palaces were now worked up into fences around holes in the rocks, the burrowing-places of the miserable Arabs.

And here, too, we saw the tokens of man's inhumanity to man; the thunder of war had been leveled against the wretched village, the habitations were in ruins, and the inhabitants whom the sword had spared were driven out and scattered no one knew whither. On the borders of the Holy Land we saw that Ibrahim Pasha, the great Egyptian soldier, whose terrible war cry had been heard on the plains of Egypt and among the mountains of Greece, in the deserts of Syria and under the walls of Constantinople, was ruling the conquered country with the same rod of iron which his father swayed in Egypt. He had lately been to this frontier village with the brand of war, and burning and desolation had marked his path.

Soon after we came to an inhabited village, the first since we left Cairo. Like the ruined and deserted village we had left, it was a mingled exhibition of ancient greatness and modern poverty; and probably it was a continuation of the same ruined Roman city. A

[3] The ruins of the Roman caravan city of Birosaba (Bershabee) located on the main crossroad to Hebron and hence on the road to Jerusalem.

large fortress, forming part of a battlement, in good preservation, and fragments of a wall formed the nucleus of a village, around which the inhabitants had built themselves huts. The rude artisans of the present day knew nothing of the works which their predecessors had built; and the only care they had for them was to pull them down, and with the fragments to build for themselves rude hovels and enclosures; and the sculptured stones which once formed the ornaments of Roman palaces were now worked up into fences around holes in the ground, the poor dwellings of the miserable Arabs.

The stranger from a more favored land, in looking at the tenants of these wretched habitations, cannot help thanking his God that his lot is not like theirs. When I rode through, the whole population had crawled out of their holes and hiding-places, and were basking in the warmth of a summer's sun; and I could not help seeing the kindly hand of a benefactor in giving to them what he has denied us, a climate where, for the greater part of the year, they may spend their whole days in the open air, and even at night hardly need the shelter of a roof. This is probably the last of the cities which once stood on the great Roman road from Jerusalem to Aqaba. While riding among the ruins and stopping for a moment to talk with some of the Arabs, I saw on the left, in the side of a mountain, an open door like those of the tombs in Egypt; a simple orifice, without any ornament or sculpture. A woman was coming out with a child in her arms, a palpable indication that here too, the abodes of the dead were used as habitations by the living. In Paul's disabled state I could ask no questions and I did not stop to explore.

I cannot leave this interesting region without again expressing my regret at being able to add so little to the stock of useful knowledge. I can only testify to the existence of the ruins of cities which have been known only in the books of historians, and I can bear witness to the desolation that reigns in Edom. I can do more, not with the spirit of scoffing at prophecy, but of one who, in the strong evidence of the fulfillment of predictions uttered by the voice of inspiration, has seen and felt the evidences of the sure foundation of the Christian faith; and having regard to what I have already said in reference to the interpretation of the prophecy, "None shall pass through it for ever and ever," I can say that I have passed *through* the land of Idumea. My route was not open to the objection made to that of Burckhardt, the traveler who came nearest to passing *through* the land; for he entered from Damascus, on the east side of the Dead Sea, and struck the borders of Edom at such a point that literally he cannot be said to have passed through it. If the reader will look at the map accompanying these pages, he will see Burckhardt's route; and he will also see that mine is not open to the critical objections made to his; and that, beyond all peradventure, I did pass directly through the land of Idumea lengthwise, and crossing its northern and southern border; and, unless the two Englishmen and Italian before referred to passed on this same route, I am the only person, except the wandering Arabs, who ever did pass through the doomed and forbidden Edom, beholding with his own eyes the fearful fulfillment of the terrible denunciations of an offended God. And, though I did pass through and yet was not cut off, God forbid that I should count the prophecy a lie: no; even though I had been a confirmed skeptic, I had seen enough, in wandering with the Bible in my hand in the unpeopled desert, to tear up the very foundations of unbelief, and scatter its fragments to the winds. In my judgment, the words of the prophet are abundantly fulfilled in the destruction and desolation of the ancient Edom, and the complete and eternal breaking up of a great public highway; and it is neither necessary nor useful to extend the denunciation against a passing traveler.[4]

[4] Keith's celebrated treatise on the Prophecies has passed through fourteen editions, differing in some few particulars. In the sixth edition he says that Sir Frederick Henniker, in his notes dated from Mount Sinai, states that Seetzen, on a vessel of paper pasted against the wall, notifies his having penetrated the country in a direct line between the Dead Sea and Mount Sinai (through Idumea), *a route never before accomplished*. In a note to the same edition, the learned divine says, "Not even the cases of two individuals, Seetzen and Burckhardt, can be stated as at all opposed to the literal interpretation of the prophecies. Seetzen did indeed pass through Idumea, and Burckhardt traversed a considerable part of it; but the former met his death not long after the completion of his journey through Idumea (he died at 'Aqaba, supposed to have been poisoned); the latter never recovered from the effects of the hardships and privations which he suffered there; and, without even commencing the exclusive design which he had in view, viz., to explore the interior of Africa, to which all his

journeyings in Asia were merely intended as preparatory, he died at Cairo. Neither of them lived to return to Europe. '*I will cut off from Mount Seir him that passeth out and him that returneth.*' " In the edition which I saw on the Nile, and which first turned my attention to the route through Idumea, I have no recollection of having seen any reference to Seetzen. It may have been there, however, without my particularly noticing it; as, when I read it, I had but little expectation of being able myself to undertake the route.—Stephens' note.

CHAPTER XXV

I HAD FOLLOWED the wandering path of the children of Israel
from the land of Egypt and the house of bondage to the borders
of the Promised Land; had tracked them in their miraculous passage across the Red Sea to the mountains of Sinai, through "the
great and terrible wilderness that leadeth to Kadesh Barnea"; and
among the stony mountains through which I was now journeying
must have been the Kadesh, the wilderness of Paran, from which
Moses sent the ten chosen men to spy out the land of Canaan, who
went "unto the brook of Eshcol, and cut down from thence a branch
with one cluster of grapes, and bare it between two upon a staff;
and though they brought of the pomegranates and figs, and said
that surely the land flowed with milk and honey, and these were the
fruits thereof, yet brought up such an evil report of the land that it
ate up the inhabitants thereof; and of the sons of Anak, the giants
that dwelt therein, that the hearts of the Israelites sank within
them; they murmured against Moses; and for their murmurings
they were sent back into the wilderness; and their carcasses, from
twenty years old and upward, were doomed to fall in the wilderness,
and the children of the murmurers to wander forty years before
they should enter the Land of Promise."[1]

I followed in the track of the spies; and, though I saw not the
Vale of Eshcol with its grapes and pomegranates, neither did I see
the sons of Anak, the giants which dwelt in the land. Indeed, the
men of Anak could not have made me turn back from the Land of
Promise. I was so heartily tired of the desert and my Bedouin

[1] Numbers xiii, 23.—Stephens' note.

companions that I would have thrown myself into the arms of the giants themselves for relief. And though the mountains were as yet stony and barren, they were so green and beautiful by comparison with the desert I had left that the conviction even of much greater dangers than I had yet encountered could hardly have driven me back. The Bedouins and the Fellahs about Hebron are regarded as the worst, most turbulent, and desperate Arabs under the government of the pasha; but as I met little parties of them coming out towards the frontier, they looked, if such a character can be conceived of Arabs, like quiet, respectable, orderly citizens, when compared with my wild protectors; and they greeted us kindly and cordially as we passed them, and seemed to welcome us once more to the abodes of men.

As we approached Hebron the sheik became more and more civil and obsequious; and, before we came in sight of the city, he seemed to have some misgivings about entering it, and asked me to secure protection from the governor for that night for himself and men, which I did not hesitate to promise. I was glad to be approaching again a place under the established government of the pasha, where, capricious and despotic as was the exercise of power, I was sure of protection against the exactions of my Bedouins; and the reader may judge of the different degrees of security existing in these regions, from being told that I looked to the protection of a Turk as a guarantee against the rapacity of an Arab. After clambering over a rocky mountain, we came down into a valley, bounded on all sides, and apparently shut in by stony mountains. We followed the valley for more than an hour, finding the land good and well cultivated, with abundance of grapes, vines, and olives, as in the day when the spies sent by Moses entered it; and I can only wonder that, to a hardy and warlike people like the Israelites, after a long journey in the desert, the rich products of Hebron did not present more powerful considerations than the enmity of the men of Anak. We turned a point of the mountain to the left; and at the extreme end of the valley, on the side of a hill, bounding it, stands the little city of Hebron, the ancient capital of the kingdom of David. But it bears no traces of the glory of its Jewish king. Thunder and lightning, and earthquakes, wars, pestilence, and famine, have passed over it; and a small town of white houses, compactly built on the side of the mountain, a mosque and two minarets, are all that mark the ancient city of Hebron.

As soon as we came in sight of the city the sheik dismounted, and, arranging his saddle, made Paul take back his dromedary and give me my horse; and placing me on his right hand, and drawing up the caravan with the order and precision of a troop of "regulars," we made a dashing entry. It was on Friday, the Mussulmans' Sabbath; and several hundred women, in long white dresses, were sitting among the tombs of the Turkish burying-ground, outside the walls. We passed this burying-ground and a large square fountain connected with the ancient city, being regarded at this day as one of the works of Solomon; and leaving the baggage camels at the gate, with our horses and dromedaries on full gallop, we dashed through the narrow streets up to the door of the citadel, and in no very modest tone demanded an audience of the governor. The Turks and Arabs are proverbial for the indifference with which they look upon everything; and though I knew that a stranger coming from the desert was a rare object, and ought to excite some attention, I was amused and somewhat surprised at the extraordinary sensation our appearance created. Men stopped in the midst of their business; the lazy groups in the cafés sprang up, and workmen threw down their tools to run out and stare at us. I was surprised at this; but I afterward learned that, since the pasha had disarmed all Syria, and his subjects in that part of his dominions wore arms only by stealth, it was a strange and startling occurrence to see a party of lawless Bedouins coming in from the desert, armed to the teeth, and riding boldly up to the gates of the citadel.

The janissary at the door told us that the governor was sick and asleep, and could not be disturbed. He was, however, a blundering fellow; and, after a few moments' parley, without giving his master any notice, he had us all standing over the sleeping invalid. The noise of our entering and the clang of our weapons roused him; and, staring round for a moment, leaning on his elbow, he fixed his eyes on the sheik, and with a voice the like of which can only issue from the bottom of a Turk's throat, thundered out, "Who are you?" The sheik was for a moment confounded, and made no answer. "Who are you?" reiterated the governor, in a voice even louder than before. "I am Ibrahim Pasha's man," said the sheik. "I know that," answered the governor; "none but Ibrahim Pasha's men dare come here; but have you no name?" "Sheik El Alouin," said the Arab, with the pride of a chief of Bedouins, and looking for a moment as if he stood in the desert at the head of his lawless tribe. "I conducted the pasha's caravan to Aqaba;" and pointing to me, "I have conducted safe through all the bad Arabs Abdel Hasis, the friend of the pasha"; and then the governor, like a wild animal balked in his spring, turned his eyes from the sheik to me, as for the first time sensible of my presence. I showed him my firman, and told him that I did not mean to give him much trouble; that all I wanted was that he would send me on immediately to Bethlehem.

I had no wish to stop at Hebron, though the first city in the Holy Land and hallowed by high and holy associations. The glory of the house of David had forever departed. I was anxious to put an outpost between myself and the desert; and I had an indefinable longing to sleep my first night in the Holy Land in the city where our Savior was born. But the governor positively refused to let me go that afternoon; he said that it was a bad road, and that a Jew had been robbed a few days before on his way to Bethlehem; and again lying down, he silenced all objections with the eternal but hateful word, "Bokhara, bokhara," "tomorrow, tomorrow." Seeing there was no help for me, I made the best of it, and asked him to furnish me with a place to lodge in that night. He immediately gave orders to the janissary; and, as I was rising to leave, asked me if I could not give him some medicine. I had some expectation and some fear of this, and would have avoided it if I could. I had often drugged and physicked a common Arab, but had never been called upon to prescribe for such pure porcelain of the earth as a governor. Nevertheless, I ventured my unskillful hand upon him; and having with all due gravity asked his symptoms, and felt his pulse, and made him stick out his tongue till he could hardly get it back again, I looked down his throat, and into his eyes, and covering him up, told him, with as much solemnity as if I was licensed to kill *secundem artem*, that I would send him some medicine, with the necessary directions for taking it. I was quite equal to the governor's case, for I saw that he had merely half-killed himself with eating, and wanted clearing out, and I had with me emetics and cathartics that I well knew were capable of clearing out a whole regiment. In the course of the evening he sent his janissary to me; and, expecting to be off before daylight, I gave him a double emetic, with very precise directions for its use; and I afterward learned that, during its operation, his wrath had waxed warm against me, but in the morning he was so much better that he was ready to do me any kindness.

This over, I followed the janissary, who conducted me around outside the walls and through the burying-ground, where the women were scattered in groups among the tombs, to a distant and separate quarter of the city. I had no idea where he was taking me; but I had not advanced a horse's length in the narrow streets before their peculiar costume and physiognomies told me that I was among the unhappy remnant of a fallen people, the persecuted and despised Israelites. They were removed from the Turkish quarter, as if the slightest contact with this once-favored people would contaminate the bigoted follower of the Prophet. The governor, in the haughty spirit of a Turk, probably thought that the house of a Jew was a fit place for the repose of a Christian; and, following the janissary through a low range of narrow, dark, and filthy lanes, mountings, and turnings, of which it is impossible to give any idea, with the whole Jewish population turning out to review us, and the sheik and all his attendants with their long swords clattering at my heels, I was conducted to the house of the chief Rabbi of Hebron.

If I had had my choice, these were the very persons I would have selected for my first acquaintances in the Holy Land. The descendants of Israel were fit persons to welcome a stranger to the ancient city of their fathers; and if they had been then sitting under the shadow of the throne of David, they could not have given me a warmer reception. It may be that, standing in the same relation to the Turks, alike the victims of persecution and contempt, they forgot the great cause which had torn us apart and made us a separate people, and felt only a sympathy for the object of mutual oppression. But, whatever was the cause, I shall never forget the kindness with which, as a stranger and Christian, I was received by the Jews in the capital of their ancient kingdom; and I look to my reception here and by the monks of Mount Sinai as among the few bright spots in my long and dreary pilgrimage through the desert.

I had seen enough of the desert, and of the wild spirit of freedom which men talk of without knowing, to make me cling more fondly than ever even to the lowest grade of civilization; and I could have sat down that night, provided it was under a roof, with the fiercest Mussulman as in a family circle. Judge, then, of my satisfaction at being welcomed from the desert by the friendly and hospitable Israelites. Returned once more to the occupation of our busy, money-making life, floating again upon the stream of business, and carried away by the cares and anxieties which agitate every portion of our stirring community, it is refreshing to turn to the few brief moments when far other thoughts occupied my mind; and my speculating, scheming friends and fellow-citizens would have smiled to see me that night, with a Syrian dress and long beard, sitting cross-legged on a divan, with the chief rabbi of the Jews at Hebron, and half the synagogue around us, talking of Abraham, Isaac, and Jacob as of old and mutual friends.

With the few moments of daylight that remained, my Jewish friends conducted me around their miserable quarter. They had few lions to show me, but they took me to their synagogue, in which an old white-bearded Israelite was teaching some prattling children to read the laws of Moses in the language of their fathers; and when the sun was setting in the west and the Muezzin from the top of the minaret was calling the sons of the faithful to evening prayers, the old rabbi and myself, a Jew and a Christian, were sitting on the roof of the little synagogue, looking out as by stealth upon the sacred mosque containing the hallowed ashes of their patriarch fathers. The Turk guards entered the door, and the Jew and the Christian are not permitted to enter; and the old rabbi was pointing

313

to the different parts of the mosque, where, as he told me, under tombs adorned with carpets of silk and gold, rested the mortal remains of Abraham, Isaac, and Jacob.

But to return to my Bedouin companions. The sheik and his whole suite had been following close at my heels, through the narrow lanes and streets, up to the very doors of the synagogue; and their swarthy figures, their clattering swords, and grim visages prevented my seeing the face of many a Hebrew maiden. I expected a scene with them at parting, and I was not disappointed. Returning to the rabbi's, they followed me into the room, and, after a few preliminaries, I counted out the price of the camels, and laid down a backsheesh for each separately. Not one of them touched it, but all looked at the money and at me alternately, without speaking a word (it was about ten times as much as I would have had to pay for the same services anywhere else); and the sheik seemed uncertain what to do. The janissary, however, whose presence I had almost forgotten, put himself forward as an actor in the scene; and, half drawing his sword and rattling it back into its scabbard, swore that it was a vile extortion; that the governor ought to know it; and that the firman of the pasha ought to protect a stranger. This brought the sheik to a decision; and taking up his own portion, and directing the rest to do the same, he expressed himself satisfied, and, without moving from his place, betook himself to smoking.

It was evident, however, that he was not altogether content; and the janissary leaving us soon after, hardly had the rattling of his steel scabbard died away along the narrow passage, when they all turned upon me and gave voice to their dissatisfaction. I told them that I had paid them an enormous price, much more than the sheik had spoken of at Cairo; that I had brought with me more money than he had given me to understand would be necessary, and that it was all gone; that it was impossible to give them any more, for I had it not to give. In fact, I had paid them extravagantly, but far below their extravagant expectations. One would not have come for two hundred dollars, another for one hundred, &c.; and from the noise and clamor which they made here, I am well satisfied that, if the denouement had taken place in the desert, they would have

314

searched for themselves whether there was something left in the bottom of my trunk; and, from what happened afterward, I am very sure that they would have stripped me of my Turkish plumage; but now I was perfectly safe. I considered a Turkish governor good protection against the rapacity of a Bedouin Arab. I did not even fear their future vengeance, for I knew that they did not dare set their feet outside of any gate in Hebron, except that which opened to their own tents in the desert; they seemed to think that they had let me slip through their fingers; and when they pushed me to desperation, I told them that I did not care whether they were satisfied or not.

As I rose the sheik fell; and when I began working myself into a passion at his exorbitant demand, he fell to begging a dollar or two in such moving terms that I could not resist. I continued yielding to his petty extortions, until, having ascertained the expense, I found that I had not a dollar more than enough to carry me to Jerusalem; and at this moment he consummated his impudence by begging my dress from off my back. The dress was of no great value; it had not cost much when new, and was travel-worn and frayed with hard usage; but it had a value in my eyes from the mere circumstance of having been worn upon this journey. I had given him nearly all my tent equipage, arms, ammunition, &c., and I had borne with all his twopenny extortions; but he urged and insisted, and begged and entreated with so much pertinacity, that my patience was exhausted, and I told him that I had borne with him long enough, and that he and his whole tribe might go to the d——l. This was not very courteous or dignified between treaty-making powers; but, considering that the immediate subject of negotiation was an old silk dress, and the parties were a single individual and a horde of Bedouins, it may perhaps be allowed to pass.

All the nice web of diplomacy was now broken; and all springing at the same moment to our feet, the whole group stood fronting me, glaring upon me like so many wild beasts. Now the long-smothered passion broke out, and, wild and clamorous as the Arabs always were, I had never seen them so perfectly furious. They raved like so many bedlamites; and the sheik, with torrents of vociferation and reproach, drew from his bosom the money he had accepted as his portion, dashed it on the floor, and swearing that no Frank should ever pass through his country again, poured out upon me a volley of bitter curses, and, grinding his teeth with rage and disappointment, rushed out of the room. I did not then know what he was saying; but I could judge, from the almost diabolical expression of his face, that he was not paying me very handsome compliments; and I felt a convulsive movement about the extreme end of my foot, and had advanced a step to help him down stairs, but his troop followed him close; and I do not know how it is, but when one looks long at the ugly figure of a Bedouin, he is apt to forego a purpose of vengeance. There is something particularly truculent and pacifying in their aspect.

A moment after he had gone I was exceedingly sorry for what had happened, particularly on account of his oath, that no European should ever pass through his country. I felt unhappy in the idea that, when I expected to be the pioneer in opening a new and interesting route, I had become the means of more effectually closing it. With a heavy heart I told Paul that I must have another interview; that the old dress must go, and anything else I had; and, in short, that I must have peace upon any terms. To dispose of this business without mixing it with other things, in about an hour the sheik returned with his brother, and, walking up to me and kissing my hand, told me that he had just heard of a robbery on the road to Jerusalem, and came to tell me of it; and, looking me in the face, added that, when he had got back to his tent, he felt unhappy at having left me in anger; that he had been so used to sitting with me, that he could not remain away, &c., &c. I was not to be outdone; and, looking him back again in the face, I introduced him to my Jewish companion as my dearest friend, the chief of the tribe of El Alouins, who had protected me with his life through the dangers of the desert, and to whose bold arm they were indebted for the privilege they then enjoyed of seeing my face. The sheik looked at me as if he thought me in earnest, and himself entitled to all that I had said; and, satisfied so far, he sat down and smoked his pipe, and at parting disclosed the object of his visit, by asking me for a letter of recommendation to the consul at Cairo, and to the friends of whom I had before spoken as intending to follow me to Petra. Glad to patch up a peace, I told him to come to me early the next morning, and I would settle everything to his satisfaction.

Before I was awake he was shaking me by the shoulder. I jumped up, and roused Paul; and now wishing to redeem my ungraciousness of the day before, I may say literally that "I parted my raiment among them," and gave away pretty much everything I had except my European clothes, completing my present with a double-barreled gun, rather given to bursting, which I gave the sheik's brother. The sheik had changed his tone altogether, and now told me that he loved me as a brother; and, pointing to the brother at his side, that he loved me as well as him; and with great warmth assured me, that if I would turn Mussulman and come and live with him in his tents in the wilderness, he would give me for wives four of the most beautiful girls of his tribe. He did not confine his offers to me, but told me that he would receive, guard, and protect any of my friends as if they were of his own blood; and warming with his own generosity, or perhaps really feeling a certain degree of kindness, he asked me for some symbol or sign which should be perpetual between us. I had just sealed a letter for Mr. Gliddon, and a stick of sealing-wax and a lighted lamp were on the low table before me. I made a huge plaster with the sealing-wax on a sheet of coarse brown paper, and, stamping it with the stock of my pistol, chased and carved in the Turkish fashion, I gave him a seal with such a device as would have puzzled the professors of heraldry, telling him that, when any one came to him with this seal, he might know he was a friend of mine; and I added, that I would never send anyone without plenty of money; so that any one who visits the Sheik El Alouin with my recommendation must expect to make up for my deficiences.

This over, we bade each other farewell, the sheik and the whole of his swarthy companions kissing me on both sides of my face. I looked after them as long as they continued in sight, listened till I heard the last clattering of their armor, and I never saw nor do I ever wish to see them again. I am sorry to entertain such a feeling

317

towards any who have been the companions of my wanderings, and I hardly know another instance, from the English nobleman down to a muleteer or boatman, at parting with whom I have not felt a certain degree of regret. But when I parted with the Bedouin chief, though he kissed me on both cheeks, though he gave me his signet and has mine in return, and though four Arabian girls are ready for me whenever I choose to put my trust in Mohammed and Sheik El Alouin, it was delightful to think that I should never see his face again.

One by one I had seen the many illusions of my waking dreams fade away; the gorgeous pictures of Oriental scenes melt into nothing; but I still clung to the primitive simplicity and purity of the children of the desert; their temperance and abstinence, their contented poverty and contempt for luxuries, as approaching the true nobility of man's nature and sustaining the poetry of the "land of the East." But my last dream was broken; and I never saw among the wanderers of the desert any traits of character or any habits of life which did not make me prize and value more the privileges of civilization. I had been more than a month alone with the Bedouins; and, to say nothing of their manners, excluding women from all companionship; dipping their fingers up to the knuckles in the same dish; eating sheep's insides, and sleeping under tents crawling with vermin engendered by their filthy habits, their temperance and frugality are from necessity, not from choice; for in their nature they are gluttonous, and will eat at any time till they are gorged of whatever they can get, and then lie down and sleep like brutes. I have sometimes amused myself with trying the variety of their appetites, and I never knew them refuse anything that could be eaten. Their stomach was literally their god, and the only chance of doing anything with them was by first making to it a grateful offering; instead of scorning luxuries, they would eat sugar as boys do sugarcandy; and I am very sure, if they could have got poundcake, they would never have eaten their own coarse bread.

One might expect to find these children of Nature free from the reproach of civilized life, the love of gold. But, fellow-citizens and fellow-worshippers of mammon, hold up your heads; this reproach must not be confined to you. It would have been a pleasing thing to me to find among the Arabs of the desert a slight similarity of taste and pursuits with the denizens of my native city; and in the early developments of a thirst for acquisition, I would have hailed the embryo spirit which might one day lead to stock and exchange boards, and laying out city lots around the base of Mount Sinai or the excavated city of Petra. But the savage was already far beyond the civilized man in his appetite for gold; and though brought up in a school of hungry and thirsty disciples, and knowing many in my native city who regard it as the one thing needful, I blush for myself, for my city, and for them, when I say that I never saw one among them who could be compared with the Bedouin. I never saw anything like the expression of face with which a Bedouin looks upon silver or gold. When he asks for backsheesh and receives the glittering metal, his eyes sparkle with wild delight, his fingers clutch it with eager rapacity, and he skulks away like the miser, to count it over alone and hide it from all other eyes.

Hebron, one of the oldest cities of Canaan, is now a small Arab town, containing seven or eight hundred Arab families. The present inhabitants are the wildest, most lawless, and desperate people in the Holy Land; and it is a singular fact, that they sustain now the same mutinous character with the rebels of ancient days, who armed with David against Saul, and with Absalom against David; in the last desperate revolution against Mohammed Ali, they were foremost in the strife, the first to draw the sword, and the last to return it to its scabbard. A petty Turk now wields the scepter of the son of Jesse, and a small remnant of a despised and persecuted people still hover round the graves of their fathers; and though degraded and trampled under foot, from the very dust in which they lie are still looking to the restoration of their temporal kingdom.

Accompanied by my Jewish friends, I visited the few spots which tradition marks as connected with scenes of Bible history. Passing through the bazars at the extreme end, and descending a few steps, we entered a vault containing a large monument, intended in memory of Abner, the greatest captain of his age, the favored and for a long time trusted officer of David, who, as the Jews told me, was

319

killed in battle near Hebron, and his body brought here and buried. The great mosque, the walls of which, the Jews say, are built with the ruins of the temple of Solomon, according to the belief of the Mussulmans and the better authority of the Jews, covers the site of the Cave of Machpelah, which Abraham bought from Ephron the Hittite; and within its sacred precincts are the supposed tombs of Abraham, Isaac, and Jacob. The doors were guarded with jealous care by the bigoted Mussulmans; and when, with my Jewish companion, I stopped for a moment to look up at the long marble staircase leading to the tomb of Abraham, a Turk came out from the bazars, and, with furious gesticulations, gathered a crowd around us; and a Jew and a Christian were driven with contempt from the sepulchre of the patriarch whom they both revered. A special firman from the pasha, or perhaps a large bribe to the governor, might have procured me a private admission; but death or the Koran would have been the penalty required by the bigoted people of Hebron.

On a rising ground a little beyond the mosque is a large fountain or reservoir, supported by marble pillars, where my companions told me that Sarah had washed the clothes of Abraham and Isaac. Leaving this, I went once more to the two pools outside the walls, and after examining them as the so-called works of Solomon, I had seen all a stranger could see in Hebron.

I cannot leave this place, however, without a word or two more. I had spent a long evening with my Jewish friends. The old rabbi talked to me of their prospects and condition, and told me how he had left his country in Europe many years before, and come with his wife and children to lay their bones in the Holy Land. He was now eighty years old; and for thirty years, he said, he had lived with the sword suspended over his head; had been reviled, buffeted, and spit upon; and, though sometimes enjoying a respite from persecution, he never knew at what moment the bloodhounds might not be let loose upon him; that, since the country had been wrested from the sultan by the Pasha of Egypt, they had been comparatively safe and tranquil; though some idea may be formed of this comparative security from the fact that, during the revolution two years before, when Ibrahim Pasha, after having been pent up several months in

Jerusalem, burst out like a roaring lion, the first place upon which his wrath descended was the unhappy Hebron; and while their guilty brethren were sometimes spared, the unhappy Jews, never offending but always suffering, received the full weight of Arab vengeance. Their houses were ransacked and plundered; their gold and silver, and all things valuable, carried away; and their wives and daughters violated before their eyes by a brutal soldiery.

During the evening a fine portly man, in the flowing Syrian dress, came to pay me a visit. His complexion proclaimed him of Coptic origin, a descendant of the ancient lords of Egypt; his inkhorn in his sash told me that he was a writer, and his cordial salutation that he was a Christian. Living among Turks, Arabs, and Jews, he greeted me as if it were a rare thing to meet a professor of the same faith, and a believer in the same God and Savior. He regretted that he had been away when I arrived, and said that he ought by right to have had me at his house, as he was the only Christian in Hebron; and he, even where proselytes were wanted, would perhaps not have passed muster according to the strict canons of a Catholic church. My Christian friend, however, was more of a Jew than any of the descendants of Israel around me; for, amid professions of friend-ship and offers of service, he was not forgetting his own interests. The European and American governments had been appointing consular agents in many of the cities of Syria, and this office, under the government of the present pasha, exempted the holder from certain taxes and impositions, to which the fellahs and rayahs were subject. America is known in the Holy Land by her missionaries, by the great ship (the Delaware) which, a year before, touched at the seaport towns, and by the respect and character which she confers on her consular agents. My Coptic Christian knew her on the last account, and told me, in confidence, that he thought America had need of a consular agent in Hebron, to protect her citizens traveling in that region. I was the first American traveler who had ever been there, and years may roll by before another follows me; but I fully concurred with him in the necessity of such an officer; and when he suggested that there was no better man than himself to hold it, I concurred with him again. Little did I think when, years before, I was seeking to climb the slippery rungs of the political ladder, that my political influence would ever be sought for the office of consul in the ancient capital of David, but so it was; and, without questioning him too closely about his faith in the principles and usages of the democratic party, the virtue of regular nominations, &c., taking his name written in Arabic, and giving him my card that he might know the name of his political benefactor, I promised to speak to the consul at Beirut in his favor; and he left me with as much confidence as if he had his commission already in his pocket.

A more interesting business followed with the old rabbi, probably induced by what had just passed between the Christian and myself. He told me that he had lately had occasion to regret exceedingly the loss of a paper which would now be of great use to him; that he was a Jew of Venice (I can vouch for it that he was no Shylock), and thirty years before had left his native city and come to Hebron with a regular passport; that for many years a European passport was no protection, and, indeed, it had been rather an object with him to lay aside the European character, and identify himself with the Asiatics; that, in consequence, he had been careless of his passport, and had lost it; but that now, since the conquest of Mohammed Ali and the government of Ibrahim Pasha, a European passport was respected, and saved its holder and his family from Turkish impositions. He mourned bitterly over his loss, not, as he said, for himself, for his days were almost ended, and the storms of life could not break over his head more heavily than they had already done; but he mourned for his children and grandchildren, whom his carelessness had deprived of the evidence of their birthright and the protection of their country. I was interested in the old man's story, and particularly in his unobtrusive manner of telling it; and drawing upon the reminiscences of my legal knowledge, I told him that the loss of his passport had not deprived him of his right to the protection of his country, and that, if he could establish the fact of his being a native of Venice, he might still sit down under the wings of the double-headed eagle of Austria.

I afterward went more into detail. Learning that there were in Hebron some of his very old acquaintances, who could testify to the fact of his nativity, I told him to bring them to me, and I would take their affidavits, and, on my arrival at Beirut, would represent the matter to the Austrian consul there; and I thought that with such evidence the consul would not refuse him another passport. He thanked me very warmly, and the next morning early, while I was waiting, all ready for my departure, he brought in his witnesses. It would have been difficult for the old man to produce deponents who could swear positively to his nativity; but of those whom he brought any one could look back farther than it is usually allowed to man. They were all over sixty, and their long white beards gave them a venerable appearance, which made me attach more importance to the proceedings than I intended. These hoary-headed men, I thought, could not speak with lying lips; and, taking my place in the middle of the floor, the witnesses seated themselves before me, and I prepared, with business-like formality, to examine them and reduce their examination to writing. Since I left home I had rarely thought of anything connected with my professional pursuits, and I could but smile as I found myself seated in the middle of a floor, surrounded by a crowd of Israelites in the old city of Hebron, for the first time in more than eighteen months resuming the path of my daily walks at home.

I placed the scribe before me, and with a little of the keenness of the hunter returning to a track for some time lost, I examined the witnesses severally, and dictated in good set form the several requisite affidavits; and then reading them over distinctly, like a commissioner authorized to take acknowledgments under the act, &c., I swore the white-bearded men upon the table of their law, a Hebrew copy of the Old Testament. I then dictated an affidavit for the rabbi himself, and was about administering the oath as before, when the old man rose, and taking the paper in his hand, and telling me to follow him, led the way through a range of narrow lanes and streets, and a crowd of people, to the little synagogue, where, opening the holy of holies, and laying his hand upon the sacred scroll, he read over the affidavit and solemnly swore to its truth. It did not need this additional act of solemnity to convince me of his truth; and when he gave me back the paper, and I saw the earnestness and

323

deep interest depicted in the faces of the crowd that had followed us, I again resolved that I would use my best exertions to gladden once more the old man's heart before he died. I added to the several affidavits a brief statement of the circumstances under which they had been taken, and, putting the paper in my pocket, returned to the house of the rabbi; and I may as well mention here, that at Beirut I called upon the Austrian consul, and before I left had the satisfaction of receiving from him the assurance that the passport should be made out forthwith, and delivered to the agent whom the old rabbi had named to me.

I had nothing now to detain me in Hebron; my mules and a kervash provided by the governor were waiting for me, and I bade farewell to my Jewish friends. I could not offer to pay the old rabbi with money for his hospitality, and would have satisfied my conscience by a compliment to the servants; but the son of the good old man, himself more than sixty, told Paul that they would all feel hurt if I urged it. I did not urge it; and the thought passed rapidly through my mind that while yesterday the children of the desert would have stripped me of my last farthing, today a Jew would not take from me a para. I passed through the dark and narrow lanes of the Jewish Quarter, the inhabitants being all arranged before their houses; and all along, even from the lips of maidens, a farewell salutation fell upon my ears. They did not know what I had done or what I proposed to do; but they knew that I intended a kindness to a father of their tribe, and they thanked me as if that kindness were already done. With the last of their kind greetings still lingering on my ears, I emerged from the Jewish Quarter, and it was with a warm feeling of thankfulness I felt, that if yesterday I had an Arab's curse, today I had a Jewish blessing.

CHAPTER XXVI

I HAD GIVEN away all my superfluous baggage, and commenced my journey in the Holy Land with three mules, one for myself, another for Paul, and the third for my baggage. The muleteer, who was an uncommonly thriving-looking, well-dressed man, rode upon a donkey, and had an assistant, who accompanied us on foot; but by far the most important person of our party was our kervash. He was a wild Arnaout, of a race that had for centuries furnished the bravest, fiercest, and most terrible soldiers in the army of the sultan; and he himself was one of the wildest of that wild tribe. He was now about forty, and had been a warrior from his youth upward, and battles and bloodshed were familiar to him as his food; he had fought under Ibrahim Pasha in his bloody campaign in Greece and his rebellious war against the sultan; and having been wounded in the great battle in which the Egyptian soldiers defeated the grand vizier with the flower of the sultan's army, he had been removed from the regular service and placed in an honorable position near the governor of Hebron. He was above the middle height, armed like the bristling porcupine, with pistols, a Damascus sabre, and a Turkish gun slung over his back, all which he carried as lightly and easily as a sportman does his fowling-piece. His face was red, a burnt or baked red; his mustaches seemed to curl spontaneously, as if in contempt of dangers; and he rode his high-mettled horse as if he were himself a part of the noble animal. Altogether, he was the boldest, most dashing, and martial-looking figure I ever saw; and had a frankness and openness in his countenance which, after the dark and sinister looks of my Bedouins, made me take to him the

325

moment I saw him. I do not think I made as favorable an impression upon him at first; for almost the first words he spoke to Paul after starting were to express his astonishment at my not drinking wine. The janissary must have told him this as he sat by me at supper, though I did not think he was watching me so closely. I soon succeeded, however, in establishing myself on a good footing with my kervash, and learned that his reading of the Koran did not forbid the winecup to the followers of the Prophet. He admitted that the Sultan, as being of the blood of the Prophet, and the viceregent of God upon earth, ought not to taste it; but as to the Pasha of Egypt, he drank good wine whenever he could get it, and this gave *his* subjects a right to drink as often as they pleased.

We were interrupted by an Arab, who told us that a party of soldiers had just caught two robbers. The kervash pricked up his ears at this, and, telling us that he would meet us at a place some distance farther on, he drove his heavy stirrups into his horse's sides, and, dashing up the hill at full gallop, was out of sight in an instant. I did not think it exactly the thing to leave us the first moment we heard of robbers; but I saw that his fiery impatience to be present at a scene could not be controlled, and I felt well assured that, if danger should arrive, we would soon find him at our side. Soon after we found him waiting with the party he had sought; the two robbers chained together, and, probably long before this, they have expiated their crime with their lives. He told us that from Hebron to Jerusalem was the most unsafe road in the Holy Land; and that Ibrahim Pasha, who hated the Arabs in that vicinity, was determined to clear it of rebels and robbers if he cut off every man in the country.

About half an hour from Hebron we came to a valley, supposed to be the Vale of Eschol, where the spies sent out by Moses found the grapes so heavy that to carry one bunch it was necessary to suspend it on a pole. On the right we passed a ruined wall, by some called the Cave of Machpelah, or sepulchre of the patriarchs, but which the Jews at Hebron had called the House of Abraham.

We were on our way to Bethlehem. I had hired my mules for Jerusalem, expecting merely to stop at Bethlehem and push on to

Jerusalem that night. The road between these oldest of cities was simply a mule-path over rocky mountains, descending occasionally into rich valleys. We had already, on this first journey in the Holy Land, found that the character given of it in the Bible is true at this day; and that the Land of Promise is not like the land of Egypt, watered by the dews of heaven, but by copious and abundant rains. Indeed, the rain was falling in torrents; our clothes were already dripping wet, but we did not mind it, for we were too full of thankfulness that continued sunshine and clear and unclouded skies had been our portion, when we most needed them, in the desert.

The heavy fall of rain made the track slippery and precarious; and it was four hours before we reached the celebrated reservoirs, known to modern travelers under the name of the Pools of Solomon. These large, strong, noble structures, in a land where every work of art has been hurried to destruction, remain now almost as perfect as when they were built. There are three of them, about 480, 600, and 660 feet in length, and 280 in breadth, and of different altitudes, the water from the first running into the second, and from the second into the third. At about a hundred yards' distance is the spring which supplies the reservoirs, as the monks say, the sealed fountain referred to in Canticles iv, 12. The water from these reservoirs is conveyed to Jerusalem by a small aqueduct, a round earthen pipe about ten inches in diameter, which follows all the sinuosities of the ground, being sometimes above the surface and sometimes under. It is easily broken; and while I was in Jerusalem an accident happened which entirely cut off the water from their pools.

There is every reason to believe that these pools have existed from the date assigned to them; and that this was the site of one of King Solomon's houses of pleasure, where he made himself "gardens, and orchards, and pools of water." The rain here ceased for a few moments, and enabled me to view them at my leisure; and as I walked along the bank, or stood on the margin, or descended the steps to the water's edge, it seemed almost the wild suggestion of a dream to imagine that the wisest of men had looked into the same pool, had strolled along the same bank, and stood on the very

327

same steps. It was like annihilating all the intervals of time and space. Solomon and all his glory are departed, and little could even his wisdom have foreseen that, long after he should be laid in the dust and his kingdom had passed into the hands of strangers, a traveler from a land he never dreamed of would be looking upon his works, and murmuring to himself the words of the preacher, "Vanity of vanities, all is vanity."

A little to the right of the pools, towards the region of the Dead Sea, is a very large grotto, supported by great pillars of the natural rock, perfectly dry, without petrifaction or stalactites; it is a perfect labyrinth within; and, as in many of the ancient catacombs, a man might easily lose himself forever in its windings. It lies in the mountainous wilderness of Engaddi, and is supposed to be the Cave of Adullam, where David received the mutinous and discontented spirits of his days, and where, when Saul was in pursuit of him, he cut off the skirts of his garment, and suffered him to go away unharmed.

In an hour more we came in sight of Bethlehem, seated on an elevation, a confused and irregular pile of white buildings. The star of the east no longer hovers over it to mark the spot where the Savior was born; and the mosque and the minaret proclaim the birthplace of Christ under the dominion of a people who reject and despise him.

Heaps of ruins and houses blackened with smoke show that the hand of war has been there. Ibrahim Pasha, on his sortie from Jerusalem and on his way to Hebron, had lingered on his path of destruction long enough to lay in ruins half the little city of Bethlehem. It is a singular fact, and exhibits a liberality elsewhere unknown in the history of the Turks or of the Mussulman religion, that the height of his indignation fell upon the Arabs. He spared the Christians for a reason that never before operated with a Turk —because they had not offended. He did, too, another liberal thing: saying that Christians and Mussulmans could not live together in unity, he drove out from Bethlehem the Arabs whom the sword had spared and left the place consecrated by the birth of Christ in the exclusive possession of his followers. True, he stained this act of clemency or policy by arbitrarily taking away thirty Christian boys, whom he sent to work at the factories in Cairo; and the simple-hearted parents, hearing that I had come from that city, asked me if I had seen their children.

It is a happy thing for the traveler in the Holy Land, that in almost all the principal places there is a Christian convent, whose doors are always open to him; and one of the largest and finest of these is in Bethlehem. Riding through the whole extent of the little town, greeted by Christians, who, however, with their white turbans and fierce mustaches and beards, had in my eyes a most unchristian appearance, and stopping for a moment on the high plain in front, overlooking the valley, and the sides of the hill all cultivated in terraces, we dismounted at the door of the convent.

Beginning my tour in the Holy Land at the birthplace of our Savior, and about to follow him in his wanderings through Judea, Samaria, and Galilee, over the ground consecrated by his preaching, his sufferings, and miracles, to his crucifixion on Calvary, I must prepare my readers for a disappointment which I experienced myself. The immediate followers of our Savior, who personally knew the localities which are now guarded and reverenced as holy places, engrossed by the more important business of their Master's mission, never marked these places for the knowledge of their descendants. Neglected for several centuries, many of them were probably entirely unknown when a new spirit arose in the East and the minds of the Christians were inflamed with a passion for collecting holy relics and for making pilgrimages to the places consecrated by the acts and sufferings of our Redeemer and his disciples; and the Empress Helena, the mother of Constantine, the first Christian empress, came as a crusader into the Holy Land, to search for and determine the then unknown localities. And the traveler is often astonished that, with so little to guide her, she was so successful; for she not only found all the holy places mentioned in the Bible, but many more; and the piety of Christians will never forget that it was through her indefatigable exertions the true cross was drawn from the bottom of a dark pit, and is now scattered in pieces all over the world, to gladden the hearts of believers. It may be that the earnest piety of the empress sometimes deceived her; but then she always covered a doubtful place with a handsomer monument, upon much the same principle that a jockey praises a bad horse and says nothing of a good one because the bad one wants praising and the good one can speak for himself. Besides, the worthy empress seemed to think that a little marble could not hurt a holy place, and a good deal might help to make holy what was not so without it; and so think most of the Christian pilgrims, for I have observed that they always kiss with more devotion the polished marble than the rude stone.

But the Christian who goes animated by the fresh, I may almost say virgin, feeling, awakened by the perusal of his Bible, expecting to see in Bethlehem the stable in which our Savior was born and the manger in which he was cradled, or in Jerusalem the tomb hewn out of the rock wherein his crucified body was buried, will feel another added to the many grievous disappointments of a traveler when he finds these hallowed objects, or at least what are pointed out as these, covered and enclosed with parti-colored marble, and bedecked with gaudy and inappropriate ornaments, as if intentionally and impiously to destroy all resemblance to the descriptions given in the sacred book.

I had intended going on to Jerusalem that afternoon; but the rain had retarded me so much that, as soon as I saw the interior of the convent, I determined to remain all night. My muleteer insisted upon proceeding, as I had arranged with him when I engaged him; but my kervash silenced him by a rap over the back with the flat of his sword, and he went off on his donkey alone, leaving behind him his companion and his mules.

Entering by the small door of the convent, I heard in the distance the loud pealing of an organ and the solemn chant of the monks; the sound transported me at once to scenes that were familiar and almost homelike, the churches and cathedrals in Italy; and the appearance of one of the brothers, in the long brown habit of the Capuchins, with his shaved head and sandals on his feet, made me feel for the moment as if I were in Europe. The monks were then at prayers; and following him through the great church, down a

330

Monastery of St. Catherine, from Laborde's *Voyage de l'Arabie Petrée*.

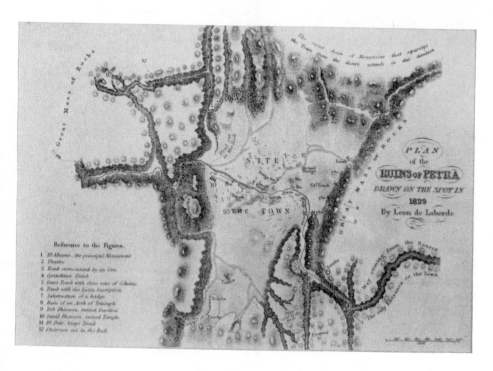

Plan of Petra, from Laborde's *Voyage de l'Arabie Petrée*.

The Khasna, ruins of Petra, from Laborde's *Voyage de l'Arabie Petrée*.

Mosque of Omar, engraved by William Finden from a drawing by Catherwood. From Finden's *Landscape Illustrations of the Bible* (London, 1836).

Interior of the Golden Gate, Jerusalem, engraved by William Finden from a drawing by Catherwood. From Finden's *Landscape Illustrations of the Bible* (London, 1836).

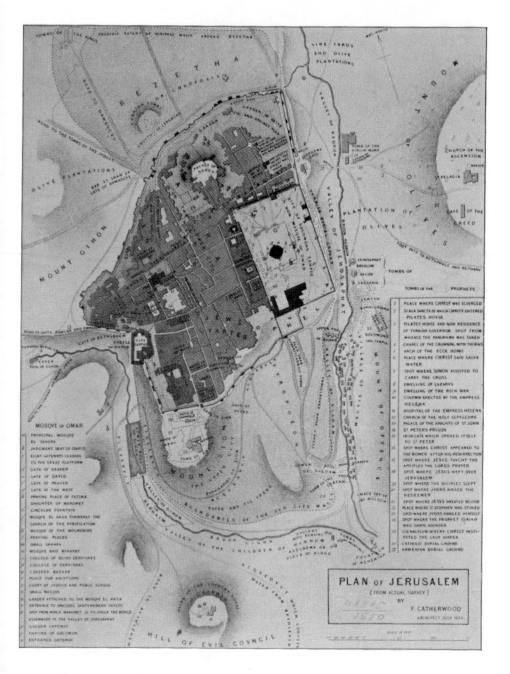

Catherwood's plan of Jerusalem.

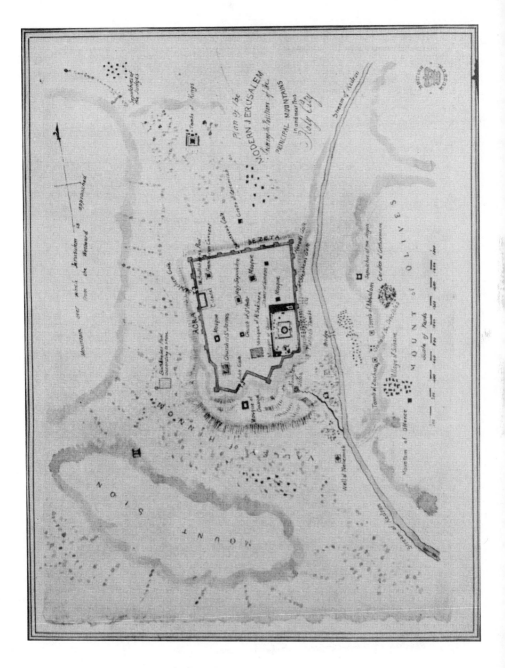

Catherwood's map of Jerusalem.

Τιμιώτατε ἀγαπητότατε ἄρχον κύριε κύρ Ἰωάν: .... σέ
ἀντῆς ψυχῆς, ᾗ καρδίας εὐχαριστεῖν χαιρετίζομεν.

f ,, Διάγομεν ἐδῶ εἰς Σιναῖς τὸ ὄρι ὀφείλετος ἀγάπην δεσ. ....
ὀφείλεις Ἁγίας Βάτου, ᾗ τῆς .... καρδιῶν ᾗ ἱστορίας Ἁγίας Αἰ-
καλ..ρίνης, ἵνα σώζῃ ᾗ Ἀδελφοί ἡμῶν ἱερευταῖς ἀ..............
.... σώτειαν, διὰ τὸ σαρκὸς ὑμῶν γράμμα. ....
ὅτι χαίρει ὅλα ἡμετέρων μέχρι ...δε. Μεσούλεος δὲ ....
τὸ σὸς πιστός κυρίω Γεωργὶς ...., διὸ βιβλιάρια, ᾗ ἕνα ....
τη .... ᾗ δουλεία... αρχι ἡμᾶς, ᾗ ....
τῶν .... αὐτῆς ...., ᾗ καρδίας ....
.... γὸ τῆς ψυχῆν σας, ᾗ .... τὸ ὄνομα τὸ Σιναίου τὸ ὄρος
γὸ τοῦ μετὰ ...., ᾗ γὸ ἡμᾶς τῆς ....
.................., χωρὶς νὰ .... ἀπὸ ἡμᾶς τὸ σαραμηκροῦ ....
....
.. .., ᾗ σε εὐχαριστῶμεν ... μύρια, ᾗ ... θέλομεν ....
τὸ νὰ ...., ᾗ νὰ σαρακαλοῦμεν τοῦ ἄγιον Θεοῦ διὰ τοῦ ὑγίαν σας.
καὶ ταῦτα μετ' εὐχιλικοῖ, ᾗ ..... ἐν Κυρίῳ.
                    τῆς ἡμετέρας ἀγάπης ὅλοι Πρόθυμοι.

.... 1839: .... 22: ....

Letter to John L. Stephens from the Mount Sinai brotherhood.

marble staircase, and along a subterranean corridor, in five minutes after my arrival in Bethlehem I was standing on the spot where the Savior of mankind was born.

The superior was a young man, not more than thirty, with a face and figure of uncommon beauty; though not unhealthy, his face was thin and pale, and his high, projecting forehead indicated more than talent. Genius flashed from his eyes, though, so far as I could judge from his conversation, he did not sustain the character his features and expression promised. He was not insensible to the advantages of his personal appearance. The rope around his waist, with the cross dangling at the end, was laid as neatly as a soldier's sword-belt; the top of his head was shaved, his beard combed, and the folds of his long coarse dress, his cowl, and the sandals on his feet, all were arranged with a precision that, under other circumstances, would have made him a Brummel. There was something, too, in the display of a small hand and long taper fingers that savored more of the exquisite than of the recluse; but I ought not to have noted him too critically, for he was young, handsome, and gentlemanly, and fit for better things than the dronish life of a convent. I am inclined to believe, too, that he sometimes thought of other things than his breviary and his missal; at all events, he was not particularly familiar with Bible history; for, in answer to his question as to the route by which I had come, I told him that I had passed through the land of Idumea; and when I expected to see him open his eyes with wonder, I found that he did not know where the land of Idumea was. I remember that he got down a huge volume in Latin, written by saint somebody, and we pored over it together until our attention was drawn off by something else and we forgot what we were looking for.

The walls of the convent contain all that is most interesting in Bethlehem; but outside the walls also are places consecrated in Bible history, and which the pilgrim to Bethlehem, in spite of doubts and confusion, will look upon with exceeding interest. Standing on the high table of ground in front of the convent, one of the monks pointed out the fountain where, when David was thirsting, his young men procured him water; and in the rear of the convent is a beautiful valley, having in the midst of it a ruined village, marking the place where the shepherds were watching their flocks at night when the angel came down and announced to them the birth of the Savior. The scene was as pastoral as it had been eighteen hundred years before; the sun was going down, the shepherds were gathering their flocks together, and one could almost imagine that, with the approach of evening, they were preparing to receive another visitor from on high. In the distance beyond the valley is a long range of mountains enclosing the Dead Sea, and among them was the wilderness of Engaddi; and the monk pointed out a small opening as leading to the shores of the sea, at the precise spot where Lot's wife was turned into a pillar of salt.

Mixed with these references to Bible history were idle legends of later days, connected with places to which the monk conducted me with as much solemnity as he had displayed when indicating the holy places of Scripture. In a grotto cut out of the rock is a chapel dedicated to the Virgin, and he told me that the mother of Christ had here concealed herself from Herod and nursed the infant Jesus forty days before she escaped into Egypt. Near this is another grotto, in which the Virgin, going to visit a neighbor with the child in her arms, took refuge from a shower, and her milk overflowed; and, now, said the monk, there is a faith among all people, Turks, Greeks, and Armenians, that if a woman to whom Nature has denied the power of nursing her child comes to this grotto and prays before the altar, the fountain of life will be opened to her. Nor was the virtue of the place confined to those who should resort to it in person; for the monks had prayed for and had obtained a delegation of the Virgin's power, and a small portion of powder from the porous rock, swallowed in a little water, would be equally efficacious to women having faith. A huge chamber had been cut away in the back of the grotto by pilgrims, who had taken with them to their distant homes some of this beautiful provision for a want of nature, and Paul and myself each took a pilgrim's share.

It was dark when I returned to the convent, followed by my wild Arnaout, whom, by the way, I have neglected for some time. I had told him on my arrival that I should not need his escort any farther;

but he swore that he had his orders and would not leave me until he saw me safe within the walls of Jerusalem; and so far he had been as good as his word, for, wherever I went, he was close at my heels, following with invincible gravity, but never intruding, the continual rattling of his steel scabbard being the only intimation I had of his presence. He was now following me through the stone court of the convent, into the room fitted up for the reception of pilgrims and travelers. I liked him, and I liked to hear the clanking of his sword at my heels; I would have staked my life upon his faith; and such confidence did he inspire by his bold, frank bearing, his manly, muscular figure, and his excellent weapons that with a dozen such I would not have feared a whole tribe of Bedouins. In another country and a former age he would have been the *beau ideal* of a dashing cavalier, and an unflinching companion at the winecup or in the battlefield.

I bore in mind our conversation in the morning about wine, and was determined that my liberal expounder of the Koran should not suffer from my abstinence. The superior, apologizing for the want of animal food, had told me to call for anything in the convent, and I used the privilege for the benefit of my thirsty Mussulman. The first thing I called for was wine; and, while supper was preparing, we were tasting its quality. He was no stickler for trifles, and accepted, without any difficulty, my apology for not being able to pledge him in full bumpers; and although most of this time Paul was away and we could not exchange a word, the more he drank the better I liked him. It was so long since I had had with me a companion I liked, that I "cottoned" to him more and more, and resolved to make the most of him. I had a plate for him at table by the side of me; and when Paul, who did not altogether enter into my feelings, asked him if he would not rather eat alone, on the floor, he half drew his sword and, driving it back into its scabbard, swore that he would eat with me if it was on the top of a minaret. We sat down to table, and I did the honors with an unsparing hand. He attempted for a moment the use of the knife and fork, but threw them down in disgust, and trusted to the means with which nature had provided him. The wine he knew how to manage, and for the

333

rest he trusted to me; and I gave him bread, olives, fish, milk, honey, sugar, figs, grapes, dates, &c., &c., about as fast as I could hand them over, one after the other, all together, pellmell, and with such an utter contempt of all rules of science as would have made a Frenchman go mad. Paul by this time entered into the spirit of the thing; and when my bold guest held up for a moment, he stood by with a raw egg, the shell broken, and turning back his head, poured it down his throat. I followed with a plate of brown sugar, into which he thrust his hand to the knuckles, sent down a huge mouthful to sweeten the egg, and, nearly kicking over the table with an ejaculation about equivalent to our emphatic "enough," threw himself upon the divan. I wound him up with coffee and pipes; and when the superior came to me in the evening, to the scandal of the holy brotherhood, my wild companion was lying asleep, as drunk as a lord, upon the divan.

Several of the monks came in to see me; and all loved to talk of the world they had left. They were all Italians; and in the dreariness and desolation of Judea, in spite of monastic vows, their hearts turned to the sunny skies of their beautiful native land. They left me at an early hour; and I trust the reader will forgive me if, in the holy city of Bethlehem, I forgot for a moment the high and holy associations connected with the place in the sense of enjoyment awakened by the extraordinary luxury of a pair of sheets, a luxury I had not known since my last night in Cairo.

Tempted as I was to yield myself at once to the enjoyment, I paused a while to look at the sleeping figure of my kervash. He lay extended at full length on his back, with his arms folded across his breast, his right hand clutching the hilt of his sword, and his left the handle of a pistol; his broad chest rose and fell with his long and heavy respirations; and he slept like a man who expected to be roused by a cry to battle. His youth and manhood had been spent in scenes of violence; his hands were red with blood; murder and rapine had been familiar to him; and when his blood was up in battle, the shrieks and groans of the dying were music in his ears; yet he slept, and his sleep was calm and sound as that of childhood. I stood over him with the candle in my hand, and flashed the light across his face; his rugged features contracted, and his sword rattled in his convulsive grasp. I blew out the light and jumped into bed. Once during the night I was awakened by his noise; by the dim light of a small lamp that hung from the ceiling I saw him stumble to the table, seize a huge jar of water and apply it to his lips; I saw him throw back his head and heard his long, regular, and continued swallows; and when he had finished the jar he drew a long breath, went to the window, came to my bedside, looked at me for a moment, probably thinking what a deal of useless trouble I took in pulling off my clothes; and, throwing himself upon the divan, in a few moments he was again asleep.

In the morning immediately after breakfast one of the monks came to conduct me through the convent. The building covered a great extent of ground; and for strength and solidity, as well as size, resembled a fortress. It was built by the Empress Helena, over the spot consecrated as the birthplace of our Savior, and was intended, so far as human handiwork could do so, to honor and reverence the holy spot. The insufficient means of the pious empress, however, or some other cause prevented its being finished according to the plan she had designed; and the charity of subsequent Christians has barely sufficed to keep it from falling to ruin. The great church would have been a magnificent building if finished according to her plan; but now, in its incomplete state, it is a melancholy monument of defeated ambition. On each side is a range of noble columns supporting a frieze of wood, which the monk told me was cedar from Lebanon, and still remaining almost as sound as the solid stone. The whole building is divided among the Catholics, Greeks, and Armenians, the three great bodies who represent, or rather misrepresent, Christianity in the East. Each has its limits, beyond which the others must not pass; and again there are certain parts which are common to all. The Turkish government exercises a control over it; and, taking advantage of the dissensions between these different professors, sells the privileges to the highest bidder. In the great church the Greeks, happening to have been the richest, are the largest proprietors, to the great scandal of the Catholics, who hate the Greeks with a most orthodox virulence.

The Grotto of the Nativity is under the floor of the church, the Greeks having an entrance directly by its side and the Catholics by a longer and more distant passage. I descended by the latter. My Arnaout was close at my heels, grave and sober as if he had never known the taste of wine and following with a respect that might have satisfied the most bigoted Christian. Indeed, it was a thing to be noted, with what respect and reverence this wild and lawless Mussulman regarded the holy places, consecrated by a religion he believed false and the worship of a people he despised. Nevertheless, Paul was scandalized at the eyes of an unbeliever being permitted to see the holy places, and stopped at the top of the staircase to urge upon me the propriety of making him stay behind. The kervash seemed to understand what he was saying and to intimate by his looks that it would not be an easy matter to turn him back. I did not think, however, that the feet of a Mussulman would be in themselves a profanation, and the monk making no objection, I silenced Paul's.

Passing through the chapel of the Catholic convent, where the monks were teaching the children of the Arab Christians the principles of the Catholic faith, I was conducted to the room of the superior, where, among other relics which I now forget, he showed me the withered hand of an infant, preserved among the treasures of the convent as having belonged to one of the innocents massacred by the order of Herod. Near the door of the chapel we descended a flight of stone steps, and then a second, until we came to an excavation in the solid rock, and, following a passage to the right, came to a little chapel, with an altar, dedicated to Joseph, the husband of Mary. At the end of this passage was a large chamber, called the school of St. Jerome, where the great Catholic saint wrote his version of the Bible, the celebrated Vulgate. Passing out through the door of this chamber, on the right is the tomb of the saint; and directly opposite are the tombs of Santa Paula and another whose name I have forgotten; very good ladies, no doubt, but who they were, or why they were buried in that holy place, I did not understand, although they must have died in the odor of sanctity, as their bodies have since been removed to the papal city. Returning into the first passage and advancing a few steps, on the left is an altar over the pit into which the bodies of the murdered innocents were thrown. Under the altar is a recess with an iron grating opening into the pit, or rather vault, below. By the light of a torch I gazed long and earnestly within, but could see nothing that gave confirmation to the story. Over the altar was a rude painting, representing the massacred infants held up by their heels, with their throats cut and their bowels gushing out, the anguish of the mothers, and all the necessary and fearful accompaniments of such a scene. A few paces farther is an altar, over the spot where Joseph sat during the birth of the divine infant, meditating upon the great event; and farther on, to the left, is the entrance to the Grotto of the Nativity.

It was the hour assigned for the use of the Armenians, and the monks were all there chanting the praises of the Redeemer. The chamber of the grotto is thirty-seven feet long and eleven wide, with a marble floor and walls, the latter adorned with tapestry and paintings. Directly in front of the door by which we entered, at the other end of the grotto, is a semicircular recess, lined and floored with small blocks of marble, and in the center a single star with the inscription, "Hic natus est Jesus Christus de Virga"—"here Christ was born of the Virgin." The star in the east which went before the wise men, says the tradition, rested over this spot; and fourteen lamps, the gifts of Christian princes, burning night and day, constantly illumine the birthplace of salvation to a ruined world. On the right, descending two steps, is a chamber paved and lined with marble, having at one end a block polished and hollowed out; and this is the manger in which our Savior was laid. Over the altar is a picture representing a stable with horses and cattle, and behind a little iron wickerwork are five lamps constantly burning. Directly opposite is the altar of the magi, where the three kings sat when they came to offer presents to the Son of God. Over it is a picture representing them in the act of making their offerings, and one of the kings is represented as an Ethiopian.

All this has but little conformity with the rude scene of the stable and the manger as described in the Bible; and, in all probability, most of the holy places pointed out in Bethlehem, and adorned and transformed by the false but well-meaning piety of Christians, have no better claim to authenticity than the credulity of a weak and pious old woman. But amid all the doubts that present themselves when we stop to ponder and reflect, it is sufficient for our enjoyment of these scenes to know that we are in "Bethlehem of Judea," consecrated by the greatest event in the history of the world, the birth of the Son of God. We know that, within the atmosphere we breathe, Christ first appeared on earth; that one of the stars of heaven left its place among the constellations, and hovered over the spot on which we stand; that the kings of the earth came here to offer gifts to the holy child; and, beholding multitudes of pilgrims from far-distant lands constantly prostrating themselves before the altar in earnestness and sincerity of undoubting faith, we give ourselves up to the illusion, if illusion it be, and are ready to believe that we are indeed standing where Christ was born.

My Arnaout behaved remarkably well, though once he broke the stillness of the grotto by an involuntary exclamation; his loud harsh voice and the rattling of his armor startled for a moment the monks and praying pilgrims. On coming out, I told him that the Christians were much more liberal than the Mussulmans, for we had permitted him to see all the holy places in the church while I had been violently driven from the door of the mosque in Hebron. He railed at the ignorance and prejudice of his countrymen, and swore, if I would go back to Hebron, he would carry me through the mosque on the point of his sword. I did not much relish this method of entering a mosque, but took it, as it was meant, for a warm expression of his willingness to serve me; and we returned to the apartment of the superior to bid him farewell. The superior accompanied us to the door of the convent; and, without meaning to be scandalous or insinuate that there was anything wrong in it, although he was a young and handsome man, I left him talking with a woman.

CHAPTER XXVII

THE TOMB OF RACHEL—FIRST VIEW OF JERUSALEM—FALLING
AMONG THIEVES—POTENT SWAY OF THE PASHA—A TURKISH DIGNI-
TARY—A MISSIONARY—EASTER IN JERUSALEM—
A LITTLE CONGREGATION

GIVING a last look to the Valley of the Shepherds, we were soon on the mountain's side, and very soon all the interest with which I had regarded Bethlehem was lost in the more absorbing feeling with which I looked forward to Jerusalem. My muleteer had gone on the night before, my Arnaout knew nothing of the holy places on the road, and we took with us a Christian boy to point them out. The first was the tomb of Rachel, a large building, with a whitened dome, and having within it a high, oblong monument built of brick and stuccoed over. I dismounted and walked round the tomb, inside and out, and again resumed my journey. All that we know in regard to this tomb is that Rachel died when journeying with Jacob from Sychem to Hebron and that Jacob buried her near Bethlehem; and whether it be her tomb or not, I could not but remark that, while youth and beauty have faded away and the queens of the East have died and been forgotten and Zenobia and Cleopatra sleep in unknown graves, year after year thousands of pilgrims are thronging to the supposed last resting place of a poor Hebrew woman.

The boy next conducted us to a stony field, by which, as he said, the Virgin once passed and asked for beans; the owner of the field told her there were none; and, to punish him for his falsehood and lack of charity, the beans were all changed into stones, and the country had remained barren ever since. Paul had been twice to Bethlehem without seeing this field, and he immediately dismounted and joined the boy in searching for the holy petrifactions. "It was wonderful," said Paul, as he picked up some little stones as much

339

like beans as anything else; "and see, too," he said, "how barren the country is." In about an hour we came to the Greek monastery of St. Elias, a large stone building standing on an eminence and commanding a fine view of Bethlehem. Stopping to water my horse at a fountain in front of the monastery, I turned to take a last look at Bethlehem; and my horse moving a few paces, when I turned again I saw in full view the holy city of Jerusalem. I did not expect it, and was startled by its proximity. It looked so small, and yet lay spread out before me so distinctly that it seemed as if I ought to perceive the inhabitants moving through the streets and hear their voices humming in my ears. I saw that it was walled all around and that it stood alone in an extensive waste of mountains, without suburbs or even a solitary habitation beyond its walls. There were no domes, steeples, or turrets to break the monotony of its aspect, and even the mosques and minarets made no show. It would have been a relief, and afforded something to excite the feelings, to behold it in ruins or dreary and desolate like Petra or with the banner of the Prophet, the blood-red Mussulman flag, waving high above its walls. But all was tame and vacant. There was nothing in its appearance that afforded me a sensation; it did not even inspire me with melancholy; and I probably convict myself when I say that the only image it presented to my mind was that of a city larger and in better condition than the usual smaller class of those within the Turkish dominion. I was obliged to rouse myself by recalling to mind the long train of extraordinary incidents of which that little city had been the theater, and which made it, in the eyes of the Christian at least, the most hallowed spot on earth. One thing only particularly struck me—its exceeding stillness. It was about midday, but there was no throng of people entering or departing from its gates, no movement of living creatures to be seen beneath its walls. All was as quiet as if the inhabitants were, like the Spaniards, taking their noonday sleep. We passed the Pools of Hezekiah and came in sight of the Mount of Olives; and now, for the first signs of life, we saw streaming from the gate a long procession of men, women, and children, on dromedaries, camels, and horses, and on foot, pilgrims who had visited Calvary and the holy sepulchre, and were now bending their steps towards Bethlehem.

At every moment the approach was gaining interest; but in a few minutes, while yet about an hour distant from the walls, my attention was diverted from the city by the sudden appearance of our muleteer, who had left us the day before in a pet and gone on before us to Jerusalem. He was sitting on the ground alone, so wan and woebegone, so changed from the spruce and well-dressed muleteer who had accompanied us from Hebron, that I scarcely recognized him. Every article of his former dress was gone, from his gay turban to his long boots; and in their stead he displayed an old yellow striped shawl, doing duty as a turban, and a ragged Bedouin gown. Late in the afternoon, while hurrying on to get in before the gates should be closed, he was hailed by four Arabs; and when he attempted to escape by pushing his donkey, he was brought to by a musket-ball passing through the folds of his dress and grazing his side. A hole in his coat, however, did not save it; and, according to the Arab mode of robbery, they stripped him to his skin, and left him stark naked in the road. From his manner of telling the story, I am inclined to think that the poor fellow had not conducted himself very valiantly, for though he did not regard the scratch on his side or the risk he had run of his life, he mourned bitterly over the loss of his garments. Arrived in the Holy Land, I had thought danger of all kinds at an end, and I could not help recognizing the singular good fortune which had accompanied me thus far, and congratulating myself upon the accident which had detained me at Bethlehem.

We were soon approaching the walls of Jerusalem, and seemed to be almost at their foot; but we were on one of the mountains that encompass the city, and the deep Valley of Jehoshaphat was yet between us and the holy city—the sacred burying-ground of the Jews, the "gathering-place of nations." Crossing this valley, we ascended on the other side, and in a few moments were on one of the seven hills on which the city is built, and entering at the Bethlehem gate. It was guarded by a Turkish soldier, and half a dozen more lay basking in the sun outside, who raised their heads as I ap-

341

proached, their long mustaches curling as they looked at me; and though they gave me no greeting, they let me pass without any molestation. On the right was the citadel; a soldier was on the walls, and a small red flag, the standard of Mohammed, was drooping against its staff. In front was an open place, irregular, and apparently formed by clearing away the ruins of fallen houses. As in all Turkish cities, the stillness was unbroken; there was no rattling of wheels over the pavements nor even the tramp of horses.

We wound around the walls and dismounted at the only asylum for strangers, the Latin Convent. I presented myself to the superior, and, after receiving from him a kind and cordial welcome with the usual apologies for meager fare on account of its being Lent, went to the room assigned me, and had just sat down to dinner when my poor muleteer entered in greater distress than ever.

Afraid of the very thing that happened, he had started immediately on his return to Hebron, and at the gate his mules were seized by a soldier for the use of the government. It was in a spirit of perfect wretchedness that the poor fellow, still smarting under the loss of his clothes, almost threw himself at my feet and begged me to intercede for him. I was, of course, anxious to help him if I could, and immediately rose to go with him; but Paul told me to remain quiet, and he would settle the matter in five minutes. Paul was a great admirer of the pasha. Wherever his government was established, he had made it safe for the traveler, and Paul's courage always rose and fell according to the subdued or unsubdued state of the population. In the city of Jerusalem the wind could scarcely blow without the leave of Ibrahim Pasha, and Paul had mounted on stilts almost as soon as we crossed the threshold of the gate. He had already been at his old tricks of pushing the unresisting Arabs about and kicking them out of the way, as in the miserable villages on the Nile; and, strong in the omnipotence of the firman, he now hurried to the gate, but he came back faster than he went. I have no doubt that he was very presuming and impudent, and richly deserved more than he got; but, at all events, he returned on a full run and in a towering passion. The soldier had given him the usual Mussulman abuse, showering upon him the accustomed "dog" and

"Christian," and, moreover, had driven him to the verge of madness by calling him a "Jew" and threatening to whip both him and his master. Paul ran away from what I am inclined to believe would have been his share, as the Arabs had taken part against him, and, burning with the indignity of being called a Jew, begged me to seek redress of the governor. I was roused myself, not so much by the particular insult to Paul as by the general intention of the thing and the disconsolate figure of my poor muleteer; and leaving my unfinished meal, with my firman in my hand and Paul and the muleteer at my heels, I started for the palace of the governor.

Old things and new are strangely blended in Jerusalem; and the residence of the Turkish governor is in the large building which to this day bears the name of Pontius Pilate. Paul told me its history as we were ascending the steps; and it passed through my mind as a strange thing, that almost the first moment after entering the city, I was making a complaint, perhaps in the same hall where the Jews had complained of Christ before Pontius Pilate, having with me a follower of that Christ, whom the Jews reviled and buffeted, burning under the indignity of being called a Jew.

The governor, as is the custom of governors in the East and probably as Pontius Pilate did in the time of our Savior, sat in a large room, ready to receive everybody who had any complaint to make; his divan was a raised platform, on an iron camp-bedstead, covered with rich Turkey rugs, and over them a splendid lion-skin. His face was noble, and his long black beard the finest I ever saw; a pair of large pistols and a Damascus sabre were lying by his side, and a rich fur cloak, thrown back over his shoulders, displayed a form that might have served as a model for a Hercules. Altogether, he reminded me of Richard in his tent on the plains of Acre. At the moment of my entry he was breathing on a brilliant diamond, and I noticed on his finger an uncommonly beautiful emerald. He received me with great politeness; and when I handed him the pasha's firman, with a delicacy and courtesy I never saw surpassed, he returned it to me unopened and unread, telling me that my dress and appearance were sufficient recommendation to the best services in his power. If the reader would know what dress and appearance

343

are a sufficient recommendation to the best offices of a Turkish governor, I will merely mention that, having thrown off, or rather having been stripped of, most of my Turkish dress at Hebron, I stood before the governor in a red tarboosh, with a long black silk tassel, a blue roundabout jacket buttoned up to the throat, gray pantaloons, boots splashed with mud, a red sash, a pair of large Turkish pistols, sword, and my Nubian club in my hand; and the only decided mark of aristocracy about me was my beard, which, though not so long as the governor's, far exceeded it in brilliancy of complexion.

The few moments I had had for observation and the courteous demeanor of the governor disarmed me of my anger; and coffee and the first pipe over, I stated my grievances very dispassionately. Paul's wrath was still dominant, and I have no doubt he represented the conduct of the soldier as much worse than it was, for the governor, turning to me without any further inquiries, asked if he should have him bastinadoed. This summary justice startled even Paul; and feeling a little ashamed of my own precipitation, I was now more anxious to prevent punishment than I had before been to procure it; and begged him to spare the soldier and merely order him to release the mules. Without another word he called a janissary, and requesting me to wait, ordered him to accompany Paul to the gate where the scene took place; and when Paul returned, the muleteer, with a thankful heart, was already on his way to Hebron. I had the satisfaction of learning, too, that the officers were on the track of the robbers who had stripped him, and before morning the governor expected to have them in custody.

Several times afterward I called upon the governor, and was always treated with the same politeness. Once, when I was walking alone outside the walls, I met him sitting on the grass with his janissaries and slaves standing up around him; and the whole Turkish population being out wandering among the tombs, he procured for me a respect and consideration which I think were useful to me afterward by calling me to a seat beside him and giving me the pipe from his own mouth. Some months afterward, at Genoa,

I saw a brief article in an Italian paper, referring to a previous article, giving an account of a then late revolution there, in which the governor was on the point of falling into the hands of the insurgents. I have never seen any account of the particulars of this revolution, and do not know whether he is now living or dead. In the East life hangs by so brittle a thread that when you part from a man in power, in all probability you will never see him again. I can only hope that the governor of Jerusalem still lives, and that his condition in life is as happy as when I saw him.

It was Saturday afternoon when I arrived at Jerusalem. I had a letter of introduction to Mr. Thompson, an American missionary, and the first thing I did was to look for him. One of the monks of the convent gave me the direction to the American priest, not knowing his name; and, instead of Mr. Thompson, I found Mr. Whiting, who had been there about a year in his place. Like the governor, Mr. Whiting did not want any credentials; but here, being among judges, it was not my dress and appearance that recommended me. I was an American, and at that distance from home the name of countryman was enough. In the city of Jerusalem such a meeting was to him a rare and most welcome incident; while to me, who had so long been debarred all conversation except with Paul and the Arabs, it was a pleasure which few can ever know, to sit down with a compatriot and once more, in my native tongue, hold converse of my native land.

Each of us soon learned to look upon the other as a friend, for we found that an old friend and schoolmate of mine had been also a friend and schoolmate of his own. He would have had me stay at his house; but I returned to the convent, and with my thoughts far away and full of the home of which we had been talking, I slept for the first night in the city of Jerusalem.

The first and most interesting object within the walls of the holy city, the spot to which every pilgrim first directs his steps, is the holy sepulchre. The traveler who has never read the descriptions of those who have preceded him in a pilgrimage through the Holy Land, finds his expectations strangely disappointed when, approaching this hallowed tomb, he sees around him the tottering houses of a ruined city, and is conducted to the door of a gigantic church.

This edifice is another, and perhaps the principal, monument of the Empress Helena's piety. What authority she had for fixing here the site of the Redeemer's burial-place I will not stop to inquire. Doubtless she had her reasons; and there is more pleasure in believing than in raising doubts which cannot be confirmed. In the front of the church is a large courtyard, filled with dealers in beads, crucifixes, and relics, among the most conspicuous of whom are the Christians of Bethlehem, with figures of the Savior, the Virgin, and a host of saints, carved from mother of pearl in all kinds of fantastic shapes. It was precisely the time at which I had wished and expected to be in Jerusalem—the season of Easter—and thousands of pilgrims, from every part of the Eastern world, had already arrived for the great ceremonies of the holy week. The court was thronged with them, crowded together so that it was almost impossible to move, and waiting, like myself, till the door of the church should be opened.

The holy sepulchre, as in the days when all the chivalry of Europe armed to wrest it from them, is still in the hands of the infidels; and it would have made the sword of an old crusader leap from its scabbard to behold a haughty Turk, with the air of a lord and master, standing sentinel at the door and with his long mace beating and driving back the crowd of struggling Christians. As soon as the door was opened, a rush was made for entrance; and as I was in the front rank, before the impetus ceased, amid a perfect storm of pushing, yelling, and shouting, I was carried almost headlong into the body of the church. The press continued behind, hurrying me along and kicking off my shoes; and in a state of desperate excitement both of mind and body, utterly unsuited to the place and time, I found myself standing over the so-called tomb of Christ, where, to enhance the incongruity of the scene, at the head of the sepulchre stood a long-bearded monk with a plate in his hand, receiving paras from the pilgrims. My dress marked me as a different person from the miserable, beggarly crowd before me; and expecting a better contribution from me, at the tomb of him who had pronounced that all men are equal in the sight of God, with an expression of contempt like the "canaille" of a Frenchman, and with kicks, cuffs, and blows, he drove back those before me and gave me a place at the head of the sepulchre. My feelings were painfully disturbed, as well by the manner of my entrance as by the irreverent demeanor of the monk; and disappointed, disgusted, and sick at heart, while hundreds were still struggling for admission, I turned away and left the church. A warmer imagination than mine could perhaps have seen, in a white marble sarcophagus, "the sepulchre hewn out of a rock," and in the fierce struggling of these barefooted pilgrims the devotion of sincere and earnest piety, burning to do homage in the holiest of places; but I could not.

It was refreshing to turn from this painful exhibition of a deformed and degraded Christianity to a simpler and purer scene. The evening before, Mr. Whiting had told me that religious exercises would be performed at his house the next day, and I hastened from the church to join in the grateful service. I found him sitting at a table, with a large family Bible open before him. His wife was present, with two little Armenian girls whom she was educating to assist her in her school; and I was not a little surprised to find that, when I had taken my seat, the congregation was assembled. In fact, Mr. Whiting had only been waiting for me; and, as soon as I came in, he commenced the service to which I had been so long a stranger. It was long since I had heard the words of truth from the lips of a preacher; and as I sat with my eyes fixed upon the Garden of Gethsemane and the Mount of Olives, I could not help thinking of it as a strangely interesting fact that here, in the holy city of Jerusalem, where Christ preached and died, though thousands were calling upon his name, the only persons who were praising him in simplicity and truth were a missionary and his wife, and a passing traveler, all from a far-distant land. I had, moreover, another subject of reflection. In Greece I had been struck with the fact that the only schools of instruction were those established by American missionaries, and supported by the liberality of American citizens; that our young republic was thus, in part, discharging the debt

347

which the world owes to the ancient mistress of science and the arts by sending forth her sons to bestow the elements of knowledge upon the descendants of Homer and Pericles, Plato and Aristotle; and here, on the very spot whence the apostles had gone forth to preach the glad tidings of salvation to a ruined world, a missionary from the same distant land was standing as an apostle over the grave of Christianity, a solitary laborer striving to re-establish the pure faith and worship that were founded on this spot eighteen centuries ago.

CHAPTER XXVIII

DURING my stay in Jerusalem a day seldom passed in which I did not visit the Church of the Holy Sepulchre; but my occupation was chiefly to observe the conduct of the pilgrims; and, if the reader will accompany me into the interior, he will see what I was in the habit of seeing every day.

The key of the church is kept by the governor of the city; the door is guarded by a Turk, and opened only at fixed hours, and then only with the consent of the three convents and in the presence of their several dragomen, an arrangement which often causes great and vexatious delays to such as desire admittance. This formality was probably intended for solemnity and effect, but its consequence is exactly the reverse; for, as soon as the door is opened, the pilgrims, who have almost always been kept waiting for some time and have naturally become impatient, rush in, struggling with each other, overturning the dragomen, and thumped by the Turkish doorkeeper, and are driven like a herd of wild animals into the body of the church. I do not mean to exaggerate the picture, the lightest of whose shades is already too dark. I describe only what I saw, and with this assurance the reader must believe me when I say that I frequently considered it putting life and limb in peril to mingle in that crowd. Probably it is not always so; but there were at that time within the walls of Jerusalem from ten to twenty thousand pilgrims, and all had come to visit the holy sepulchre.

Supposing, then, the rush to be over, and the traveler to have recovered from its effects, he will find himself in a large apartment, forming a sort of vestibule; on the left, in a recess of the wall, is a

large divan, cushioned and carpeted, where the Turkish doorkeeper is usually sitting, with half a dozen of his friends, smoking
the long pipe and drinking coffee and always conducting himself
with great dignity and propriety. Directly in front, surmounted by
an iron railing, having at each end three enormous wax candles
more than twenty feet high, and suspended above it a number of
silver lamps of different sizes and fashions, gifts from the Catholic,
Greek, and Armenian convents, is a long flat stone, called the "stone
of unction"; and on this, it is said, the body of our Lord was laid
when taken down from the cross and washed and anointed in
preparation for sepulture. This is the first object that arrests the
pilgrims on their entrance; and here they prostrate themselves in
succession, the old and the young, women and children, the rich man
and the beggar, and all kiss the sacred stone. It is a slab of polished
white marble; and one of the monks, whom I questioned on the
subject as he rose from his knees, after kissing it most devoutly told
me that it was not the genuine stone, which he said was under it, the
marble having been placed there as an ornamental covering and to
protect the hallowed relic from the abuses of the Greeks.

On the left is an iron circular railing in the shape of a large par-
rot's cage, having within it a lamp and marking the spot where the
women sat while the body was anointed for the tomb. In front of
this is an open area, surrounded by high square columns, supporting
a gallery above. The area is covered by a dome, imposing in appearance and effect; and directly under, in the center of the area,
is an oblong building, about twenty feet long and twelve feet high,
circular at the back, but square and finished with a platform in
front; and within this building is the holy sepulchre.

Leaving for a moment the throng that is constantly pressing at
the door of the sepulchre, let us make the tour of the church. Around
the open space under the dome are small chapels for the Syrians,
Copts, Maronites, and other sects of Christians who have not, like
the Catholics, the Greeks, and Armenians, large chapels in the body
of the church. Between two of the pillars is a small door, opening to
a dark gallery, which leads, as the monks told me, to the tombs of
Joseph and Nicodemus, between which and that of the Savior there

is a subterranean communication. These tombs are excavated in the rock, which here forms the floor of the chamber. Without any expectation of making a discovery, I remember that once, in prying about this part of the building alone, I took the little taper that lighted the chamber and stepped down into the tomb; and I had just time to see that one of the excavations never could have been intended for a tomb, being not more than three feet long, when I heard the footsteps of pilgrim visitors, and scrambled out with such haste that I let the taper fall, put out the light, and had to grope my way back in the dark.

Farther on, and nearly in range of the front of the sepulchre, is a large opening, forming a sort of court to the entrance of the Latin Chapel. On one side is a gallery, containing a fine organ, and the chapel itself is neat enough and differs but little from those in the churches of Italy. This is called the chapel of apparition, where Christ appeared to the Virgin. Within the door, on the right, in an enclosure, completely hidden from view, is the pillar of flagellation, to which our Savior was tied when he was scourged before being taken into the presence of Pontius Pilate. A long stick is passed through a hole in the enclosure, the handle being outside, and the pilgrim thrusts it in till it strikes against the pillar, when he draws it out and kisses the point. Only one half of the pillar is here; the other half is in one of the churches at Rome, where may also be seen the table on which our Savior ate his last supper with his disciples and the stone on which the cock crowed when Peter denied his master!

Going back again from the door of the chapel of apparition and turning to the left, on the right is the outside of the Greek chapel, which occupies the largest space in the body of the church; and on the left is a range of chapels and doors, the first of which leads to the prison where, they say, our Savior was confined before he was led to crucifixion. In front of the door is an unintelligible machine, described as the stone on which our Savior was placed when put in the stocks. I had never heard of this incident in the story of man's redemption, nor, in all probability, has the reader; but the Christians in Jerusalem have a great deal more of such knowledge than they gain from the Bible. Even Paul knew much that is not recorded in the sacred volume, for he had a book, written by a priest in Malta and giving many particulars in the life of our Savior which all the evangelists never knew, or knowing, have entirely omitted.

Next is the chapel where the soldier who struck his spear into the side of the Redeemer as he hung upon the cross retired and wept over his transgression. Beyond this is the chapel where the Jews divided Christ's raiment and "cast lots for his vesture." The next is one of the most holy places in the church, the chapel of the cross. Descending twenty-eight broad marble steps, the visitor comes to a large chamber eighteen paces square, dimly lighted by a few distant lamps; the roof is supported by four short columns with enormous capitals. In front of the steps is the altar, and on the right a seat on which the Empress Helena, advised by a dream where the true cross was to be found, sat and watched the workmen who were digging below. Descending again fourteen steps, another chamber is reached, darker and more dimly lighted than the first and hung with faded red tapestry; a marble slab, having on it a figure of the cross, covers the mouth of the pit in which the true cross was found. The next chapel is over the spot where our Savior was crowned with thorns; and under the altar, protected by an iron grating, is the very stone on which he sat. Then the visitor arrives at Mount Calvary.

A narrow marble staircase of eighteen steps leads to a chapel about fifteen feet square, paved with marble in mosaic, and hung on all sides with silken tapestry and lamps dimly burning; the chapel is divided by two short pillars, hung also with silk and supporting quadrangular arches. At the extremity is a large altar, ornamented with paintings and figures, and under the altar a circular silver plate, with a hole in the center, indicating the spot in which rested the step of the cross. On each side of the hole is another, the two designating the places where the crosses of the two thieves were erected; and near by, on the same marble platform, is a crevice about three feet long and three inches wide, having brass bars over it and a covering of silk; removing the covering, by the aid of a lamp I saw beneath a fissure in a rock; and this, say the monks, is the rock which was rent asunder when our Savior, in the agonies of death, cried out from the cross, "My God, my God, why hast thou forsaken me?" Descending to the floor of the church, underneath is an iron grating which shows more distinctly the fissure in the rock; and directly opposite is a large monument over the head of—Adam.

The reader will probably think that all these things are enough to be comprised under one roof; and, having finished the tour of the church, I returned to the great object of the pilgrimage to Jerusalem —the Holy Sepulchre. Taking off the shoes on the marble platform in front, the visitor is admitted by a low door, on entering which the proudest head must needs do reverence. In the center of the first chamber is the stone which was rolled away from the mouth of the sepulchre—a square block of marble, cut and polished; and though the Armenians have lately succeeded in establishing the genuineness of the stone in their chapel on Mount Zion (the admission by the other monks, however, being always accompanied by the assertion that they stole it), yet the infatuated Greek still kisses and adores this block of marble as the very stone on which the angel sat when he announced to the women, "He is not dead; he is risen; come see the place where the Lord lay." Again bending the head, and lower than before, the visitor enters the inner chamber, the holiest of holy places. The sepulchre "hewn out of the rock" is a marble sarcophagus, somewhat resembling a common marble bathing-tub, with a lid of the same material. Over it hang forty-three lamps, which burn without ceasing night and day. The sarcophagus is six feet, one inch long, and occupies about one half of the chamber; and one of the monks being always present to receive the gifts or tribute of the pilgrims, there is only room for three or four at a time to enter. The walls are of a greenish marble, usually called verd-antique, and this is all. And it will be borne in mind that all this is in a building above ground, standing on the floor of the church.

If I can form any judgment from my own feelings, every man other than a blind and determined enthusiast, when he stands by the side of that marble sarcophagus, must be ready to exclaim, "This is not the place where the Lord lay"; and yet I must be wrong, for sensible men have thought otherwise; and Dr. Richardson, the most

353

cautious traveler in the Holy Land, speaks of it as the "Mansion of victory, where Christ triumphed over the grave, and disarmed death of all its terrors." The feelings of a man are to be envied who can so believe. I cannot imagine a higher and holier enthusiasm, and it would be far more agreeable to sustain than to dissolve such illusions; but, although I might be deceived by my own imagination and the glowing descriptions of travelers, I would at least have the merit of not deceiving others. The sepulchre of Christ is too holy a thing to be made the subject of trickery and deception, and I am persuaded that it would be far better for the interests of Christianity that it had remained forever locked up in the hands of the Turks, and all access to it been denied to Christian feet.

But I was not disposed to cavil. It was far easier, and suited my humor far better, to take things as I found them; and in this spirit, under the guidance of a monk and accompanied by a procession of pilgrims, I wandered through the streets of Jerusalem, visited the Pool of Bethesda where David saw Bathsheba bathing, the five porches where the sick were brought to be healed, the house of Simon the Pharisee where Mary Magdalene confessed her sins, the prison of St. Peter, the house of Mary the mother of Mark, the mansion of Dives, and the house of Lazarus (which, by the way, not to be skeptical again, did not look as if its tenant had ever lain at its neighbor's gate, and begged for the "crumbs which fell from the rich man's table"); and entering the Via Dolorosa, the way by which the Savior passed from the judgment hall of Pilate to Calvary, saw the spot where the people laid hold of Simon the Cyrene, and compelled him to bear the cross; three different stones on which Christ, fainting, sat down to rest; passed under the arch called Ecce homo, and looked up at the window from which the Roman judge exclaimed to the persecuting Jews, "Behold the man."

But if the stranger leaves the walls of the city, his faith is not so severely tested; and, for my own part, disposed to indemnify myself for my unwilling skepticism, the third day after my arrival at Jerusalem, on a bright and beautiful morning, with my Nubian club in my hand, which soon became the terror of all the cowardly dogs in Jerusalem, I stood on the threshold of St. Stephen's Gate. Paul was with me; and stopping for a moment among the tombs in the Turkish burying-ground, we descended towards the bridge across the brook Kedron, and the mysterious Valley of Jehoshaphat. Here I was indeed among the hallowed places of the Bible. Here all was as nature had left it, and spared by the desecrating hand of man; and as I gazed upon the vast sepulchral monuments, the tombs of Absalom, of Zachariah, and Jehoshaphat, and the thousands and tens of thousands of Hebrew tombstones covering the declivity of the mountain, I had no doubt I was looking upon the great gathering place, where, three thousand years ago, the Jew buried his dead under the shadow of the Temple of Solomon; and where, even at this day, in every country where his race is known, it is the dearest wish of his heart that his bones may be laid to rest among those of his long-buried ancestors.

Near the bridge is a small table-rock, reverenced as the spot where Stephen the Martyr was stoned to death, but even here one cannot go far without finding the handiwork of the Lady Helena. A little to the left is the tomb of Joseph and Mary. Descending a few steps to a large marble door, opening to a subterraneous church, excavated from the solid rock, and thence by a flight of fifty marble steps, each twenty feet long, we came to the floor of the chamber. On the right, in a large recess, is the tomb of the Virgin, having over it an altar, and over the altar a painting representing her deathbed, with the Son standing over her to comfort her and receive her blessing. This is an interesting domestic relation in which to exhibit a mother and her son, but rather inconsistent with the Bible account of the Virgin Mother being present at the crucifixion of our Lord. Indeed, it is a singular fact that with all the pious homage which they pay to the Son of God, adoring him as equal with the Father in power and goodness, and worshiping the very ground on which he is supposed to have trodden, there is still among the Christians of the East a constant tendency to look upon him as a man of flesh. In a community like ours, governed by a universal sentiment of the spiritual character of our Savior, it would be regarded as setting at defiance the religious impressions of the people even to repeat what is talked of familiarly by the people of the East;

355

but, at the risk of incurring this reproach, it is necessary, to illustrate their character, to say that I have heard them talk of the Savior and of every incident in his history as a man with whom they had been familiar in his life; of the Virgin nursing the "little Jesus"; of his stature, strength, age, the color of his hair, his complexion, and of every incident in his life, real or supposed, from his ascension into heaven down to the "washing of his linen."

At the foot of the hill, on the borders of the Valley of Jehoshaphat, beneath the Mount of Olives, we came to the Garden of Gethsemane. Like the great battle-grounds where kingdoms have been lost and won, the stubborn earth bears no traces of the scenes that have passed upon its surface; and a stranger might easily pass the Garden of Gethsemane without knowing it as the place where, on the night on which he was betrayed, the Savior watched with his disciples. It was enclosed by a low, broken stone fence, and an Arab Fellah was quietly turning up the ground with his spade. According to my measurement, the garden is forty-seven paces long and forty-four wide. It contains eight olive trees, which the monks believe to have been standing in the days of our Savior, and to which a gentleman, in whose knowledge I have confidence, ascribed an age of more than eight hundred years. One of these, the largest, barked and scarified by the knives of pilgrims, is reverenced as the identical tree under which Christ was betrayed; and its enormous roots, growing high out of the earth, could induce a belief of almost any degree of antiquity. A little outside the fence of the garden is a stone, reverenced as marking the hallowed place where Christ, in the agony of his spirit, prayed that the cup might pass from him; a little farther, where he "sweat great drops of blood"; and a little farther is the spot to which he returned, and found the disciples sleeping; and no good pilgrim ever passes from the Garden of Gethsemane to the Mount of Olives without doing reverence in these holy places.

In company with a long procession of pilgrims, who had been assembling in the garden, we ascended the Mount of Olives. The mount consists of a range of four mountains, with summits of unequal altitudes. The highest rises from the Garden of Gethsemane, and is the one fixed upon as the place of our Savior's ascension. About halfway up is a ruined monastery, built, according to the monks, over the spot where Jesus sat down and wept over the city and uttered the prediction which has since been so fearfully verified. The olive still maintains its place on its native mountain, and now grows spontaneously upon its top and sides, as in the days of David and our Savior. In a few moments we reached the summit, the view from which embraces, perhaps, more interesting objects than any other in the world: the Valley of Jehoshaphat, the Garden of Gethsemane, and the city of Jerusalem, the Plains of Jericho, the Valley of the Jordan, and the Dead Sea.

On the top of the mountain is a miserable Arab village, in the center of which is a small octagonal building, erected, it is said, over the spot from which our Savior ascended into heaven; and the print of his foot, say the monks, is still to be seen. This print is in the rock, enclosed by an oblong border of marble; and pilgrims may at any time be seen taking, in wax, impressions of the holy footstep; and for this, too, they are indebted to the research and bounty of the Empress Helena.

Descending again to the ruined monastery, at the place where our Savior, more than eighteen hundred years ago, wept over the city and predicted its eternal ruin, I sat down on a rough stone to survey and muse over the favored and fallen Jerusalem. The whole city lay extended before me like a map. I could see and distinguish the streets, and the whole interior to the inner side of the farther wall; and oh! how different from the city of our Savior's love. Though even then but a mere appendage of imperial Rome, it retained the magnificent wonders of its Jewish kings, and, pre-eminent even among the splendid fanes of heathen worship, rose the proud temple of the great King Solomon. Solomon and all his glory have departed; centuries ago the great temple which he built, the "glory of the whole earth," was a heap of ruins; in the prophetic words of our Savior, not one stone was left upon another; and, in the wanton spirit of triumph, a conquering general drove his plough over its site. For years its very site lay buried in ruins, till the Saracen came with his terrible war-cry, "The Koran or the sword"; and the great mosque of Omar, the holy of holies in the eyes of all true believers, now rears its lofty dome upon the foundations of the Temple of Solomon.

From the place where I sat, the mosque of Omar was the only object that relieved the general dullness of the city, and all the rest was dark, monotonous, and gloomy; no spires reared their tapering points to the skies, nor domes, nor minarets, the pride and ornament of other Turkish cities. All was as still as death; and the only sign of life that I could see was the straggling figure of a Mussulman, with his slippers in his hand, stealing up the long courtyard to the threshold of the mosque. The mosque of Omar, like the great mosque at Mecca, the birthplace of the Prophet, is regarded with far more veneration than even that of St. Sophia, or any other edifice of the Mohammedan worship; and to this day the Koran or the sword is the doom of any bold intruder within its sacred precincts. At the northern extremity of the mosque is the Golden Gate, for many years closed, and flanked with a tower, in which a Mussulman soldier is constantly on guard; for the Turks believe that, by that gate, the Christians will one day enter and obtain possession of the city—city of mystery and wonder, and still to be the scene of miracles! "It shall be trodden down by the Gentiles until the time of the Gentiles be fulfilled"; and the time shall come when the crescent shall no longer glitter over its battlements, nor the banner of the Prophet wave over its walls.

Returning to the Valley of Jehoshaphat and passing along its eastern side, we came to the great burying place of the Jews. Among its monuments are four, unique in their appearance and construction, and known from time immemorial as the tombs of Absalom, Jehoshaphat, St. James, and the Prophet Zachariah. All are cut out of the solid rock; the tomb of Absalom is a single stone, as large as an ordinary two-story house, and ornamented with twenty-four semi-columns of the Doric order, supporting a triangular pyramidal top. The top is battered and defaced; and no pilgrim, whether Jew or Christian, ever passes through the Valley of Jehoshaphat without casting a stone at the sepulchre of the rebellious son. No entrance to this sepulchre has ever been discovered, and the only way of getting into the interior is by a hole broken for the purpose in one of the sides.

Behind the tomb of Absalom is that of Jehoshaphat, "the King of Judah, who walked in the ways of the Lord." It is an excavation in the rock, the door being its only ornament. The interior was damp, the water trickling from the walls, and nearly filled with sand and crumbling stones. The next is the tomb of St. James, standing out boldly in the side of the mountain, with a handsome portico of four columns in front, an entrance at the side, and many chambers within. After this is the tomb of Zachariah, like that of Absalom hewn out of the solid rock, and like that, too, having no known entrance. Notwithstanding the specific names given to these tombs, it is altogether uncertain to what age they belong; and it is generally considered that the style of architecture precludes the supposition that they are the work of Jewish builders.

Leaving them after a cursory examination, we descended the valley; and, following the now dry bed of the Kedron, we came to "Siloa's Brook, that flowed fast by the oracle of God," which, coming from the foot of Mount Zion, here presents itself as a beautiful stream, and runs winding and murmuring through the valley. Hundreds of pilgrims were stretched on its bank; and a little above is the sacred pool issuing from the rock, enclosed by stone walls, with a descent by two flights of steps. "Go wash in the Pool of Siloam," said Christ to the man who was born blind; and, like myself, a number of pilgrims were now bending over the pool and washing in its hallowed waters. Passing by the great tree under which the Prophet Isaiah was sawed asunder, I turned up towards the city, and in a few minutes was standing on Mount Zion.

CHAPTER XXIX

THE FIELD OF BLOOD—A TRAVELER'S COMPLIMENT—SINGULAR
CEREMONY—A RAGGED RASCAL—OSTENTATIOUS HUMILITY—
PRIDE MUST HAVE A FALL—AN ANCIENT RELIC—
SUMMARY LEGISLATION

ALL that is interesting about Jerusalem[1] may be seen in a few days. My health compelled me to remain there more than three weeks, during which I made two excursions, one to the ancient city of Joppa and the other to the Dead Sea. As soon as I could do so, however, I visited all the places, to see which is the business of a pilgrim to the holy city. The fourth morning after my arrival I went out at the Bethlehem Gate, and, crossing the valley of the sons of Hinmon, on the side of the opposite mountain I came to the Aceldama, or field of blood, the field bought with "the thirty pieces of silver," which to this day remains a public burying place or potter's field. A large chamber excavated in the rock is still the charnel-house of the poor and unhonored dead of Jerusalem. The fabulous account is that the earth of that field will in forty-eight hours consume the flesh from off the bones committed to it.

Leaving this resting-place of poverty and perhaps of crime, I wandered among the tombs on the sides of the mountain, tombs ornamented with sculpture and divided into chambers, the last abodes of the great and rich of Jerusalem; but the beggar, rudely thrown into the common pit in the potter's field and the rich man

---

[1] A Plan of Jerusalem (see illustration) made by F. Catherwood in 1835 was used by Stephens, as he acknowledges in the preface to the eighth edition of *Arabia Petraea*, which he said he found more useful than any other such available in Jerusalem. Later, Stephens visited the Panorama of Jerusalem, exhibited in London, drawn by Catherwood and Robert Burford, and there made the acquaintance of the architect-artist who with him would change archaeological history.

laid by pious hands in the sculptured sepulchre of his ancestors, are alike nothing.

Outside the Damascus Gate, and about half a mile distant, is what is called the Sepulchre of the Kings of Judah. This sepulchre is hewn out of the rock, and has in front a large square excavation, the entrance to which is under a small arch. To the left, on entering, is a large portico, nine paces long and four wide, with an architrave, on which are sculptured fruit and flowers, much defaced; and at the end, on the left, a hole, filled up with stones and rubbish, barely large enough to enable one to crawl through on hands and knees, leads to a chamber eight paces square; and from this chamber there are three doors, two directly opposite and one to the right. Entering that to the right, we found ourselves in another chamber, on each of the three sides of which was a large door, with smaller ones on either side opening to small receptacles, in each of which were places for three bodies. The door of this chamber, now lying on the floor, was a curious work. It had been cut from the solid rock and made to turn on its hinges or sockets without having ever been removed from its place. On the right, a single door leads down several steps into a dark chamber, where we found the lid of a sarcophagus elegantly carved. The other doors opening from the great chamber lead to others inferior in size and workmanship. On coming out of one of them, at the very moment when I extinguished my light, the hole of the entrance was suddenly darkened and stopped up. I had left a strange Arab at the door; and remembering the fearful thought that had often come over me while creeping among the tombs in Egypt, of being shut up and entombed alive, my first impulse was to curse my folly in coming into such a place and leaving myself so completely in the power of a stranger. But I was taking the alarm too soon. It was only the Arab himself coming in. He, too, had his apprehensions; and, from my remaining so long within, began to fear that I had crawled out some back way and given his backsheesh the slip.

But enough of the tombs. I leave the abodes of the dead and turn to the living, and among the living in Jerusalem there are few who live better than the monks. Chateaubriand, in his poetical description of his pilgrimage to the Holy Land, gives an exceeding interest to the character of these monks. "Here reside," said he, "communities of Christian monks whom nothing can compel to forsake the tomb of Christ; neither plunder, nor personal ill treatment, nor menaces of death itself. Night and day they chant their hymns around the holy sepulchre. Driven by the cudgel and the sabre, women, children, flocks, and herds seek refuge in the cloisters of these recluses. What prevents the armed oppressor from pursuing his prey and overthrowing such feeble ramparts? The charity of the monks. They deprive themselves of the last resources of life to ransom their suppliants," &c.

The first glance at the well-fed superior of the convent of Jerusalem dispelled in my mind all such poetic illusions, though the beautiful rhapsody was fully appreciated by those of whom it was uttered. On my first interview with the superior, an old monk entered the room who was in the convent at the time of the visit of Chateaubriand, and both said that they had read the accounts of several travelers in the Holy Land, and none could be compared with his. I do not mean to speak harshly of them personally, for they were my hosts, and every Eastern traveler knows the comfort of a cell in a convent compared with any other shelter he can find in the Holy Land. Particularly I would not speak harshly of the superior of the convent at Jerusalem, towards whom I have an exceedingly kind feeling and with whom I was on terms of rather jocose intimacy. The second time I saw him he railed at me with much good-natured indignation for having taken off two or three inches of my beard; and, during the whole time I was in Jerusalem, I was in the habit of calling upon him almost every day. I owe him something, too, on Paul's account, for he did that worthy man of all work a most especial honor.

Since our arrival at the convent, Paul had returned to the essence of his Catholic faith, to wit, the strict observance of its forms. In the desert he had often grumbled at being obliged to go without animal food; but no sooner did he come within the odour of burning incense than he felt the enormity of ever having entertained so impious a thought, and set himself down like a martyr to the table of the

362

convent. He was, in his way, an epicure; and it used to amuse me, while playing before him the breast of a chicken, to see him turn his eyes wistfully towards me and choke himself upon pulse and beans. He went through it all, however, though with a bad grace; and his piety was not lost upon the superior, who sent for him a few mornings after our arrival and told him that a grand ceremony of washing the feet of the disciples was to take place in the chapel, and desired him to officiate as one of them. It was amusing to see Paul's altered manner on his return. With a dignity and, at the same time, a respect, which he seemed all at once to have acquired from his clear understanding of his relative duties, he asked me whether I could spare him the next afternoon, stating the reason and the honor the superior had done him. I told him, of course, that I would not interfere with his playing such an important part, and as it would be a new character for him to appear in, I should like to be present at the representation. The next day he came to me with his coat buttoned tight across his breast, his boots polished, and hat smoothed to a hair, and told me, with great gravity, that the superior had sent me his particular compliments and an invitation to be present at the ceremony; and turning away, he remarked, with an air of nonchalance, that a Sicilian priest, who had just left me and who was arranging to accompany me to the Dead Sea, was to be one of his associates in the ceremony.

Paul was evidently very much lifted up; he was constantly telling Elias, the cook of the convent, that he wanted such and such a thing for tomorrow afternoon, begging me not to make any engagement for tomorrow afternoon; and, in due season, tomorrow afternoon came. I entered my room a little before the time, and found him at rehearsal, with a large tub of water before him, prudently washing his feet beforehand. I was a good deal disposed to bring down his dignity, and told him that it was well enough to rehearse his part, but that he ought to leave at least one foot unwashed, as a sort of bonus for his friend the superior. Paul was a good deal scandalized at my levity of manner, and got out of my reach as soon as he could. Afterward, however, I saw him in one of the corridors, talking with the Sicilian with a greater accession of dignity than ever. I saw him again in the chapel of the convent, standing in line with his associates; and, excepting him, the Sicilian priest, and one monk, who was put in to fill up, I never saw a set of harder-looking scoundrels.

This ceremony of washing the feet of the disciples, intended by our Savior as a beautiful lesson of humility, is performed from year to year, ostensibly to teach the same lesson; and in this case the humility of the superior was exalted shamefully at the expense of the disciples. Most of the twelve would have come under the meaning, though inexplicable, term of "loafer"; but one, a vagrant Pole, was, beyond all peradventure, the greatest blackguard I ever saw. A black muslin frock-coat, dirty and glossy from long use, buttoned tight across the breast and reaching down to his ankles, and an old foxy, low-crowned hat, too big for him and almost covering his eyes and ears, formed his entire dress, for he had no trousers, shoes, or shirt; he was snub-nosed, pock-marked, and sore-eyed, wore a long beard, and probably could not remember the last time he had washed his face; think, then, of his feet. If Paul had been dignified, *he* was puffed up almost to bursting, and the self-complacency with which he looked upon himself and all around him was admirable beyond description. By great good fortune for my designs against Paul, the Pole stood next and before him in the line of the *quasi* disciples; and it was refreshing to turn from the consequential and complacent air of the one to the crestfallen look of the other and to see him, the moment he caught my eye, with a suddenness that made me laugh, turn his head to the other side; but he had hardly got it there before he found me on that side too, and so I kept him watching and dodging, and in a perpetual fidget. To add to his mortification, the Pole seemed to take particularly to him, and as he was before him in the line, was constantly turning round and speaking to him with a patronizing air; and I capped the climax of his agony by going up in a quiet way and asking him who was the gentleman before him. I could see him wince, and for a moment I thought of letting him alone; but he was often on stilts, and I seldom had such an opportunity of pulling him down. Besides, it was so ludicrous, I could not help it.

If I had had anyone with me to share the joke, it would have been exquisite. As it was, when I saw his determination to dodge me, I neglected everything else, and devoted myself entirely to him; and, let the poor fellow turn where he would, he was sure to find me leaning against a pillar, with a smile on my face and my eyes intently fixed upon him; occasionally I would go up and ask him some question about his friend before him; and finally, as if I could not joke about it any more and felt on my own account the indignity offered to him, I told him that, if I were he, I would not stand it any longer; that I was ashamed to see him with such a pack of rascals; that they had made a cat's-paw of him, and advised him to run for it, saying that I would stand by him against a bull from the pope. He now spoke for the first time, and told me that he had been thinking of the same thing; and, by degrees, actually worked himself up to the desperate pitch of incurring the hazard of excommunication, if it must needs be so, and had his shoes and stockings in his hands ready for a start when I brought him down again by telling him it would soon be over; and, though he had been shamefully treated, that he might cut the gentleman next to him whenever he pleased.

After goading him as long as he could possibly bear, I left him to observe the ceremony. At the upper end of the chapel, placed there for the occasion, was a large chair, with a gilded frame and velvet back and cushion, intended as the seat of the nominal disciple. Before it was a large copper vase, filled with water, and a plentiful sprinkling of rose leaves; and before that, a large red velvet cushion, on which the superior kneeled to perform the office of lavation. I need not suggest how inconsistent was this display of gold, rose water, and velvet with the humble scene it was intended to represent; but the tinsel and show imposed upon the eyes for which they were intended.

One after the other the disciples came up, seated themselves in the chair, and put their feet in the copper vase. The superior kneeled upon the cushion, with both hands washed the right foot, wiped it with a clean towel, kissed it, and then held it in his hands to receive the kisses of the monks and of all volunteers that offered. All went on well enough until it came to the turn of Paul's friend and forerunner, the doughty Pole. There was a general titter as he took his place in the chair, and I saw the superior and the monk who assisted him hold down their heads and laugh almost convulsively. The Pole seemed to be conscious that he was creating a sensation and that all eyes were upon him, and sat with his arms folded, with an ease and self-complacency altogether indescribable, looking down in the vase and turning his foot in the superior's hands, heel up, toe up, so as to facilitate the process; and when the superior had washed and kissed it and was holding it up for others to kiss, he looked about him with all the grandeur of a monarch in the act of coronation. Keeping his arms folded, he fairly threw himself back into the huge chair, looking from his foot to the monks, and from the monks to his foot again, as one to whom the world had nothing more to offer. It was more than a minute before anyone would venture upon the perilous task of kissing those very suspicious toes, and the monk who was assisting the superior had to go round and drum them up; though he had already kissed it once in the way of his particular duty, to set an example he kissed it a second time; and now, as if ashamed of their backwardness, two or three rushed forward at once; and, the ice once broken, the effect seemed electric, and there was a greater rush to kiss his foot than there had been to any of the others.

It was almost too hard to follow Paul after this display. I ought to have spared him, but I could not. His mortification was in proportion to his predecessor's pride. He was sneaking up to the chair, when, startled by some noise, he raised his head, and caught the eye which, above all others, he would have avoided. A broad laugh was on my face, and poor Paul was so discomfited that he stumbled, and came near pitching headlong into the vase. I could not catch his eye again; he seemed to have resigned himself to the worst. I followed him round in the procession as he thrice made the tour of the chapel and corridors with a long lighted candle in his hand; and then we went down to the superior's room, where the monks, the superior, the twelve, and myself, were entertained with coffee. As the Pole, who had lagged behind, entered after we were all seated, the superior, with the humor of a good fellow, cried out, "Viva Polacca"; all broke out into a loud laugh, and Paul escaped in the midst of it. About an hour afterward I met him outside the Damascus Gate. Even then he would have shunned me; but I called him, and, to his great relief, neither then nor at any other time referred to the washing of the feet of the disciples.

The reader may remember the kindness with which I had been received by the chief rabbi at Hebron. His kindness did not end there; a few days after my arrival, the chief rabbi of Jerusalem, the high priest of the Jews in the city of their ancient kings, called upon me, accompanied by a Gibraltar Jew who spoke English and who told me that they had come at the request of my friend in Hebron to receive and welcome me in the city of their fathers. I had already seen a great deal of the Jews. I had seen them in the cities of Italy, everywhere more or less oppressed; at Rome, shut up every night in their miserable quarters as if they were noxious beasts; in Turkey, persecuted and oppressed; along the shores of the Black Sea and in the heart of Russia, looked down upon by the serfs of that great empire of vassalage; and, for the climax of misery, I had seen them contemned and spit upon even by the ignorant and enslaved boors of Poland. I had seen them scattered abroad among all nations, as it had been foretold they would be, everywhere a separate and peculiar people; and everywhere, under all poverty, wretchedness, and oppression, waiting for, and anxiously expecting, the coming of a Messiah, to call together their scattered tribes and restore them to the kingdom of their fathers; and all this the better fitted me for the more interesting spectacle of the Jews in the holy city. In all changes and revolutions, from the day when the kingdom of Solomon passed into the hands of strangers, under the Assyrian, the Roman, the Arab, and the Turk, a remnant of that once-favored people has always hovered around the holy city; and now, as in the days of David, old men may be seen at the foot of Mount Zion, teaching their children to read from that mysterious book on which they have ever fondly built their hopes of a temporal and eternal kingdom.

The friends made for me by the rabbi at Hebron were the very friends above all others whom I would have selected for myself.

While the Christians were preparing for the religious ceremonies of Easter, the Jews were making ready for the great feast of the Pass-over, and one of the first offers of kindness they made me was in invitation to wait and partake of it with them. The rabbi was an old man, nearly seventy, with a long white beard, and Aaron him-self need not have been ashamed of such a representative. I would have preferred to attach myself particularly to him; but, as I could speak neither Arabic nor Hebrew and the English Jew was not willing to play second and serve merely as interpreter, I had but little benefit of the old man's society.

The Jews are the best topographers in Jerusalem, although their authority ends where the great interest of the city begins; for, as their fathers did before them, they deny the name of Christ and know nothing of the holy places so anxiously sought for by the Christians. That same morning they took me to what they call a part of the wall of Solomon's temple. It forms part of the southern wall of the mosque of Omar, and is evidently older than the rest, the stones being much larger, measuring nine or ten feet long; and I saw that day, as other travelers may still see every Friday in the year, all the Jews in Jerusalem clothed in their best raiment, wind-ing through the narrow streets of their quarter; and under this hallowed wall, with the sacred volume in their hands, singing, in the language in which they were written, the Songs of Solomon and the Psalms of David. White-bearded old men and smooth-cheeked boys were leaning over the same book; and Jewish maidens, in their long white robes, were standing with their faces against the wall, and praying through the cracks and crevices. The tradition which leads them to pray *through* this wall is that during the building of the temple a cloud rested over it so as to prevent any entrance; and Solomon stood at the door and prayed that the cloud might be re-moved and promised that the temple should be always open to men of every nation desiring to offer up prayers, whereupon the Lord removed the cloud and promised that the prayers of all people offered up in that place should find acceptance in his sight; and now, as the Mussulman lords it over the place where the temple stood and the Jews are not permitted to enter, they endeavor to insinuate their prayers through the crevices in the wall, that thus they may rise from the interior to the Throne of Grace. The tradition is characteristic and serves to illustrate the devoted constancy with which the Israelites adhere to the externals of their faith.

Returning to the convent, and passing through one of the bazars, we saw an Arab mounted on a bench and making a proclamation to the crowd around him; and my friend, the Gibraltar Jew, was immediately among them, listening earnestly. The subject was one that touched his tenderest sensibilities as a dealer in money; for the edict proclaimed was on changing the value of the current coin, reducing the tallahree or dollar from twenty-one to twenty piasters, commanding all the subjects of Mohammed Ali to take it at that value, and concluding with the usual finale of a Turkish proclamation, "Death to the offender." My Jew, as he had already told me several times, was the richest Israelite in Jerusalem, and consequently took a great interest in everything that related to money. He told me that he always cultivated an intimacy with the officer of the mint, and, by giving him an occasional present, he always got intimation of any intended change in time to save himself. We parted at the door of the convent, having arranged that I should go with him the next day to the synagogue and afterward dine at his house.

CHAPTER XXX

ABOUT nine o'clock the next morning I was with him, and in a few moments we were sitting in the highest seats in the synagogue, at the foot of Mount Zion. My old friend the rabbi was in the desk, reading to a small remnant of the Israelites the same law which had been read to their fathers on the same spot ever since they came up out of the land of Egypt. And there they sat, where their fathers had sat before them, with high, black, square-topped caps, with shawls wound around, crossed in front, and laid very neatly; long gowns fastened with a sash, and long beards, the feeble remnant of a mighty people; there was sternness in their faces, but in their hearts a spirit of patient endurance and a firm and settled resolution to die and be buried under the shadow of their fallen temple.

By the Jewish law the men and women sit apart in the synagogues, and, as I could not understand the words of exhortation which fell from the lips of the preacher, it was not altogether unnatural that I should turn from the rough-bearded sons of Abraham to the smooth faces of their wives and daughters. Since I left Europe, I had not been in an apartment where the women sat with their faces uncovered; and, under these circumstances, it is not surprising that I saw many a dark-eyed Jewess who appeared well worthy of my gaze; and it is not a vain boast to say, that while singing the songs of Solomon, many a Hebrew maiden turned her bright black orbs upon me; for, in the first place, on entering we had disturbed more than a hundred sitting on the steps; secondly, my original dress, half-Turk, half-Frank, attracted the eyes even of the men; and, thirdly, the alleged universal failing of the sex is not wanting among the daughters of Judah.

The service over, we stopped a moment to look at the synagogue, which was a new building, with nothing about it that was peculiar or interesting. It had no gold or silver ornaments, and the sacred scroll, the table of the Law, contained in the holy of holies, was all that the pride of the Jew could show. My friend, however, did not put his own light under a bushel; for, telling me the amount he had himself contributed to the building, he conducted me to a room built at his own expense for a schoolroom, with a stone in the front wall recording his name and generosity.

We then returned to his house, and, being about to sit down to dinner with him, I ought to introduce him more particularly to the reader. He was a man about fifty-five, born in Gibraltar to the same abject poverty which is the lot of most of his nation. In his youth he had been fortunate in his little dealings and had been what we call an enterprising man, for he had twice made a voyage to England, and was so successful and liked the country so much that he always called himself an Englishman. Having accumulated a little property or, as he expressed it, having become very rich, he gratified the darling wish of his heart by coming to Jerusalem, to die and be buried with his fathers in the Valley of Jehoshaphat. But this holy purpose in regard to his death and burial did not make him undervalue the importance of life and the advantages of being a great man now. He told me that he was rich, very rich; that he was the richest and, in fact, the only rich Jew in Jerusalem. He took me through his house, and showed me his gold and silver ornaments and talked of his money and the uses he made of it; that he lent to the Latin Convent on *interest*, without any security, whenever they wanted; but as for the Greeks—he laughed, laid his finger on his nose, and said he had in pledge jewels belonging to them of the value of more than twenty thousand dollars. He had had his losses too; and while we were enjoying the luxuries of his table, the leaven of his nature broke out, and he endeavored to sell me a note for fifteen hundred pounds of the Lady Esther Stanhope, which he offered at a discount of 50 per cent, a bargain which I declined, as being out of the line of my business.

I remember once the American fever came upon me in Athens, when, sitting among the ruins of the Acropolis, upon a broken column of the Parthenon, I speculated upon the growth of the city. I bought, in imagination, a piece of ground, and laid it out in lots, lithographed, and handsomely painted, red, blue, and white, like the maps of Chicago, Dunkirk, and Hinsdale; built up the ancient harbor of the Piraeus, and ran a railroad to the foot of the Acropolis; and I leaned my head upon my hand and calculated the immense increase in value that must attend the building of the king's new palace and the erection of a royal residence on the site of Plato's academy. I have since regretted that I did not "go in" for some up-town lots in Athens; but I have never regretted not having shaved the note of the Queen of the East, in the hands of the richest Jew in Jerusalem.

It was Saturday, the Jewish Sabbath. The command to do no work on the Sabbath day is observed by every Jew, as strictly as when the commandment was given to his fathers; and to such an extent was it obeyed in the house of my friend that it was not considered allowable to extinguish a lamp which had been lighted the night before and was now burning in broad daylight over our table. This extremely strict observance of the law at first gave me some uneasiness about my dinner; but my host, with great self-complacency, relieved me from all apprehensions by describing the admirable contrivance he had invented for reconciling appetite and duty—an oven, heated the night before to such a degree that the process of cooking was continued during the night and the dishes were ready when wanted the next day. I must not forget the Jew's family, which consisted of a second wife, about sixteen, already the mother of two children, and his son and son's wife, the husband twelve and the wife ten years old. The little gentleman was at the table and behaved very well, except that his father had to check him in eating sweetmeats. The lady was playing on the floor with other children, and I did with her what I could not have done with a bigger man's wife—I took her on my knee and kissed her. Among the Jews, matches are made by the parents; and, immediately upon the marriage, the wife is brought into the household of the husband. A young gentleman was tumbling about the floor who was engaged to the daughter of the chief rabbi. I did not ask the age of the lady, of course, but the gentleman bore the heavy burden of three years. He had not yet learned to whisper the story of his love to his blushing mistress, for, in fact, he could not talk at all; he was a great bawling boy, and cared much more for his bread and butter than a wife; but his prudent father had already provided him.

On the morning of the twenty-first I set out for Jaffa, the ancient Joppa. It was a bright and beautiful morning when I left the Bethlehem Gate; but, before I had been an hour on my way, it began to rain and continued nearly the whole day. About three hours from Jerusalem we came to the village of Abougos, the chief of the most powerful families of Fellahs in the Holy Land. Nearly all his life he had been more or less in arms against the government; and his name was known among all the Christians in the East as the robber of the pilgrims to the Holy Sepulchre. I had met and spoken with him outside of the walls of Jerusalem, and during the rain, as I approached his village, I determined to stop and throw myself upon his hospitality for the night; but the returning sunshine deceived me, and I passed on, admiring the appearance of his village, which had much the best of any I had seen in the Holy Land. About an hour afterward I was repenting, under a merciless rain, that I had not fulfilled my purpose.

Riding three hours longer, stopping from time to time under a rock or tree, I was ascending the last range of mountains; before me were the fertile plains of Sharon, and across the plain, still at a great distance, was Ramla, the ancient Arimathea, the city of "Joseph the counsellor, the good man, and just." To the right, bordering the sea, was the range of Mount Carmel; but the rain was pelting in my eyes so that I could see nothing of it. I had been eight hours on the back of one of the most stubborn mules that ever persisted in having their own way, toiling with all my might, with blows and kicks, but finding it impossible to make him move one step faster than he pleased;

and when the tower, the mosque, and the minaret of Ramla were before me, at the other side of a level plain, and an hour's smart riding would have carried me there, I was completely worn out with urging the obstinate brute; and with muttered threats of future vengeance wound my cloak around me, and hauling my umbrella close down and grinding my teeth, I tried to think myself resigned to my fate.

A strong wind was driving the rain directly in my face, and my mule, my cursed mule, stopped moving when I stopped beating; and, in the very hardest of the storm, when I would have rushed like a bird on the wing, turned off from the path, and fell quietly to browsing on the grass. Afraid to disarrange my umbrella and cloak, I sat for a moment irresolute, but the brute turned his face round and looked at me with such perfect nonchalance that I could not stand it. I raised my club for a blow; the wind opened my cloak in front, puffing it out like a sail, caught under my umbrella, and turned it inside out; and the mule suddenly starting, under a deluge of rain I found myself planted in the mud on the plains of Sharon. An hour afterward I was drying my clothes in the house of our consular agent at Ramla. There was no fireplace in the room; but I was hovering over a brazier of burning charcoal. I spent that night and all the next day in Ramla, although a quarter of an hour would have been sufficient to see all that it contained, which was simply nothing more than is to be found in any other village. The consul gave me a dry coverlet, and while some of his friends came in to look at and welcome the stranger, I laid myself down upon the divan and went to sleep.

The next morning I was unable to move; the fatigue, and particularly the rain of the preceding day, had been too much for me, and I remained all the morning in an upstairs room, with a high ceiling and a stone floor, lying on a rug in one corner, cold, desponding, and miserable. In the afternoon I went down into the large room, to talk with the consular agent. But a year before he had flourished in all the pomp and pride of office. The arms of our country were blazoned over his door, and the stars and stripes had protected his dwelling; but a change had come over him. The

Viceroy of Syria had ordered the flags of the consuls to be taken down at Ramla, and forbidden any of his subjects to hold the office except in the seaport towns. I could not help thinking that he was perfectly right, as it was merely allowing them the benefit of a foreign protection to save them and their families, with two or three janissaries, from their duties to himself; but I listened attentively to the complaints of the poor agent. His dignity had been touched, and his pride humbled in the eyes of his townsmen, for the governor had demanded the usual duty from his sons and had sent his executive officers with the summary order, the duty or the bastinado. The agent owed his appointment to Commodore Patterson, and talked of him and Captain Nicholson as friends who would see justice done him if he could communicate with them. I was afterward struck with a display of delicacy and a sense of propriety that I had not expected from him; for, although he charged me with many messages to Commodore Patterson, he requested me not to mention his difficulties in the matter of the agency, as he had already made representations to the consul at Beirut, who had laid them before Commodore Porter at Constantinople; and an application in another quarter would look like distrusting their ability or their willingness to resent what he called an indignity offered to the American flag. Annoyed at seeing the women dodging by, with their faces covered and always avoiding me, I told him that, being a Christian and holding an appointment under our government, he ought to conform to our customs and treat his women more as companions, or, at least, to let them come into the same room and sit at the same table with him. He listened, but could not see any reason in my proposition. He said it might do for us; for with us the wives always brought their husbands money (the ignorant, uninformed barbarian), but in Syria (he sighed as he said it) they never added a para to the riches of their lords.

The next morning I set out again for Jaffa. The road lies through a rich plain; and in three hours, passing a large detachment of Turkish soldiers encamped outside and waiting a transport to carry them to Alexandria, I was entering the gate of the ancient city of Joppa. Believed to have existed before the deluge, the city where

375

Noah dwelt and built his ark, whence Jonah embarked for Tarshish when he was thrown overboard and swallowed by a whale, the port used by Solomon to receive timber from Tyre for the building of the temple, and by all the kings of Judah to connect the city of Jerusalem with foreign people, Jaffa is now a small Turkish town on the shores of the Mediterranean, built on a little eminence projecting into the sea, and containing a population of from ten to fifteen thousand Turks, Arabs, Jews, and Christians. It has a fine climate and a fine country around it, and the orange gardens are the finest on the shores of the Mediterranean. Although the seaport of Jerusalem, its harbor has always been bad; and when I was there the wreck of a Turkish man-of-war was lying on the beach; and that same night, there being a severe storm, the little Greek pilgrim vessels were considered in great danger.

There is nothing of interest in the modern city of Jaffa. Its history is connected with the past. The traveler must stand on the shore and fill the little harbor with the ships of Tarshish, or imagine Noah entering the ark with his family, by whom the earth was to be repeopled; or wander through the narrow streets and ask himself, Where is the house of Tabitha, whom Peter "raised from the dead"? or that of Simon the tanner, where Peter "tarried many days"? and he may feel a less holy, but hardly less powerful interest, in standing by the gate where, for many years, a large pyramid of skulls attested the desperate struggle of Napoleon; or, in walking through the chambers of the Greek convent, then used as a hospital for the French, and the monks will show him an apartment where, when all hearts were sinking within them for fear, he visited and touched the sick of the plague, restored the drooping courage of his soldiers, and almost raised the dying from their bed of death.

Besides the interest attached to this place by reason of its great antiquity, and the many important events of which it has been the scene, I remember it with much kindness on account of the American consular agent,[1] and the cordial manner in which he received

---

[1] For a long time the consular agent at Jaffa, the main port for Palestine, was Murad Arrutin, a rich Armenian who spoke no English. In his house in 1844, wrote the American naval officer, Francis Schroeder, "the American eagle and shield were

me. He was not at home when I arrived; but in a few moments he came in, and, taking both my hands in his, pointed to the American arms on the wall, ordered the stars and stripes to be hoisted on the top of his house, and, with all the extravagance of the East, told me that all he had was mine. I had a great mind to take him at his word, and begin by appropriating a beautiful emerald that I saw on his finger; but, for the present, I contented myself with asking merely for a dinner, which was soon prepared; and I sat down to dine in the ancient city of Joppa, with my country's arms before me, and my country's banner waving above.

The agent was an Armenian, and a strict observer of all the requisitions of his exacting creed; he was rich, and had no children; and, what I never before heard from the lips of man, he said that he was perfectly happy. I was the first American who had visited him since he had received his appointment, and it seemed as if he could not do enough for me.[2] He had repaired and reconstructed the whole road from Jaffa to Jerusalem; and when I asked him what reward he promised himself for this, he answered that he had done it for God, the pilgrims, and his own honor. I remained with him that night, and would have gone early the next morning, but he would

emblazoned on the wall, and prints of General Jackson and Mr. Van Buren and a map of the United States decorated the salon. . . . He showed me an album in which are inscribed the names of all Americans who have been in Jaffa during his consulate." The map was a gift from Stephens, who had passed through eight years before.— David H. Finnie *Pioneers East* (Cambridge, Mass., Harvard University Press, 1967).

[2] Later the agent wrote to John L. Stephens regarding a visitor to Jaffa:

Jaffa April 18th, 1840

Dear Sir

Your kind letter by the hands of Mr. Moore came to hand two days since, and it afforded me much pleasure to hear from you once more. The gentleman whom you introduce to me, I am sorry to say I could not treat with those attentions which both for his sake and because he is your friend I should have felt most happy in showing him. His stay in Jaffa was only for one night, and as he was travelling in company with an English gentleman, he saw fit to put up at the Greek Convent, where I had the pleasure of seeing him only for a short time on the day of his setting out for Jerusalem.

I shall ever be gratified in meeting any of your friends who may at any time pass this way, and esteem it a pleasure to wait upon them.—It will also always rejoice me to learn of your health and prosperity.

Your obedt. Servant
Murad Arrutin

not part with me so soon; I dined with him again; and in the afternoon, escorted to the gate by two janissaries, each with a large silver-headed mace in his hand, I left, probably forever, my Armenian friend and the ancient city of Joppa. I do not know when I parted from a man with more regret.[3]

I slept that night at Ramla; and the next day, about four o'clock, in company with several hundred pilgrims, I was again entering the Bethlehem Gate. Notwithstanding the munificence of my Armenian friend, the road from Jerusalem to Jaffa, a road traveled from the time when Jonas [sic] went thither to embark for Tarshish, is now a mere mule-path, on which I was several times obliged to stop and turn aside to let a loaded mule pass by.

I had seen everything in Jerusalem that it was the duty of a traveler to see. My time was now my own, for idling, lounging, or strolling, in the luxurious consciousness of having nothing to do. In this humor I used to set forth from the convent, never knowing where I should go or what I should do; and, whenever I went out with the deliberate intention of doing nothing, I was always sure of finding enough to occupy me. My favorite amusement in the morning was to go out by St. Stephen's Gate and watch the pilgrims as they began their daily round of visits to the holy places. Frequently, if I saw a group that interested me, I followed them to the Garden of Gethsemane and the Mount of Olives; sometimes I stopped in the Valley of Jehoshaphat and, sitting down on the grave of an Israelite, watched the Jewish pilgrims. One morning, I remember, Paul and I were together, and we saw a young girl kissing the tomb of Zachariah and weeping as if her heart would break. Paul asked her, rather roughly, what she was crying about; and the poor girl, looking at him for a moment, burst into a flood of tears, and told him that she was weeping over the tomb of the blessed prophet.

But there are few things connected with my journeying in the Holy Land which I look back upon with a more quiet satisfaction than my often repeated and almost daily walk around the walls of

[3] The town of Jaffa has since been destroyed by an earthquake, and of fifteen thousand inhabitants, thirteen thousand were buried in the ruins. Has my Armenian friend escaped?—Stephens' note.

Jerusalem. It was a walk of between three and four miles; and I always contrived, about half an hour before the gates were closed, to be sitting on a favorite tombstone near St. Stephen's Gate. The great Turkish burying-ground is outside the wall, near this gate; and regularly, on a fine afternoon, towards sunset, the whole Turkish population, in all their gay and striking costumes, might be seen wandering among the tombs. Few things strike a traveler in the East more than this, and few are to us more inexplicable. We seldom go into a graveyard except to pay the last offices to a departed friend, and for years afterward we never find ourselves in the same place again without a shade of melancholy coming over us. Not so in the East; today they bury a friend, tomorrow they plant flowers over his grave, and the next day, and the next, they tend and water them, and once a week, regularly, they sit by the grave. On every holyday it is a religious duty to go there; and as often as they walk out for health or pleasure, they habitually turn their footsteps to the burial-ground. To them the grave is not clothed with the same terrors. It is not so dark and gloomy as to us. They are firmer believers than we are, though, as we think, in a false and fatal creed; and to them there is a light beyond the grave, which we of a better faith can seldom see. It was a beautiful picture to behold the graveyard thronged with Turkish women, in their long white veils. It would, perhaps, be too poetical to look upon them all as mourners. Perhaps, indeed, it would not be too much to say that, of the immense multitude who, day after day, are seen flitting among the tombs, many a widowed fair one, over the tomb of a dead lord, is dreaming of a living lover.

But there was one whom I noticed every day; she was always sitting by the same stone, and I always noticed her as one of the first to come out and one of the last to return. She was a young Sciote girl, mourning over the tomb of her young lord; and well she might, for he had been to her a friend and protector, and she had been his only bride. When her father's house was laid in ruins, and her gray-headed sire and her manly brothers were slain before her eyes, he had saved her from the bloody scimitar or from a fate worse than death; and he had wooed her, not as a Turk and master, but as a

379

lover. He had won her young heart, and she had forgotten her kindred and her country; he had died with his bloody scimitar in his hand, and she thought only of the dead when she stood beside his grave.

CHAPTER XXXI

DESERT OF ST. JOHN—A MIDNIGHT PROCESSION—ROAD TO JERICHO—
A COMMUNITY OF WOMEN—A NAVIGATOR OF THE DEAD SEA—
A DANCE BY MOONLIGHT—A RUDE LODGING

IN COMPANY with Mr. Whiting, I started for the Desert of St. John the Baptist. Passing the Pool of Gihon, where Saul was anointed king by Zadoc and Nathan, we came to the Convent of the Holy Cross, the great altar of the chapel being erected, as the monks pretend, over the spot where grew the tree from which the cross was made. Moving on among hills and valleys, on our right was a distant view of Ramah, the country of Samuel the seer; and before us, crowning the very top of a high hill, were the ruins of the palace and the burial-place of the warlike Maccabees. The Convent of St. John is built on the spot where John the Baptist was born. There is no doubt of this, say the monks; for beneath the great altar of the church is a circular slab of marble, with an inscription almost effaced: "Hic natus est precursor dei," here the forerunner of the Lord was born. This convent is in a fine situation; a small Christian village is attached to it; the top commands a beautiful view of the mountains, cultivated in terraces; and directly in front is the great Valley of Turpentine, or Elah, the battle-ground of the Israelites and Philistines, of David and Goliath. Taking a Christian boy with us as guide, we entered the valley; and, following the stream to its source, in about two hours we came to the place where, it is said, Saul and the men of Israel pitched by the Valley of Elah, and set the battle in array against the Philistines. It was precisely the spot where the scene, so graphically recorded in Scripture, might have taken place. "And the Philistines stood on a mountain on the one side, and Israel stood on a mountain on the other side, and there was a valley between them." On each side of me was a mountain, and the brook was still running near from which the shepherd boy gathered the five smooth stones. The boy who accompanied us told me that the precise stones had never yet been found, though the monks had often searched for them.

At the extreme end of the valley is the Desert of St. John, where was heard, for the first time, the voice of one crying in the wilderness, "Prepare ye the way of the Lord; make his paths straight." Directly in front, at the top of the mountain bounding the valley, is an open door in the rock, leading to the grotto in which the prophet lived. There is no appearance of a desert in this place, except solitude; and if it be merely a locality fixed upon by the monks, they could not have selected one more inappropriate. It is one of the prettiest and best-cultivated spots in the Holy Land; and sitting in the door of the grotto, with an Armenian pilgrim by my side and looking out upon the valley and the mountains, all around terraced and cultivated to the very summits, all still and beautiful, I thought I had never seen a place better qualified to inspire a pious, philosophic, and happy state of mind than this Desert of St. John. We returned by a different road, searching on our way for the pool where Philip baptized the eunuch of Queen Candace; but, after losing ourselves once or twice and fearing a threatening shower, we returned to the city unsuccessful.

At about ten o'clock that evening, the monks, under a guard of soldiers and a crowd of pilgrims, each with a candle in his hand, left St. Stephen's Gate in solemn procession. With a loud chant they crossed the Valley of Jehoshaphat, wound around the foot of the Mount of Olives to Bethpage and Bethany, said mass in the tomb of Lazarus, and returning, prayed and chanted on the Mount of Olives and in the Garden of Gethsemane; and at about daylight the next morning returned to the convent.

For several days I had been preparing for a journey to the Dead Sea; but a mysterious influence seemed still to hang about the borders of that water; and now, when all the rest of the Holy Land was perfectly tranquil, the Fellahs were in commotion among the barren mountains around it. I had waited two or three days at the request of the governor; but, hearing of nothing in particular to prevent me, I determined to set out. The Sicilian priest who had proposed to accompany me could not go; and at about eight o'clock I was sitting on my horse alone, outside the St. Stephen's Gate, waiting for Paul, who had gone to the governor for a letter which he had promised me to the aga of Jericho. Attracted by the uncommon beauty of the morning, half the population of Jerusalem had already gathered without the walls. Joining a party of pilgrims, I followed once more the path I had so often trodden across the Brook Kedron and the Valley of Jehoshaphat; and, parting with them at the foot of the Mount of Olives, I wound around its base, and fell into the road to Jericho and the Jordan. We must have passed Bethpage, though there is nothing to mark where it stood; and in about an hour we came to Bethany, now a ruined Arab village, though the monks still show the house of Martha and Mary, the tomb of Lazarus, and even the barren fig-tree which was cursed by our Lord. The tomb of Lazarus is a large excavation in the rock; and the sepulchral chamber is at the foot of a staircase of ten or twelve steps.

Not far from Bethany we came to a fountain enclosed with marble, and soon after to a valley, where, the monks say, our Savior, in coming from beyond the Jordan, at the prayer of the sisters of Lazarus, reposed with the disciples. In about two hours we were among the mountains. The scene every moment became wilder and more rugged; and, except in the wilderness of Sinai and among the wastes of Idumea, I never traveled so dreary a road as in "going down to Jericho." It is on this desolate route that our Savior lays the scene of the parable of the good Samaritan, and nowhere could a more forcible illustration be given of the heartlessness of the priest and the Levite, in "passing by on the other side." Ascending for some distance by the precipitous side of a yawning chasm, where a false movement of my horse might have dashed me to atoms, from the top of the Mountains of Desolation I looked to the left upon a higher and still wilder and more dreary range; and, towering above all the rest, in gloomy grandeur, its naked sides pierced with doors for the cells of hermits, was the mountain of our Savior's fasting and temptation; before me were the plains of Jericho, the Valley of the

Jordan, the Mountains of Arabia, and the Dead Sea. A high, square building, like a tower, marked the site of Jericho, and a small stream, running between two banks of sand, was the hallowed Jordan.

Descending the mountain, on our left, directly at the foot, were the remains of an aqueduct and other ruins, which, in all probability, were part of the ancient city of Jericho. The plain commences at the foot of the mountains; the land is fertile and well watered with streams emptying into the Jordan, but for the most part wild and uncultivated. About halfway across we passed the edge of a stagnant pool, nearly covering a Mussulman burying-ground; the tombstones were washed from their places, and here and there the ghastly skeletons were visible above the muddy water. In one place, crossing a stream, we met three Abyssinians, who had come from the remotest point in the interior of Africa where the name of Christian is known, to bathe in the sacred Jordan. Two or three times we were obstructed by brick fences, intended as ramparts to protect the inhabitants and their flocks against the incursions of wolves; and at about four o'clock we arrived at the ruined village of Jericho.

I have observed that travelers generally, when they arrive at any place of extraordinary interest, find the right glow of feeling coming over them precisely at the proper moment. I never had any difficulty in Italy; for there, in the useful guidebook of Madame Starke, beautifully interspersed with valuable information about hotels, post-horses, and the price of washing linen, the reader may find prepared for him an appropriate catalogue of sensations for almost every possible situation and object, from a walk in the Colosseum by moonlight to a puppet-show at San Carlino in Naples; but, in a country like this, a man is thrown upon his own resources; and, notwithstanding the interest attached to the name of Jericho, I found it a hard matter to feel duly excited.

Jericho was the first city in Canaan which fell into the hands of the Israelites. It was long the second city of Judea, and, according to the Jewish Talmud, contained twelve thousand priests. It had its hippodrome and amphitheatre, and in its royal palace Herod the

Tetrarch died. But the curse of Joshua seems to rest upon it now: "Cursed be the man before the Lord who shall rebuild Jericho." It consists of fifty or sixty miserable Arab houses, the walls of which on three sides are of stones, piled up like the stone fences of our farmers, most of them not so high as a man's head, and the front and top either entirely open or covered with brush.

The old fortress in which I expected to sleep I found entirely abandoned, and the apartments used as a shelter for sheep and goats. I expected to find there the aga, quietly smoking his pipe and glad to receive and gossip with a stranger; but I had mounted to the top and looked out upon the extensive plains of Jericho and the Valley of the Jordan without meeting a single person, and it was not until I had gone out of the gate, and, with the bridle in my hand, was walking back into the village, that I noticed the remarkable circumstance, so different from the usual course of matters in Arab villages, that no throng of idlers had gathered around me. In fact, I had passed through the village, gone to the fortress, and come back without seeing a man; and soon found that there was not a male in the village above ten years old, except the aga and one passing Arab. It had numbered sixty men, of whom Ibrahim Pasha had ordered a levy of twenty-four for his army. The miserable inhabitants had decided among themselves upon nineteen who could best be spared; and, unable to supply the rest, in a spirit of desperation had abandoned their village; and, taking with them all the boys above ten years old, fled to the mountains around the Dead Sea, where they were now in arms, ripe for rebellion, robbery, and murder.

I found myself very much at a loss; the aga was a stranger there and knew nothing of the localities, and I could not find a boy old enough to conduct me to the Well of Elisha. Some of the women knew where it was, but they would not go with me, though I asked them in all courtesy; and, taking my direction from them, and fixing my eyes on the naked top of the mountain of our Savior's temptation, in about half an hour I reached the miraculous fountain where, at the request of the men of Jericho, Elisha "cast salt into the spring and healed the water." It is enclosed in a large marble basin, and several streams, constantly running from it, refresh and fertilize the plains of Jericho. Riding on a short distance farther, I came to an aqueduct and the ruins of a Greek convent, at the base of the "exceeding high mountain" from whose top the devil showed our Savior all the kingdoms of the world. The naked sides of the mountain are studded with doors, opening to the cells of anchorites and hermits, who there turned their backs upon temptation, and, amid desolation and solitude, passed their days in penance and prayer.

It was dark when I returned to Jericho. Before going away, the aga had taken me to his hut, and wished me to pass the night with him; but, as two horses had already taken their places before me and the hut was perfectly open, having merely a roof of branches and nothing at all in front, I had looked round and selected another for my lodging-place, chiefly from the circumstance of its having a small boat set up on its side before it so as to form a front wall.

That boat told a melancholy tale. It was the only one that had ever floated on the Dead Sea. About eight months before, Mr. Costigan, an Irish traveler who had been some years in the East, had projected a most interesting journey, and, most unhappily for himself and the interests of science, died almost in the moment of its successful accomplishment. He had purchased his boat at Beirut, and, with a Maltese sailor for his servant, in spite of many difficulties and impediments from the Arabs, had carried it across the country on a dromedary and launched it on the Sea of Galilee; he had explored this most interesting water, and entering the Jordan, followed it down until he narrowly escaped with his life among the rocks and rapids of that ancient but unknown river; and then constantly obstructed by the Arabs, even the governor of Damascus refusing him any facilities, with great difficulty he succeeded in bringing his boat by land to the Dead Sea. In the middle of July he had embarked with his servant to make the tour of the sea, and eight days afterward the old woman in whose tent I lodged had found him lying on the shore alone, gasping for breath. She had him carried to her hut, where he lay till the Rev. Mr. Nicolaisen, the English missionary at Jerusalem, came for him, and the second day after his arrival in Jerusalem he died. With his dying breath he bore the same testimony to the kindness of woman under the burning sun of

Syria that our countryman Ledyard did in the wilds of Siberia; for, while lying upon the shores of the Dead Sea, the Arabs gathered round him only to gaze, and would have left him to die there if this old woman had not prevailed upon two of her sons to carry him to her hut.

That boat was interesting to me for another reason. Nothing, not even the thought of visiting Petra and the land of Idumea, affected me so strangely as the idea of making the tour of this sea; and, notwithstanding the miserable state of my health, shattered by my journey in the desert, as soon as I heard, after my arrival at Jerusalem, that there was a boat at Jericho, I began to think of taking advantage of it. If I had succeeded in this, I should consider my tour the most perfect and complete ever made by any oriental traveler. I had hunted up the oars, sail, &c.; but on my return from Jaffa I was compelled to abandon all thoughts of making the attempt. Still, when I saw the boat, all my ardor revived; and never, in my lonely journeyings in the East, did I wish so earnestly for the comfort and support of a friend. With a companion, or even with a servant who would encourage and support me, in spite of my health I should certainly have undertaken it; but Paul was particularly averse to the attempt; the boat was barely large enough for two; and I was compelled to give up the thought.

That evening I saw at Jericho what I never saw before. It was a beautiful moonlight night, and all the women were out of doors singing and dancing. The dance was altogether indescribable, consisting not of wanton movements, like those of the dancing girls in Egypt, but merely in joining hands and moving round in a circle, keeping time to the music of their own voices. I had never seen so gay and joyous a scene among the women in the East; and though their fathers, and brothers, and husbands, and lovers were away among the mountains, I did not feel disposed to judge them harshly. It was so rare, in that unhappy country, to see anything like gaiety of heart that if they had been dancing over the graves of their husbands I should have been inclined to join them. And they did not shun us as the Moslem women generally do; they talked with us with their faces uncovered; and I remember a young Arab girl, not more than sixteen, who had a child in her arms and who told me that its father had fled to the mountains, and she put the child in my arms while she joined in the dance. In fact, my situation began to be peculiar; the aga had gone off to look for someone who would accompany me to the Dead Sea; and among perhaps more than a hundred women, that night Paul, and I and my muleteers were the only men in Jericho. In justice to the poor Arab women, however, I would remove from them any imputation of want of feeling or hardness of heart; for I have no doubt the young girl who left her child in my arms loved its father as warmly as if they all clad in purple and fine raiment every day.

I would have been better satisfied, however, if that night they had ceased their merriment at an earlier hour, for long after I had lain down on my stony bed their song and laugh prevented my sleeping, and when they had retired, other noises followed: the lowing of cattle, the bleating of sheep and goats, the stamping of horses, the crying of children, and the loud barking of the watch dog; and, finally, the fierce assault of the voracious insects that always swarm in an Arab's hut drove me from my bed and out of doors. The cool air refreshed and revived me, and I walked by the light of a splendid moon among the miserable huts of the village, hunted and barked at by the watching wolf-dog, and perhaps exciting the apprehensions of the unprotected women.

I leaned against a high fence of brush enclosing some of the huts and mused upon the wonderful events of which this miserable place had been the scene, until my eyes began to close; when, opening a place among the brushes, I drew my cloak around me and crawled in, and soon fell fast asleep. Once during the night I was worried and almost dragged out of my burrowing-place by the dogs, but I kicked them away and slept on. At daylight the aga was pulling me by the shoulder, armed to the teeth, and ready to escort me. I shook myself and my toilet was made, and before the laughers and singers and dancers of the previous night had waked from their slumbers, we were mounted and on our way to the Jordan.

388

CHAPTER XXXII

Moving directly from the ruined village, we soon left the
fertile plains of Jericho and entered the barren valley of
the Jordan. It was washed and torn by the mountain torrents, full
of gullies and large sandhills; and in about an hour and a half we
were standing on the banks of the river, at the most hallowed spot
on the margin of that sacred stream, where, eighteen hundred years
ago, John baptized the Redeemer of the world; and where, year
after year, thousands of pilgrims throw themselves into the river
with the blind belief that, by bathing in its waters, they wash away
their sins. As a pious pilgrim, it would have been my duty, perhaps,
to do the same; but the reader will please remember that it was the
last day of March, that I had slept in a bush, that my limbs were
stiff, and that it was not yet six o'clock in the morning, and that I
had not breakfasted. Sitting down, then, on the bank, I made my
morning meal, and drank as devoutly of its water as any pilgrim
who ever stood by the Jordan.

I afterward followed the river close along its bank till it emptied
into the Dead Sea, and nowhere found any spot that, for beauty of
scenery, could be compared with this consecrated bathing place of
the pilgrims. The bank here is about ten or twelve feet high, a clear,
level table of land, covered with rich grass, and large bushes on the
edge overhanging the river. Judging by the eye, the river is here
about thirty paces broad; the current is very rapid, and the pilgrim,
in bathing, is obliged to hold on by the bushes to avoid being carried
away. Here, it is said, the wild beast still has his haunt; and the
traveler sometimes, when the river is rising, may realize the ex-

389

pression, "He shall come up like a lion out of the swelling of Jordan." Opposite, the bank is low, and the bushes grow down to the water's edge. Immediately below this the river narrows to ten paces; and there is not another spot on the line of the Jordan which can attract the eye of the traveler. It is a small, broken, and muddy stream, running between banks of barren sand, without bloom or verdure; and if it were not for the associations connected with it, a man would turn from it as the most uninteresting of rivers. In one place I saw an Arab wading across, and the river there, so far as I could judge, had not fallen more than two feet. I followed it as closely as the cracks and gullies would allow, cutting off none of the bends. For the last two or three miles it runs between perpendicular banks of sand, from five to ten feet high, and its pure waters are already corrupted by the pestiferous influence of the bituminous lake. On the left it stops even with the shore; but on the right the bank runs out to a low, sandy point, round which a quantity of driftwood is collected; and here, with a gentle ripple of its waters, the Jordan is lost in the Dead Sea.

I followed it almost to the very point, until my horse's feet sank above his fetlocks in the wet sand. It was the old opinion, and was counted among the wonders of the Lake Asphaltites, that the river passed through without mingling with the waters of the lake; and Pococke says, "I thought I saw the stream of a different color"; but Pococke did not follow the river down to the extreme point. I did; and could see most distinctly the very spot where the waters mingled; instead of the river keeping its way through, its current was rather stopped at once by the denser water of the lake; and, in fact, for two or three miles above its mouth, the Jordan is impregnated with the salt and bituminous matter of the lake.

Almost at the moment of my turning from the Jordan to the Dead Sea, notwithstanding the long-credited accounts that no bird could fly over without dropping dead upon its surface, I saw a flock of gulls floating quietly on its bosom; and when I roused them with a stone, they flew down the lake, skimming its surface until they had carried themselves out of sight. From the point on which I stood, near its eastern shore, the sea was spread out before me, motionless as a lake of molten lead, bounded on either side by ranges of high and barren mountains, and on its southern extremity by the great desert Valley of El Ghor, constantly receiving the waters of the Jordan, but, unlike other waters, sending no tribute to the sea. Pliny, Diodorus Siculus, and Josephus describe it as more than sixty miles long; but Mr. Banks and his companions, by observation from elevated heights, make it not more than thirty; and, as the ancients were better acquainted with it than modern geographers, it has been supposed that the lake has contracted in its dimensions and that part of the Valley of El Ghor was once covered by its waters. Moving on slowly from the point of the Jordan, the shores low and sandy, strewed with brush and driftwood, and rising in a slope to the sandy plain above, I rode along nearly the whole head of the lake, with my horse's feet in the water, and twice picked up a large piece of bitumen, almost like common pitch, supposed to be thrown up from the bottom of the lake. The sand is not bright like that of an Atlantic or Mediterranean beach, but of a dirty, dark brown. The water is exceedingly clear and transparent, but its taste and smell are a compound of all that is bad.

It was now the last day of March, and even before we left the plains of the Jordan the sun had been intensely hot; without a branch or leaf to break its force, it poured upon the dreary waste around the Dead Sea with a scorching and withering heat. It was on this shore that the Knight of the Leopard encountered the Saracen Emir; and in the sandy plain above is the beautiful scene of the Diamond of the Desert, in the opening of Scott's Crusaders. The general features of the scenery along the northern shore of the Dead Sea are admirably described. The Diamond of the Desert is, of course, the creation of the author's fancy; and the only actual error is in placing the wilderness of Engaddi, which Scott has confounded with the mountains of Quarantania, but which is really halfway down the borders of the sea.

It was two o'clock when my guards, having conducted me along the head of the sea, proposed returning to Jericho. I had already had some difficulty with them. Twice disappointed in my purposed exploration of this sea; once in my wish, conceived on the top of

391

Mount Hor, to strike it at its southern extremity, and coast along its borders; and then, in the still more attractive project of exploring it in a boat, instead of returning to Jericho, my desire was to go down the borders of the sea and turn up among the mountains to the convent of Santa Saba. At Jerusalem I could not hire horses for this convent because, as they said, it was a dangerous route, and I took them for Jericho, hoping in some way or other still to accomplish my object. By accident, an Arab from Santa Saba had come to Jericho during the night; and in the morning I told the aga and his companion that I would not have them as my escort at all unless they would go with me to the convent. They at first objected, but afterward promised to go as far as I wanted them; now they again made objections. I thought it was merely to enhance the value of their services; but in a few moments they told me they would not go any farther; that the order of the governor was to protect me to the Dead Sea and back to Jericho. The worst of it was that my muleteers refused to go without the guard; and, although we had a guide with us who told us there was no danger, though we had not met a single Arab since we left Jericho, and though we could see many miles down the lake and plainly distinguish the wild track up the bare side of the mountain to the open country above, they were "afraid of the bad Arabs." I was determined, however, not to go back to Jericho. I had no idea of sleeping in the bushes again; and, spurring my horse, I told Paul to follow me, and they might do as they pleased. The aga and his companion bade me farewell, and, dashing over the arid plain, were soon hidden from view by hillocks of sand. I continued along the shore; and, after a few moments' consultation, my Arabs quietly followed me.

Since early in the morning, I had had the sea constantly before my eyes. While riding along the northern shore, the general aspect was very much the same; but, as soon as I turned the head, and began to move along its side, the mountains every moment assumed a different aspect, although everywhere wild, rugged, and barren. At three o'clock we were approaching a place where the mountain rises precipitously from the lake, leaving no room for a passage at its foot; my eyes were fixed upon the lake, my thoughts upon its mysterious properties. The ancients believed that living bodies and even heavy metals would not sink in it, and Pliny and Strabo have written of its extraordinary buoyancy. Before I left Jerusalem, I had resolved not to bathe in it, on account of my health; and I had sustained my resolution during the whole of my day's ride along its shore; but, on the point of turning up among the mountains, I could resist no longer. My clothes seemed to come off of their own accord, and, before Paul had time to ask me what I was going to do, I was floating on its waters. Paul and the Arabs followed, and, after splashing about for a while, we lay like a parcel of corks upon its surface.

From my own experience, I can almost corroborate the most extravagant accounts of the ancients. I know, in reference to my own specific gravity, that in the Atlantic or Mediterranean I cannot float without some little movement of the hands, and even then my body is almost totally submerged; but here, when I threw myself upon my back, my body was half out of water. It was an exertion even for my lank Arabs to keep themselves under. When I struck out in swimming, it was exceedingly awkward, for my legs were constantly rising to the surface and even above the water. I could have lain there and read with perfect ease. In fact, I could have slept, and it would have been a much easier bed than the bushes at Jericho. It was ludicrous to see one of the horses. As soon as his body touched the water he was afloat, and turned over on his side; he struggled with all his force to preserve his equilibrium; but the moment he stopped moving he turned over on his side again, and almost on his back, kicking his feet out of water, and snorting with terror. The worst of my bath was, after it was over, my skin was covered with a thick, glutinous substance, which it required another ablution to get rid of; and after I had wiped myself dry, my body burnt and smarted as if I had been turned round before a roasting fire. My face and ears were incrusted with salt; my hairs stood out, "each particular hair on end"; and my eyes were irritated and inflamed, so that I felt the effects of it for several days. In spite of all this, however, revived and refreshed by my bath, I mounted my horse a new man.

Modern science has solved all the mystery about this water. It has been satisfactorily analyzed, and its specific gravity ascertained to be 1.211, a degree of density unknown in any other, the specific gravity of fresh water being 1.000; and it has been found to hold in solution the following proportions of salt to one hundred grains of water—

	Grains
Muriate of lime	3.920
Muriate of magnesia	10.246
Muriate of soda	10.360
Sulphate of lime	0.054
	24.580

Except the ruined city of Petra, I never felt so unwilling to leave any place. I was unsatisfied. I had a longing desire to explore every part of that unknown water; to spend days upon its surface, to coast along its shores, to sound its mysterious depths, and search for the ruins of the guilty cities. And why not? If we believe our Bible, that bituminous lake covers the once fertile Vale of Siddom and the ruins of Sodom and Gomorrah; and why may we not see them? The ruins of Thebes still cover for miles the banks of the Nile; the pyramids stand towering as when they were built, and no man knows their builders; and the traveler may still trace, by "the great river, the Euphrates," the ruins of the Tower of Babel. Besides, that water does not destroy; it preserves all that it touches; the wood that falls into it becomes petrified by its action; and I can see no good reason why it should hide forever from man's eyes the monuments of that fearful anger which the crimes of the guilty had so righteously provoked.

Except to the summit of Mount Hor, I never had so desperate a climb as up the barren mountain on the borders of the Dead Sea. We had not found any water fit to drink since we left the Jordan, and turned up a little before we reached the place we had intended, the guide telling us that here we would find a spring. We were soon obliged to dismount; and even our sure-footed horses, trained as they were to climbing mountains, slipped, faltered, and completely failed. Our guide told us that he had never ascended with horses before; and, looking forward, the attempt seemed utterly impossible; but the noble animals climbed with the intelligence of men, holding on with the forefeet as if they were hands, and the Arabs above pulling them by the mane or pushing from below. One of them, in climbing an almost perpendicular height, fell over backward. I thought he was killed; and my Arabs, irritated by toil, thirst, and the danger to their horses, sprang upon the guide, and I believe would have killed him if Paul and I had not interfered. Taking off the enormous saddle, we all joined above and below, and hoisted and pushed him up almost bodily.

It was nearly dark when we reached the top of the mountain, and I sat down for a moment to take a last look at the Dead Sea. From this distance its aspect fully justified its name. It was calm, motionless, and seemingly dead; there was no wave or ripple on its surface, nor was it hurrying on, like other waters, to pay its tribute to the ocean; the mountains around it were also dead; no trees or shrubs, not a blade of grass grew on their naked sides; and, as in the days of Moses, "Brimstone and salt, it is not sown, nor beareth, nor any grass groweth thereon."

One thing had especially attracted my attention in ascending the mountain; on attaining a particular point, we had a clear view of the whole sea, and at the extreme end we saw distinctly what Paul and I both at once called an island. Mr. Seetzen, one of the earliest modern travelers who visited this sea, imagined that he had discovered a large island in the same direction; and though no one believed in its reality, I had then seen no satisfactory explanation of its appearance. I could not be deceived in what I saw. There never was anything that looked more like an island, and I afterward received an explanation which to me at least was perfectly satisfactory. It comes from one who ought to know, from the only man who ever made the tour of that sea and lived to tell of it; and, relying upon the interesting nature of the subject, I make no apology for introducing it here.

When the unhappy Costigan[1] was found by the Arabs on the shore of the Dead Sea, the spirit of the enterprising Irishman was fast fleeting away. He lived two days after he was carried to the convent at Jerusalem, but he never once referred to his unhappy voyage. He had long been a traveler in the East, and long preparing for this voyage; had read every book that treated of the mysterious water, and was thoroughly prepared with all the knowledge necessary for exploring it to advantage. Unfortunately for the interests of science, he had always been in the habit of trusting greatly to his memory; and, after his death, the missionaries in Jerusalem found no regular diary or journal, but merely brief notes written on the margins of books, so irregular and confused that they could make nothing of them; and, either from indifference, or because they had no confidence in him, they allowed Costigan's servant to go without asking him any questions.

I took some pains to trace out this man; and afterward, while lying at Beirut, suffering from a malady which abruptly put an end to my travels in the East, Paul hunted him out and brought him to me. He was a little, dried-up Maltese sailor; had rowed around that sea without knowing why, except that he was paid for it; and what he told me bore the stamp of truth, for he did not seem to think that he had done anything extraordinary. He knew as little about it as any man could know who had been over the same water; and yet, after all, perhaps he knew as much as any one else could learn. He seemed, however, to have observed the coast and the soundings with the eye of a sailor, and I got him to make me a map, which has been engraved for this work, and on which I marked down the particulars as I received them from his lips.

The reader will see by it that they had completed the whole tour

[1] "Mr. Costigan" lived as obscurely as he died. Nothing at all is known of him. His memory is preserved only in so far as Stephens obtained from his companion, a Maltese sailor, Costigan's maps of the Dead Sea (see illustration). Whatever Stephens gathered, it was sufficient for Captain William F. Lynch U.S.N., commander of an expedition, author of *Narrative of the United States Expedition to the River Jordan* (Washington, 1843), to acknowledge that "To Mr. Stephens of New York, the author of one of the most interesting books of travels which our language can produce I return in this public manner my acknowledgements for a timely letter written when the equipment of the expedition was under consideration."

of the lake. They were eight days in accomplishing the task, sleeping every night on shore except once, when, afraid of some suspicious Arabs whom they saw on the mountains, they slept on board, beyond the reach of gunshot from the land. He told me that they had moved in a zigzag direction, crossing and recrossing the lake several times; that every day they sounded, frequently with a line of 175 brachia (about six feet each); that they found the bottom rocky and of very unequal depth, sometimes ranging thirty, forty, eighty, twenty brachia all within a few boats' length;[2] that sometimes the lead brought up sand, like that of the mountains on each side; that they failed in finding bottom but once, and in that place there were large bubbles all around for thirty paces, rising probably from a spring; that in one place they found on the bank a hot sulphur spring; that at the southern extremity Mr. Costigan looked for the River of Dogs, but did not find it; that in four different places they found ruins, and could clearly distinguish large hewn stones, which seemed to have been used for buildings; and in one place they saw ruins which Mr. Costigan said were the ruins of Gomorrah.

Now I have no doubt that Mr. Costigan talked with him as they went along, and told him what he told me, and that Mr. Costigan had persuaded himself that he did see the ruins of the guilty city; he may have been deceived, and probably was, but it must have been the most intensely interesting illusion that ever any man had. But of the island, or what Paul and I had imagined to be such:— He said that they too had noticed it particularly; and when they came towards the southern extremity of the lake, found that it was an optical deception, caused by a tongue of high land that put out for a long distance from the middle of the southern extremity, as in the map; and being much higher than the valley beyond it, intercepted the view in the manner we had both noticed; this tongue of land, he said, was composed of solid salt, tending to confirm the

[2] I would suggest whether this irregularity does not tend to show the fallacy of the opinion that the cities of the plain were destroyed by a volcanic eruption, and that the lake covers the crater of an extinct volcano. I have seen the craters of Vesuvius, Solfatara, Etna, and Monte Rosso, and all present the same form of a mountain excavated in the form of a cone, without any of the irregularities found in the bottom of this sea.—Stephens' note.

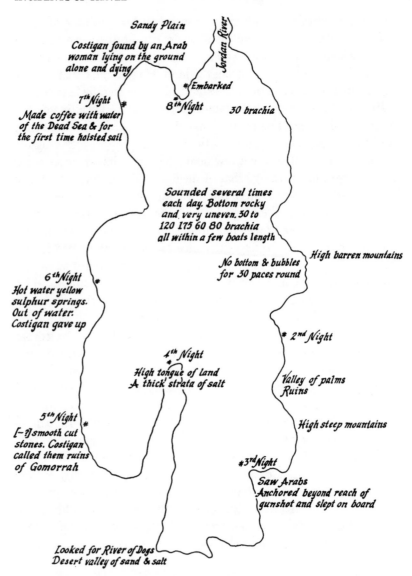

Sandy Plain

*Costigan found by an Arab
woman lying on the ground
alone and dying*

Jordan River

Embarked

7ᵗʰ Night

*Made coffee with water
of the Dead Sea & for
the first time hoisted sail*

8ᵗʰ Night   *30 brachia*

*Sounded several times
each day. Bottom rocky
and very uneven. 30 to
120 175 60 80 brachia
all within a few boats length*

High barren mountains

*No bottom & bubbles
for 30 paces round*

6ᵗʰ Night
*Hot water yellow
sulphur springs.
Out of water.
Costigan gave up*

2ⁿᵈ Night

4ᵗʰ Night
*High tongue of land
A thick strata of salt*

*Valley of palms
Ruins*

High steep mountains

5ᵗʰ Night
*[-?] smooth cut
stones. Costigan
called them ruins
of Gomorrah*

3ʳᵈ Night

*Saw Arabs
Anchored beyond reach of
gunshot and slept on board*

*Looked for River of Dogs
Desert valley of sand & salt*

Costigan's journey on the Dead Sea

Redrawn from Stephens' *Incidents of Travel in . . . Arabia
Petraea . . .* (1837)

assertion of Strabo, to which I referred in my journey through Idumea, that in the great valley south of the Dead Sea there were formerly large cities built entirely of salt. The reader will take this for what it is worth; it is at least new, and it comes from the only man living who has explored the lake.

He told me some other particulars; that the boat, when empty, floated a palm higher out of the water than on the Mediterranean; and that Costigan lay on the water, and picked a fowl, and tried to induce him to come in; that it was in the month of July, and from nine to five dreadfully hot, and every night a north wind blew, and the waves were worse than in the Gulf of Lyons; and, in reference to their peculiar exposures and the circumstances that hurried poor Costigan to his unhappy fate, he said that they had suffered exceedingly from the heat, the first five days Costigan taking his turn at the oars; that on the sixth day their water was exhausted, and Costigan gave out; that on the seventh day they were obliged to drink the water of the sea, and on the eighth they were near the head of the lake, and he himself exhausted and unable any longer to pull an oar. There he made coffee from the water of the sea; and a favorable wind springing up, for the first time they hoisted their sail and in a few hours reached the head of the lake; that, feeble as he was, he set off for Jericho, and, in the meantime, the unhappy Costigan was found by the Arabs on the shore a dying man, and, by the intercession of the old woman, carried to Jericho. I ought to add that the next time he came to me, like Goose Gibbie, he had tried whether the money I gave him was good, and recollected a great many things he had forgotten before.

The reader cannot feel the same interest in that sea which I did, and therefore I will not detain him longer. In three hours, crossing a rich and fertile country where flowers were blooming, and Arab shepherds were pasturing their flocks of sheep and goats, we had descended the bed of a ravine, where the Kedron passes from Jerusalem to the Dead Sea, at the foot of the mountains of Santa Saba. It was night when we arrived; and, groping our way by the uncertain light of the moon, we arrived at the door of the convent, a lofty and gigantic structure, rising in stories or terraces, one above the other, against the sides of the mountain, to its very top; and then crowned with turrets that, from the base where I stood, seemed, like the tower at which the wickedness of man was confounded, striving to reach to heaven.

We "knocked, and it was opened to us"; ascended two or three flights of steps, climbed up a ladder, crawled through a small door, only large enough to admit one at a time, and found ourselves in an antechamber, surrounded by more than a hundred Greek pilgrims. A monk conducted us up two or three flights of steps to the chamber of the superior, where we took coffee. In a few moments we followed him again up two or three more flights of steps to a neat little room with a divan and a large pile of coverlets.

I thought of the bush in which I had lodged the night before, spread out a few of the coverlets, crawled in among them, and in a few moments the Dead Sea, and the Holy Land, and every other land and sea were nothing to me.

CHAPTER XXXIII

CONVENT OF SANTA SABA—A STRANGE PICTURE—CELEBRATION OF
GOOD FRIDAY—PALM SUNDAY—A STRUGGLE FOR LIFE—THE GRAVE OF
A FRIEND—A CONVERT—BURIAL OF A MISSIONARY

I SLEPT till nine o'clock the next morning. The first thing I did after breakfast was to mount to the tower at the top of the convent. This is the largest Greek convent in the Holy Land; and I remarked that it was in a good state of repair, and that large and expensive improvements were then in progress. The tower commanded a view of the whole convent, built in terraces, in a sort of amphitheatre, in the side of the mountain. All around, particularly in the mountain opposite, were ranges of grottoes, formerly the residences of anchorites and hermits, admirably situated for cherishing pious thoughts and leading a holy life. An old, white-bearded monk, leaning on his staff, was toiling up its sides, leading a long procession of pilgrims, probably to some very holy place; and below me, apparently growing out of the rock, was a large palm-tree, planted, as they say, by Santa Saba himself in the fourth century. The cemetery is about halfway down, in a vault under an open area. The flat stone that covered the entrance was fastened down with cement. The monk told me that the bodies of the dead were laid on stone benches, where lime was thrown over them, and, as soon as decomposition had taken place, the bones were removed and thrown upon a pile in another part of the cemetery.

The chapel, like all the other Greek chapels, was full of gaudy and ridiculous ornaments and paintings; and, among the latter, there was one that attracted the particular admiration and reverence of the pilgrims. At the top of the picture sat the Father, surrounded by angels, and patriarchs, and good men; and on his right was a range of two-story houses, St. Peter standing before them with the keys in

401

his hand. Below the Father was a large, powerful man, with a huge pair of scales in his hand, weighing sinners as they came up and billeting on each the weight of his sins; below him were a number of naked figures, in a sitting posture, with their arms spread out and their legs enclosed in long boxes extended horizontally. On the left a stream of fire was coming down from the Father and collecting in the mouth of a huge nondescript sea monster, while in front stood a great half-naked figure, pitching in the sinners just as the fireman on board a steamboat pitches in the long sticks of wood, and the damned were kicking about in the flames. On the right was Elias doing battle with Antichrist; and below was a representation of the last day, and the graves giving up their dead, in almost every conceivable variety of form and situation.

In another chapel, dedicated to John of Damascus, who formerly lived there, behind an iron grating in a grotto of the rock was a large pile of skulls and bones, the remains of fourteen thousand hermits who dwelt among the mountains and were slain by the Turks.

The superior had been waiting some time to accompany me to Jerusalem. Will the reader believe it? This man had lived twenty years in the convent, and had never been to the Dead Sea! I was so disgusted with him that I rode on and left him; and, following the Valley of the Kedron, meeting on the way hundreds of Greek pilgrims, in three hours I was again in Jerusalem.

The next night being Good Friday, the monks of the Latin Convent performed the ceremony of the Crucifixion. The doors were open at an early hour for a short time and then closed for the night, so that we were obliged to be there two or three hours before the ceremony began. Most of the pilgrims had prepared against the tediousness of waiting by bringing with them their beds, mats, and coverlets; and all around the floor of the church, men, women, and children were taking an intermediate nap. The proceedings commenced in the chapel of the Latin Convent, where priests, monks, pilgrims, Paul, and myself, all assembled, everyone holding in his hand a long lighted candle. The superior, with his gold mitre and black velvet cloak trimmed with gold, my friend the Sicilian priest, and some other dignitaries of the church were present, very richly dressed. On a large cross was the figure of a man, representing the Savior, the crown of thorns on his head, nails in his hands and feet, blood trickling from them, and a gaping wound in his side. Before setting out on the procession the lights were extinguished; and, in total darkness, a monk commenced a sermon in Italian. After this the candles were relighted, banners and crucifixes raised, and the procession moved round the church towards Calvary. Stopping at the Pillar of Flagellation, at the prison where they say Christ was confined, where the crown of thorns was put upon his head, where his raiment was divided, &c., and giving a chant and an address by one of the monks at each place, they wound round the church until they came to the staircase leading to Calvary; and, leaving their shoes below, mounted barefoot to the place of crucifixion. Here they first went to an altar on the right, where, as they have it, Christ was nailed to the cross; and laying the figure down on the floor, although they had been bearing it aloft for more than two hours, they now went through the ceremony of nailing it; and, returning to the adjoining altar, passed the foot of the cross through the marble floor, and, with the bleeding figure upon it, set it up in the hole in the natural rock according to the tradition, in the very spot where, eighteen hundred years ago, Christ was crucified. At the foot of the cross a monk preached a sermon in Italian, warm, earnest, and impassioned, frequently turning round, and, with both hands extended, apostrophizing the bleeding figure above him. In spite of my skepticism and incredulity and my contempt for the monkish tricks, I could not behold this scene unmoved. Every attendant upon the crucifixion was represented; for the Governor of Jerusalem was present, with a smile of scorn upon his handsome features, and Turkish and Mussulman soldiers, breaking the stillness of the scene with loud laughs of derision; and I could almost imagine that I heard the unbelieving Jews, with gibes and sneers, crying out, "If he be the King of Israel, let him come down from the cross!"

After the body had remained some time suspended, two friars, personating Joseph of Arimathea and Nicodemus, approached the foot of the cross; and one of them on the right, with a long pair of pincers, took the crown of thorns from the head, waved it around slowly with a theatrically mournful air, kissed it, and laid it down on a table before him; he then drew long spikes from the hands and feet, and moving them around, one by one, slowly as before, kissed them, and laid them also on the table. I never saw anything more affecting than this representation, bad as it was, of the bloody drama of the crucifixion; and as the monks drew out the long nails from the hands and feet, even the scoffing Mussulmans stopped their laugh of derision. I stood by the table while they laid the body upon it and wrapped it in a clean linen cloth; followed them when they carried it down from Calvary to the stone of unction; stood by the head of the stone while they washed and anointed it and prepared it for burial, and followed it to the door of the sepulchre. It was now near two o'clock; the ceremony was ended, the Mussulman soldiers had retired, and Paul and I returned to the convent. We had no lamp; and as, in all the Turkish cities, everyone is obliged to carry a lamp at night, and, in fact, it is necessary for his own security, we walked through the narrow streets of Jerusalem bearing the same long candles with which we had figured in the procession of the crucifixion.

On Sunday morning, being Easter, or Palm Sunday [sic], I visited, for the last time, the Church of the Holy Sepulchre. It was more crowded than I had ever yet seen it. The courtyard literally swarmed with vendors of amulets, crucifixes, and holy ornaments, and within the church were tables of oranges, figs, dates, &c. The Arab baker was walking about, with a large tray on his head, crying his bread; and in each of the altars was a sort of shop, in which Greeks were making and selling chaplets and wreaths of palm-leaves. It was altogether a lively image of the scene when Christ went into the temple, and "cast out them that bought and sold, and overthrew the tables of the money-changers." The ceremonies of the day were in commemoration of that on which our Savior entered into Jerusalem, riding upon an ass, when the multitude followed him, strewing their garments and branches of palm trees in his path, and crying, "Hosannah to the Son of David!" When I entered, the monks of the Latin convent were celebrating grand mass before the

404

holy sepulchre; and, in the meantime, the Greeks were getting ready for their turn. Their chapel was crowded, and all along the corridors the monks were arranging the people in procession and distributing banners, for which the young Greeks were scrambling; and in one place a monk, with a standard in his hand, which had just been handed down from above, with his back against the wall, was knocking and kicking away a crowd of young Greeks, struggling to obtain it for the procession.

As soon as the Latins had finished, the Arab soldiers whom I always found regular attendants at these scenes, as if they knew what was coming when the Greeks began, addressed them with loud shouts of "Yellah, yellah—come on, come on." A large banner was stationed at the door of the sepulchre; and the rush of the pilgrims to prostrate themselves before it, and to touch it with their palm branches, was tremendous. A tall young Greek, with a large turban on his head, while his left hand supported the banner, was laying about him with his right as if he were really defending the sepulchre itself from the hands of the infidels. The procession advanced under a loud chant, preceded by a body of Turkish officers to clear the way; then came the priests, wearing their richest dresses, their mitres and caps richly ornamented with precious stones, and carrying aloft sacred banners, and one of them sprinkling holy water. Wherever he came the rush was terrible; the Greeks became excited to a sort of frenzy in their eagerness to catch a drop; and one strapping fellow, bursting through the rear ranks, thrust his face over my shoulder, and bawled out, "Papa, papa," in such an agonizing voice, that the "papa" aimed at him a copious discharge, of which my face received the principal benefit. When the largest banner came round, the struggle to touch it with the palm-branches was inconceivable. A Turkish officer had, until this time, covered me with his body, and by dint of shouting, kicking, and striking furiously about him, saved me till the procession passed by; but after this the rush became dreadful. I could feel my ribs yielding under the pressure, and was really alarmed when a sudden and mighty surge of the struggling mass hurried me into the stock in trade of a merchant of dates and oranges. Instead of picking up his goods, the fellow grappled at

405

me, but I got out of his clutches as well as I could; and, setting up for myself, kicked, thumped, and scuffled until I made my way to the door; and that was my last visit to the Church of the Holy Sepulchre.

I had regretted that I could not stay for the great Greek jugglery, the drawing down fire from heaven, when every pilgrim considers himself bound to light his taper at the sacred flame; and those who light first are considered the most fortunate and the most favored in the sight of God. I could imagine the wild and frantic struggling among more than ten thousand bigots and fanatics for the first rays of the heavenly light; but, from what I saw that day, I felt that it would be putting life and limb in peril to be among them. Two years before a horrible catastrophe had happened at the enactment of this ceremony. The air of the church had become so contaminated by the exhalations from the bodies of the thousands crowded within it that respiration became difficult; terror, confusion, and a rush for the door ensued; Ibrahim Pasha was carried out senseless, over the heads of the people, by a strong body of his soldiers; and between two and three hundred pilgrims were trodden down and trampled to death. Their bodies were laid out the next morning in the court of the church; and so degraded is the character of these Christian pilgrims that, as I was told by Mr. Nicolaisen, the English missionary to the Jews, who was looking among them for a servant of his own, the friends and relatives of the slain carried them away in triumph, as martyrs in the cause of Christ.

My last visit in Jerusalem was to Mount Zion. I believe I have not mentioned that on this hill stands the tomb, or the supposed tomb, of David. It is covered by a mosque; the tomb is walled in, and, as the Arab doorkeeper told me, even the eyes of the pasha are not permitted to look within the holy place. Here, too, is the caenaculum, or chamber, where our Savior ate his last supper with his disciples; in the Armenian chapel is the real stone that was rolled from the door of the sepulchre; and here also is the house of Caiphas the high-priest, with a tree marking the spot where the cock crew when Peter denied his master.

But there was one spot on Mount Zion far more interesting to me than all these, or even than anything in Jerusalem. It was the grave of my early friend, whom I had tracked in his wanderings from the Cataracts of the Nile, through the wilderness of Sinai, to his last resting-place in Jerusalem. Years had rolled away since I bade him farewell in the streets of our native city. I had heard of him in the gay circles of Paris as about to wed with one of the proudest names in France; again, as a wanderer in the East, and then as dead in Palestine. But a few short years had passed away, and what changes! My old schoolmates, the companions of my youth and opening manhood, where were they? Gone, scattered, dispersed, and dead; one of them was sleeping in the cold earth under my feet. He had left his home and become a wanderer in strange lands, and had come to the Holy Land to die, and I was now bending over his grave. Where were the friends that should have gathered around him in the awful hour of death? Who closed his dying eyes? Who received his parting words for his friends at home? Who buried him on Mount Zion? Once I had been present there at a scene which almost made me weep; the burial of an Armenian pilgrim. He was brought for burial in the clothes in which he had died; the grave was too small, and had to be enlarged; the priest stood at the head of the grave under a heavy shower of rain, and, as he offered me his snuff-box, grumbled at being obliged to wait; and when the grave was enlarged and the body thrown in and the wet dirt cast upon it, he mumbled a short prayer, and then all hurried away. And this was by the grave of my friend; and I could not but ask myself who had buried him, and who had mourned over his grave. The inscription on his tombstone afforded but vague answers to my questions, and they were of a painful character. It ran thus:

D.O.M.

Hic jacet,

C——— B———, ex Americae,

Regionibus

Lugduni Galliae Consul Hyerosolomis tactus intrinsecus

sponte

Erroribus Lutheri et Calvini abjectis, Cathlicam
religionem professus svnanche correptus
E vita decessit IV. nonas Augusti, MDCCCXXX, aetatis
suae XXV.
Amici moerentes posuere
Orate pro eo.[1]

He had died at the convent, and died alone. His traveling companion had accidentally remained at Jaffa, had not heard of his sickness, and did not arrive in Jerusalem until poor B[radford] was in his grave. It was necessary to be wary in my inquiries, for the Catholics here are ever on the watch for souls and with great ostentation had blazoned his conversion upon his tomb. The first time I inquired about him, a young monk told me that he remembered him well, as on the day of his arrival, a fine, handsome young man, full of health and spirit, and that he immediately commenced talking about religion, and three days afterward they said mass and took the sacrament together in the chapel of the convent. He told me the story so glibly, that I was confident of its falsity, even without referring to its improbability. I had known B[radford] well. I knew that, like most young men with us, though entertaining the deepest respect and reverence for holy things, in the pride of youth and health he had lived as if there was no grave; and I could imagine that, stretched upon his bed of death in the dreary cell of the convent, with "no eye to pity and no arm to save," surrounded by Catholic monks and probably enfeebled in mind by disease, he

---

[1] This was the tomb of Cornelius Bradford, New Yorker (c. 1805–30). Stephens had inscribed his name under his on the rock-surface of Aswan on the Nile. A translation of the inscription:

To Greatest and Best God.
Deus Optime Maxime,
Here lies Cornelius Bradford, from America.
Consul to the regions of Lyon in France, who,
inwardly moved of his own free will, rejected
the errors of Luther and Calvin and took up
the Catholic religion. Worn away by disease
he died on the 4th day of the Nones of August
[eleventh?], 1830, aged 25. This monument was
set up by —— friends. Pray for him.

[Editor's Translation]

had, perhaps, laid hold of the only hope of salvation offered him; and when I stood over his grave, and thought of the many thorns in his pillow in that awful hour—the distracting thoughts of home, of the mother whose name had been the last on his lips; the shuddering consciousness that, if he died a Protestant, his bones would be denied the rites of burial, I pitied, I grieved for, but I could not blame him. But when suspicion was aroused by the manner of the monk, I resolved to inquire further; and, if his tale should prove untrue, to tear with my own hands the libellous stone from my friend's grave, and hurl it down Mount Zion. I afterward saw the monk who had shrived him, and was told that the young man with whom I had conversed was a prater and a fool; that he himself had never heard B[radford] speak of religion until after his return from the Dead Sea with the hand of death upon him; that he had administered the sacrament to him but three days before his death, when all hope of life was past, and that even yet it might be a question whether he did really renounce his faith, for the solemn abjuration was made in a language he but imperfectly understood; and he never spoke afterward, except, in the wildness of delirium, to murmur the name of "Mother."

I have said that, in his dying moments, his feelings were harrowed by the thought that his body would be denied a Christian burial. Mr. Whiting, who accompanied me on my first visit to his grave, told me that the Catholics would not have allowed him a resting-place in consecrated ground; and, leading me a short distance to the grave of a friend and fellow-missionary who had died since he had been at Jerusalem, described to me what he had seen of the unchristian spirit of the Christians of the holy city. Refused by the Latins, the friends of Dr. Dodge had asked permission of the Greeks to lay his body for a little while in their burying-ground; and, negotiating with the dragoman of the convent, they thought that permission had been granted; but, while they were in the act of performing the funeral service, a messenger came in to tell them that the grave had been filled up. They protracted the service till the delay excited the attention of his unhappy widow, and they were obliged to tell her that they had no place where they could lay

409

the head of her young husband. A reluctant permission was at length granted, and they buried him by the light of torches; and although there had been no graves in that part of the ground before, the Greeks had buried all around, to prevent any application for permission to lay by his side the body of another heretic.

THE NEXT DAY I left Jerusalem; but, before leaving it, I was witness to another striking scene, which I shall never forget: the departure of the pilgrims, fifteen or twenty thousand in number, for the Jordan. At an early hour I was on horseback, outside St. Stephen's Gate. It was such a morning as that on which I started for the Dead Sea, clear, bright, and beautiful; the streets of the city were deserted, and the whole population were outside the walls, sitting under the shadow of the temple, among the tombs of the Turkish burying-ground; the women in their long white dresses, with their faces covered, and the men in large flowing robes, of gay and varied colors, and turbans of every fashion, many of them green, the proud token of the pilgrimage to Mecca, with pipes and swords and glittering arms; the whole Valley of Jehoshaphat was filled with moving beings in every variety of gay apparel, as if the great day of resurrection had already come and the tenants of the dreary tombs had burst the fetters of the grave and come forth into new life and beauty.

I had received an invitation from the governor to ride in his suite; and, while waiting for him at the gate, the terrible Abougos, with his retainers, came out and beckoned me to join him. I followed him over the Brook Kedron and the Valley of Jehoshaphat to the Garden of Gethsemane, where I stopped, and, giving my horse to an Arab boy, I stepped over the low fence, and seating myself on the jutting root of the tree marked by the knives of pilgrims as that under which our Savior was betrayed, looking over the heads of the Turkish women seated on the fence below, I saw the whole proces-

411

sion streaming from the gate, crossing the Valley of Jehoshaphat, and filing along the foot of the garden. They were on foot and on horseback, on donkeys, mules, dromedaries, and camels, and here and there were well-equipped caravans, with tents and provisions for the monks of the different convents. It would be impossible to give any idea of this strange and extraordinary procession; here might be seen a woman on horseback, with a child on each arm; there a large pannier on each side of a mule, with a man in one and a woman in the other; or a large frame on the high back of a camel, like a diminutive ark, carrying a whole family, with all their quilts, coverlets, cooking utensils, &c. Among them, riding alone on a raw-boned horse, was a beggarly Italian, in a worn and shabby European dress, with a fowling-piece and a game-bag, and everybody made way for him; and there was a general laugh wherever he came. And now a body of Turkish horsemen, with drawn scimitars in their hands, rushed out of the gate, dashed down the valley and up the sides of the mountains at full gallop, clearing the way for the governor; and then came the governor himself, under a salute from the fortress, on a horse of the best blood of Arabia, riding as if he were part of the noble animal, preceded by the music of the Turkish drum and bowing with a nobility and dignity of manner known only in the East, and which I marked the more particularly as he stopped opposite to me and beckoned to me to join him. Then came the pilgrims again, and I sat there till the last had gone by. Galloping back to the gate, I turned to look at them for the last time, a living, moving mass of thousands, thousands of miles from their homes, bound for the sacred Jordan, and strong in the faith that, bathing in its hallowed waters, they should wash away their sins.

In a few moments I was at the convent; and, sending Paul before me to the Damascus Gate, I went to take my leave of the superior. He told me that, though I was an American (the only Americans he had seen were missionaries, and he did not like them), he liked me; and, bidding me a kind and affectionate farewell, he put into my hands a pilgrim's certificate, which follows in these words—

FR. FRANCISCUS XAVERIUS A MELITA.

Ordinis minorum regularis observantiae s. p. n. Francisci; custodiae Melitensis lector theologus; ex-definito; sacrae congregationis propagandae fidei responsalis; missionum aegypti et cypri praefectus; in partibus orientis commisarius apostolicus; sacri montis Sion, et santissimi sepulcri d.n. Jesu Christi guardianus; totius terrae sanctae custos, visitator, et humilis in Domino servus:

Illustrissimo Domino —— — ——, Americano libenter hoc presens testimonium damus, et omnibus, ac singulis hos praesentes nostras litteras lecturis, vel inspecturis notum, fidemque facimus, Laudatum Illustrissimum Dominum Jerusalem pervenisse, et omnia principaliora loca, quae in tota Palestina visitari solent, presertim Ssm Sepulchrum Dom. H. Jesu Christi, Calvariae Montem, Praesepim Bethlehemiticum, etc., visitasse. Et quod ita sit, attestationem manu nostra subscribimus, et sigillo majori officii nostri munitam expediri mandamus.

Datis Jerusalem, ex hoc Venerabili Conventu Sancti Salvatoris die. 3 Aprilis, Anno Domini 18 trigesimo-sexto.

Fr. Franciscus Xaverius a Melita, Custs Terrae Sanctae.

De Mandato Rendmi in Xpto Patris,

FR. PERPETUUS A SOLERIO

Secretarius Terrae Sanctae.

Which, being interpreted, is as follows:—

Brother Francis Xavier, of Malta, of the order of monks of the regular rule of our Father Saint Francis; theological reader of the order of Malta; expounder, missionary of the Sacred Congregation for propagating the faith; Prefect of the Missions of Egypt and Cyprus; apostolical commissary in the Eastern world; guardian of

413

the holy Mount Zion and of the most Holy Sepulchre of our Lord Jesus Christ; keeper and visitor of all the Holy Land, and humble servant in the Lord:

To the most illustrious Lord John L. Stephens, an American, we give this present testimonial; and to all and every one who shall read or inspect these our present letters, we do make known and certify that this celebrated and most illustrious lord has come through Jerusalem, and has visited all the principal places which are accustomed to be visited in all Palestine, especially the most Holy Sepulchre of our Lord Jesus Christ, the Mount of Calvary, the Convent at Bethlehem, &c.; and that it is so we subscribe this attestation with our hand, and cause it to be put forth fortified by the great seal of our office.

Given at Jerusalem, from this venerable convent of the Holy Savior, on the third day of April, in the year of the Lord one thousand eight hundred and thirty-six.

Brother Francis Xavier, of Malta, Guardian of the Holy Land.

Given by command, in the private office of the
Father,

FRANCIS S. SOLERIO,
Perpetual Secretary of the Holy Land.

Whereby the reader will see that, whatever may be his fate hereafter, a pilgrimage to the holy city gives a man temporal honors, and has transformed a republican citizen of America into an "illustrissimus dominus."

With this evidence of my pilgrim character, I mounted my horse for the last time at the door of the convent. I lost my way in going to the Damascus Gate, but a friendly Jew conducted me to it; a Jew was the first to welcome me to the Holy Land, and a Jew was the last to speed me on my way from the holy city of Jerusalem. Paul was waiting for me, and for half a mile we passed mounds of ruins, the walls of the old city having extended some distance beyond the Damascus Gate. In about three quarters of an hour, a little to the right, we came to what are called the Tombs of the Judges, excavations in the rock, one of them full of water. I have no satisfaction in the recollection of these tombs, for there I lost my old companion, the terror of evil dogs, my Nubian club; which, since I bought it in Nubia, had seldom been out of my hand. In about three hours we were mounting Djebel Samyel, the highest mountain about Jerusalem, crowned with the ruins of Ramah, the birthplace and tomb of Samuel the seer. A few Arab huts are around the ruins, and a ruined mosque, the minaret of which has fallen, is the most prominent building on the mountain. We entered the mosque; at the farther end was a door locked, but with the key in it. I turned the key and entered a dark chamber. By the light from the door I could see at the far end a dark, somber-looking object, and groped my way to the tomb of Samuel; I kept my hands on it and walked around it; and, hearing some of the villagers at the door, I tore off a piece of the pall, as I had done from the tomb of Aaron, and hurried out. I stopped for a moment on the top of the mountain and, looking back towards the holy city, saw for the last time the Mosque of Omar, rising proudly over the ruins of the Temple of Solomon, the Church of the Holy Sepulchre, the walls of Jerusalem, and the Dead Sea. My first view of this latter had been from the tomb of Aaron, and I considered it a not uninteresting coincidence that I was now looking upon it for the last time from the tomb of Samuel.

In about an hour, riding over a rough road, we came to the village of Beer, supposed to be the Beer to which Jotham fled "for fear of his brother Abimelech." A ruined khan was at the entrance of the village, and near it a large fountain, at which the women were washing. About an hour beyond this, to the right, on a little elevation, are the ruins of Beteel, the ancient Bethel. It was here that the bears came out and tore in pieces the children that mocked the bald-headed prophet Elisha, and it was here that Jacob took "the stones of the place for his pillow, and dreamed, and beheld a ladder reaching to heaven, and the angels of God ascending and descending thereon." Though surrounded by stony mountains, it was prettily

415

situated; I rode among the ruins without dismounting. The place was solitary and deserted, and not a human being appeared to dwell in it. At one end were the ruins of a church, and near it was a large fountain in a stone reservoir; a single cow was drinking at the fountain, and at the moment a boy was driving past a flock of goats to his village home in the mountains. He was a Christian, and called me Christian and hadji or pilgrim, and gave me a wild flower which he plucked from under my horse's feet. It was a beautiful afternoon, and all was so still and quiet that I felt strongly tempted to lie down and sleep where Jacob did; but I had given away my tent and camp equipage, and I reflected that while I was sure of the patriarch's pillow of stone, I had but little prospect of being blessed with the promise that softened it, "that the land on which he lay should be given to him and his seed, and that in him all the families of the earth should be blessed."

In about an hour we came to the village of Einbroot, prettily situated on an eminence, and commanding on all sides a view of fertile and well-cultivated valleys. We were looking for Einbroot, and as the village to which we had come lay a little off the road, we were not sure it was the place we wanted. A woman told us it was not, a man assured us that the sheik was not at home, and there seemed clearly a disposition to send us on farther; and this determined us to stop. We rode up to the village and inquired for the sheik; the villagers gave us evasive answers, one saying that he was away, and another that he was sick; but a little boy, pointing with his finger, told us that he was there, praying; and, looking up, we saw him on the top of the house, on his knees, praying with all his might, and occasionally looking over his shoulder at us. By his not coming to welcome me, I saw that he did not wish me to stay; and, after my scenes with the Bedouins in the desert, having a comparative contempt for dwellers in houses, I dismounted and sat down, determined to see who would get tired first. In the meantime the villagers gathered around, as spectators of our contest, and the sheik, as if ashamed of himself, at length finished his prayers and came down to receive me. He told me that he had no place for us, and showed me to a large room, fifty or sixty feet square, which seemed to be the common resort and sleeping place of all who had no particular home. After the comforts of the convent at Jerusalem, I did not like the looks of things in the beginning of my journey; but, consoling myself with the reflection that it was only for one night, I spread my mat in a corner, and had just time to stroll around the village before dark.

The houses were built of rough stone, a single story in height, with mud roofs, many of them overgrown with grass, and now presenting, towards sundown, the singularly picturesque spectacle, which I had often noticed in Syria, of the inhabitants sitting out upon the terraces and roofs of their houses, or, perhaps, the still more striking picture of a single old white-bearded, patriarchal figure sitting alone upon his housetop. One of these venerable personages called me up to his side; and I was well rewarded for my trouble, and could fully appreciate the satisfaction with which the old man, day after day, looked out upon the beautiful and well-cultivated valley, the terraces, and the smiling villages on the mountain side.

Several of the villagers were following us, and among them a fine old man, the brother of the sheik and formerly sheik himself. He told me that, since the stormy times of Mohammed Ali, he had resigned the sheikdom, and comforted himself for the loss of station in the arms of a young wife; and before we parted we were on such good terms that he told me the reason of their unwillingness to receive us, namely, that they thought we were officers of Mohammed Ali, sent to spy out their condition and ascertain the number of their men able to bear arms; but, satisfied that we were merely travelers and warmed by my honest disclaimer of the imputed character, he invited me to his house, and both he and the sheik and all the villagers seemed striving now to atone for the churlishness of their first reception.

The old man was as kind as a man could be; in fact, his kindness oppressed me, for, having but one room in his house, he sent both his wives out of doors to sleep at a neighbor's. In vain I told him not to disarrange himself on my account; to make no stranger of me; to let them stay; and that it was nothing to me if the whole harem of the sultan was there; he was positive and decided. I catechized him about his wives, and he said that he had been a poor man all his life, and could never afford to keep more than one till lately; and now the companion of his youth and the sharer of his poverty was thrust away into a corner, while with all simplicity and honesty he showed me the best place in the house, appropriated to his young bride. He talked as if it had been the hardest thing in the world that he had been obliged to content himself so long with his first wife. Thus, it seems, that here, as with us, extravagance comes with wealth; and whereas with us, when a man grows rich, he adds another pair of horses to his establishment, so the honest Mussulman indulges himself with another helpmate.

Two Turks and an Arab slept in the room with us; and before going to bed, that is, before lying down on the mud floor, and the first thing in the morning, they turned their faces to the tomb of the Prophet, kneeled down, and prayed. In the evening one of them had complained of a headache, and another, standing over him and pressing his temples with the palms of his hands, repeated a verse of the Koran, and the headache went away. I asked him whether that was good for a sore throat; he told me that it was, but, after giving me a verse or two, said that his remedy could only have full effect upon true believers.

Early in the morning I set off, my host and the sheik and half the village gathering around me to bid me farewell and invoke blessings upon me. I did not know the extent of the sacrifice my host had made for me until at the moment of parting, when I got a glimpse of his young wife.

We were now entering the region of Samaria, and, though the mountains were yet stony, a beautiful country was opening before us. We soon came into a smiling valley full of large olive-trees, and rode for some time in a pleasant shade. Everywhere we were meeting streams of pure water, tempting us perpetually to dismount after the sandy desert through which we had been so long traveling. We passed, too, several villages, among which I remember was the village of Cowara, beautifully situated on the side of the mountain, overlooking a fertile valley, and all the women of the village were in the field picking the tares from the grain.

I was now about entering one of the most interesting countries in the Holy Land, consecrated by the presence of our Savior in the body and by the exercise of his divine and miraculous powers. The Bible was again in my hand, and I read there that Jesus Christ had left "Judea and departed into Galilee; that he must needs pass through Samaria, and that he came to a city of Samaria called Sychar, near to the parcel of ground that Jacob gave to his son Joseph." And "Jacob's well was there, and Jesus, being weary with his journey, sat down on the well, and it was about the sixth hour. And there cometh a woman of Samaria to draw water; and Jesus saith unto her, Give me to drink." It is with no irreverent feeling that I draw the parallel, but I was following in the very footsteps of the Savior; I too had left "Judea, and had departed into Galilee"; I too "must needs go through Samaria"; and I too was now coming to the city of Samaria called Sychar, and, before entering the city, I would fain sit down on the well of Jacob, where our Savior talked with the Samaritan woman.

At Cowara I took a guide to conduct me to this well. In about two hours we were winding along the side of Mount Gerizim, whose summit was covered with the white dome of the tomb of an Arab saint; and passing one well on the declivity of the mountain, going down to the valley at its base, we came to Jacob's well, or the Beer Samarea of the Arabs. I knew that there was a difference of opinion as to the precise site of this interesting monument; but, when I found myself at the mouth of this well, I had no wish to look farther; I could feel and realize the whole scene; I could see our Savior coming out from Judea and traveling along this valley; I could see him, wearied with his journey, sitting down on this well to rest, and the Samaritan woman, as I saw them at every town in the Holy Land, coming out for water. I could imagine his looking up to Mount Gerizim, and predicting the ruin of the temple, and telling her that the hour was coming when neither on that mountain nor yet in Jerusalem would she worship the God of her fathers. A large column lay across the top of the well, and the mouth was filled up with huge stones. I could see the water through the crevices; but, even with the assistance of Paul and the Arabs, found it impossible to remove them. I plucked a wild flower growing in the mouth of the well and passed on.

The ground which I was now treading is supposed to be the "parcel of ground" which Jacob bought of the sons of Hamor, the father of Shechem, for a hundred pieces of silver and gave to his son Joseph. Turning the point of the mountain, we came to a rich valley, lying between the mountains of Gerizim and Ebal. Crossing this valley, on the sides of the mountains of Ebal is a long range of grottoes and tombs, and a little before coming to them, in a large white building like a sheik's tomb, is the sepulchre of Joseph, as it is written, "the bones also of Joseph, which the children of Israel brought up with them out of Egypt, buried they in Shechem." I dismounted and entered the building, and it is a not uninteresting fact that I found there a white-bearded Israelite, kneeling at the tomb of the patriarch, and teaching a rosy-cheeked boy (his descendant of the fourth generation) the beautiful story of Joseph and his brethren.

It was late in the afternoon when I was moving up the valley of Naplous. The mountains of Gerizim and Ebal, the mountains of blessings and curses, were towering like lofty walls on either side of me; Mount Gerizim fertile, and Mount Ebal barren, as when God commanded Joshua to set up the stones in Mount Ebal and pronounced on Mount Gerizim blessings upon the children of Israel "if they would hearken diligently unto the voice of the Lord, to observe and do all his commandments,"[1] and on Ebal the withering curses of disobedience. A beautiful stream, in two or three places filling large reservoirs, was running through the valley, and a shepherd sat on its bank, playing a reed pipe, with his flock feeding quietly around him. The shades of evening were gathering fast as I approached the town of Naplous, the Shechem or Sychem of the Old Testament, and the Sychar of the New. More than a dozen lepers were sitting outside the gate, their faces shining, pimpled and bloated, covered with sores and pustules, their nostrils open and filled with ulcers, and their red eyes fixed and staring; with swollen

[1] Deuteronomy xxviii., 1.—Stephens' note.

feet they dragged their disgusting bodies towards me, and with hoarse voices extended their deformed and hideous hands for charity.

We rode up the principal street, and at the door of the palace I met the governor just mounting his horse, with a large retinue of officers and slaves around him. We exchanged our greetings on horseback. I showed him my firman, and he sent a janissary to conduct me to the house of a Samaritan, a writer to the government, where I was received, fed, and lodged better than in any other place in the Holy Land, always excepting the abodes of those suffering martyrs, the Terra Santa monks.

I had just time to visit the Samaritan synagogue. Leaving my shoes at the door, with naked feet I entered a small room, about fifteen feet square, with nothing striking or interesting about it except what the Samaritans say is the oldest manuscript in the world, a copy of the Pentateuch, written by Abishua, the grandson of Aaron, three years after the death of Moses, or about 3,300 years ago. The priest was a man of forty-five, and gave me but a poor idea of the character of the Samaritans, for he refused to show me the sacred scroll unless I would pay him first. He then brought down an old manuscript, which, very much to his astonishment, I told him was not the genuine record, giving him very plainly to understand that I was not to be bamboozled in the matter. I had been advised of this trick by the English clergyman whom I met in Jerusalem; and the priest, laughing at my detection of the cheat, while some of his hopeful flock who had followed me joined in the laugh, brought down the other preserved in a tin case. It was written in some character I did not understand, said to be the Samaritan, tattered and worn, and bearing the marks of extreme age; and, though I knew nothing about it, I admitted it to be the genuine manuscript; and they all laughed when I told the priest what a rogue he was for trying to deceive me; and this priest they believe to be of the tribe of Levi, of the seed of Aaron. If I had left Naplous then I should probably have repeated the words that our Savior applied to them in his day, "No good thing can come out of

Samaria"; but I spent a long evening and had an interesting conversation with my host and his brother, and in their kindness, sincerity, and honesty, forgot the petty duplicity of the Levite.

Much curiosity has existed in Europe among the learned with regard to this singular people, and several of the most eminent men of their day, in London and Paris, have had correspondence with them, but without any satisfactory result. The descendants of the Israelites who remained and were not carried into captivity, on the rebuilding of the second temple were denied the privilege of sharing the labor and expense of its reconstruction at Jerusalem, and, in mortification and revenge, they built a temple on Mount Gerizim, and ever since a deadly hatred has existed between their descendants the Samaritans and the Jews. Gibbon, speaking of them in the time of Justinian, says, "The Samaritans of Palestine were a motley race, an ambiguous sect, rejected as Jews by the pagans, by the Jews as schismatics, and by the Christians as idolaters. The abomination of the cross had already been planted on their holy mount of Gerizim, but the persecution of Justinian offered only the alternative of baptism or rebellion. They chose the latter; under the standard of a desperate leader, they rose in arms and retaliated their wrongs on the lives, the property, and the temples of a defenseless people. The Samaritans were finally subdued by the regular forces of the East; twenty thousand were slain, twenty thousand were sold by the Arabs to the infidels of Persia and India, and the remains of that unhappy nation atoned for the crime of treason by the sin of hypocrisy." About sixty families are all now remaining, and these few relics of a once powerful people still dwell in their ancient capital, at the base of Mount Gerizim, under the shadow of their fallen temple.

The brother of my host was particularly fond of talking about them. He was very old, and the most deformed man I ever saw who lived to attain a great age. His legs were long, and all his limbs were those of a tall man, but he was so hump-backed that in sitting he rested upon his hump. He asked me many questions about the Samaritans in England (of America he had no knowledge), and seemed determined to believe that there were many in that country, and told me that I might say to them, wherever I found them, that there they believed in one omnipotent and eternal God, the five Books of Moses, and a future Messiah, and the day of the Messiah's coming to be near at hand; that they practiced circumcision, went three times a year up to Mount Gerizim, "the everlasting mountain," to worship and offer sacrifice, and once a year pitched their tents and left their virgins alone on the mount for seven days, expecting that one of them would conceive and bring forth a son, who should be the Messiah; that they allowed two wives, and, in case of barrenness, four; that the women were not permitted to enter the synagogue, except once a year during fast, but on no account were they permitted to touch the sacred scroll; and that, although the Jews and Samaritans had dealings in the market-places, &c., they hated each other now as much as their fathers did before them.

I asked him about Jacob's well; he said he knew the place, and that he knew our Savior, or Jesus Christ, as he familiarly called him, very well; he was Joseph the carpenter's son, of Nazareth; but that the story which the Christians had about the women at the well was all a fiction; that Christ did not convert her; but that, on the contrary, she laughed at him, and even refused to give him water to drink.

The information I received from these old men is more than I have ever seen in print about this reduced and singular people, and I give it for what it may be worth. I cannot help mentioning a little circumstance, which serves to illustrate the proverb that boys will be boys all the world over. While I was exploring the mysteries of the Samaritan creed, it being the season of Easter, a fine chubby little fellow came to me with a couple of eggs dyed yellow, and trying them on his teeth, just as we used to do in my boyish days (did we learn it from them or they from us?)—gave me a choice; and, though it may seem a trifling incident to the reader, it was not an uninteresting circumstance to me, this celebration of my "paas" in the ancient Sychem, cracking eggs with a Samaritan boy.

CHAPTER XXXV

SEBASTE—RUINS OF THE PALACE OF HEROD—MOUNT TABOR—NAZ-
ARETH—SCRIPTURAL LOCALITIES—TIBERIAS—AN ENGLISH SPORTS-
MAN—BETHSAIDA AND CHORAZIN—CAPERNAUM—ZAFFAD—
ARRIVAL AT ACRE

AT ABOUT eight o'clock in the morning we left Naplous; the
lepers were lying at the gate as before, not permitted to enter
the walls of the city, but living apart and perpetuating among themselves their loathsome race. The valley of Naplous was, if possible,
more beautiful by morning than by evening light, shaded by groves
of figs, olives, almonds, and apricots in full bloom, and bounded by
lofty mountains, with a clear and beautiful stream winding and
murmuring through its center. Until I came to this place I had
frequently said to myself that I would not give the estate of a
wealthy gentleman in Geneseo for the whole kingdom of David, but
there was a rare and extraordinary beauty here, even in the hands of
the Arab Fellahs. Men and women were stealing among the trees, in
gaily-colored apparel, and, instead of the turban or tarboosh, the
men wore a long red cap, with the tassel hanging jauntily like that
of a Neapolitan. For more than an hour we followed the course of
the stream, and nothing could be more beautifully picturesque than
the little mills on its banks; low, completely imbosomed among
trees, and with their roofs covered with grass, and sometimes the
agreeable sound of a waterfall was the first intimation we had of
their presence. There was something exceedingly rural and poetic
in their appearance. I went down to one of them, more than usually
beautiful, hoping to be greeted by some lovely "maid of the mill";
but, as if it were determined that everything like illusion in the East
should be destroyed for my especial benefit, the sight of one chamber, filled with sacks of grain, sheep and goats, and all kinds of filth,
and a young girl sitting in the door, with the head of an old woman

in her lap, occupied as is constantly seen in every miserable town in Italy, drove me away perfectly disgusted.

Leaving the valley, we turned up to the right, and, crossing among the mountains, in two hours came in sight of the ruins of Sebaste, the ancient Samaria, standing upon a singularly bold and insulated mountain, crowned with ruins. The capital of the ten tribes of Israel, where Ahab built his palace of ivory; where, in the days of Jereboam, her citizens sat in the lap of luxury, saying to their masters "come and let us drink," destroyed by the Assyrians, but rebuilt and restored to more than its original splendor by Herod, now lies in the state foretold by the prophet Amos, "her inhabitants and their posterity are taken away." The ancient Samaritans are all gone, and around the ruins of their palaces and temples are gathered the miserable huts of the Arab Fellahs. Climbing up the precipitous ascent of the hill, we came to the ruins of a church, or tower, or something else, built by our old friend the Lady Helena, and seen to great advantage from the valley below. The Lady Helena, however, did not put together all this stone and mortar for the picturesque alone; it was erected over, and in honor of, the prison where John the Baptist was beheaded, and his grave. I knew that this spot was guarded with jealous care by the Arabs, and that none but Mussulmans were permitted to see it; but this did not prevent my asking admission; and, when the lame sheik said that none could enter without a special order from the pasha, Paul rated him soundly for thinking we would be such fools as to come without one; and, handing him our traveling firman, the sheik kissed the seal, and, utterly unable to determine for himself whether the order was to furnish me with horses or admit me to mosques, said he knew he was bound to obey that seal and do whatever the bearer told him, and hobbled off to get the key.

Leaving our shoes at the door in one corner of the enclosure, we entered a small mosque with whitewashed walls, hung with ostrich eggs, clean mats for the praying Mussulmans, a sort of pulpit, and the usual recess of the Kebla. In the center of the stone floor was a hole opening to the prison below, and, going outside and descending a flight of steps, we came to the prison chamber, about eight paces

425

square; the door, now broken and leaning against the wall, like the doors in the sepulchres of the kings at Jerusalem, was a slab cut from the solid stone and turning on a pivot. On the opposite side were three small holes, opening to another chamber, which was the tomb of the Baptist. I looked in, but all was dark; the Mussulman told me that the body only was there; that the prophet was beheaded at the request of the wife of a king, and I forget where he said the head was. This may be the prison where the great forerunner of the Lord was beheaded; at least no man can say that it is not; and leaving it with the best disposition to believe, I ascended to the ruined palace of Herod, his persecutor and murderer. Thirty or forty columns were still standing, the monuments of the departed greatness of its former tenant. On one side, towards the northeast, where are the ruins of a gate, there is a double range of Ionic columns. I counted more than sixty, and, from the fragments I was constantly meeting, it would seem as if a double colonnade had extended all around.

The palace of Herod stands on a table of land, on the very summit of the hill, overlooking every part of the surrounding country; and such were the exceeding softness and beauty of the scene, even under the wildness and waste of Arab cultivation, that the city seemed smiling in the midst of her desolation. All around was a beautiful valley, watered by running streams and covered by a rich carpet of grass, sprinkled with wild flowers of every hue, and beyond, stretched like an open book before me, a boundary of fruitful mountains, the vine and the olive rising in terraces to their very summits; there, day after day, the haughty Herod had sat in his royal palace; and looking out upon all these beauties, his heart had become hardened with prosperity; here, among these still towering columns, the proud monarch had made a supper "to his lords, and high captains, and chief estates of Galilee"; here the daughter of Herodias, Herod's brother's wife, "danced before him, and the proud king promised with an oath to give her whatever she should ask, even to the half of his kingdom." And while the feast and dance went on, the "head of John the Baptist was brought in a charger and given to the damsel." And Herod has gone, and Herodias,

426

Herod's brother's wife, has gone, and "the lords, and the high captains, and the chief estates of Galilee" are gone; but the ruins of the palace in which they feasted are still here; the mountains and valleys which beheld their revels are here; and oh, what a comment upon the vanity of worldly greatness, a fellah was turning his plough around one of the columns, I was sitting on a broken capital under a fig-tree by its side, and I asked him what were the ruins that we saw; and while his oxen were quietly cropping the grass that grew among the fragments of the marble floor, he told me that they were the ruins of the palace of a king—he believed, of the Christians; and while pilgrims from every quarter of the world turn aside from their path to do homage in the prison of his beheaded victim, the Arab who was driving his plough among the columns of his palace knew not the name of the haughty Herod. Even at this distance of time I look back with a feeling of uncommon interest upon my ramble among those ruins, talking with the Arab ploughman of the king who built it, leaning against a column which perhaps had often supported the haughty Herod, and looking out from this scene of desolation and ruin upon the most beautiful country in the Holy Land.

Descending from the ruined city, we continued our way along the valley. In about an hour we came to the village of Beteen, standing on the side of a mountain, overlooking a fertile valley: the women were in the fields, as I had seen them before, picking the tares from the wheat. Riding along through a succession of beautiful valleys, nearly all the way close to the banks of a running stream, and stopping under a fine shade of olives for our noonday meal, we came to Sanpoor, standing on an insulated hill, commanding an extensive view of the country, and once a strongly fortified place, with a tower and walls, supposed to have been built during the time of the crusades, but now totally demolished and in ruins. About three years ago it was taken, after a six months' siege, by Abdallah Pasha, the great soldier of the sultan; the insurgent inhabitants were put to the sword, and their houses burnt and razed to the ground. A little beyond this, the continued falls of rain have formed a small lake. In an hour and a half we passed the village of Abattia;

427

and late in the afternoon we fell in with a party of Turkish travelers, one of whom was the "biggest in the round" of all the men I had seen in the East. His noble horse seemed to complain of his extraordinary burden. At about six o'clock we had left the beautiful country of Samaria, and were entering the little town of Jennin, or Janeen, standing on the borders of Galilee, at the commencement of the great plain of Jezreel.

Early in the morning, leaving the village of Janeen, we entered almost immediately the great plain of Jezreel. The holy places were now crowding upon me in rapid succession. I was on my way to Nazareth, the city of Joseph and Mary, where Christ spent nearly all his life; but I turned off the direct road to do homage on Mount Tabor, recognized as the scene of our Savior's transfiguration. We passed two miserable villages, looking at a distance like little mounds or excrescences on the surface of the great plain; and, turning to the right, around the mountains of Samaria, saw afar off the lofty summit of Hermon, crowned with a sheik's tomb. On the right, towards the Sea of Galilee, was the village of Bisan, the Bethshan of the Bible, where the Philistines fastened the bodies of Saul and his three sons to the walls after they had fallen in Mount Gilboa.[1]

Before us, and the most striking and imposing object on the whole of the great plain of Esdraelon, was Mount Tabor. It stands perfectly isolated; rising alone from the plain in a rounded tapering form, like a truncated cone, to the height of three thousand feet, covered with trees, grass, and wild flowers from the base to its summit and presenting the combination so rarely found in natural scenery of the bold and the beautiful. At twelve o'clock we were at the miserable village of Deborah, at the foot of the mountain, supposed to be the place where Deborah the prophetess, who then judged Israel, and Barak and "ten thousand men after him, descended upon Sisera, and discomfited him and all his chariots, even nine hundred chariots of iron, and all the people that were with him." The men and boys had all gone out to their daily labor, and we tried to persuade a woman to guide us to the top of the mountain,

[1] Joshua, xvii., 11; 1 Samuel, xxxi., 12; Kings, iv., 12.—Stephens' note.

428

but she turned away with contempt; and, having had some practice in climbing, we moved around its sides until we found a regular path, and ascended nearly to the top without dismounting. The path wound around the mountain and gave us a view from all its different sides, every step presenting something new, and more and more beautiful, until all was completely forgotten and lost in the exceeding loveliness of the view from the summit.

Stripped of every association and considered merely as an elevation commanding a view of unknown valleys and mountains, I never saw a mountain which, for beauty of scene, better repaid the toil of ascending it; and I need not say what an interest was given to every feature when we saw in the valley beneath the large plain of Jezreel, the great battle-ground of nations; on the south the supposed range of Hermon, with whose dews the psalmist compares the "pleasantness of brethren dwelling together in unity"; beyond, the ruined village of Endor, where dwelled the witch who raised up the prophet Samuel; and near it the little city of Nain, where our Savior raised from the dead the widow's son; on the east, the mountains of Gilboa, "where Saul, and his armor-bearer, and his three sons fell upon their swords, to save themselves from falling into the hands of the Philistines"; beyond, the Sea of Galilee, or Lake of Genesareth, the theatre of our Savior's miracles, where, in the fourth watch of the night, he appeared to his terrified disciples, walking on the face of the waters; and to the north, on a lofty eminence, high above the top of Tabor, the city of Saphet, supposed to be the ancient Bethulia, alluded to in the words "a city that is set on a hill cannot be hid."

But, if the tradition be true, we need not go beyond the mountain itself, for it was on this high mountain that "Jesus Christ took Peter, and James, and John his brother apart," and gave them a glimpse of his glory before his death, when "his face did shine as the sun, and his raiment was white as the light; and a voice out of the cloud was heard, saying, This is my beloved son, in whom I am well pleased." I stood on the very spot where this holy scene was enacted. Within the walls of an old fortress is a ruined grotto with three altars, built as Peter had proposed, one for Christ, one for

Moses, and one for Elias; where, once a year, the monks of the convent and all the Christians of Nazareth, ascending in solemn procession, offer adoration and praise to the Savior of the world. The top of the mountain is an oval, about half a mile long and encompassed by a wall built by Josephus when he was governor of Galilee; within this enclosure is a table of luxuriant grass and wild flowers, sending forth such an odor and looking so clean and refreshing that, when my horse lay down and rolled in it, I felt the spirit of boyhood coming over me again, and was strongly tempted to follow his example.

We descended and hurried on towards Nazareth. Winding along the valley, an accidental turn brought the mountain again full before me, alone, and strongly defined against the sky; the figure of a man could have been seen standing on the top as on a pedestal. I know not whether, in the splendid effort of Raphael that now adorns the Vatican, he had any idea of this particular mountain; but I remember that, looking back upon it at this time, it struck me that it was exactly the scene which the daring genius of the painter might have selected for the transfiguration of the Son of God.

In two hours and a half we were in the vale of Naszera, and approaching the city of Nazareth. The valley is fertile, surrounded by hills, and the city stands at the extreme end on the side of an elevation. The houses are white, and in the place of Christ's residence, as of his birth, the mosque with its minaret is the most conspicuous object, and next to that the convent. A little on this side is a Greek church, built, as the Greeks say, over the spot where the angel Gabriel appeared to the Virgin Mary and announced to her the birth of a son "of whose kingdom there should be no end." A little farther is a fountain, where the Virgin is said to have been in the habit of going for water; a procession of women, with large jars on their heads, was coming out from the city, and one of them, a Christian woman, gave us to drink; a comfortable-looking monk, taking his afternoon's promenade in the suburbs, was the first to greet us, and following him, we dismounted at the door of the convent—one of the largest in the Holy Land.

In the city where Joseph and Mary lived, and where our Savior passed thirty years of his life, there is of course no lack of holy places, and, as in the case of the Church of the Holy Sepulchre, as many of these places as possible have, with admirable economy, been brought under one roof. The Church of the Annunciation, within the walls of the convent, next to the Church of the Holy Sepulchre, is the finest in the Holy Land. There are two organs, and the walls and pillars are hung with red damask. Under the principal altar is the house of Joseph and Mary, consisting of several grottoes, kitchen, parlor, and bedroom. In front of the same altar are two granite columns, designating the spots where the angel and the Virgin stood at the time of the annunciation. One of them is broken off below, and the upper part hangs from the roof—the monks say by a miracle, but others by mortar; and all over Galilee the miraculous pillar is celebrated for its virtue in curing diseases. Outside the convent are the workshop where Joseph wrought at his carpenter's trade and the synagogue where Christ, by reading the book of Isaiah and applying to himself the words of the prophet, so exasperated the Jews that they rose up and thrust him out of the city. A lamp was burning dimly at the altar, and an Arab Christian prostrating himself before it; and, lastly, I saw the table on which, say the monks, our Lord dined with his disciples both before and after the resurrection, a large flat stone about three feet high and fifteen paces in circumference. I was about knocking off a piece as a memorial when the friar checked me, and, turning round a nail in one of the many holes in the surface, he worked off a little powder, laid it carefully in a paper, and gave it me.

In my humor there was no great interest in visiting these so-called holy places; but here was the city in which our Savior had been brought up; I could walk in the same streets where he had walked, and look out upon the same hills and valleys; and a man of warm and impassioned piety might imagine that, in breathing the same atmosphere, he was drawing nearer to the person of the Savior. I went back to the convent, joined the monks at vespers, listened to the solemn chant and the majestic tones of the organ, and went to bed.

Early in the morning, changing for the first time the horses with which I had come from Jerusalem, I took a Christian of Nazareth for my guide and started for Tiberias and the Sea of Galilee. In about an hour we came to Cana of Galilee, where our Savior performed his first miracle by turning water into wine. At the entrance of the village is a fountain, where the women were drawing water in large jars, and near it a Greek church, built over the house of the young man at whose wedding the miracle was performed. Here, too, are large stone jars, being, as the monks say, the identical vessels in which the water was changed. War, bloody and relentless war, has swept over the little Cana of Galilee; fire and sword have laid waste and destroyed the peaceful village in which Christ met the rejoicing wedding party.

In about two hours, leaving Mount Hermon and Mount Tabor on our right, we passed through the field where the disciples plucked the corn on the Sabbath day; about half an hour farther on is the mountain of the Beatitude, where Christ preached the sermon on the mount. Whether the tradition be true or no, it was just the place where, in those primitive days, or even in the state of society which exists now in the Holy Land, such an event might have taken place; the preacher standing a little distance up the hill, and the multitude sitting down below him. Indeed, so strikingly similar in all its details is the state of society existing here now to that which existed in time of our Savior that I remember, when standing on the ruins of a small church supposed to cover the precise spot where Christ preached that compendium of goodness and wisdom, it struck me that if I or any other man should preach new and strange things, the people would come out from the cities and villages to listen and dispute, as they did under the preaching of our Lord.

Half an hour farther on we came to a large stone, on which, tradition says, our Savior sat when he blessed the five loaves and two fishes, and the immense multitude ate and were filled. These localities may be, and probably are, mere monkish conjectures; but one thing we know, that our Savior and his disciples journeyed on this road, that he looked upon the same scenes, and that, in all probability, somewhere within the range of my eye these deeds and miracles were actually performed. At all events, before me, in full view, was the hallowed Lake of Genesareth. Here we cannot be wrong; Christ walked upon that sea, and stilled the raging of its waters, and preached the tidings of salvation to the cities on its banks. But where are those cities now? Chorazin and Bethsaida, and thou too, Capernaum, that wast exalted unto heaven! The whole lake is spread out before me, almost from where the Jordan enters unto where that hallowed stream passes on to discharge its waters in the bituminous lake which covers the guilty cities; but there is no city, no habitation of man; all is still and quiet as the grave. But I am wrong; towards the southern extremity of the lake I see the city of Tabbereeah, the miserable relic of the ancient Tiberias, another of the proud cities of Herod, standing on the very shore of the sea, a mere speck in the distance, its walls and turrets, its mosques and minarets telling that it is possessed by the persecutors and oppressors of the followers of Christ.

We descended the mountains and, passing under the walls of the city, continued on about half an hour to a large bath erected by Ibrahim Pasha over the hot springs of Emmaus, celebrated for their medicinal properties; and, finding that we could pass the night there, left our baggage and returned to the city. The walls and circular towers, Moorish in their construction, gave it an imposing appearance; outside the gate was the tent of a harlot, that unhappy class of women not being permitted, by the Mussulman law, to enter the walls; within, all was in a most ruined and desolate condition; a great part being entirely vacant, and, where the space was occupied, the houses or huts were built far apart.

Tiberias was the third of the holy cities of the Jews; and here, as at Jerusalem and Hebron, the unhappy remnant of a fallen people still hover around the graves of their fathers, and, though degraded and trampled under foot, are still looking for the restoration of their temporal kingdom. There were two classes of Jews, Eastern and European, the latter being Muscovites, Poles, and Germans; all had come merely to lay their bones in the Holy Land, and were now supported by the charity of their brethren in Europe. There were two synagogues and two schools or colleges, and it was an interesting sight to see them, old men tottering on the verge of the grave and beardless boys studying in the same mysterious book what they believed to be the road to heaven.

I inquired for their rabbi, and they asked me whether I meant the Asiatic or European. I told them the greater of the two, and was conducted by a crowd to his house. I had no diffidence in those days, and invited myself to sit down and talk with him. He was an old man, and told me that they were all poor, living upon precarious charity; and that their brethren in America were so far off that they had forgotten the land of their fathers. Everything looked so comfortable in his house that I tried to get an invitation to stay all night, but the old rabbi was too cunning for me. It was a fête day, but my notes are so imperfect that I cannot make out whether it was their Sabbath. All were dressed in their best apparel, the women sitting in the doors or on the terraces, their heads adorned with large gold and silver ornaments, and their eyes sparkling like diamonds.

Returning, I noticed more particularly the ruins beyond the southern wall. They extend for more than a mile, and there is no doubt that this ground was covered by the ancient city. The plain runs back about half a mile to the foot of the mountain, and in the sides of the mountain are long ranges of tombs. It was from one of these tombs, said our guide, that the man possessed of devils rushed forth when our Savior rebuked the unclean spirits, and made them enter into a herd of swine, which ran violently down a steep place into the sea, and were drowned.

Passing the bath, I walked on to a point where I could see the extreme end of the lake, forming near the other side into the Jordan. It was a beautiful evening, still and quiet as the most troubled spirit could wish. The sides of the mountains were green and verdant, but there were no trees, and no rustling of the wind among the branches; not a boat was upon the lake; and, except in the city of Tiberias, which, enclosed within its walls, gave no signs of life, I was the only living being on its shores; I almost felt myself alone in the world; and surely, if ever there was a spot where a man might be willing to live alone, it would be there. There was no desolation, but rather beauty in the loneliness; and when the sun was setting I was bathing my feet in the waters of the hallowed lake, and fast falling into the belief that I could sit me down on its banks "the world forgetting, by the world forgot"; but just then I saw filing under the walls of Tiberias a long procession of men. They were coming to the baths of Emmaus; and, in a few moments, I, that was musing as if I were alone in the world, was struggling with naked Arabs for a place in the bathing apartment.

A large bathing-house has been built over the hot springs by Ibrahim Pasha; a circular building, with a dome, like the baths at Constantinople; and under the dome a large marble reservoir, twenty feet in diameter and nearly six feet deep, into which the Arabs slipped off from the sides like turtles, darkening the white marble and the clear water with their swarthy skins. I could not bear the heat, which seemed to me scalding. A separate room, with a single bath, had been built expressly for the precious body of Ibrahim Pasha; and, as he was not at hand to use it, I had it prepared for myself. Here was a theme for moralizing! I had stood on the top of the pyramids, on Mount Sinai, and the shores of the Dead Sea; I had been in close contact with greatness in the tombs of Augustus, Agamemnon, and the Scipios; but what were these compared with bathing in the same tub with the great bulldog-warrior of the East, the terrible Ibrahim Pasha? I spread my rug in an adjoining chamber; the long window opened directly upon the Sea of Galilee; for more than an hour my eyes were fixed upon its calm and silvery surface; and the last sounds that broke upon my ears were the murmurs of its waters.

Early in the morning we started. Stopping again at Tiberias, the soldier at the gate told us that a European had arrived during the night. I hunted him out and found him to be an Englishman, as I afterward learned, a merchant of Damascus, and a sportsman, equipped with shooting-jacket, gun, dog, &c. He was in a miserable hovel, and, having just risen, was sitting apart from the Arab family; his rug and coverlet were lying on the mud floor not yet rolled up; and he seemed in a most rueful mood, objurgating all travel for pleasure, and whistling earnestly "There's no place like home." I knew his humor, for I had often felt it myself and could hardly keep

435

from laughing. He was not more than half dressed, and reminded me of the caricature of an Englishman standing in his nether garment, with a piece of cloth in one hand and a pair of scissors in the other, as not being resolved after what fashion to have his coat cut.

> "I am an English gentleman, and naked I stand here,
> Musing in my mind what raiment I shall wear;
> For now I will wear this, and now I will wear that,
> And now I will wear—I cannot tell what."

We spent half an hour together, and parted. He was an old stager, and did not travel for scenery, associations, and all that, but he could tell every place where he had bagged a bird, from Damascus to the Sea of Galilee.

Stopping for a moment at the only monument of antiquity, the church of St. Peter, a long building with a vaulted stone roof, built, as the monks say, over the place where the house of St. Peter stood, and the cornerstone laid by our Savior; a burly monk was in the confessional, and a young Christian girl pouring into his greedy ears perhaps a story of unhappy love, we left for the last time the gate[2] of the city, the tent of the harlot standing there still, and commenced our journey along the shore of the sea.

A short distance from Tiberias we crossed the point of a mountain running down into the lake, and in about an hour came to a small Mohammedan village, called Magdol, supposed to be the Magdala into which our Savior came when he had sent away the multitude after feeding them with the seven loaves and two fishes. It was along this shore that Jesus Christ began to preach the glad tidings of salvation to a ruined world; eighteen hundred years ago, walking by this sea, he saw two brethren, "Simon Peter and Andrew his brother, casting their nets into the sea, toiling all day and catching no fish; and he told them to thrust forth from the land; and their nets brake and their ships sank with the multitude of fish; and he said unto

2 About six months after this gate was swallowed up by an earthquake; the wall and the whole of that quarter of the city were thrown down and demolished, and a great portion of the inhabitants buried under the ruins.—Stephens' note.

them, Follow me, and I will make you fishers of men; and they for-
sook all and followed him."

We were now crossing a rich valley, through which several
streams were running and emptying into the lake; and towards the
other end, at some distance from the sea, we came to a small mound
of crumbling bricks and stones, almost overgrown with grass; and
this is all that remains of the city of Bethsaida, the city of Peter,
and Andrew, and Philip. If we had diverged a hundred yards one
way or the other, I should have passed without seeing it. A short
distance off, among the hills that border the plain, alike in ruins, is
her sister city Chorazin. Leaving the valley and crossing a rude
point of the mountain which runs boldly to the lake, the road being
so narrow that we were obliged to unload the baggage-horse, we
descended to the plains of Genesareth, the richest and most fertile
plain on the shores of the lake, and, perhaps, for a combination of
natural advantages, soil, beauty of scenery, climate, and temperature, exceeded by no place in the world. A short distance across the
plain we came to a little mill, set in motion by a large, clear, and
beautiful stream, conveyed in two stone aqueducts. Four or five
Arab families lived there, in huts made with palm leaves; the men
lay stretched on the ground, lulled to sleep by the murmur of the
falling waters.

From here to Talhoun, the supposed site of Capernaum, the rich
plain of Genesareth was lying a wild and luxuriant waste, entirely
uncultivated and neglected, except in one place, where an Arab was
ploughing a small plot for tobacco. Approaching, the single Arab
footpath becomes lost, and the road which our Savior had often
followed upon his great errand of redemption was so overgrown
with long grass, bushes, and weeds that they rose above the back
of my horse, and I found it easier to dismount and pick my way
on foot.

The ruins of Capernaum extend more than a mile along the shore
and back towards the mountain, but they were so overgrown with
grass and bushes that it was difficult to move among them. Climbing
upon a high wall, which, though ruined itself, seemed proud of its
pre-eminence above the rest, I had a full view of the ruins of the

437

city, of the plains of Genesareth, and the whole extent of the Sea of
Galilee, from where the Jordan comes down from the mountains
until it passes out and rolls on to the Dead Sea. It is about sixteen
miles long and six wide; at each end is the narrow valley of the
Jordan; on the east a range of mountains, rising, not precipitously,
but rolling back from the shore, green and verdant, but destitute of
trees; on the west are mountains, in two places coming down to the
lake, and the rest is a rich and beautiful, but wild and uncultivated
plain. It was by far the most imposing view I had enjoyed, and I am
not sure that in all my journeying in the East I had a more interesting moment than when I sat among the ruins of Capernaum, looking out upon the Lake of Genesareth.

Travelers have often compared this lake with the Lake of
Geneva. I could see very little resemblance; it is not so large, and
wants the variety of scenery of the Lake of Geneva, and, above all,
the lofty summit of Mount Blanc. The banks of the Lake of Geneva
are crowded from one end to the other with villages and villas, and
its surface is covered with boats, and all the hurry and bustle of a
traveling population; this is in all the wildness of nature, all neglected and uncultivated; and, except the little town of Tiberias,
not a habitation, not even an Arab's hut, is seen upon its banks, not
a solitary boat upon its waters. A single pelican was floating at my
feet, and, like myself, he was alone. He was so near that I could
have hit him with a stone; he was the only thing I saw that had life,
and he seemed looking at me with wonder and asking me why I
still lingered in the desolate city. I was looking upon the theatre of
mighty miracles; it was here that, when a great tempest arose, and
the ship was covered with waves, and his disciples cried out, "Save
us, or we perish," Christ rose from his sleep, and rebuked the wind
and the sea, and there was a great calm and here too it was that in
the fourth watch of the night he appeared to his terrified disciples,
walking on the face of the sea, and crying out to them, "It is I, be
not afraid"; and again the wind ceased, and there was a calm.

But this scene was not always so desolate. The shores of this lake
were once covered with cities, in which Christ preached on the
Sabbath day, healed the sick, gave sight to the blind, cleansed the

lepers, cast out devils, and raised the dead. Bethsaida and Chorazin I had passed, and I was standing among the ruins of Capernaum, the city that was exalted to heaven in our Savior's love; where Christ first raised his warning voice, saying, "Repent, for the kingdom of heaven is at hand"; and I could feel the fulfillment of his prophetic words, " Wo unto thee, Chorazin, wo unto thee Bethsaida; it shall be more tolerable for Tyre and Sidon in the day of judgment than for you. And thou, Capernaum, which art exalted unto heaven, shall be brought down to hell, and it shall be more tolerable for the land of Sodom in the day of judgment than for thee." I am aware that lately there has been some dispute whether this be the site of Capernaum, but I had now passed along the whole western shore of the lake, and, if this be not Capernaum, my horse's hoofs must have trampled upon the city of our Savior's love without my knowing where that city stood.

I thought to enhance the interest of this day's journey by making my noonday meal from the fish of the Lake of Genesareth; obliged to go back by the mills and having on my way up seen a net drying on the shore, I had roused the sleeping Arabs, and they had promised to throw it for me; but, when I returned, I found that, like Simon Peter and the sons of Zebedee, "they had toiled all day, and had caught no fish."

Here we turned away from the consecrated lake and fixed our eyes on the end of my day's journey, the towering city of Zaffad. But the interest of the day was not yet over. Ascending for about an hour from the shore of the lake, we came to the great caravan road from Jerusalem to Damascus, and a little off from this to a large khan; and within this khan, according to tradition, is the pit into which Joseph was thrown by his brethren before they sold him to the Ishmaelites. The khan, like all other caravansaries, is a large stone building enclosing a hollow square, with small chambers around it for the accommodation of caravan travelers. The pit is a solid piece of masonwork, like a well; and, when I saw it, was nearly full of water. Both Mussulmans and Christians reverence this as a holy place; near it are a Mussulman mosque and a Christian chapel; and few travelers pass this way, whether Mussulmans or Christians, without prostrating themselves before the altar of Joseph the Just.

In all probability, the legend establishing this locality has no better foundation than most of the others in the Holy Land; but I cannot help remarking that I do not attach the importance assigned by others to the circumstance of its distance from Hebron, at that time Jacob's dwelling-place. We know that Joseph's brethren were feeding their father's flock at Shechem; and, when Joseph came thither "wandering in the field, he inquired after his brethren, and a man told him they are departed hence, for I heard them say, Let us go to Dothan; and Joseph went after his brethren, and found them in Dothan." If there be any good reason for calling this place Dothan, to me it does not seem at all strange that, in the pastoral state of society which existed then and still exists unchanged, Jacob's sons had driven their flocks to a pasture-ground two days farther on; and, affording a striking illustration of the scene supposed to have taken place here, while we were loitering around the khan, a caravan of merchants from Damascus came up, on their way to Egypt, and the buying or selling of slaves, white or black, being still a part of the trade between these places, I have no doubt that, if I had offered Paul for sale, they would have bought him and carried him to Egypt, where, perhaps, he might have risen to be a grand vizier. From hence we continued mounting again, the city of Zaffad seeming to detach itself more and more, and to rise higher and higher above surrounding objects, and the atmosphere growing perceptibly colder; and at four o'clock we had reached the city.

Zaffad is the last of the four holy cities of the Jews. My intercourse with the Jews in the Holy Land had been so interesting that I determined to prolong it to the last, and, having heard a favorable report of a Jew, the English consular agent at Zaffad, I rode directly to his house. He was a very poor and very amiable man. I went with him to the governor, showed my firman, and demanded permission to see the grotto of Jacob. The governor was sick, and told me that God had sent me there expressly to cure him. Since my successful experiment upon the governor of Hebron, I began to think doctoring governors was my forte, and, after feeling his pulse, and making him stick out his tongue, upon the principle that a governor was a governor, and what was good for one was good for another, I gave him an emetic which almost turned him inside out, and completely cured him. One thing I cannot help observing, not with a view of impeaching anything that is written but as illustrating the state of society in the East, that if a skillful physician, by the application of his medical science, should raise an Arab from what, without such application, would be his bed of death, the ignorant people would be very likely to believe it a miracle and to follow him with that degree of faith which would give credence to the saving virtue of touching the "hem of his garment."

From the palace of the governor we ascended to the ruined fortress crowning the very top of the hill, and from one of the windows of the tower I looked down upon an extensive prospect of hills and valleys; the Lake of Genesareth seemed almost at my feet; the stately and majestic Tabor was far below me, and beyond was the great plain of Jezreel, stretching off to the mountains of Carmel and the shores of the Mediterranean. In all my wanderings in the most remote places, I had been constantly seeing what I may call the handwriting of Napoleon. In Italy, Poland, Germany, and the burnt and rebuilt capital of the tzars, at the pyramids and cataracts of the Nile, and now, on this almost inaccessible height, the turrets of the fortress were battered by the French cannon.

We descended again to the Jews' quarter. Their houses were on the side of the hill, overlooking a beautiful valley. It was the last day of eating unleavened bread, and the whole Jewish population, in their best attire, were sitting on the terraces and on the tops of their houses, in gay, striking, and beautiful costumes, the women with their gold and silver ornaments on their heads and around their necks, enjoying the balmy mildness of a Syrian sunset; and, when the shades of evening had driven them to their houses, I heard all around me, and for the last time in the Holy Land, rising in loud and solemn chants the Songs of Solomon and the Psalms of David.

There are about two hundred families of Israelites in Zaffad; they come there only to lay their bones in the land of their fathers, have no occupation or means of livelihood, spend all their time in reading the Bible and Talmud, and live upon the charity of their European brethren. The agent told me that during the late revolution they had been stripped of everything; that, as at Hebron, they had suffered robbery, murder, and rapine; that the governor had allowed them to take refuge in the fortress, where they remained, three thousand in number, without a mat to lie on or bread to put in their mouths; many of them had died of starvation, and the living remained beside the bodies of the dead till the whirlwind passed by; that, thinking himself safe under his foreign protection, he had remained below, but that his hat with the consular cockade had been torn off and trampled under foot; and his wife, a lovely young woman sitting by our side, then not more than nineteen, had been thrown down, whipped, and he did not tell me so, but I inferred that far worse had befallen her; and the brutal Turk who committed the outrage still lived, and he met him in the streets every day.

During the evening a Christian from Nazareth came in, and it struck me as an interesting circumstance that I was introduced to him as a brother Nazarene.

A Jew welcomed me to the first of the holy cities, and a Jew accompanied me on my exit from the last. Both received me into their houses and gave me the best that they had, and both refused to accept a price for their hospitality. I had a hard day's journey before me. My Jewish friend had told me that it would be necessary to make a very early start to arrive at Acre that night, but it so happened that I set off late. We had a ravine to cross, the worst I had met in Syria. Paul and I were some distance ahead, when we heard the shouting of our muleteer; our baggage mule had fallen and caught on the brink of a precipice, where he was afraid to move until we came to his help; and this and the exceeding roughness of the road detained us so much that, when we reached the other side of the ravine, my guide told me that it would be utterly impossible to reach Acre that day. I would have returned, but I did not want to throw myself again upon the hospitality of my Jew friend. I was in a bad condition for roughing it; but, at the risk of being obliged to sleep in some miserable Arab hut or perhaps under the walls of Acre, I pushed on.

For two or three hours there was no improvement in the road; we were obliged to dismount several times, and could not do more than pick our way on a walk. We then came to the village of Rinah, situated in a fine olive grove. The villagers told us it would be impossible to reach Acre before night, but a bribe to my guide induced him to lead off on a brisk trot. Of every man we met we asked the distance; at length we came to one who told us he thought we might do it. I could almost always tell beforehand the answer we should get; when we came to a lazy fellow, sprawling on the ground and basking in the sun, he invariably said no; and when we met an Arab, riding nimbly on his mule or striding over the ground as if he had something to do and meant to do it, his answer was always yes, and so we were alternately cheered and discouraged. We watered our horses at the stream without dismounting. About midday Paul handed me a boiled fowl, holding on by one leg while I pulled at the other; the fowl came apart, and so we dined on horseback without stopping. I am not sure, but I do not think that there was anything particularly interesting on the road; once, riding over a fine, well-cultivated valley, we saw at a distance on the right two handsome villages, and standing alone, something which appeared to be a large white mosque or sheik's tomb.

At about four o'clock we came in sight of the Mediterranean, the great plain of Acre, the low circular shore extending to Caipha and Mount Carmel, and before us, at a great distance, on an extreme point in the sea, the ancient Ptolemais, the St. Jean d'Acre of Richard and the Crusaders. Still we were not safe. The sun was settling away towards my distant home when we reached the shore of the sea. I shall never forget my sensations at the moment when I gained that shore; after the Red Sea and the Dead Sea and the Sea of Galilee, it seemed an old acquaintance, and I spurred my horse into the waters to greet it. But I had no time to dally, for as yet I was not secure. I joined the last of the loungers outside the walls; the heavy gates were swung to as I entered; and when I pushed my jaded horse over the threshold of the gate I felt as happy as the gallant leader of the Crusaders when he planted the banner of England upon the walls of Acre. Soon in the peaceful cell of the convent, I forgot my toil and anxiety as well as Richard and the holy wars. The night before I had slept by the quiet waters of Galilee, and now the last sounds that I heard were the rolling waves of the Mediterranean.

CHAPTER XXXVI

I ROSE next morning much fatigued. My strength had been greatly impaired by sickness and exposure, and I intended to give
myself a day of rest, instead of which I committed an act of folly.
The night before I left Jerusalem I had seen, at the house of my
friend Mr. Whiting, the poetical pilgrimage of M. de la Martine; I
had not time to read it through, and by chance opened it at the
chapter containing the particulars of his visit to Caipha, and the
glowing account which he gave of the two sisters of the Sardinian
consul had inflamed in some degree my imagination. I had found it
one of the most annoying circumstances attendant upon traveling
in the East that, in spite of the poetical accounts of Eastern beauty,
though I had seen Georgian and Circassian women, I had never yet
met with anything that to my mind was equal to the beauty of the
European and American women. I had passed Caipha, and it was a
direct retrograde movement to go there; but early in the morning,
as I was walking on the ramparts of Acre, I looked back towards
the little city and the beautiful creations of the poet rose before me
in most ravishing colors. I was worn down. There was no physician
in Acre, and, perhaps, to bask an hour in the sunshine of beauty
might revive and restore me. Paul too was under the weather; ever
since his fall from the dromedary he had wanted bleeding, and it
might do him good. In short, I had been rambling for months among
ruins and old cities, working as hard as if I were to be paid for it by
the day; I had had enough of these things, and one glimpse of a
beautiful girl was worth more to me at that moment than all the
ruins of the Holy Land; but I would not admit to myself, much less

445

to Paul, that I was making this retrograde movement merely to see a couple of pretty faces, and I ordered horses for Caipha and Mount Carmel. Horses, however, were not to be had, and we were obliged to take donkeys, which I considered unlucky. For the first time since I left Jerusalem, I brushed my tarboosh, my blue jacket, and gray pantaloons.

I started on donkeyback. Caipha is distant a ride of about three hours and a half from Acre, all the way along the shore of the sea. About half an hour from Acre we crossed the river Belus in a boat. It was on the banks of this stream that Elijah killed the four hundred prophets of Baal, gathered unto Mount Carmel by the orders of Ahab. A dead level plain, fertile but uncultivated, stretched back for many miles into the interior and in the front to the foot of Mount Carmel. We rode close along the shore, where the sand was every moment washed and hardened by the waves. The sea was calm, but the wrecks on the shore, of which we counted seventeen on our way to Caipha, told us that the elements of storm and tempest might lurk under a fair and beautiful face, all which was àpropos to my intended visit. On the way I thought it necessary to let Paul into part of my plans, and told him that I wanted to stop at the house of the Sardinian consul. Paul asked me whether I had any letter to him; I told him no, and, by degrees, disclosed to him the reason of my wanting to go there; and he surprised me by telling me that he knew the young ladies very well; and when I asked him how and when, he told me that he had assisted them in their cooking when he stopped there three years before with Mr. Wellesley. This was rather a damper; but I reflected that Haidee, on her beautiful little island, prepared with her own hands the food for the shipwrecked, and revived at the thought.

We were now approaching Caipha. The city was walled all around; without the walls was a Mohammedan burying-ground; and the gate, like the shields of Homer's heroes, was covered with a tough bull's hide. I rode directly to the consul's house; it was a miserable-looking place, and on the platform directly before the door stood a most unpoetical heap of dirt and rubbish; but I didn't mind that; the door was open, and I went in. The table was set for

446

dinner, and I could not help remarking a few rather questionable spots on the table-cloth, but I didn't mind that; knives, forks, and plates were a spectacle to which I had long been unaccustomed, and my heart warmed even to the empty platters. I thought I had come at the witching moment, and I felt as sure of my dinner as if I had it already under my jacket. The consul was sitting on a settee, and I began the acquaintance by asking him if there was an American consul there. He told me no; at which I was very much surprised, as we had one at Jaffa, not so much of a place as Caipha; and I invited myself to a seat beside the consul and made myself agreeable. I soon found, however, that I was not so pleasant a fellow as I thought. The consul answered my questions, but his manner might be interpreted, "Don't you see you are keeping the dinner waiting?" I didn't mind that, however, but talked about the necessity of my government having a consul there, to entertain American travelers, and suggested that at Jaffa the government had given the appointment to the then acting Sardinian consul; still my friend was impenetrable. I tried him upon several other topics, but with no great success. During this time the mother entered, evidently in dishabillé, and occasionally I got a glimpse of a pair of fine black eyes peeping at me through the door. At last, when I found that he was bent on not asking me to dine, I rose suddenly, made a hundred apologies for my haste, shook him cordially by the hand, and, with most consummate impudence, told him I would call again on my return from Mount Carmel. Paul rather crowed over me, for he had met and spoken to the young ladies, and in the same place where he had seen them before.

In about an hour we had reached the top of Mount Carmel; this celebrated mountain is the only great promontory upon the low coast of Palestine, and it is, beyond all comparison, the finest mountain in the Holy Land. The traveler at this day may realize fully the poetical description by the inspired writers, of the "excellency" of Mount Carmel. The pine, oak, olive, and laurel grew above a beautiful carpet of grass and wildflowers, and from amid this luxuriance I looked out upon the plains of Acre, the little city stretching out on a low point, like a mere speck in the water; and

447

beyond, the mountains of Lebanon; on the left, along the shore of
the Mediterranean to the ruins of Caesarea, the once proud city of
Herod and of Cornelius the Centurion, where Paul made Felix
tremble; in front, the dark blue sea, on whose bosom two trans-
ports, with Egyptian soldiers on board, were at that time stretching
under easy sail from Acre to Alexandria; and behind, the great
plain of Jezreel.

One word with regard to this great plain. I had traveled around
and about and across it; had looked at it from hills and mountains,
and I was now on the point of leaving it forever. This plain, com-
puted to be about fifteen miles square, is the "mighty plain," as it
is called, of the ancients, and celebrated for more than three thousand years as the "great battle-ground of nations." From here
Elijah girded up his loins and ran before Ahab to the entrance of
Jezreel; it was on this plain that Barak went down, and ten
thousand men after him, and discomfited Sisera and all his chariots;
it was here that Josiah, king of Judah, disguised himself, that he
might fight with Necho, king of Egypt, and fell by the arrows of
the Egyptian archers. The Assyrian and the Persian, Jews and
Gentiles, Crusaders and Saracens, Egyptians and Turks, Arabs and
Frenchmen, warriors of every nation, have poured out their blood
on the plains of Esdraelon; and here, said a gentleman whom I met
in Palestine skilled in the reading and interpretation of the prophecies, will be fought the great final battle with antichrist, when
circumstances which are now supposed to be rapidly developing
themselves shall bring together a mighty army of the followers of
Christ, under the banner of the cross, to do battle in his name and
sweep from the earth his contemners and opposers.

The convent on Mount Carmel is worthy of the place where it
stands, and, like the mountain itself, is the best in the Holy Land.
The church, which is unfinished, is intended to be a very fine building, and the interior of the convent is really beautiful. I could hardly
believe my own eyes when I saw, in rooms provided for travelers,
French bedsteads with curtains and French dressing-tables. The
rules of their order forbid the Carmelite friars to eat meat, but they
set me down to such a dinner, to say nothing of the wines of Mount

Lebanon, that, so far as regarded the eating and drinking merely, I was glad I had not invited myself to dine with my friend the consul at Caipha. From my seat at the table I looked out upon the distant sea; the monks were all gathered around me, kind, good men, happy to receive and talk with a stranger; and it is no extravagance to say that, after having been buffeted about for months, I felt at the moment that I could be almost willing to remain with them forever. I ought not to tell it, but the fact is, the extraordinary comfort of the convent, and the extraordinary beauty of the scene, drove away all the associations connected with this gathering-place of the prophets. I wanted nothing but what I saw before me. The monks told me that there was fine shooting on the mountain. I could throw myself into the clearest of waters, and bathe, or, with my little boat, could glide over to Caipha or Acre. For an invalid in search of retirement, with every beauty that climate and natural scenery can offer, I know no place superior to the convent at Mount Carmel. It is one of the few places I ever saw where a man could be cheerful and happy in perfect seclusion. Books, the mountain, the sky and the sea would be companions enough. It would be the sweetest spot on earth for a *very* young couple to test the strength of their poetic dreams; and knocked about and buffeted as I had been, when the superior told me that, in spite of the inscription over the doors of their convents, "clausura per le donna [*sic*]," I might build a house on the spot where I stood, and bring whom I pleased there, it instantly brought to my mind the beautiful birds of Paradise of De la Martine, and my engagements with my friend the consul at Caipha. The whole of the fraternity accompanied me down the side of the mountain; and I beg to except them all, including the cook, from anything I may have said bearing harshly upon the monastic character. The recollection of my engagement, however, began to hurry me. The friars were pussy and shortwinded; one by one they bade me good-by; and the cook, a most deserving brother and unnaturally lean for his profession and position in the convent, was the only one who held out to the foot of the mountain. I crossed his hand with a piece of money; Paul kissed it and, after we had started,

449

turned his head and cried out to the holy cook, "Orate pro mihi," "Pray for me."

At Caipha we found the consul in the street. I do not know whether he was expecting us or not; but, whether or no, I considered it my duty to apologize for having stayed so long on the mountain, and accompanied him to his house. Unluckily, it was so late that Paul said if we stopped we should be shut out from Acre; and when I looked at the sun and the distant city I had great misgivings, but it was only for a moment. The sisters were now dressed up, and standing in a door as I passed. Their dresses were Asiatic, consisting, from the waist downward, of a variety of wrappers, the outermost of which was silk, hiding the most beautiful figures under a mere bundle of habits. I went into the room and took a glass of lemonade with my watch in my hand. I would not speak of her in the morning, but now, in full dress, the interesting mother, so glowingly described by M. de la Martine,[1] appeared in a costume a great deal beyond what is usually called low in the neck. I do not mention it as a reproach to her, for she was an Arab woman, and it was the custom of her country; and as to the young ladies—M. de la Martine had never been in America.

I had intended this for a day of rest; but I had, if possible, a harder task than on the preceding day to reach the city before the gates were closed. We pushed our donkeys till they broke down, and then got off and whipped them on before us. It was like the Irishman working his passage by hauling the towline of the canal boat; if it was not for the name of the thing, we might as well have walked; and when I lay down that night in my cell in the convent, I prayed that age might temper enthusiasm; that even the imagination of M. de la Martine might grow cool; and that old men would pay respect to their lawful wives and not go in ecstasies about young girls.

---

[1] A.M.L. de la Martine (1790–1869), poet and statesman, was reared in ultra-royalist principles. He published his first poems, *Meditations*, in 1820, accepted consular posts in Europe, and made a tour of the Levant which produced *Souvenirs d'Orient*. He continued to oppose all democratic change and was involved in the 1848 uprising, but remained unreconciled to the regime of Louis Napoleon. The rest of his life was given to writing and editing.

CHAPTER XXXVII

I SHALL SAY but little of Acre. The age of chivalry is gone forever, but there is a green spot in every man's memory, a feeble but undying spark of romance in every heart; and that man's feelings are not to be envied who could walk on the ramparts of St. Jean d'Acre without calling up Richard and Saladin, the Crusaders and the Saracens; and when the interval of centuries is forgotten, and the imagination is reveling in the scenes of days long passed away, his illusion rises to the vividness of reality as he sees dashing by him a gallant array of Turkish horsemen, with turbans and glittering sabres, as when they sallied forth to drive back from the walls the chivalry of Europe. Near the city is a mount which is still called Richard Coeur de Lion, and from which Napoleon, pointing to the city, said to Murat, "The fate of the East depends upon yonder petty town." Constantinople and the Indies, a new empire in the East, and a change in the face of the whole world! Eight times he led his veteran soldiers to the assault; eleven times he stood the desperate sallies of the Mameluke sabres. British soldiers under Sir Sidney Smith came to the aid of the besieged; the ruins of a breached wall served as a breastwork, the muzzles of British and French muskets touched each other, and the spearheads of their standards were locked together. The bravest of his officers were killed, and the bodies of the dead soldiers lying around putrefied under the burning sun. The pasha (Djezzar the Butcher) sat on the floor of his palace, surrounded by a heap of gory heads, distributing money to all who brought in the heads of Frenchmen, and he who was destined to overturn every throne in Europe was foiled under

451

the walls of Acre. Three years ago it sustained, under Abdallah Pasha, a long and bloody siege from Ibrahim Pasha, and, when it fell into his hands, was given up to pillage and the flames. It has since been rebuilt, fortified with skill and science, and is now almost impregnable; full of the élite of the Egyptian army under Colonel Sêve (formerly aid to Marshal Ney), now Suliman Pasha, and constantly stored with five years' provisions. The pasha has lately been building fine hospitals for his soldiers, and an Italian apothecary, licensed to kill secundem artem, is let loose upon the sick at the low rate of a hundred dollars per annum.

I was so much pleased with the old Arab muleteer who went with me to Mount Carmel that I hired his donkeys again for another journey. He was an old Egyptian from Damietta; four of his children had been taken for soldiers, and he and his old wife and three donkeys followed them about wherever they went. He had had two wives and sixteen children, and these were all that were left. They were all now stationed at Acre, and, when we started, two of them, not on duty at the time, were with the old man at the convent, arranging the baggage while he was taking his coffee and pipe; they accompanied us to the gate, received the old man's benediction, and returned.

A short distance from the gate we met a Turkish grandee, with his officers, slaves, and attendants. He had formerly been a collector of taxes under Abdallah Pasha, and would have done well as an officeholder under a civilized government, for he had abandoned the falling fortunes of his master in time to slip into the same office under his successor.

Looking back, Acre appeared to much better advantage than from the other side, and the mosque and minaret of Abdallah Pasha were particularly conspicuous. We rode for some distance by the side of an aqueduct, which conveys water from the mountains twenty miles distant to the city of Acre. In the plain towards Acre two upright pillars, in which the water rose and descended, formed part of the aqueduct. Our road lay across a plain, and several times we picked up musket balls and fragments of bombs, left there by the French and Napoleon. We passed two palaces of Abdallah

Pasha, where the haughty Turk had reveled with his fifty or a hundred wives in all the luxuries of the East. The plain was very extensive, naturally rich, but almost entirely uncultivated. Over an extent of several miles we would perhaps see a single Arab turning up what on the great plain appeared to be merely a few yards; and the oppressive nature of the government is manifest from the fact that, while the whole of this rich plain lies open to anyone who chooses to till it, hundreds prefer to drag out a half-starved exist- ence within the walls of Acre; for the fruits of their labor are not their own, and another will reap where they sow; the tax-gatherer comes and looks at the products, and takes not a fifth, or a sixth, nor any other fixed proportion, but as much as the pasha needs; and the question is not how much he shall take, but how little he shall leave. Taxation, or rather extortion, for it is wrong to call it by so mild a name, from cantars of olives down to single eggs, grinds the Arab to the dust; and yet, said the old man, even this is better than our lot under the sultan; even this we could bear if the pasha would only spare us our children.

Along this plain we passed a large house, in a garden of oranges, lemons, almonds, and figs, with a row of cypress-trees along the road; formerly the residence of the treasurer of Abdallah Pasha. He himself had been a great tyrant and oppressor and had fallen into the hands of a greater, and now wanders, with both his eyes out, a beggar in the streets of Cairo.

In about five hours we came upon the sea, on a bold point project- ing out like Carmel, the white promontory of Pliny, the ancient Scala of the Syrians. On this point stood an old khan, and we sat down under the shadow of the wall for our noonday lunch. From here, too, the view was exceedingly fine. On the left were Acre and Mount Carmel; on the right the Turkish city of Sour, the ancient Tyre; and, in front, the horizon was darkened by the island of Cyprus. Almost at my feet was the wreck of a schooner, driven on the rocks only the night before, her shivered sails still flying from the masts, and the luckless mariners were alongside in a small boat, bringing ashore the remnant of the cargo. Near me, and, like me, looking out upon the movements of the shipwrecked sailors and

453

apparently bemoaning his own unhappy lot, was a long, awkward, dangling young man, on his way to Acre; sent by the sheik of his village to work in Ibrahim Pasha's factory for three rolls of bread a day. I asked him why he did not run away, but where could he go? If he went to a strange village, he would immediately be delivered up on the never-failing demand for soldiers. There was no help for him. He did not know that there were other lands, where men were free; and, if he had known it, the curse of poverty rested upon him, and bound him where he was. I had seen misery in Italy, Greece, Turkey, Russia, and gallant, but conquered and enslaved Poland, but I saw it refined and perfected under the iron despotism of Mohammed Ali.

From hence the road continued, for about two hours, over a rocky precipice overhanging the sea, and so narrow that, as I sat on my horse, I could look down the steep and naked sides into the clear water below. In one place were the ruins of an old wall, probably, when the city before me was in its glory, defending the precipice. In the narrowest place we met a caravan of camels, and from here descended into a sandy plain, and, passing small rivulets and ruins of castles or fortresses, came to a fine stream, on the banks of which were soldiers' barracks; the horses, with their gay accouterments, were tied near the doors of the tents, constantly saddled and bridled, and strains of military music were swelling from a band among the trees.

Near this are what are called Solomon's cisterns, supposed to have been built by King Solomon in payment for the materials furnished by Hiram, king of Tyre, towards the building of the temple. Circumstances, however, abundantly prove that these cisterns, and the aqueduct connecting them with Tyre, have been built since the time of Alexander the Great.

On the extreme end of a long, low, sandy isthmus, which seems to have crawled out as far as it could, stands the fallen city of Tyre, seeming, at a distance, to rest on the bosom of the sea. A Turkish soldier was stationed at the Gate. I entered under an arch, so low that it was necessary to stoop on the back of my horse, and passed through dark and narrow streets, sheltered by mats stretched over

454

the bazars from the scorching heat of a Syrian sun. A single fishing-boat was lying in the harbor of "the crowning city, whose merchants were princes, whose traffickers were the honorable of the earth."

I left the gate of Tyre between as honest a man and as great a rogue as the sun ever shone upon. The honest man was my old Arab, whom I kept with me in spite of his bad donkey; and the rogue was a limping, sore-eyed Arab, in an old and ragged suit of regimentals, whom I hired for two days to relieve the old man in whipping the donkeys. He was a dismissed soldier, turned out of Ibrahim Pasha's army as of no use whatever, than which there could not be a stronger certificate of worthlessness. He told me, however, that he had once been a man of property, and, like honest Dogberry, had had his losses; he had been worth sixty piasters (nearly three dollars), with which he had come to live in the city; and been induced to embark in enterprises that had turned out unfortunately, and he had lost his all.

On my arrival at Sidon I drove immediately to the Arab consular agent, to consult him about paying a visit to Lady Esther Stanhope.[1] He told me that I must send a note to her ladyship, requesting permission to present myself, and wait her pleasure for an answer, that sometimes she was rather capricious and that the English consul from Beirut had been obliged to wait for two days. The state of my health would not permit my waiting anywhere upon an uncertainty. I was but one day from Beirut, where I looked for rest and medical attendance; but I did not like to go past, and I made my application perhaps with more regard to my own convenience and feelings than the respect due to those of the lady. My baggage, with my writing materials, had not yet arrived. I had no time to lose; the Arab agent gave me the best he had; and writing a note about as "big as a book" on a piece of coarse Arab paper with a reed pen, and sealing it with a huge Arab wafer, I gave it to a

---

[1] Lady Esther Stanhope (1776–1839) was the white-robed Sibyl of Lebanon. When young she became mistress of the establishment of her uncle, William Pitt. On his death, in 1806, the king settled a pension of £1,200 on her. She left England, lived with the Bedouins, toured the Levant, settled on Mount Lebanon, and had for many years had ascendency over the tribes about her. Misery and abject poverty surrounded her last years.

messenger, and, tumbling him out of the house, told him he must bring me an answer before daylight the next morning.

He probably reached Lady Stanhope's residence about nine or ten o'clock in the evening; and I have no doubt he tumbled in, just as he had been tumbled out at Sidon, and, demanding an immediate answer, he got one forthwith, "Her ladyship's compliments," &c.; in short, somewhat like that which a city lady gives from the head of the stairs, "I'm not at home." I have since read M. de la Martine's account of his visit to her ladyship, by which it appears that her ladyship had regard to the phraseology of a note. Mine, as near as I can recollect it, was as follows:—"Mr. S., a young American, on the point of leaving the Holy Land, would regret exceedingly being obliged to do so without first having paid his respects to the Lady Esther Stanhope. If the Lady Esther Stanhope will allow him that honor, Mr. S. will present himself *tomorrow*, at any hour her ladyship will name." If the reader will compare this note with the letter of M. de la Martine, he will almost wonder that my poor messenger, demanding, too, an immediate answer, was not kicked out of doors.

My horses were at the door, either for Beirut or her ladyship's residence; and, when obliged to turn away from the latter, I comforted myself with a good gallop to the former. Her ladyship was exceedingly lucky, by the way, in not having received me, for that night I broke down at Beirut; my travels in the East were abruptly terminated; and, after lying ten days under the attendance of an old Italian quack, with a blue frock-coat and great frog buttons, who frightened me to death every time he approached my bedside, I got on board the first vessel bound for sea, and sailed for Alexandria.

At Beirut I received a letter from the friend who had taken me on board his boat at Thebes, advising me of the sickness of his lady, and that he had prevailed upon the English doctor at Beirut to accompany him to Damascus and Baalbek; here, too, I heard of the death of Mr. Lowell,[2] a gentleman from Boston, who had preceded

2 John Lowell (b. in Boston 1800–d. 1836) left Boston in grief over his wife's death and gave himself over to world traveling. With a Swiss artist, G. C. Cleyre, he

me in many parts of my tour in the East; and who had everywhere left behind him such a name that it was a pleasure for an American to follow in his steps; and here, too, I heard of the great fire, which, by the time it reached this distant land, had laid the whole of my native city in ruins. In the midst of my troubles, however, I had three things that gave me pleasure. I met here my two friends with whom I had mounted the cataracts of the Nile, one of whom I hope one day to see in my own country; I received from the Austrian consul an assurance that the passport of my Jew friend at Hebron should be made out and delivered forthwith to his friend there; and I saw Costigan's servant, from whom I obtained a map of the Dead Sea before referred to. For ten days I lay on the deck of a little Austrian schooner watching the movements of a pair of turtle doves, and on the morning of the eleventh I was again off the coast of Egypt and entering the harbor of Alexandria. Here I introduced myself to the reader; and here, if he have not fallen from me by the way, I take my leave of him, with thanks for his patient courtesy.

arrived in Egypt in February, 1836. But he traveled alone up the Nile and began to collect antiquities. From Egypt he was moved to create in his will the Lowell Institute, "a beacon of Bostonian adult education to this day." Later he went by camel to the Red Sea, was then shipwrecked and rescued, but took a fever and died aboard a steamer going to Bombay on March 24, 1836. His portrait in Turkish costume is in the Boston Museum of Fine Arts.

Index

459

65, 266, 267, 274, 280, 310, 312, 314, 320, 330, 336, 344, 347, 350, 351, 355, 358, 359, 360, 379, 406, 408, 411, 419, 420, 434, 435; of sheiks, 79, 244, 420, 428, 443; of kings, 110, 132; of pharaoh, 112; in Egypt, 126, 261, 361; of the caliphs, 141, 146, 149; of the Prophet, 143, 144, 161, 231, 275, 300, 418; of a saint, 167; public, 223; of Aaron, 247, 263, 266, 268, 274, 275, 277–79, 415; the doors of, 254, 305; at Thebes, 262; in Petra, 264; of the first high priest of Israel, 271; Arabs living in, 301; of Rachel, 339; of Christ, 346, 362; of Joseph, 350, 355; of Nicodemus, 350; of Mary, 355; of Zachariah, 359, 378; of St. James, 359; in Jerusalem, 361; of Lazarus, 382, 383; of the Judges, 415; of Samuel, 415; of John the Baptist, 426

Tor, Egypt: 161, 162

Toualeb (Bedouin): 150, 151, 164, 167, 171, 173, 184, 210, 211, 213, 214, 217, 224, 230, 232, 239, 242

Tower of Babel: 394

Trail, Mr. (in the service of Ibrahim Pasha): 30

Trajan, Roman emperor: 246n., 249n.; road of, 232n., 284n.

Trans-Oceanic Honduras Railway: *xxix* n.

Turkey: 149, 156, 367, 454

Turkish bath: 47–49

Turkish gun: 325

Turks: 321, 332, 367, 376, 448; Stephens' attitude toward, *xxi*, history of the, 328; soldiers, 375, 403

Turpentine, Valley of: *see* Elah

Tutankhamen, king of Egypt: 110n.

Tyre, Lebanon: 44n., 248, 376, 439, 453–55

United States of America: *xxv*, 377n.

Uxmal, Mexico: *xlii*

Van Buren, Martin: *xxxvii*, 377n.

Vatican: 430

Vesuvius, Mount: 32, 188, 397n.

Via Dolorosa: 354

Via Hadriana nova: 37n.

Virgin Mary: 18, 104, 336, 337, 339, 346, 351, 355, 356, 430, 449, 450 & n.; chapel dedicated to, 185, 332; tomb of, 355

Vistula River, Russia: *xxvii*

Volney, Comte Constantin François de Chasseboeuf de: *xxix*, *xxxviii*, 8

Vulgate, the: 336

Vyse, Colonel (English gentleman of fortune): 37

Wadi-el-Butm: 246n.

Wadi Hammamat: 125n.

Wadi Musa, Jordan: 235, 246 & n., 251, 265, 266, 278, 280–82, 284n., 295; *see also* Petra

Waghorn, Mr. (Stephens' friend): 11 & n., 14, 140, 155, 157

Wahabees: 24

Waldeck, Jean Frédéric de: *xli* & n.

Walne, Dr. (English vice-consul at Cairo): 27 & n., 228

Warsaw, Poland: *xxvii*

Warwick vase: 10

Washington Parade Ground: 32

Weed, Mr. (guide): *xvii*

Weehawken, N.J.: *vi*

Welford, Charles: *xli*

Well of Saladin: *see* Joseph's Well

Wellesley (natural son of the Duke of Wellington): 278, 446

West Indian campaign in 1795: 9n

Weston, Conn.: *xliv*

Wheeling, W. Va.: *xvi*

Whiting (American missionary): 345, 347, 381, 409, 445

Wilkinson, Sir John Gardner: *xxx* n.

Wolff, Rev. Joseph: 281 & n.

Xavier, Brother Francis: 413, 414

Youssouff (son of Mehemet Ali): 25

Yucatán, Mexico: *xlii*, *xliv*; exploration of suggested to Stephens, *xli*

Zachariah: 355, 358; tomb of, 359, 378

Zadoc: 381

Zaffad: 439–41

Zebedee: 439

Zenobia: 339

Zion, Mount: 359, 369, 370, 406, 407, 409, 414; chapel on, 353

Zuyder Zee, Netherlands: 282